Representing Childhood and Atrocity

Representing Childhood and Atrocity

Edited by

Victoria Nesfield

and

Philip Smith

SUNY PRESS

Cover image by Stephanie Stella.

Published by State University of New York Press, Albany

© 2023 State University of New York

All rights reserved

Printed in the United States of America

No part of this book may be used or reproduced in any manner whatsoever without written permission. No part of this book may be stored in a retrieval system or transmitted in any form or by any means including electronic, electrostatic, magnetic tape, mechanical, photocopying, recording, or otherwise without the prior permission in writing of the publisher.

For information, contact State University of New York Press, Albany, NY
www.sunypress.edu

Library of Congress Cataloging-in-Publication Data

Names: Nesfield, Victoria, 1984– editor. | Smith, Philip, 1983– editor.
Title: Representing childhood and atrocity / Victoria Nesfield, Philip Smith.
Description: Albany : State University of New York Press, [2022] | Includes
   bibliographical references.
Identifiers: LCCN 2022009665 | ISBN 9781438490755 (hardcover : alk. paper) |
   ISBN 9781438490762 (ebook) | ISBN 9781438490748 (pbk. : alk. paper)
Subjects: LCSH: Children in literature. | Atrocities in literature. | Genocide in
   literature. | Children and genocide.
Classification: LCC PN56.5.C48 R47 2022 | DDC 700/.4552—dc23/eng/20220727
LC record available at https://lccn.loc.gov/2022009665

10 9 8 7 6 5 4 3 2 1

In the process of finalizing this volume's manuscript we were deeply saddened to learn of the passing of Dr. Rosemary Horowitz. With a research profile that spanned Yiddish writers, Holocaust studies and Elie Wiesel's writing, Rosemary Horowitz's work influenced many scholars, including the editors of this volume. In addition, she was a supporter of our own endeavors, contributing to our previous publication *The Struggle for Understanding: The Novels of Elie Wiesel*. It is with gratitude and appreciation to Rosemary, her family, and her colleagues that we are able to include her chapter in this volume.

Contents

List of Illustrations — ix

Introduction — 1
    Victoria Nesfield and Philip Smith

Part 1: Late Twentieth-Century Genocides

1. Children's Humanitarian Arts and the Genocide in Darfur: Drawing Loss and Atrocity — 21
    Chigbo Arthur Anyaduba

2. Framing the Unframeable: *Deogratias* and the Horror of Genocide — 51
    Kaitlyn Newman

3. Tracing Trauma: Childhood, Innocence and Memory in Cypriot Children's Literature since 1974 — 69
    Maria Chatzianastasi

Part 2: The Holocaust

4. Beyond the Ovens: The Changing Nature of Holocaust Children's Literature — 99
    Barbara Krasner

5. Gendered Behavior in Uri Orlev's and Kathy Kacer's Literature about the Holocaust for Children — 121
    Rosemary Horowitz

6. A Sonnet of Atrocity: A Consideration of a Poem Written
by a Child at the Terezín Concentration Camp   143
   Mary Catherine Mueller

Part 3: Dictatorships

7. Communism for Children: Fiction Mediation and
Representations of Past Wrongdoings   161
   Simona Mitroiu

8. The Uses of Allegory to Tell Youth Disappearance and
Mortality under Spain's Dictatorship in Ana María Matute's
1956 *Los niños tontos* (*The Foolish Children*)   179
   Lora L. Looney

9. Confronting Atrocity Through Geometry: Franco's First
Illustrated Biography   201
   María Porras Sánchez

Part 4: Institutions and Domestic Structures

10. Picture Books and Parrhesia: Canadian Residential Schools
and Answering the TRC's Calls to Action   225
    Caroline Bagelman

11. Hidden Atrocities in Cinematic Representations of Chinese
Girlhoods   253
    Chengcheng You

12. Nursery Atrocities: The Australian Children's Classic
The Magic Pudding   273
    Jayson Althofer and Brian Musgrove

13. Freedom in Fiction: Trickster Tales and Enslavement
in the United States   297
    Megan Jeffreys

Contributors   315

Index   321

Illustrations

Figures

1.1 Photograph showing the seventeen Darfuri child artists at the Farchana refugee camp. Source: United States Holocaust Memorial Museum.   26

1.2 Drawing by an art teacher living in the Farchana refugee camp in Chad. He explained that the drawing represents the beauty of his native home in Darfur. Source: United States Holocaust Memorial Museum. Photograph Number: N13664, COC Exhibitions and Historic Photographs, July 2007.   29

1.3 Drawing by Darfurian child living in a refugee camp in Chad depicting daily life in Darfur before the civil war. Source: United States Holocaust Memorial Museum. Photograph Number: N13671, COC Exhibitions and Historic Photographs, July 2007.   31

1.4 Drawing of an attack on a Darfurian village drawn by a child living in the Farchana refugee camp in Chad. Source: United States Holocaust Memorial Museum. Photograph Number: N13661, COC Exhibitions and Historic Photographs, July 2007.   33

1.5 Drawing of an attack on a Darfurian village drawn by a child living in the Farchana refugee camp in Chad. Source: United States Holocaust Memorial Museum. Photograph Number: N13670, COC Exhibitions and Historic Photographs, July 2007.   34

1.6 Drawing of an attack on a Darfurian village drawn by a child living in the Farchana refugee camp in Chad. Source: United States Holocaust Memorial Museum. Photograph Number: N13660, COC Exhibitions and Historic Photographs, July 2007.   34

1.7 Drawing of an attack on a Darfurian village drawn by a child living in the Farchana refugee camp in Chad. Source: United States Holocaust Memorial Museum. Photograph Number: N13667, COC Exhibitions and Historic Photographs, July 2007.   35

1.8 Drawing of a helicopter attack on a Darfurian village drawn by a child living in the Farchana refugee camp in Chad. Source: United States Holocaust Memorial Museum. Photograph Number: N13677, COC Exhibitions and Historic Photographs, July 2007.   36

1.9 Drawing of an attack on a Darfurian village drawn by a child living in the Farchana refugee camp in Chad. Source: United States Holocaust Memorial Museum. Photograph Number: N13675, COC Exhibitions and Historic Photographs, July 2007.   37

1.10 Drawing of an attack on a Darfurian village drawn by a child living in the Farchana refugee camp in Chad. Source: United States Holocaust Memorial Museum. Photograph Number: N13672, COC Exhibitions and Historic Photographs, July 2007.   38

1.11 Drawing of an attack on a Darfurian village drawn by a child living in the Farchana refugee camp in Chad. Source: United States Holocaust Memorial Museum. Photograph Number: N13665, COC Exhibitions and Historic Photographs, July 2007.   40

1.12 Drawing of an attack on a Darfurian village drawn by fourteen-year-old Mahamad Ahmat Haron living in the Farchana refugee camp in Chad. Source: United States Holocaust Memorial Museum. Photograph Number: N13666, COC Exhibitions and Historic Photographs, July 2007.   41

3.1 Illustration no. 1 from the book *The Wolves and Red Riding Hood* (foreword, p. 7).   81

4.1 Number of Children's Holocaust Books Published in North America by Year. Source: Barbara Krasner, Holocaustkidlit.com.   102

4.2 Number of Children's Holocaust Books by Genre, 2002–16. Source: Barbara Krasner, Holocaustkidlit.com.   103

4.3 Number of Titles by Age Group, 2002–16. Source: Barbara Krasner, Holocaustkidlit.com.   103

4.4 Number of Titles by Geography. Source: Barbara Krasner, Holocaustkidlit.com.   112

9.1 Abadía, Ximo, *Frank: La increíble historia de una dictadura olvidada* (Madrid: Dibbuks, 2018), front and back covers.   202

9.2 Abadía, Ximo, *Frank: La increíble historia de una dictadura olvidada* (Madrid: Dibbuks, 2018), 7–8.   209

9.3 Abadía, Ximo, *Frank: La increíble historia de una dictadura olvidada* (Madrid: Dibbuks, 2018), 21–22.   210

9.4 Abadía, Ximo, *Frank: La increíble historia de una dictadura olvidada* (Madrid: Dibbuks, 2018), 35–36.   213

9.5 Abadía, Ximo, *Frank: La increíble historia de una dictadura olvidada* (Madrid: Dibbuks, 2018), 44–45.   214

Table

4.1 Categories by Year, 2002–16. Source: Barbara Krasner, Holocaustkidlit.com.   104

Introduction

Victoria Nesfield and Philip Smith

> But what, then, is a naturalistic writer for children to do? Can he present the child with evil and an insoluble problem . . . To give a child a picture of . . . gas chambers . . . or famines or the cruelties of a psychotic patient, and say, "Well, baby, this is how it is, what are you going to make of it?"—that is surely unethical. If you suggest that there is a "solution" to these monstrous facts, you are lying to the child. If you insist that there isn't, you are overwhelming him with a load he is not strong enough yet to carry.
>
> —Ursula Le Guin, *The Language of the Night*, 1992[1]

> [A]ll of the best children's literature, if anyone has been paying attention, hinges on betrayal, the heartlessness of nature, and death.
>
> —Laura van den Berg, "The Pitch" 2019[2]

This volume concerns literary and other media that describe and mediate children's experience and knowledge of atrocity. It is, we hope, not redundant to note here that many children do experience (per the OED) "savage enormity [and] horrible or heinous wickedness" both on a global scale, as victims of mass catastrophic events, and within the often-hidden space of the domestic sphere. In many cases, as with the United States' program of separating migrant children from their parents, atrocity is often orchestrated on a global scale, but its effects, particularly for those who lack the knowledge to place their suffering in context, are private and specific. As author Gavriel Savit argues, "human beings encounter the same problems throughout all phases of life"—trauma does not discriminate by age.[3] As the quote from Ursula Le Guin above suggests, however, managing the confluence of childhood in and atrocity in fiction is a difficult, if not impossible, task; parsing the experience of catastrophe through a child protagonist and/or in a format that a child can understand is an undertaking fraught with pitfalls.

Many critics have argued that literature is an eminently suitable site to play out the childhood experience of atrocity. Bruno Bettelheim asserts that fairy stories for children should include evil acts for children to understand and process—that working through fictional traumas is a means to rehearse the working-through of real traumas.[4] His argument centers on works created for child readers but is equally applicable to works created for adult readers who may still be coming to terms with childhood trauma.[5] The literature of childhood, as Kenneth B. Kidd similarly observes, is not insulated from violence:

> Fairy tales are considered potentially traumatizing because of their sometimes severe scenes and themes (violence, infanticide, child abandonment) even as they are also positioned as therapeutic or cathartic. Picturebooks, including those of Maurice Sendak, are increasingly focused on the child's experience of and responses to loss and trauma. The adolescent novel [. . .] trends toward traumatic subjects in more ways than one. Even Golden Age aftertexts move toward as much as away from certain kinds of trauma writing, especially sexual-abuse narratives.[6]

The literature of childhood, then, has not historically served to insulate potential child readers, but to present potential sources of trauma in a controlled context. A child who has learned about death through literature has some context for understanding the death of a grandparent or pet, whereas a child who has never been introduced to death through fiction must make sense of it as they cope with grief when it springs unexpected and uninvited into their own life. An adult, similarly, may turn to a work of literature, and in particular literature that centers on a child's experience, to provide order to their own grief.

Many, echoing Le Guin, add a note of caution; as Lydia Kokkola, among others, argues, if literature of atrocity is not presented in an appropriate context, child readers may fail to disentangle the truth of its setting from the fictionality of its specifics. Children, as Hester Burton argues, are not less intelligent than adults but possess less knowledge.[7] This lack of experience can lead to a failure to distinguish between works that seek to describe a historical object and those that are pure invention; children often mistake fact for fiction and fiction for fact. This is even more fraught when a work moves between the two, offering fictional characters operating in an environment that is sketched from true events.

Fiction, we may then reasonably conclude, is an effective supplement to historical studies. This assertion is not limited to children's literature but can extend to works for adults that include child protagonists. Whether we imagine the experiences of Florence Horner through Nabokov's *Lolita* (1955) or the experience of the children indoctrinated with Nazi ideology in *Jojo Rabbit* (2019), narrative can make history personal: rather than simply stating what occurred, literature can imbue the historical object with a sense of felt experience. Indeed, child focalizers are, as many of the chapters in this volume suggest, a convenient way to introduce readers to a historical event because the child, like the reader or viewer, lacks the knowledge required to put the events being described into context.

Literature presents us with the moral conundrums and impossible decisions experienced by historical subjects and, as such, can be a vehicle for the exploration of atrocity. We can read the facts of the Holocaust, but these facts are made all the more vivid by Primo Levi's pained recollection of secretly sharing a water supply with an Italian compatriot; Elie Wiesel's horror upon seeing Akiba Drumer abandoned by his son to die in the snow in the death march from Auschwitz, only later to find himself resenting his own father's plaintive, dying, cries; the contrived and cruel Nazi methods of placing some Jewish prisoners in positions of power over others, crafting a hierarchy that pits victim against victim for so-called privileges. As Paula T. Connolly argues, similarly, "fiction often becomes a way not simply to 'story' a scene of slavery but to allow authors to imagine the lives that could not be fully expressed in antebellum slave narratives, particularly the lives of those who did not escape or survive slavery."[8] Fiction can bring the historical object to life, as it were—and it can provide a controlled space to explore what otherwise might be emotionally damaging.

Fiction, then, can manage a reader's experience and suggest means of interpretation, and so an effective literature of atrocity can, as Kokkola argues, "provide a new focus" for the reader's "grief."[9] It is perhaps these qualities that led to the outpouring of Holocaust literature for children from the 1980s onward, prompting Kidd to comment that "there seems to be consensus now that children's literature is the most rather than the least appropriate form for trauma work."[10]

And yet narrative can also distort our understanding of a historical object. Connolly observes, for example, that children's stories that concern slavery often avoid direct representations of violence. In some instances, such as *The Child's Story of the Negro* (1938) by Jane Dabney Shackleford, Connolly argues, such editing threatens to contribute to the erasure of enslavement from American cultural consciousness. As Kokkola asserts (and Connolly would no doubt concur), attempts to fictionalize atrocity bear a "greater moral obligation to be historically accurate."[11] To omit the worst parts of the transatlantic slave trade, the Holocaust, the Rwandan genocide, or similar acts of widescale violence is to misrepresent those events and to present a sanitized version that is simply untrue.

Conversely, to include the horrors of atrocity in full may also be detrimental. In the case of children's literature, violent material will be upsetting for some young readers, but this, of course, is not the only possible outcome; when Ursula Le Guin writes in the quote that opens this introduction of "a load [that the child reader] is not strong enough yet to carry," we might imagine a range of possible ways in which a child might signal their failure to bear such a burden. The danger is not only of children being upset by violent content, but also of them reacting with merriment or playful reenactment; children, as J. M. Barrie elegantly asserts, are "gay and innocent and heartless."[12] One is reminded of the famous incident, for example, from 1994 of students from Castlemont High School, Oakland, being ejected from a screening of *Schindler's List* (1993) for laughing during the film. This may be a case of students responding negatively to the tone of the work with which they are engaged. As David L. Russell argues, "Children's books about the Holocaust are unabashedly didactic—they have an overt moral purpose and because of that they are delivered with the same fervor as those Puritan tales of James Janeway or Benjamin Keath that many modern readers find so startling."[13] Geoffrey Short reports that when they are first introduced to the Holocaust, children often either blame victims or suggest that the perpetrators may have been justified in their actions.[14] The danger, in other words, is not simply of child readers being upset, but of them reacting in a manner, or of receiving a message, other than that which the creator intended.

There is evidence to suggest that, while our fears about exposing children to the worst of our history may not be unfounded, they may be exaggerated. Jefrey L. Derevensky and Ursula F. Sherman, for example, both describe classrooms in which children aged ten and older successfully engaged with Holocaust literature.[15] Both report that the children they worked with, counter to Short's arguments, grasped the key events and facts of what occurred. Their work suggests that our concern with potentially negative outcomes may obscure the far more significant benefits of teaching atrocity through children's literature

Kokkola asserts that children should be exposed to atrocity through literature but that the process should be mediated by an adult to avoid undesirable responses. She further acknowledges that withholding information can lead to confusion but sees potential for literature that omits certain information and relies on the presence of an adult to elaborate on what is implied or otherwise mediate the child reader's experience. Connolly echoes this assertion, noting instances where the psychological and physical violence of enslavement is implied in certain texts without being depicted directly, communicating the brutality of enslavement while, to use a favorite term from the discipline, "sparing the child." Both Kokkola and Connolly advocate for a kind of fiction that leaves productive gaps (what Perry Nodelman calls a "shadow text") to which the work alludes but does not make explicit.[16] Kokkola argues that "The events of the Holocaust are simply too large to be intelligently condensed into a single narrative. Expecting adults to mediate a child reader's comprehension only becomes irresponsible when the resulting text is incomprehensible without such intervention."[17] She advocates for texts that are complete narratives but call attention to their omissions, prompting the child reader to approach an adult for answers. Such a strategy is useful for engaging a child's curiosity but, perhaps dangerously, assumes the presence of an adult who is capable of providing the words that the text omits.

The tension between these two positions—the need to inform and the need to protect—lies at the heart of many discussions of atrocity and the literature of childhood. As Kidd argues: "On the one hand, we continue to believe that children should be protected from trauma, but increasingly we also seem to expect that trauma must be experienced in order to be understood, so that books about trauma can only be effective if they frighten and even endanger the child."[18] The question, to return once again to Le Guin's quote above, seems impossible to resolve; to suggest a solution is to lie, yet to refuse to offer a solution is cruel. In *Sparing the Child*, Hamida Bosmajian offers a taxonomy of sorts for strategies to mitigate the experience of trauma through fiction such as the reader proxy who witnesses but is not subject to violence, or the "trading places" scenario in which the protagonist experiences only temporary danger before a return to normal. Such strategies can be effective, yet by mitigating the trauma they risk, as with the reliance on an adult who can "fill the gaps," misrepresenting their subject.[19]

One might argue, of course, that interventions are important, even at the risk of cruelty, because there is a significant danger of adults deliberately misinforming children. As Connolly persuasively argues, children's literature has historically served as a political tool and a battleground over the ways in which young people understand the world. The 1838 publication *A Slave's Friend*, for example, encourages readers to become politically active by petitioning their congressman, arranging fundraisers, and forming antislavery societies for young people. Literature, however, is a weapon anyone can wield:

> for slavery proponents, children's literature offered potentially limitless possibilities both to protect their racialised view of nationhood and to justify their position [. . .] Despite the obvious disagreements between antebellum slavery opponents and supporters, they both believed that to win the child was to win the future of the nation.[20]

The consequences of misrepresentation can be severe; one might think, for example, of the 2018 controversy over the worksheet titled "The Life of Slaves: A Balanced View" distributed to students in the eighth grade at Great Hearts Monte Vista in San Antonio that included a space for the respondent to list "positive" aspects of enslavement. As the texts described in Donnarae McCann's *White Supremacy in Children's Literature* or Hamida Bosmajian's *Sparing the Child*, children's literature can be a powerful tool in enabling and perpetuating atrocity.[21] As Edward L. Sullivan argues:

> Neo-Nazi and other white supremacist organisations prey upon alienated, angry, impressionable youth. They tap into the anger and ignorance of these young people and teach them how to hate. They fill the voids in their lives with it; hate gives their lives a sense of direction and purpose.[22]

It is entirely prescient given that at present many adults, including 41 percent of millennials, do not know the basic facts of the Holocaust.[23] In a world where we encounter various shades of Holocaust denial or the kind of willful misrepresentation of enslavement found in, for example, Disney's *Song of the South*, as Jeffreys discusses in detail, many of my students argue that we have a duty to tell children the truth, even the worst parts of the truth, before someone else tells them lies.

Even if we are resolved to tell the truth, the path still remains difficult. Accounts based on true events may still be too myopic to present a complete picture. As Connolly argues, stories that end with a formerly enslaved person escaping to the North "risk suggesting that escape from slavery was always successful, potentially implying that if slaves had only enough determination they would have freed themselves"[24] Such accounts are not inaccurate—many did escape their enslavement—but collectively they suggest that such escape was the norm. Kokkola similarly warns against texts that may be "historically accurate" but present unusual cases such that "the pattern which emerges from the corpus is not."[25] If we teach children that the truly brave escaped enslavement and the death camps, what, then, are we teaching them of those who did not escape or survive?

An additional fold, of course, in the ethics of representing atrocity is in the question of whether such representation is even possible. As Hayden White, among others, warns, any attempt to describe a historical object unavoidably imbues that object with qualities and meanings not inherent in the object itself. As soon as we attempt to render an event in language, photography, visual art, or any other medium, we transform it, organizing it within the conventions of the medium we have chosen. While this is true of any reimagining of history, it can often be more acute and more contested when we consider atrocity. A key contention in the study of Holocaust literature is that fiction around the Holocaust can, at best, approximate its scale and violence. As Berel Lang asserts, "traditional forms—the developmental order of the novel, the predictability of prosody, the comforting representations of landscape or portrait in painting—are quite inadequate for the images of a subject with the moral dimensions and impersonal will of the Holocaust."[26] The true dimensions of genocide ultimately lie beyond our understanding. Children's literature and the literature of childhood must serve, as Adrienne Kertzer claims, "our need for hope and happy endings," yet what happy ending can possibly be drawn from the torture, humiliation, and murder of millions of people?[27] One recalls the words of Tim O'Brien, writing about the Vietnam War:

> A true war story is never moral. It does not instruct, nor encourage virtue, nor suggest models of proper human behavior, nor restrain men from doing the things men have always done. If a story seems moral, do not believe it. If at the end of a war story you feel uplifted, or if you feel that some small bit of rectitude has been salvaged from the larger waste, then you have been made the victim of a very old and terrible lie. There

is no rectitude whatsoever. There is no virtue. As a first rule of thumb, therefore, you can tell a true war story by its absolute and uncompromising allegiance to obscenity and evil.[28]

Deborah R. Geis, similarly, argues that attempts to force atrocity to conform to traditional structures threaten to:

> [S]anitize and codify the Shoah in Hollywood terms so that a kind of catharsis results from the closing reunion, where (as in *Jurassic Park*) the ultimate sense is that the audience members have vicariously been "saved" and can go home safely without having to worry about the threat, whether of Nazis or Velociraptors.[29]

The question is not simply of presenting atrocity the "correct" way—free from a sense of catharsis, for example, or using a format that resists easy answers—but of recognizing the failure of language itself to adequately describe such a subject. Lawrence Langer argues that "language alone cannot give meaning to Auschwitz . . . The depth and uncontained scope of the Nazi ruthlessness poisoned both Jewish and Christian precedents and left millions of victims without metaphors to imagine, not to say justify, their fate."[30]

The impossibility of fully articulating atrocity is reflected in the ways in which we memorialize it for young people. Students visiting Auschwitz from UK schools and colleges in a government-sponsored initiative are presented with—by means of orientation around the sites of Auschwitz and Birkenau—examples of literature as diverse as Kitty Hart-Moxon's typically unsentimental recollection of being tasked to the "*scheisse kommando*," Elie Wiesel's famous seven declarations that "never again" would he forget his first night in camp, and Leonard Cohen's poem about the inconspicuous ordinariness of Adolf Eichmann. Moving from one site or artifact of atrocity to another, be it the glass cabinet of decaying hair shorn from women prisoners, the empty tins of Zyklon B, Kommandant Hoess's family home overlooking the gas chamber of Auschwitz I, or the railway line within the Birkenau gatehouse, young visitors attempt to reconcile a vast and diverse history with fragments of literature, glimpses into the lives, memories, and identities of victims, survivors, even perpetrators. From this jigsaw they are asked to draw out the moral imperative to stand up to racism, intolerance, and persecution, and encourage their peers to do likewise.

Many of the chapters in this volume discuss the unrepresentable nature of atrocity, or the manner in which the authors, illustrators, and filmmakers negotiate representing children's experience of atrocity. That this question recurs throughout the breadth of contexts here, demonstrates that it remains a live issue. Our concern, of course, is not simply of whether atrocity can be communicated through any form of art, but whether it can be communicated specifically through art for and about children.

The question of audience can have dramatic implications for our understanding of the audience for texts that address atrocity not least because there are some children and adults who have experienced atrocity directly and for whom literature is not a preemptive measure but a source of retrospective understanding. Children whose lives have been affected by war or forced migration—children, in our contemporary moment, who are fleeing Syria, for example—may need literature even more urgently to help them make sense of their experience. Various writers, Arthur Frank among them, have argued that narrative can be an effective means to heal the damage of trauma.[31] In *My Mother's Voice* Adrienne Kertzer describes learning about her own family history through literature and the value of narrative as a means to allow readers to come to an understanding of events that are otherwise unavailable to them.[32] The body of literature in which children work through their own trauma, such as the collection of art and essays *The Day Our World Changed* that addresses the September 11 terrorist attacks, remains small and undertheorized.[33]

This volume asks if atrocity can be represented in a way that is truthful and respectful of the victims and, if so, what should we include and what should we omit? How can a child's experiences of atrocity through literature be appropriately managed? What considerations should we make for readers who are victims of atrocity? And how do we ensure that children reach an appropriate and true understanding of atrocity? None of these questions have easy answers, nor should they. They are difficult because we (we as adults, we as a society), ourselves, have not yet come to terms with, or even developed an appropriate language to discuss, the atrocities that shape our history and our present.

A History

The fairy tales and folk tales that, for centuries, were transmitted orally for all audiences and have, from the eighteenth century onward come to make up the canon of children's literature, contain a great deal of violence including murder, sexual assault, and war; Perrault's retelling of Red Riding Hood in *Histoires ou contes du temps passé* (1697), for example, concludes with an explicit warning to young girls that leaves little doubt as to the threat that "wolves" present. If we are to understand the origins of childhood, as we now understand it, as the eighteenth century, with John Newbery's *A Little Pretty Pocket Book* (1744) among the first such works, then the literature of childhood took less than six decades to explicitly engage historical trauma.[34] *The Little Reader's Assistant* (1790) by Noah Webster, includes two abolitionist essays. It was followed by works such as *The Slave's Friend* (1836–1838) and *The Anti-Slavery Alphabet* (1846). While such works took an abolitionist stance, they ran a wide political spectrum, including from those who agreed with many pro-enslavement arguments and advocated for a gradual move away from enslavement. They also, Connolly argues, often communicate an implicit message of white superiority even as they advocate for black emancipation.[35]

Early abolitionist texts for children also precede, in Jane Thrailkill's terms, literature that addresses the trauma. Thrailkill argues that Mark Twain's realist fiction opened a path from the literary suffering child to a modern theory of trauma.[36] As scholars such as Patricia Pace and Kenneth B. Kidd have argued, the exploration of trauma through the literature of childhood is dependent on literary explorations of interiority that only began in the late nineteenth century.[37] Kidd argues that it is no coincidence that children's literature as a widespread genre emerged during the interwar years in concert with the most important work from the pioneers of psychotherapy for children Anna Freud and Melanie Klein. He thus conceives of a children's literature of atrocity as an "ongoing collaborative project of psychoanalysis and literature."[38]

Identifying the first work to address the Holocaust through a child protagonist takes us into the problematic question of how we define children. Horst Rosenthall created a series of picture books within the Gurs camp; his heavy use of irony and the absence of a young audience suggests that his first readers were adults, yet Mickey's innocent perspective, as well as his proportions, is unmistakably childlike.[39] Young poets in the Terezín camp, discussed in this volume by Mary Catherine Muller, also describe the Holocaust through a child's perspective. Similarly, Anne Frank's diary, which first appeared in English in 1952 as *The Diary of a Young Girl*, similarly describes a child's experience of atrocity and is perhaps the first work of Holocaust literature to be read by children on a large scale. Ruth Franklin asserts "[a]s a child, I was obsessed with Anne Frank's Diary. Like Anne, I wanted to grow up to be a writer; like her, I kept a diary (though less faithfully), which for a time I addressed, following her model, as Kitty; like her, I agonized over how little my mother understood me and longed to swoon in a boy's arms."[40]

While Anne Frank may be the most famous Jewish child in the history of literature for young people, Hamida Bosmajian questions whether the success of the *Diary* was that it was not necessarily a record of Jewish life in hiding so much as an adolescent in hiding. As Franklin recalls, Anne's ambitions, her character, her temperament, spoke to her young readers, and while her Jewish identity is present and never disguised, and although it is the precise reason the diary has been so widely adopted by educators, the religious and cultural aspects of the Franks' Jewish life are not central to the narrative. Anne's preoccupations in hiding spoke to a wider audience than other diaries of murdered Jewish youth found after the war.[41] Lawrence Langer makes a similar argument in *Using and Abusing the Holocaust*, in which he argues that Anne Frank's diary has been used "to force us to construe the reality of an event before we have experienced it, to confirm an agenda in advance in order to discourage us from raising disturbing questions that might subvert the tranquility of our response."[42] Anne Frank, he asserts, has been mobilized, improperly, as a figure of hope and used as part of a grand project that runs throughout American culture of refusing to confront the realities and implications of genocide.

Anne Frank's *Diary of a Young Girl* represents another trait common to literature of the Holocaust that concerns young people, in that it was written "at the periphery of the disaster."[43] As Bosmajian asserts, it is the fate of Jewish victims that literature of the Holocaust fixates on, yet that fate is played out "off-stage" and rarely to the central protagonist.[44] The peripheral role of the child emerges as a motif that Sue Vice, in *Children Writing the Holocaust*, notes is accompanied by several characterizations: "defamiliarization; errors of fact and perception; attention to detail at the expense of context" among them, and—particularly evident in Anne Frank's *Diary of a Young Girl*—"age-specific concerns with the nature of writing and memory."[45] As Vice recognizes with particular reference to Binjamin Wilkomirski's *Fragments*, these motifs problematize a critical understanding of the text when they become transplanted into fraudulent testimonies, and the reader, accustomed to the characteristics of a naive and traumatized child writer—the reliance more on "acts of personal cruelty than on the institutional attrition"—accepts the validity of the text.[46]

Other early media consumed by children to address the Holocaust were horror comics. "Corpse of the Jury," published in *Voodoo #5* in 1953, and Bernard Krigstein's "Master Race," which was published in *Impact* in 1955, were both set, in part, in death camps.[47] Whether these should be considered childhood adjacent, however, remains open to debate. Creator Al Feldstein asserts that horror comic creators "were writing for teenagers and young adults; we were writing it for the guys in the army."[48] Many of his contemporaries, the highly influential psychologist Dr. Frederick Wertham among them, argued that horror comics were reaching the hands of children, and readership data from the period bear out such a claim.[49] Perhaps the first work of Holocaust fiction that was accessible to (although not explicitly written for) young readers is Herman H. Field's *Angry Harvest* (1958), another text at the periphery of disaster, which concerns a girl hiding from the Nazis on a farm in occupied Poland.[50]

While Anne Frank's diary was a best seller in Britain, the Holocaust did not truly enter into public discourse until the trial of Adolf Eichmann in 1961. A steady stream of Holocaust histories, (auto)biographies, fiction, drama, and documentary followed. By 1987, more than three hundred books had been published in the United States that addressed the Holocaust and World War II.[51] The Six Day War in 1967 was a formative moment in shaping a new, empowered postwar Jewish identity, both in Israel and the diaspora, particularly in the United States. In this period, some of the earliest works to depict and be read by children were published, including *Miriam* by Aimee Sommerfelt, first published in English in 1963; *The Long Escape* by Irving Werstein (1964); and Martha Bennet Stiles's *Darkness Over Land* (1966). The field of Holocaust literature was transformed by second-generation Holocaust survivor Art Spiegelman's comic book auto/biography of his father *Maus* (serialized 1980–91)—a book that successfully grapples with both the emotional weight of trauma and the impossibility of re-creating Auschwitz on the page. As famous, although not as critically celebrated, is John Boyne's *The Boy in the Striped Pyjamas*, a text that has been heavily criticized for its inaccurate depiction of life in the death camps and yet has, inarguably, had a tremendous impact on readers both in book form and in the film that followed.[52]

The outpouring of children's literature to engage with the Holocaust has informed responses to other atrocities. Yoo Kyung Sung, notes, for example, that Korean picture books that describe the experience of "comfort women"—those held in sexual slavery by the Japanese military—tend to follow similar themes to children's literature of the Holocaust.[53] We might look, too, to depictions of the bombing of Hiroshima and Nagasaki in children's literature, including, most famously, Toshi Maruki's *Hiroshima No*

Pika (1982). The relationship between different literatures of atrocity has not always flowed in one direction only—Keiji Nakazawa's manga *Barefoot Gen* (1972–87), while not a direct inspiration, preceded Art Spiegelman's *Maus* by almost a decade.

Children's literature has grown to encompass atrocities beyond the Holocaust, the transatlantic slave trade, and the bombing of Hiroshima and Nagasaki. Forchuk Skrypuch's *The Hunger* (1999), for example, addresses the Armenian genocide, and Jean-Philippe Stassen's *Deogratias* (2006), discussed in this volume, centers on the Rwandan genocide. The September 11 terrorist attacks prompted a large number of children's novels and novels concerning childhood, among them Jonathan Safran Foer's *Extremely Loud & Incredibly Close* (2005), *Fireboat: The Heroic Adventures of the John J. Harvey* by Maira Kalman (2002), and *On That Day* by Andrea Patel (2002). Kidd characterizes the works to immediately follow the attacks, enmeshed as they were in the politics of their time, as "the worst sort of literary-psychological merger, and in the service of reactionary politics."[54] It took some time for works to emerge that escaped what many, Kidd among them, saw as the oversentimentalized nationalism of the early 2000s. Marvel's *Mz Marvel* (2014–present) is one such example, imagining as it does the life of an American-Pakistani Muslim teenager who develops superpowers. *Mz Marvel* explores the traumas of Islamophobia and racism and uses superherodom as a way to explore these themes.[55]

Representing Childhood and Atrocity

As Marah Gubar asserts, children's literature represents a "richly heterogenous group of texts" that cannot be identified by a set of necessary and sufficient conditions, but by a group of family resemblances.[56] This volume encompasses representations of atrocity in media by children, media for children, and media with child protagonists. These are forms with overlapping but distinct audiences and goals. Many of the works discussed are intended for an audience of young readers and viewers, but not all. *Deogratias: A Tale of Rwanda*, *Angels Wear White*, and *Einstein and Einstein* prominently feature the experiences of young people, but their depiction of atrocity suggests the expectation of a (perhaps young) adult audience. If we are to accept Perry Nodelman's description of children's literature as providing child readers with an adult's account of childhood experience (or rather childhood as conceived by an adult), then children's poetry from the Terezín camp, discussed by Mary Catherine Mueller, and the drawings by child survivors from Darfur/Farchana, discussed by Chigbo Arthur Anyaduba, also would not be considered children's literature.[57] What unites these texts is that they present childhood experiences of atrocity. While we acknowledge that including a wide range of works forces us to straddle the often-disparate fields of childhood studies and children's literature, we feel that the dialogue that emerges from placing these studies in the same volume is worthwhile.

The types of atrocity found within these pages are also different; every chapter describes a system of violence that operates on a societal or international scale. Within this broad definition, however, there are significant differences. The concepts of *dongshi* and *guai*, as You argues, are used to justify the emotional and physical abuse of Chinese girls; this violence is different in kind from the massacre of Tutsi in Rwanda in 1994. The Holocaust, as has often been argued, resists all comparison.[58] At the level of the individual's internality—the space in which literature and other media often operates—an atrocity does not produce a single experience, but a variety of specific and personal experiences. This is particularly true of the experiences of children, who often lack the ability to understand their suffering in context. In this sense, then, these chapters do not, and should not, seek to present a totalizing account of atrocity. They are united in that they all address media that describes children suffering.

We did not set out with a structure for this volume in mind, but as we worked with our authors four broad categories presented themselves. The first section of this book concerns texts addressing late twentieth-century genocides and atrocities, those that have taken place as the world continued to insist "never again," and when the canon of Holocaust literature was well established. The opening chapter of the volume specifically questions how effectively a contemporary genocide may be engaged with when viewed through the lens of Holocaust memorialization. The second section considers texts on the Holocaust—the genocide of Jews and massacres of other groups carried out by Germany and its allies and collaborators in the buildup to and during World War II. The dedication of a section of the volume solely to this genocide is not intended to present the Holocaust as the ur-atrocity, but rather to recognize that children's literature that concerns the Holocaust has a longer history and, at present, represents a larger corpus than that devoted to other genocides. It is further the case that much of the theoretical and literary groundwork in the field of atrocity studies more broadly emerged in response to the Holocaust. In retrospect, a critical mass of works on this subject was inevitable: so many books and films concern children's experiences of the Holocaust that it has defined the genre of a literature of atrocity and exerts a gravitational pull on all that has followed. Naturally, Holocaust memory's presence in the global public domain remains a live issue, but it is also one that can offer a platform to articulate other histories. Michael Rothberg terms this "multi-directional memory" and draws on both Holocaust and postcolonial studies in exploring how various histories may be remembered via Holocaust memory rather than being subsumed by it.[59] In the UK at present, decolonizing the curricula is high on the agenda in schools, colleges, and universities, a legacy of the Black Lives Matter movement that has entered the global public domain with significant momentum and rightfully demands serious and sustained focus on the transatlantic slave trade and its global impact. There is, to borrow from Michael Rothberg's more recent text *The Implicated Subject: Beyond Victims and Perpetrators*, a growing recognition that worldwide we are all "implicated subjects" in various contexts and histories.[60] This volume, while inevitably and invaluably informed by the wealth of scholarship on the Holocaust, richly benefits from the knowledge, experience, and expertise of its contributors across a global context.

The third section concerns other inter/national atrocities that occurred under dictatorial regimes, ranging from Spain under Franco to Soviet states. Here, children serve as witnesses to the violence of the regimes, and their disillusionment mirrors the ideological collapse of the regimes being described. The first section concerns childhood experiences of war, namely the Rwandan genocide, the Greek Cypriot War, and the genocide in Darfur. In these texts, young protagonists and witnesses document the working-through of violence they witnessed. The final section concerns social institutions and domestic structures; the racist, sexist, and colonialist systems that oppress, tyrannize, and kill marginalized groups. While the aftershocks and intergenerational trauma of the events described in earlier chapters remain palpable, it is these chapters, in many cases describing places where we and our contributors have lived and worked, where atrocity feels at its most immediate and urgent.

Chigbo Arthur Anyaduba opens the volume with a reading of a series of drawings produced by refugee children from Darfur/Farchana, held in the archives of the United States Holocaust Memorial Museum. The drawings are firsthand accounts by young eyewitnesses to a very recent atrocity, and Anyaduba argues in "Children's Humanitarian Arts and the Genocide in Darfur: Drawing Loss and Atrocity" that providing traumatized children with the chance to testify with images rather than words offers the young artists a way to capture a snapshot of their traumatic memories. Not only that, but the spectator to the artwork is challenged with confronting scenes of atrocity as they occurred to and in front of young eyes and deciphering the imagery that is presented without narrative or context and without editorial interference. Anyaduba also challenges the notion of multidirectionality posed by Rothberg, identifying the varying cultural capital of different atrocities, particularly when comparing the Holocaust with African genocides.

Remaining in Africa, J. P. Stassen's *Deogratias: A Tale of Rwanda* is an important and much-celebrated work that explores the Rwandan genocide from the perspective of a perpetrator. In "Framing the Unframeable: *Deogratias* and the Horror of Genocide," Kaitlyn Newman explores the text through the lens of unspeakability, demonstrating that Stassen uses metaphor and conspicuous omissions to suggest that which lies beyond representation.

Maria Chatzianastasi considers a collection of stories not widely recognized in literature outside its geographical context—that of the occupation of Cyprus and the division between Greek and Turkish Cypriots. In "Tracing Trauma: Childhood, Innocence, and Memory in Cypriot Children's Literature since 1974," Chatzianastasi interrogates and tackles themes of trauma, occupation, disenfranchisement, and fractured relationships in this as-yet untranslated Greek-language literature, with the authors of these books writing from experience and reliving these experiences through the lens of youth.

Barbara Krasner opens the following section with an overview of the contemporary landscape of Holocaust literature for young readers. "Beyond the Ovens: The Changing Nature of Holocaust Children's Literature" draws on Krasner's extensive work tracking recent publications in the field to present a wider context, identifying twelve subcontexts in which children's literature about the Holocaust set their scenes. Arguing against the critics who claim that the field of Holocaust literature for the young is oversaturated, Krasner identifies the spaces for further thoughtful interrogation on the Holocaust and other atrocities.

Considering Holocaust literature for young readers, Rosemary Horowitz's chapter "Gendered Behavior in Uri Orlev's and Kathy Kacer's Literature about the Holocaust for Children" considers the role of gender in a collection of texts by Orlev and Kacer. Identifying that gender is a critical factor in understanding the traumas and memories of adult survivors, Horowitz argues for the same recognition of how gendered identity is formed for children and how this shapes Holocaust narratives.

Child art and other juvenilia can reveal a great deal about children's internal lives free of the expectations and literary constructs imposed by adults. Mary Catherine Mueller's "A Sonnet of Atrocity: A Consideration of a Poem Written by a Child at the Terezín Concentration Camp" seeks to understand children's experience of the Holocaust in their own terms. In a close analysis of one poem by a young poet identified only by first name and accommodation block, she identifies the recurring themes of absence: absence of home, absence of beauty in nature, and absence of names.

In "Communism for Children: Fiction Mediation and Representations of Past Wrongdoings," Simona Mitroiu examines two texts that examine childhoods in post-Communist countries, *Marzi: A Memoir* by Marzena Sowa and *Breaking Stalin's Nose* by Eugene Yelchin (both 2011). Both texts, she demonstrates, document the indoctrination of children and describe the author's disillusionment with a totalitarian regime.

Lora Looney's chapter, "The Uses of Allegory to Tell Youth Disappearance and Mortality Under Spain's Dictatorship in Ana María Matute's 1956 *Los niños tontos* (*The Foolish Children*)," examines the allegorical depiction of children and childhood in post-Civil War–era Spain. The text, she argues, attests to the suffering, disappearance, and death of children. They resist not only the erasure of these deaths but also the rhetoric of the Franco regime.

María Porras Sánchez considers the representation of Spanish history in Ximo Abadía's *Frank: La increíble historia de una dictadura olvidada* (2018). In her chapter, "Confronting Atrocity through Geometry: Franco's First Illustrated Biography," she argues that the book uses an abstract and geometric visual rhetoric to describe not only Franco's rise to power but also the atrocities, many of them still unknown in scope, committed by his regime. The text, she demonstrates, articulates the violence of Spanish history in a manner that is apprehensible for child readers.

The fourth section opens with "Picture Books and Parrhesia: The Role of Multi-modal Texts in Examining Canada's Colonial Violence." Caroline Bagelman writes from a Canadian perspective, exploring Canada's treatment of indigenous children in the residential school system. The Canadian Truth and Reconciliation Commission recognized the need to acknowledge Canada's past treatment of indigenous young people; however, Bagelman's chapter recalls the reluctance she encountered to tackle this through pedagogical initiatives, and her own educational model, using picture books to engage children in their country's history and diversity.

In "Hidden Atrocities in the Cinematic Representations of Chinese Girlhood," Chengcheng You considers the representation of Chinese girlhoods in the films *Angels Wear White* (2017) and *Einstein and Einstein* (2018). Both films, she argues, grapple with the problems of filial piety and socially sanctioned abuse in many Chinese households. Each film, in different ways, depicts young Chinese women seeking to negotiate an identity within a toxic environment. You's chapter is the only one to consider film and refers to a notion of atrocity that, prima facie, is more muted than the historical contexts of war or dictatorial regimes discussed elsewhere. The fact that the abusive treatment and sexual violence encountered by the characters in the films You identifies appear to have become normalized is precisely what makes them atrocities.

In "Nursery Atrocities: The Australian Children's Classic *The Magic Pudding*," Jayson Althofer and Brian Musgrove identify the colonial attitudes and agendas at work in a widely read and popular children's book, *The Magic Pudding*. Althofer and Musgrove read in Norman Lindsay's 1918 fantasy story—one of anthropomorphized animals and talking food which was widely praised at its publication for its wholesome and entertaining appeal to Australian children—the sinister undertones of racism and veiled allusions to the "historic atrocity" against the Aboriginal population.

Finally, in "Freedom in Fiction: Trickster Tales and Enslavement in the United States," a chapter that tackles the transatlantic slave trade discussed here and the multiple purposes of narratives of slavery, Megan Jeffreys focuses on enslavement in the American South and a series of stories made famous for young audiences by Walt Disney and the *Song of the South* film. More than entertaining stories of anthropomorphic animals and their adventures, Joel Chandler Harris's trickster stories of Brer Rabbit and his ploys to overcome Brer Fox and Brer Wolf were stories of resistance, caution, and education for enslaved adults and children.

Notes

1. Ursula Le Guin, *The Language of the Night: Essays on Fantasy and Science Fiction* (New York: Ultramarine Publishing, 1979), 69–70.
2. Laura Van Den Beerg, "The Pitch," *McSweeny's #55* (2019): 91.
3. The Guardian Children's Books Podcast "Gavriel Savit," March 16, 2019.
4. Bruno Bettleheim, *The Uses of Enchantment: The Meaning and Importance of Fairy Tales* (New York: Vintage, 2010). C. S. Lewis offers a similar argument in his essay "On Three Ways of Writing for Children" found in, among other volumes, *Of Other Worlds* (Harcourt, 2002).
5. There exists a rich literature on "bibliotherapy" as a treatment for PTSD in both children and adults. See Calla E. Y. Glavin and Paul Montgomery, "Creative Bibliotherapy for Post-traumatic Stress Disorder (PTSD): A Systematic Review," *Journal of Poetry Therapy* 30, vol. 2 (2017): 95–107.

6. Kenneth B. Kidd, *Freud in Oz* (Minneapolis: University of Minnesota Press, 2011), 184.

7. Hester Burton, "The Writing of Historical Novels," *The Horn Book Magazine* (XLV) 3 (1969): 271–76, 276.

8. Paula T. Connolly, *Slavery in American Children's Literature 1790—2010* (Iowa City: University of Iowa Press, 2013), 201. We maintain the integrity of quoted material in this instance, but recognize throughout this volume that *enslavement* is now the preferred terminology to *slavery*.

9. Lydia Kokkola, *Representing the Holocaust* (New York and London: Routledge, 2009), 173.

10. Kidd, *Freud in Oz*, 181.

11. Kokkola, *Representing the Holocaust*, 3.

12. James Matthew Barrie, *Peter Pan* (New York: Signet Classics, 1987), 154.

13. David L. Russell, "Reading the Shards and Fragments," *The Lion and the Unicorn* 21, no. 2 (1997).

14. Geoffrey Short, "The Holocaust in the National Curriculum: A Survey of Teachers Practices and Attitudes," *Journal of Holocaust Education* 4, no. 2 (1995): 167–88.

15. Jefrey L. Derevensky, "Introducing Children to Holocaust Literature: A Developmental Approach," *Judaica Librarianship* 4 (Fall 1987–Winter 1988): 53–54; Ursula F. Sherman. "Why Would a Child Want to Read about That: The Holocaust Period in Children's Literature," in *How Much Truth Should We Tell the Children? The Politics of Children's Literature*, ed. Betty Bacon (Minneapolis: MEP Publications, 1988).

16. Perry Nodelman, *The Hidden Adult: Defining Children's Literature* (Baltimore: Johns Hopkins University Press, 2008).

17. Kokkola, *Representing the Holocaust*, 39.

18. Kidd, *Freud in Oz*, 191.

19. Hamida Bosmajian, *Sparing the Child: Grief and the Unspeakable in Youth Literature about Nazism and the Holocaust* (London: Psychology Press, 2002).

20. Connolly, *Slavery in American Children's Literature*, 4–212.

21. Children's literature in Nazi Germany included Elvira Bauer's *Trau Keinem Fuchs auf grüner Heid und keinem Jud aufi seinem Eid* (Trust No Fox on his Green Meadow and No Jew on his Oath) (1936). See Donnarae McCann, *White Supremacy in Children's Literature* (New York: Taylor and Francis, 2002); and Bosmajian, *Sparing the Child*.

22. Edward T. Sullivan, *The Holocaust in Literature for Youth* (Lanham, MD: Scarecrow Press, Inc, 1999), 2.

23. Maggie Astor, "Holocaust Is Fading from Memory, Survey Finds," *New York Times*, April 12, 2018.

24. Connolly, *Slavery in American Children's Literature*, 202.

25. Kokkola, *Representing the Holocaust*, 81.

26. Berel Lang, ed., *Holocaust Representation: Art within the Limits of History and Ethics* (Baltimore: John Hopkins University Press, 2000), 10.

27. Adrienne Kertzer, *My Mother's Voice* (Peterborough, Ontario: Broadview Press, 2001), 75.

28. Tim O'Brien, *The Things They Carried* (New York: Mariner Books, 2009), 65–66.

29. Deborah R. Geis, "Introduction," in *Considering Maus: Approaches to Art Spiegelman's "Survivor's Tale" of the Holocaust*, ed. Deborah R. Geis (Tuscaloosa: University of Alabama Press, 2003), 4. Kidd, similarly, warns that the worst examples of children's literature to address trauma are "simplistic narratives of character empowerment adapted from self-help literature" (*Freud in Oz*, 185).

30. Lawrence Langer, *Versions of Survival: The Holocaust and the Human Spirit* (New York: Holmes and Meier, 1988), 1.

31. Arthur Frank, *The Wounded Storyteller: Body, Illness and Ethics* (Chicago: University of Chicago Press, 1995).

32. Kertzer, *My Mother's Voice*.

33. Robin F. Goodman and Andrea Henderson Fahnestock, *The Day Our World Changed* (New York: Goodman and Fahnestock, 2002) Kidd describes the book as "relentlessly pop-therapeutic" (*Freud in Oz*, 201).

34. The question of a "first" book of children's literature depends on the problematic question of how we define children's literature. If children's literature is understood purely as works written for child readers (as opposed to a mass medium with certain genre characteristics), then *Schoole of Virtue and Book of Good Nourture for Chyldren and Youth to Learn Theyr Duite By* (1557) precedes Newbery by almost two centuries.

35. Kidd, *Freud in Oz*, 184.

36. Jane F. Thrailkill, "Traumatic Realism and the Wounded Child," in *The American Child: A Cultural Studies Reader*, ed. Caroline F. Levander and Carol J. Singley (New Brunswick, NJ: Rutgers University Press, 2003), 128–48.

37. Patricia Pace, "All Our Lost Children: Trauma and Testimony in the Per-formance of Childhood," *Text and Performance Quarterly* 18, no. 3 (July 1998): 233–47; Kidd, *Freud in Oz*.

38. Kidd, *Freud in Oz*, 185.

39. Philip Smith, "'Un livre pour enfants': *Mickey au Camp de Gurs* as Picture Book," *Children's Literature* 47 (2019): 104–19.

40. Ruth Franklyn, "How Should Children's Books Deal with the Holocaust?," *New Yorker*, July 23, 2018.

41. Bosmajian, *Sparing the Child*, 139.

42. Lawrence Langer, *Using and Abusing the Holocaust* (Bloomington: Indiana University Press, 2006), 21.

43. Bosmajian, *Sparing the Child*, 175.

44. Bosmajian, *Sparing the Child*, 133–34.

45. Sue Vice, *Children Writing the Holocaust* (Basingstoke: Palgrave Macmillan, 2004), 2.

46. Vice, *Children Writing the Holocaust*, 1.

47. See Michael Goodrum and Philip Smith, *Printing Terror: American Horror Comics as Cold War Commentary and Critique* (Manchester: Manchester University Press, 2021).

48. Benton, *The Comic Book in America*, 48.

49. Frederick Wertham, *Seduction of the Innocent* (New York: Rinehart & Company, 1954); Ruth Morris Bakwin, "Psychological Journal of Pediatrics: The Comics," *Journal of Pediatrics* (1953): 633; Shirley Biagi and Marilyn Kern-Foxworth, *Facing Difference: Race, Gender, and Mass Media* (Thousand Oaks, CA: Pine Forge Press, 1997).

50. Sullivan recommends *Angry Harvest* for grades nine to twelve.

51. Barbara Harrison, "Howl Like the Wolves," *Children's Literature* 15 (1987): 67–90.

52. The most notable critic being Rabbi Benjamin Blech. See Benjamin Blech, "The Boy in the Striped Pajamas," Aish.com, October 23, 2008, https://www.aish.com/ci/a/48965671.html.

53. Yoo Kyung Sung, "Hearing the Voices of 'Comfort Women': Confronting Historical Trauma in Korean Children's Literature," *Bookbird: A Journal of International Children's Literature* 50, no. 1 (2012): 20–30.

54. Kidd, *Freud in Oz*, 204.

55. See Mel Gibson. "'Yeah. I Think There's Still Hope': Youth, Ethnicity, Faith, Feminism, and Fandom in *Mz Marvel*," *Gender and the Superhero Narrative*, ed. Michael Goodrum, Tara Prescott, and Philip Smith (Jackson: University Press of Mississippi, 2018), 23–44.

56. Marah Gubar, "On Not Defining Children's Literature," *PMLA* 126, no. 1 (2011): 209–16.

57. Perry Nodelman, *The Hidden Adult: Defining Children's Literature* (Baltimore: Johns Hopkins University Press, 2008), 101. Conversely, one might argue that audience is key—Anne Frank's *Diary of a Young Girl*, for example, is so ubiquitous on school syllabi that its readers are, in the majority, children, making it a work of children's literature in practice if not design.

58. See, for example, Steven T. Katz, *The Holocaust in Historical Context, Volume 1: The Holocaust and Mass Death before the Modern Age* (Oxford: Oxford University Press, 1994).

59. Michael Rothberg, *Multidirectional Memory: Remembering the Holocaust in the Age of Decolonization* (Stanford: Stanford University Press, 2009), 3.

60. Michael Rothberg, *The Implicated Subject: Beyond Victims and Perpetrators* (Stanford: Stanford University Press, 2019).

Part 1
Late Twentieth-Century Genocides

Chapter 1

Children's Humanitarian Arts and the Genocide in Darfur

Drawing Loss and Atrocity

CHIGBO ARTHUR ANYADUBA

The archives of the United States Holocaust Memorial Museum (USHMM) in Washington, DC, hold a collection of eighteen drawings by refugee children and a teacher from Darfur in Sudan.[1] The drawings show episodes of violence presumably occurring in Darfur during the crisis years in Sudan. The drawings were brought to the USHMM in 2007. At the time, the USHMM in partnership with Google had launched an initiative called the Genocide Prevention Mapping Initiative. The project was meant to explore "how web and mapping technology can be used to help prevent and respond to threats of genocide and crimes against humanity."[2] The Initiative's first project focused on the crisis in Sudan at the time. The USHMM had sent a team to the region to gather "facts" on the atrocities perpetrated in Sudan, particularly in the Darfur region. At a refugee camp located in the town of Farchana in neighboring Chad where several Sudanese people had sought refuge, the project coordinator, Michael Graham, met a group of students aged between nine and fourteen and their art teacher, all refugees at the camp. According to Graham, the students and their teacher had volunteered that rather than *talk* about their experiences of atrocities in Darfur they preferred to provide artistic illustrations in the form of *drawings*. The following day, the class handed over to Graham eighteen A2-sized crayon/

marker-colored paper drawings—seventeen drawn by the students and one by the art teacher (figure 1.1).

What prompted the class to present their experiences through drawing can only be a matter of speculation. What seems most evident is the group's conviction that art offered better prospects for them to convey their traumatic experiences than their oral testimonies could. Graham himself thought that the drawings presented an "honest" depiction of the children's experiences and, as artworks, offered a powerful tool with which to represent difficult experiences.[3] The kinds of strong reaction the drawings produced in those who saw them (in comparison to the photographs and oral testimonies that the project's team gathered) led Graham to collect the drawings and donate them to the USHMM. The museum used some of the drawings in its special exhibition that same year and subsequently to raise awareness of and to condemn atrocities taking place in Darfur at the time.

The 2007 project was not the first time people collected "atrocity" drawings from African children (particularly from Sudan) and donated them to the USHMM.[4] In 2004, for example, Jerry S. Erlich, who was volunteering with Doctors Without Borders, collected more than one hundred drawings

Figure 1.1. Photograph showing the seventeen Darfuri child artists at the Farchana refugee camp. Source: United States Holocaust Memorial Museum.

from Sudanese children (aged between eight and eleven) who were residing in an internally displaced people's camp at the time. There was no record of how (if at all) the USHMM used these drawings from 2004, except that the drawings are digitally stored in the museum's archives. What is hardly in doubt, however, is the testimonial function these drawings served and perhaps still serve for international humanitarian activism.[5] There are several overlaps in the 2004 and 2007 drawings, including, as I go on to elaborate in the context of the latter, the strokes, scales, and colors used by children to represent atrocity.[6]

My preference for the Darfur/Farchana refugee children's drawings is only a matter of the contextual information available regarding their production and uses. While my aim in part is to *interpret* some of the formal features of the drawings by way of showing how the artists use them to represent and testify against atrocity, the underlying argument I develop throughout this chapter from this reading of form is essentially based on a constructivist reading. In particular, I hope to show that any meanings adumbrated to the drawings as humanitarian arts about genocide have been shaped by their relation to the Holocaust. I show, therefore, that the transnational production, reproduction, and uses of the Darfur children's drawings as humanitarian exhibits at the USHMM underline a process of *entanglement* of traumatic memories of the Holocaust and genocides in African conflict zones. I argue that this process of entanglement, which Michael Rothberg has described in other contexts as signaling a multidirectional process of memory, underlines a guised ritual of renewal through which Holocaust memory/consciousness consistently revitalizes *itself* in contemporary humanitarian practices.

Reading Darfur/Farchana Children's Drawings

It is important to approach these drawings by putting them in context. They were produced by child victims of genocidal atrocities. The children created these artworks not in the aftermath of their experiences of suffering but instead within a temporal space when they continued to suffer violence. The Farchana refugee camp where the children and their teacher lived at the time of the drawings was located in the middle of a desert. Starvation, dehydration, sickness, and death were commonplace at the camp, not to mention violence. This context of suffering seems crucial for appreciating the drawings, their representations of violence and suffering, their testimonial significance, and the forms of politics underpinning the children's overall artistic project at the time.

There is rarely a historical or methodological model one can use as a precedent, especially in the African context, to read children's atrocity artworks. The rather commonplace approach to children's art (in the context of atrocity experiences) has often been to highlight children's artworks as psychotherapeutic arts and in part as a way to understudy children's cognitive development and healing from trauma.[7] The psychoanalytic and psychotherapeutic approaches appear, to me, inadequate for reading the Darfur/Farchana children's drawings, most especially because we know very little about each individual child artist. In addition, reading therapy into the artworks does not adequately capture the full scope, artistic significance, and politics suggested in these artworks.

Based on the photograph of the children that I found in the USHMM archive, I believe that the drawings were produced by three girls and fourteen boys.[8] I do not notice any significant differences between the drawings produced by the boys and those by the girls. The drawings appear to me to share a lot in common rather than diverge along gendered lines. Of the eighteen artworks in the collection, only two do not depict physical violence. These two highlight what I consider a marked element of nostalgia underlying the children's drawings. The remainder of the drawings depict scenes of violence. These other drawings showing violence reveal how the children represent genocide as a form of total war.

Drawing Loss: On Nostalgia and the Darfur Atrocity Arts

The two drawings showing nonviolent scenes contain elements of the nostalgic, suggested in the artists' focus on stable familial and communal lives and on vegetal environments prior to the violence. In these two drawings, loss figures as a recollected life prior to catastrophe, showing an environment teeming with rich vegetation and food. The drawing by the art teacher exemplifies this mode of nostalgic representation of loss.[9] The drawing depicts a landscape abounding in rich natural life: a dense blue sky paralleling a blue stream of water snaking in and out of the frame; the landscapes bestriding the stream are lush green with thriving palms and other trees and blooming flowers, plants, and grass. The drawing offers what one may think of as a romantic view of the natural environment. The USHMM description accompanying this artwork declares that the teacher's drawing "represents the beauty of his native home in Darfur" (figure 1.2).[10]

Figure 1.2. Drawing by an art teacher living in the Farchana refugee camp in Chad. He explained that the drawing represents the beauty of his native home in Darfur. Source: United States Holocaust Memorial Museum. Photograph Number: N13664, COC Exhibitions and Historic Photographs, July 2007.

If one were uninformed about the context of the drawing's production and if the drawing was not being used as an atrocity testimonial artwork at the USHMM, one would easily mistake the drawing for an innocent portrayal of a beautiful landscape. Nothing in the drawing immediately suggests loss and genocide. This is precisely the reason it is important to read the drawings historically and in the context of their production and uses as testimonial and commemorative artworks. In this way, it becomes possible to *see* the teacher's drawing as a testament against chaos and destruction and as an attempt to recuperate from imaginative memory a lost past whose reality serves to condemn a present of chaos and suffering. By rendering this romantic past visible in the present, the teacher's drawing, through a kind of artistic fiat, pushes the violent present away from view. This artistic displacement of a chaotic present in favor of an idyllic past serves to commemorate what has been lost in the present as well as to accord the recuperated past validity as a moment of beauty.

The recovery of this past serves at once historical, political, and commemorative functions. In its historical function, it portrays the Darfur environment in temporal reality as a place that was once peaceful, stable, and rich in life. This historical vision is political because it challenges some of the international media narratives at the time describing Darfur (and by extension the Sudan) as a place historically in a state of enduring chaos.[11] By placing Darfur within a temporal continuum (*at a time of beauty and plenty*), the teacher's drawing provides an imaginative horizon for humanitarian and political intervention in Darfur: Darfur ceases to be a place in perpetual chaos and instead becomes a place begging to be restored to a prior normative state of stability and peace.

At the same time, the drawing represents what it is not showing. Its portrayal of an idyllic past makes sense in the context of this reading only because the viewer understands the present (at that time) to be one of chaos. Understood thus, the drawing works to summon the *good* past to testify against and to indict the violent present. This commemorative function is even more important when we understand that at the time of the drawing, the teacher was living in a refugee camp that was stationed in a desert. The rich vegetation and friendly atmosphere of the teacher's drawing contrast remarkably with the hostile conditions of the desert.

The artwork's evocative sense of loss is further made more cogent by an ink pen inscription at the top center of the drawing: "Compo for Shaṅa [or Shaka/Shaxa]." The inscription is perhaps the teacher's dedication of his work to someone, probably a dead relative or friend, perhaps to a child born and living a horrendous desert life at the Farchana refugee camp, a child who is not privileged to experience the beautiful life that the teacher knew before the genocide and war. One may not immediately have known (or will ever know) what the dedication is meant for and to whom it is addressed. Speculation seems to be the only response the artwork forces on its regular, uninformed viewer. Any regular viewer of the drawing (either as an exhibition artifact or as an archival object at the USHMM) will most likely not know the precise circumstances of the teacher's dedication. This lack of contextual information about the drawing adds contemplative power to the artwork because the viewer is tasked to speculate on multiple possibilities of meaning. The one encountering the drawing as a humanitarian artwork that is testifying and protesting against genocidal atrocity is, therefore, tasked to contemplate the loss and suffering of victims. In this way too, the drawing evokes in its viewer a sense of the loss the artist is attempting to recuperate and commemorate: lost home, lost friends and family, stolen innocence.

Unlike the teacher who appears in his drawing more preoccupied by a romance with the natural environment, the children in theirs seem interested in a more holistic artistic vision and commitment. Their own drawings encompass the human and the natural worlds. The second drawing in the collection showing a scene of nonviolence provides detail of a pre-genocide/war experience.[12] This second drawing presents a picture of banal village life: outdoor cooking, a horse or a donkey casually grazing at the corner of a household, a mother and her two children riding on a horse, a man (farmer most likely) heading to or returning from the farm, a woman hawking her wares or simply bearing food items home, thriving farms and lush vegetation all around. What seems most prominent in the drawing is the presence of food. Understood as the work of a child living in a famine-prone, drought-ravaged refugee camp in a desert, it is perhaps not difficult to guess that the child is propelled by a nostalgic desire to return to a time and place of food and security. Yet the nostalgia that the drawing appears to be evoking has to be located further within the context of a genocide and war that already destroyed the world that the drawing is showing (figure 1.3). Like the art teacher's drawing, the temporal moment

Figure 1.3. Drawing by Darfurian child living in a refugee camp in Chad depicting daily life in Darfur before the civil war. Source: United States Holocaust Memorial Museum. Photograph Number: N13671, COC Exhibitions and Historic Photographs, July 2007.

and space that the drawing portrays underline a deeper sense of loss when put in the context of the catastrophe the drawing is responding to (but not showing). One should remember too that the drawing is after all a direct response not to the past it is depicting but to the chaotic present of anguish at the time of its production. Hence its imaginative retrieval of a stable past may be read as a critique and a moral condemnation of the violence that ruined this stable past.

A third drawing in the collection presents in part a similar nostalgic vision and representation of loss as the two discussed above.[13] If one were to organize the eighteen drawings into some kind of a linear narrative showing a trajectory from a stable to a chaotic stage, this third drawing would be a fitting bridge between the two stages. A third of this particular drawing—in a separate frame on the right—shows a peaceful village: a man seemingly summoning two boys to the homestead or perhaps urging them on somewhere, an older man minding a boiling kettle, colorful huts, and lush vegetation. The larger frame of the drawing, behind the one showing the village, shows an invading military force: heavily armed soldiers on horseback and an armored truck. The military force is headed in the direction of the oblivious villagers.

This drawing is remarkable for how it brings together two distinct spatial realities to construct for the viewer what may be considered a subtle narrative of an impending catastrophe. A possible narrative suggested by the drawing is that the looming catastrophe is marked by massacres of targeted and unarmed villagers. The casualness and obliviousness of the villagers in comparison to the preparedness and evident resolve of the military force underline a story of genocide and atrocity against innocent civilian populations (figure 1.4). In this sense, one observes further that the drawing depicts the villagers using a different complexion (or seemingly racial hue) in comparison to the soldiers: the villagers have thick black hair and are dark-complexioned, which the artist portrays using a gray color; the soldiers, on the other hand, appear fair-complexioned, portrayed using an orange color. This difference in complexion between uniformed killers and civilian victims is not an isolated, distinctive feature of this particular drawing. It recurs (and quite prominently) in all the other drawings. As several scholars have shown, racism was a major factor in the ideological underpinnings of violence against Darfuris. The view has been that the African-Arab-run state of Sudan was executing a heinous program aiming to Arabize Sudan and eliminate its Black Africans who are indigenous to the region.[14] The children's drawings appear to validate this

Children's Humanitarian Arts and the Genocide in Darfur / 33

Figure 1.4. Drawing of an attack on a Darfurian village drawn by a child living in the Farchana refugee camp in Chad. Source: United States Holocaust Memorial Museum. Photograph Number: N13661, COC Exhibitions and Historic Photographs, July 2007.

view of the crisis by portraying perpetrators as fair-complexioned Arabs and victims as autochthonous Blacks. This portrayal presents a picture of racially homogenous groupings that are markedly different from each other. Hence the mark of racial difference in the drawings evokes an atmosphere of catastrophe that is underpinned by identity politics.

Drawing Genocidal Atrocity

In the drawings showing violent scenes, there are significant overlaps in the children's representations. Many of the drawings show heavily armed men in military uniforms and military machinery (including fighter aircrafts) unleashing brutality on civilians. The drawings depict perhaps recollected or imagined episodes of massacres of civilians; of men, women and children fleeing and being shot from behind; of houses and the natural environment bombed, machine-gunned, and set ablaze by soldiers.[15] Observe too that the soldiers are fair in complexion and the civilian victims darker in complexion. The bulk of the drawings show scenes of attacks that take place in the villages: people fleeing their homes in desperate haste, evidenced in flip-flops left behind in flight (figures 1.5, 1.6, and 1.7).

Figure 1.5. Drawing of an attack on a Darfurian village drawn by a child living in the Farchana refugee camp in Chad. Source: United States Holocaust Memorial Museum. Photograph Number: N13670, COC Exhibitions and Historic Photographs, July 2007.

Figure 1.6. Drawing of an attack on a Darfurian village drawn by a child living in the Farchana refugee camp in Chad. Source: United States Holocaust Memorial Museum. Photograph Number: N13660, COC Exhibitions and Historic Photographs, July 2007.

Children's Humanitarian Arts and the Genocide in Darfur / 35

Figure 1.7. Drawing of an attack on a Darfurian village drawn by a child living in the Farchana refugee camp in Chad. Source: United States Holocaust Memorial Museum. Photograph Number: N13667, COC Exhibitions and Historic Photographs, July 2007.

That these scenes of violence come out firmly in the children's drawings may underline a similarity in the children's own experiences: having to flee brutal violence in a haste. In one particularly arresting portrait,[16] there is an illustration that may be described as signaling heroic sacrifice—an old man (possibly a grandfather) who is unable to flee and leaning on his walking stick is urging a child (possibly his grandchild) to flee. The viewer of this drawing (at the USHMM) does not know if this illustration precisely describes the child artist's own experience of escape. It is a possibility. The fact of such a possibility adds even more exigency and emotional weight to the drawing.

A closer reading of this particular drawing reveals that the lace design on the old man's footwear resembles the figure *100*. Was it possible that the artist was using this illustrative form to inform about the old man's age, a reason he could not escape with the boy? On the top left of the portrait is an ink inscription: *2004*. Could this be the date the illustrated episode occurred? Because we know that the drawing was produced in 2007, the closest possible guess of the significance of the inscribed date is that it was the momentous year of the violent scenario depicted in the drawing (figure 1.8). As one finds in the other drawings, a notable feature of this particular drawing is the loss of home. The captured moment in the drawing shows the moment of a child's orphaning. This moment of great loss of home (of orphaning) is a recurring feature in virtually all the drawings, suggestive perhaps of a trauma plaguing the children's memories and imaginations of their experience.

In addition, each of the violent scenes in the drawings shows a pattern of chaos that represents violence as a total existential threat. There seems to be an implicit desire manifest in the drawings to show violence as targeting not only humans but also the environment, houses, plants, and trees. In this way, the drawings reject an anthropocentric representation of violent experiences. In the drawings, humans, houses, grasses, and trees, even the sky, bleed from violence.[17] The sense of chaos that the drawings show underscores the point about the atrocity in Darfur at the time as unfolding in the manner that Raphael Lemkin would call a total war,[18] a kind of war that

Figure 1.8. Drawing of a helicopter attack on a Darfurian village drawn by a child living in the Farchana refugee camp in Chad. Source: United States Holocaust Memorial Museum. Photograph Number: N13677, COC Exhibitions and Historic Photographs, July 2007.

makes no distinction between combatants and noncombatants. The familiar landscapes and villagescapes nostalgically recollected in the first two drawings discussed earlier have become transformed (as depicted in these other drawings) into scenes of brutality and chaos. In these scenes, the familiar world that the children once knew has been replaced with an unfamiliar one, an unfamiliarity that the children portrayed in their works as a consequence of the defamiliarizing acts of violence. The defamiliarization suggested in the drawings (through showing violence and destruction of families and houses) further reveals the form of alienation that I described earlier as orphaning. In a sense, it is possible to read each of these drawings as in some form a return to the moment of orphaning, when each child lost home, family, community, and natural environment as they used to be.

Even more curious, the drawings present scenes of violence at their active moments. In the drawings, the bullets are still visibly in motion, the fires are still raging on buildings and trees, victims are still in desperate flight, and killers are in assault positions unleashing horrendous terror (figures 1.9 and 1.10). The children's drawings refuse to present horror as unimaginable,

Figure 1.9. Drawing of an attack on a Darfurian village drawn by a child living in the Farchana refugee camp in Chad. Source: United States Holocaust Memorial Museum. Photograph Number: N13675, COC Exhibitions and Historic Photographs, July 2007.

Figure 1.10. Drawing of an attack on a Darfurian village drawn by a child living in the Farchana refugee camp in Chad. Source: United States Holocaust Memorial Museum. Photograph Number: N13672, COC Exhibitions and Historic Photographs, July 2007.

as something withdrawn into the dark from where representation can only attempt to evoke feelings of an experience that is otherwise ungraspable. Representations of this kind often imply the work of a secondary witness to the aftermath of horror—displays of debris, dead bodies, and so forth. Such representations seem to be underpinned by a consciousness resolved to viewing horror as unimaginable. The children in their drawings present themselves not as secondary witnesses but as eyewitnesses to genocide.

By returning the viewer (or spectator, if you will) to the scene of horror, the drawings insist on particular ways of being looked at, one of which is that they refuse to put carnage in a temporal past. In the drawings, carnage is present, in motion, unending. The drawings subject the viewer to *see* carnage in motion, thereby constructing a visual field for the viewer. This field presents the atrocities within the visual frame as ongoing. The viewer is not looking at the detritus of atrocities past but atrocities in progress, atrocities begging for humanitarian intervention.

Seen thus, the drawings can be considered as motion drawings showing the dramatic moments of horror unfolding, moments perhaps when the child artists narrowly escaped death if one accepts that the drawings are testimonies of the children's own experiences. In this sense of the drawings as testimonial art, too, the violent moments portrayed in the drawings assume a form: they may be attesting to the encounters with atrocity that remained enduring in the children's minds as unending vignettes of chaos. The troubling violent episodes in the drawings may indeed comprise moments when the children experienced severe horrors, moments they returned to in the attempt to give testimonies of their own experiences.

Another important point of note borders on the nature of emotional power that the drawings provoke (at least for me). It is very possible to easily mistake the exuberant colorfulness of the drawings as the product of such overflowing carefreeness one finds in children's arts in general. The exaggerated scales of figures and colors, the artistic strokes sometimes tending to caricatures, and the overall visual beauty (or appeal) of the drawings are not entirely unfamiliar features of children's artworks. Under different circumstances, these drawings could easily be seen as children's creative re-creation of war and action films that they have seen. As a child, I myself drew similar sketches after watching, say, Arnold Schwarzenegger or Sylvester Stallone action-hero films. Those drawings of mine brought a certain form of creative pleasure and afforded me a freedom of mind to express myself. By contrast, the Darfur/Farchana children's drawings come, however, from a different encounter, one that derives from the lived experiences of violent atrocities, at least given the context of my encounter of the drawings—as archival materials at the USHMM. If ever there were any *pleasure* to derive from drawing these experiences, it certainly was different from the kind of pleasure that I knew as a child drawing my own re-creation of action films. As artworks showing what I might easily have mistaken as a child's re-creation of an action film, the drawings evoke a reminiscence of my own childhood (that is, a relatable experience that is sentimental and convenient). But as exhibits attesting to atrocity, they provoke a troubling discomfort for me, one bordering on a jarring recognition of how what could easily be mistaken as an *innocent* creative practice of childhood could become a product attesting to heinous cruelty. This recognition leads to my final point in the next section regarding the kinds of agencies that went into the production of these drawings, suggested most trenchantly perhaps in the formal elements used by the children to represent killers and victims.

Drawing Killers, and Their Victims

There is a noticeable difference in how the children portrayed victims and killers (including killing objects such as guns, armored trucks/tanks, and fighter jets).[19] The children seem to have expended colors and shades in drawing killers, in contrast with how they drew the civilian victims. With the exception of illustrations of blood from victims' bodies, victims do not figure in most of the drawings in conspicuously colorful shapes. Their clothes in many of the drawings when compared to those of the killers bear no varieties of colorful patterns that readily call attention to them. The dominant color on many illustrations of victims in the drawings (especially wounded or dead victims) is a bright red color evidently signaling blood (figure 1.11). An easy conclusion regarding this observation about how the drawings represent victims and killers is perhaps that the child artists paid more attention to the action/activity of killers (and their killing machines) than to victims and victims' suffering.

Figure 1.11. Drawing of an attack on a Darfurian village drawn by a child living in the Farchana refugee camp in Chad. Source: United States Holocaust Memorial Museum. Photograph Number: N13665, COC Exhibitions and Historic Photographs, July 2007.

Such a conclusion may not be entirely ill-fitted because, as one can observe, the artists depict killers in their drawings using extravagant embellishments. The drawings give details of the killers' uniforms with colors and patterns, their caps, their guns and boots, their armored cars and fighter jets. In other words, the drawings are not content with illustrating the fact of killing; they also produce *beautiful* killers. Military uniforms and weaponry appear gorgeous and colorfully illustrated.[20] The soldiers are also generally much bigger than their victims. In some of the drawings, the killers' images dwarf even the houses and trees they are destroying (figure 1.12). Yet the drawings do not portray the military killers' large size as monstrous. If anything, the soldiers look fully human and much more beautifully rendered than other figures (e.g., civilian victims) in some of the drawings.

For this reason, I am inclined to argue that the drawings highlight an unconscious *captivation* for brutal power. In making this point I am by no means suggesting that the captivation for killers as underpinned by the

Figure 1.12. Drawing of an attack on a Darfurian village drawn by fourteen-year-old Mahamad Ahmat Haron living in the Farchana refugee camp in Chad. Source: United States Holocaust Memorial Museum. Photograph Number: N13666, COC Exhibitions and Historic Photographs, July 2007.

drawings implies that the children have a positive disposition toward the murderous military or the militia. Instead, I see this captivation for killers in the drawings as a traumatic commentary on power. The word *captivation* derives from its root, *captive*. To be captivated in the sense that I intend is to be held captive, to be made a prisoner of power. In the drawings, as I have outlined above, power is exercised through guns and bombs and bullets, through military uniforms, through muscular, gigantic masculinity. This expression of power is brutally total because it sets out to annihilate people and their environment. This power's totality is manifest in its invasion of the children's memory and imagination, insisting on being the determining force of the drawing, imposing itself on the child's self-representation (or self-drawing) as the author of terror. This total power turns the child into what Achille Mbembe has described as a "hallucinated subject."[21] The hallucinated subject is the *captive* of brutal power; this subject is power's beast of burden, the subject through whom brutal power projects its horrors and terrors. This total power is so diffused that even the struggle to resist or escape it by way of testifying against it becomes, ironically, an exercise in mimicking it, in affirming its supremacy, in reproducing (*representing*) its terrors.

This reading of the children as captives of brutal power seems to me useful because it allows for a critical assessment of the drawings instead of an uncritical treatment or *consumption* of the drawings as objects calling for sympathy. It underscores (even as it unpacks) the agencies underpinning these artworks. It helps to call into question the agencies that entered into the process of creating and disseminating the artworks. If we consider that the children and their art teacher opted to *tell* about their experiences through drawing, then we need to take more seriously the agencies that they bring into their works, agencies that, while encouraging reading these artworks as serving some testimonial and commemorative functions, equally suggest other possibilities of reading. Paying attention to the formal features of the drawings alone easily tempts one to read the drawings as reflections/resemblances/imitations of an objective reality that the children experienced in their own lives. My semiformalist interpretation of the drawings—speculative, at best—precisely gestured toward these mimetic interpretations.

To be certain, a mimetic reading of the drawings is valuable and, in fact, necessary. One cannot deny with any sense of certainty that there is an obvious relationship in the children's drawings to their actual experiences. The mimetic focus does not, however, provide the whole picture because it operates under the assumption that there is a "truth" or "fact" or "meaning" in the world that art in this form aims to reflect as it is. The mimetic inclination will treat these drawings as serving a precisely testimonial function, one that attempts to tell the truth about genocide in the Sudan. There is nothing wayward about this reading. It simply isn't far-reaching, especially in explaining other *associative* meanings that *we* come to ascribe to these drawings, such as the peculiar ideas about genocide and atrocity that we think the drawings adumbrate.

By underlining agency here, I am by no means claiming that the artists *intended* certain meanings for their works that any serious interpretation must aim to reveal. To make such a claim will invariably lead to the fallacy of intentionalism: that meaning resides with the author. This is not to say that the artists did not create their works to convey certain feelings, ideas, and meanings. Instead, I am more concerned with highlighting the relational processes through which we come to make sense of the drawings in peculiar ways. We knew very little (if at all) about the children and their teacher, about what they intended to convey in the drawings, about their feelings at the time of drawing. We only have the drawings to interact with and to make sense of what they might be *signaling*. It seems to me, therefore, that understanding the process through which we come to attribute meanings to these drawings matters significantly.

My point here is that meaning does not have an objective reality, nor is it immanent in the *thing*. Rather, it is a product of "a signifying practice," a construct that results from a social process.[22] What matters really is the [social] process that shapes and determines the meanings we ascribe to objects such as the Darfur/Farchana children's drawings. To understand this process, one may need to look at the *relations* of the drawings to their use as gathered "facts" or "evidence" of genocidal atrocity and as exhibition artifacts at the USHMM.

The Darfur Children's Drawings as Exhibition Artifacts at the US Holocaust Memorial Museum

While reading the drawings in relation to their uses at the USHMM as material cultures of genocide privileges a constructivist reading, it is important, however, to state that I do not mean by any chance to challenge or revise the representational claims that the drawings make as products resulting from actual experiences of atrocity. Instead, I intend to highlight the social/symbolic processes through which we come to *make sense* of the drawings in peculiar ways that shape our relations with them. In focus here is the use of the drawings as material culture of atrocity at the USHMM. One is encouraged to consider the USHMM as a social actor (or, more accurately, a social vector) for the conceptualization of these drawings as humanitarian arts attesting to a genocide. Some scholars have told us that museums are not innocent spaces for the collection and storage of material cultures. As Henrietta Lidchi puts it: "Museums do not simply issue objective descriptions or form logical assemblages; they generate representations and attribute value and meaning in line with certain perspectives or classificatory schemas which are historically specific. They do not so much reflect the world through objects as use them to mobilize representations of the world past and present."[23] In other words, museums are conceptual sites able to produce meanings that are underpinned by certain ideologies and perceptions.

In the conceptual space of the USHMM, the Darfur/Farchana children's drawings become testimonial objects—a kind of ethnographic material signaling genocidal atrocity in Sudan. This signaling process is made possible because the USHMM serves as an institution concerned with the material cultures of the Holocaust. As a cultural institution of one of the most iconized and globalized genocides in the world, the conceptual world of the USHMM allows the translation of the Darfur children's drawings into objects of atrocity testimony and imbues them with a special meaning—as signifiers of genocide. In this way, too, the drawings become floating signifiers attaching themselves to the cultural ideas of the Holocaust. As such, the drawings enter into a conceptual world of atrocities and genocides all made to hold together by the Holocaust. As we look upon these artworks—whether during their displays on the museum's walls or in the museum's archives—we unconsciously *witness* the Holocaust anew while simultaneously encountering a peculiar representation (as a genocide) of the atrocities in Darfur.

This pattern of entanglement of the Darfur/Farchana children's drawings and Holocaust memories underscores what Michael Rothberg has explained as a "multidirectional" process through which atrocity memories and representations mutually shape one another. According to Rothberg, the emergence of the Holocaust as a popular cultural icon of genocide reveals a multidirectional process, which he explains as a kind of cross-referencing of memories/ideas of the Nazi genocide of Jews in Europe with memories/ideas of violent atrocities occurring in other conflict zones, especially during the years of decolonization in Africa and elsewhere. A notable example in this regard is the 1954–62 Algerian War of Independence against colonial

France during which antiwar activists in Europe and decolonization thinkers compared the violence against Algerians with the Nazis' torture and murder of Jews during World War II.[24] Through such entanglements, according to Rothberg, the Holocaust facilitated the articulation of other histories of suffering at the same time that it developed into an icon of suffering able to shed light on events having little or nothing to do with it. For Rothberg, the entanglement of Holocaust memories with other atrocities is possible because "the public sphere" of atrocity representation is "a malleable discursive space in which groups do not simply articulate established positions but actually come into being through their dialogical interactions with others."[25]

However, as the case of the Darfur/Farchana children's drawings shows, the notion of multidirectionality is misleading because it propagates a convenient vision of meaning by association, whereby we are to understand atrocity memories as shaping one another in a symbiotic and largely unproblematic way. Because the relation of the genocidal atrocities in Darfur and the Holocaust is based on unequal cultural capitals, what appears as a multidirectional process begins to look more like a process by which cultural memories of the Holocaust subsist by appropriating the memories of atrocities in contemporary [African] conflict zones. This process is underpinned by social and cultural domination serving the interests of those (Western political, economic, and cultural establishments) with the cultural capital to provoke and shape the peculiar meanings (or forms of recognition) of atrocity representations from Africa.

While on the one hand the Holocaust provided an analogue conducive to comprehending the suffering in Darfur as a genocide, images of Darfur suffering seems instead to have provided Western audiences at the USHMM with striking visuals of suffering and anguish *related* to those inflicted on Jews by the Nazis. Such implicit symbolic/visual comparisons underline a social process through which the Holocaust continues to entrench its cultural memories as the ur-genocide.

Notes

1. This work was the product of a chance encounter during my residency as the J. B. and Maurice C. Shapiro fellow at the Jack, Joseph and Morton Mandel Center for Advanced Holocaust Studies, United States Holocaust Memorial Museum. I benefited immensely from the incredible support and guidance provided to me by the museum staff and other researchers.

2. United States Holocaust Memorial Museum, "Michael Graham," Confront Genocide, https://www.ushmm.org/confront-genocide/speakers-and-events/biography/michael-graham.

3. Michael Graham (former coordinator of the USHMM's Genocide Prevention Mapping Initiative) in discussion with the author, October 2018.

4. Throughout, I use atrocity in the context of the Darfur children's drawings in the same way scholars now describe photographs of war and mass violence as atrocity photographs. The notion of atrocity in this context, as several scholars have explained, has been evolving within a public discourse of humanitarianism largely centered on visual cultures and photographic practices. The discourse is underpinned by a rather cultural understanding of violence and human suffering (usually about "Others" in relation to Western audiences) based on spectatorial practices that beckoned to [Western] viewers for humanitarian actions. This discourse has focused nearly exclusively on the role of photography in mobilizing visual codes of affects for humanitarian actions, but not usually on such drawings as the Darfur children's drawings and not usually on the central role children's experiences and "images" play in the process of this mobilizing practice of affect. On some of the major stakes of scholarly positions on atrocity photography and humanitarianism, see, for example, Heide Fehrenbach and David Rodongo, *Humanitarian Photography: A History* (Cambridge: Cambridge University Press, 2015). See also Christina Twomey, "Framing Atrocity: Photography and Humanitarianism," *History of Photography* 36, no. 3 (2012): 255–64; Carolyn J. Dean, "Atrocity Photographs, Dignity, and Human Vulnerability," *Humanity: An International Journal of Human Rights, Humanitarianism, and Development* 6, no. 2 (2015): 239–64.

5. The Darfur children's drawings are a part of several material cultures in the USHMM's archive collected from different atrocity zones across the world. As part of its aims to support genocide awareness and prevention, the USHMM played an active role throughout the first decade of the 2000s, especially through the work of its Committee on Conscience, in advocating for humanitarian intervention and for supporting the recognition of the atrocities taking place in Sudan (Darfur in particular) as a genocide.

6. Also, these drawings by Sudanese children are curiously similar to the drawings that one finds, for example, in an edited book collection of drawings by child survivors of the 1994 Rwandan genocide: see Richard A. Salem, ed., *Witness to Genocide: The Children of Rwanda (Drawings by Child Survivors of the Rwandan Genocide of 1994)* (New York: Friendship Press, 2000).

7. On the subject of children's art and cognitive psychology, see, for example, Spencer Eth and Robert S. Pynoos, eds., *Post-Traumatic Stress Disorder in Children* (New York: American Psychiatric Publishing, 1985); Maureen Cox, *Children's Drawings* (London, 1992). See also Rocco Quaglia, Claudio Longobardi, Nathalie O. Iotti, and Laura E. Prino, "A New Theory on Children's Drawings: Analyzing the Role of Emotion and Movement in Graphical Development," *Infant Behavior & Development* 39 (2015): 81–91. See also Kenneth B. Kidd's *Freud in Oz*, which

highlights the relations or entanglements of children's literature of trauma/atrocity and psychoanalysis.

8. See figure 1.1.

9. See figure 1.2.

10. Throughout, I have retained the original descriptions used by the USHMM to document and display the drawings.

11. On international responses to the crisis in Sudan and Western mainstream media representations of atrocity in Darfur, see, for example, Amanda F. Grzyb, ed., *The World and Darfur: International Response to Crimes Against Humanity in Western Sudan*, 2nd ed. (Montreal: McGill Queens University Press, 2010).

12. See figure 1.3.

13. See figure 1.4.

14. On scholarly accounts of the Darfur crisis as a genocide, see Samuel Totten and Eric Markusen, eds, *Genocide in Darfur: Investigating Atrocities in the Sudan* (New York: Routledge, 2006); John Hagan and Wenona Rymond-Richmond, *Darfur and the Crime of Genocide* (Cambridge: Cambridge University Press, 2009); Jane Gangi, "Children's and Young Adult Literature of Darfur," in *Genocide in Contemporary Children's and Young Adult Literature: Cambodia to Darfur* (New York: Routledge, 2014). See also Alex de Waal, ed., *War in Darfur and the Search for Peace* (Cambridge, MA: Global Equity Initiative, 2007). Some other scholars dismissed the claims of genocide in Darfur as part of a Western politics of naming: see, e.g., Mahmood Mamdani, "The Politics of Naming: Genocide, Civil War, Insurgency," *London Review of Books* 29, no. 5–8 (2007): 5–8.

15. See figures 1.5, 1.6, and 1.7.

16. See figure 1.8.

17. See, e.g., figure 1.9. Another possible reading may be to consider the violence as an attack on the land itself, whereby the land and its inhabitants are represented in the drawings as entwined. Such an imagination aligns with an understanding of nativity as autochthonous, i.e., people as intertwined with the soil on which they live. In this sense, genocide encompasses a form of violence directed not merely at the human inhabitants but also at the people and the totality of their environment.

18. See Raphael Lemkin, *Axis Rule in Occupied Europe: Laws of Occupation, Analysis of Government, Proposals for Redress*, 2nd ed. (New Jersey: The Law Book Exchange, 2008).

19. See figures 1.10, 1.11, and 1.12.

20. There are impressive works done on the appeal of military paraphernalia on the minds of the young, particularly in the context of the Holocaust. See, e.g., Hamida Bosmajian, *Sparing the Child: Grief and the Unspeakable in Youth Literature about Nazism and the Holocaust* (New York: Routledge, 2002).

21. Achille Mbembe, *On the Postcolony* (Berkeley: University of California Press, 2001), 167.

22. See, for example, Stuart Hall, ed., *Representation: Cultural Representations and Signifying Practices* (London: Sage, 1997).

23. Henrietta Lidchi, "The Poetics and the Politics of Exhibiting Other Cultures," in Hall, *Representation*, 160.

24. Michael Rothberg, *Multidirectional Memory: Remembering the Holocaust in the Age of Decolonization* (Stanford, CA: Stanford University Press, 2009), 175–98.

25. Rothberg, *Multidirectional Memory*, 5. There is no consensus regarding how the Holocaust emerged to become a cultural icon of genocide following World War II. The controversies hover around two broad claims: those suggesting that the distinct nature and enormity of violence perpetrated against Jews by the Nazis is the reason for the Holocaust's iconic status (see, e.g., Steven Katz, *The Holocaust in Historical Context: Volume 1: The Holocaust and Mass Death Before the Modern Age* (Oxford: Oxford University Press, 1994); Avishai Margalit and Gabriel Motzkin, "The Uniqueness of the Holocaust," *Philosophy & Public Affairs* 25, no. 1 (1996): 65–83, and those contending that the Holocaust became a powerful icon of suffering through complex social and political processes aided by representation and comparison with atrocities elsewhere. See, e.g., Rothberg, *Multidirectional Memory*; Jeffrey C. Alexander, *Remembering the Holocaust: A Debate* (Oxford: Oxford University Press, 2009); Daniel Levy and Natan Sznaider, *The Holocaust and Memory in the Global Age* (Philadelphia: Temple University Press, 2006). My own discussion aligns precisely within the latter discourse. It is noteworthy that the debate in support of Holocaust exceptionalism arose in response to perceived threats of other groups appropriating the cultural capital of the Holocaust. The irony, as my study of the Darfur children's drawings suggests, is that the cultural value of the Holocaust seems to depend on its associations with other genocides.

Works Cited

Alexander, Jeffrey C. *Remembering the Holocaust: A Debate*. Oxford: Oxford University Press, 2009.

Bosmajian, Hamida. *Sparing the Child: Grief and the Unspeakable in Youth Literature about Nazism and the Holocaust*. New York: Routledge, 2002.

Cox, Maureen. *Children's Drawings*. London, 1992.

de Waal, Alex, ed. *War in Darfur and the Search for Peace*. Cambridge, MA: Global Equity Initiative, 2007.

Dean, Carolyn J. "Atrocity Photographs, Dignity, and Human Vulnerability." *Humanity: An International Journal of Human Rights, Humanitarianism, and Development* 6, no. 2 (2015): 239–64.

Eth, Spencer, and Pynoos, Robert S., eds. *Post-Traumatic Stress Disorder in Children*. New York: American Psychiatric Publishing, 1985.

Fehrenbach, Heide, and Rodongo, David. *Humanitarian Photography: A History*. Cambridge: Cambridge University Press, 2015.

Gangi, Jane. "Children's and Young Adult Literature of Darfur." In *Genocide in Contemporary Children's and Young Adult Literature: Cambodia to Darfur*. New York: Routledge, 2014.

Graham, Michael. Personal correspondence, October 2018.

Grzyb, Amanda F., ed. *The World and Darfur: International Response to Crimes against Humanity in Western Sudan*. 2nd ed. Montreal: McGill Queens University Press, 2010.

Hagan, John, and Rymond-Richmond, Wenona. *Darfur and the Crime of Genocide*. Cambridge: Cambridge University Press, 2009.

Hall, Stuart, ed. *Representation: Cultural Representations and Signifying Practices*. London: Sage, 1997.

Katz, Steven. *The Holocaust in Historical Context: Volume 1: The Holocaust and Mass Death Before the Modern Age*. Oxford: Oxford University Press, 1994.

Kidd, Kenneth B. *Freud in Oz: At the Intersections of Psychoanalysis and Children's Literature*. Minneapolis: University of Minnesota Press, 2011.

Lemkin, Raphael. *Axis Rule in Occupied Europe: Laws of Occupation, Analysis of Government, Proposals for Redress*. 2nd ed. New Jersey: The Law Book Exchange, 2008.

Levy, Daniel, and Sznaider, Natan. *The Holocaust and Memory in the Global Age*. Philadelphia: Temple University Press, 2006.

Lidchi, Henrietta. "The Poetics and the Politics of Exhibiting Other Cultures." In *Representation: Cultural Representations and Signifying Practices*, ed. Stuart Hall. London: Sage, 1997.

Margalit, Avishai, and Motzkin, Gabriel. "The Uniqueness of the Holocaust." *Philosophy & Public Affairs* 25, no. 1 (1996): 65–83.

Mamdani, Mahmood. "The Politics of Naming: Genocide, Civil War, Insurgency." *London Review of Books* 29, no. 5–8 (2007): 5–8.

Mbembe, Achille. *On the Postcolony*. Berkeley: University of California Press, 2001.

Quaglia, Rocco, Claudio Longobardi, Nathalie O. Iotti, and Laura E. Prino. "A New Theory on Children's Drawings: Analyzing the Role of Emotion and Movement in Graphical Development." *Infant Behavior & Development* 39 (2015): 81–91.

Rothberg, Michael. *Multidirectional Memory: Remembering the Holocaust in the Age of Decolonization*. Stanford, CA: Stanford University Press, 2009.

Salem, Richard A., ed., *Witness to Genocide: The Children of Rwanda (Drawings by Child Survivors of the Rwandan Genocide of 1994)*. New York: Friendship Press, 2000.

Totten, Samuel, and Markusen, Eric, eds. *Genocide in Darfur: Investigating Atrocities in the Sudan*. New York: Routledge, 2006.

Twomey, Christina. "Framing Atrocity: Photography and Humanitarianism." *History of Photography* 36, no. 3 (2012): 255–64.

United States Holocaust Memorial Museum. "Michael Graham." Confront Genocide. https://www.ushmm.org/confront-genocide/speakers-and-events/biography/michael-graham.

Chapter 2

Framing the Unframeable
Deogratias and the Horror of Genocide

Kaitlyn Newman

Belgian writer Jean-Philippe Stassen's graphic novel *Deogratias*, which tells the story of a Hutu boy by the same name, is targeted at a young adult audience. The comic deals with surprisingly difficult themes for young readers, such as alcoholism, death, corruption, and prostitution, among others, and it does not attempt to shield them from the horrors of what occurred in Rwanda in 1994. Furthermore, there is no happy ending for Deogratias; the novel ends with him symbolically becoming a dog, revealing how he sees himself after the genocide. However, it is just this lack of closure that makes *Deogratias* a valuable contribution to genocide literature for young adults. *Deogratias* gives us a glimpse into what happened in Rwanda, but it also alludes to that which escapes representation in words or images, what Holocaust scholar Lawrence Langer and others, such as philosopher Jean-François Lyotard, have argued must remain beyond the possibility of representation in words or images: the unpresentable. In what follows, I explore Lyotard's account of the unpresentable and how it is at work in Stassen's novel. I then explain why the unpresentable is important not only for adult literature on genocide, but also for literature targeted at young adults.

Deogratias: Fragmentary Imagery and Words

As Michelle Bumatay and Hannah Warman recognize, *Deogratias* is targeted at a young Western readership (originally a French-speaking readership, though the novel has since been translated into English, Spanish, Portuguese, and Italian).[1] Though *Deogratias* addresses concrete historical-political events, it does not require that its readers have any significant knowledge of those circumstances and instead introduces readers to an event that is less often discussed than the Holocaust in the Western context: the Rwandan genocide.[2] The comic is accessible for a wide variety of young Western readers; its graphics are bright, engaging, and intriguing, and it does not require that its readers be experts on its topic to understand the plot.[3]

Deogratias moves between "present-day" Rwanda (post-genocide) and the periods shortly before and during the genocide. Stassen indicates the shifts in timeline through the novel's graphics: he uses a black border around the illustrated panels to indicate when the novel is in the present (the border is absent in the panels of flashbacks). The reader can also use the condition of Deogratias's clothing to distinguish between the present day and a flashback. In the present day, his clothing is worn, dirty, and full of holes; in the past, it is white and pristine. Despite these clear indicators that mark the transitions between past and present, *Deogratias* operates on a difficult timeline. If readers do not pay careful attention to the graphics, they may miss the numerous shifts between past and present. The shifts in time are rarely indicated through the dialogue. Though the lack of a straightforward chronology can be disconcerting for readers, the timeline of the story is important because its jumbled nature mirrors the state of Deogratias's mind in the aftermath of the genocide. Deogratias himself is constantly shifting back and forth between past and present, in an alcohol (*urwagwa*, banana beer)-induced haze often marked by delusions and paranoia. This temporal oscillation is similar to what Rick Iadonisi terms "temporal seepage" in an article on *Maus*; it is an uneasy state of movement in which the past intrudes upon the present.[4] And in fact this temporal disruption is constitutive, for Roger Luckhurst, of "the trauma novel." This is "because a traumatic event confounds narrative knowledge," and so "the inherently narrative form of the novel must acknowledge this in different kinds of temporal disruption."[5] As a (graphic) novel that deals explicitly with experiences of trauma and its aftermath, *Deogratias* addresses the way in which that trauma affects the memories and identities of those whom it impacts.

Many of the academic studies that reference *Deogratias* describe Deogratias the character (whose name essentially means "thanks to God") as an "ethically difficult figure" at best.[6] As Jesse Arseneault acknowledges, this makes him easily cast aside and discounted by Western liberal notions of concern that rely on sympathy. Deogratias is ethically "gray"; he is neither clearly good nor clearly bad. Though Stassen clearly expects that readers will, at the very least, pity Deogratias's circumstances, it is also difficult for readers to fully empathize with a *genocidaire,* a perpetrator. Stassen does show Deogratias in a more sympathetic light at certain points throughout the text. One scene, set prior to the genocide, shows Deogratias in school with Benina and Apollinaria, two Tutsi girls.[7] After forcing the class to raise their hands and identify their ethnicity (as either Hutu, Tutsi, or Twa), the teacher professes that the Hutu are "proud and honest farmers" who turned Rwanda into "the wonderful garden that feeds us all."[8] By contrast, the teacher refers to the Tutsi as foreigners "from the faraway North" who arrived in Rwanda "much later" and "took advantage of the poor Hutu peasants and treacherously enslaved them." This scene is presented in such a way as to make it clear that the teacher is repeating the propaganda of Hutu extremists. As writers like Fergal Keane and Nigel Eltringham have recognized, the "ethnic" divisions in Rwanda were concretized with the colonial Belgian introduction of ID cards in the early 1930s.[9] The narrative that the teacher presents reflects a common myth: that the Tutsi were "foreigners" from Ethiopia who came to Rwanda and oppressed the Hutu. After class, Deogratias approaches Benina and Apollinaria and tells them that "the teacher is a fool," making it clear that he does not agree with the anti-Tutsi ideology that was rampant in Rwanda during this time. In addition, we see Deogratias standing up for Benina at a checkpoint where a French officer attempts to detain her after seeing her Tutsi ID card.[10] Stassen also indicates that Deogratias is pressured by his Hutu friends to join them in carrying out the genocide; the novel depicts a group (likely members of the Interahamwe) knocking on his door in the night after President Habyarimana's plane was shot down and demanding that he come with them to set up a roadblock (presumably a roadblock to check the ID cards of anyone passing through in order to find and detain Tutsis). One of the friends demands that Deogratias come to "show the true color of [his] blood."[11] Finally, we see that Deogratias attempts to shield Benina from the violence by hiding her in his room (she eventually runs away). Scenes such as these give readers pause and allow them to consider the way in which Deogratias became involved in the genocide and question how many of his choices can be attributed to his own agency and how many must be attributed to forces outside his control.

Despite these moments, the reader's ability to sympathize with Deogratias's actions is further complicated by the fact that the novel does not shy away from discussions of violence.[12] We come to understand that

Deogratias was present for (and possibly participated in; his confession is unclear on this point) the rape and murder of Benina and Apollinaria.[13] His choices during the genocide do not allow the reader to easily sympathize with him, but they also do not bar us from feeling empathy for his predicament. The morally gray areas, and even the scenes of violence, make *Deogratias* an important graphic novel for young adults because they expose readers to difficult events that nevertheless must be encountered. As Ursula Sherman reminds us, it is better for youth to be exposed to events like the Rwandan genocide and knowledgeable about them than to remain ignorant, even if that means exposing them to depictions and descriptions of violence.[14] Along similar lines, Suzanne Keen writes that, if *Deogratias* were a movie, it could very well earn an R rating, but, "far from receiving a warning label, it earned the Goscinny Prize at the Angoulême International Comics Festival in 2000, the award of ALA Best Book for Young Adults, and YALSA Great Graphic Novel, establishing it as appropriate, indeed recommended reading for teenagers."[15] In *Freud in Oz*, Kenneth Kidd argues that children's literature should find a way to engage with traumatic subjects without traumatizing its readers. *Deogratias* walks a rather thin line in this respect, and some of its topics certainly are not suitable for a very young reader. Because of this, it is helpful to make a distinction between children's literature and young adult literature, which Perry Nodelman argues are similar to one another as well as "similarly different" from other forms of literature.[16] Nodelman describes young adult literature as a distinct variation of literature for younger children and states that, while it has many similar qualities, it also incorporates more "adolescent ideas." Roberta Trites argues that "children's literature often affirms the child's sense of Self and her or his personal power," but young adult literature involves "a recognition that social institutions are bigger and more powerful than individuals."[17]

In addition, young adult literature begins with the standard polarities of children's fiction (such as good versus evil) but has the potential, at least, to deconstruct them.[18] *Deogratias* clearly falls into Nodelman's young adult literature category. Its subject matter is too explicit for very young readers, but by presenting a protagonist who is at once bad (a perpetrator) and sympathetic, it allows young adult readers to begin to appreciate the complexity of the Rwandan genocide. As Elizabeth Baer insists, children's literature must, when dealing with traumatic subjects, be confrontational and grapple directly with the "evil" of the event.[19]

After the killing has ceased, Deogratias finds himself in the "Zone Turquoise," a "safezone" set up by French and Senegalese forces in southwest Rwanda. Deogratias leaves the zone against the advice of his friends, and the reader learns that, since his departure, he has begun to struggle with his memories of the traumatic events in which he participated. We learn that Deogratias often believes himself to be a dog. This is significant because, as is indirectly revealed in the novel, stray dogs often had to be shot by soldiers in Rwanda after the genocide because they ate the bodies of the dead and became violent toward humans. Deogratias views himself as no better than these dogs and often imagines—especially at night—that he is actually one of them. The illustrations even show Deogratias during these periods as a dog-like being. He is depicted in a crouched position, and his face and teeth are elongated to resemble those of a dog. In some illustrations, his hands and feet also appear to be paws. Arseneault posits that Deogratias's portrayal as a dog could easily serve to indicate that he exists outside the norms of ethical, human behavior, but to read the novel in this way is an oversimplification. Arseneault believes that the way in which Deogratias sees himself indicates his feelings about his complicity in the genocide and potentially also a feeling of responsibility for the deaths of his two friends.[20] This reading of the novel seems most likely, as Deogratias is obsessed throughout with the dogs he saw eating the bodies of the dead. We return to Deogratias's belief that he is a dog in the next section, as I argue that it serves to indicate moments when the unpresentable is at play in the text.

Deogratias is so troubled by his complicity in the genocide that he begins to take extreme steps to erase all memories of these actions. He attempts to poison those individuals who recall his actions as a genocidaire, and the novel concludes with him being arrested, in dog form, by the police, who have evidence of his recent string of poisonings. A Catholic priest and friend, Brother Philip, who witnesses his arrest comments that "he *was* a creature of God."[21] The use of the past tense here is significant, but it is worth noting that Brother Philip does not call Deogratias a "man of God"—he refers to him as a "creature," like a dog.

Behind *Deogratias*: The Unpresentable

It is by now an accepted fact that no single novel, narrative, film, or other representation of a genocide like the one which occurred in Rwanda can capture the entirety of the event.[22] At best, these stories and recollections give us only brief glimpses into the horror that occurred in these places, which continues to haunt both victims and perpetrators today. However, as we will see, novels such as *Deogratias*, in their very presentation of the events they describe and depict, indicate and allude to that which escapes representation: what Langer and others have termed "the unpresentable." This term receives significant attention in the post-Holocaust work of French philosopher Jean-François Lyotard in particular. In his work, the unpresentable is linked closely with an understanding of memory and what it means to remember a genocide. It is therefore an important concept for all who encounter post-genocide works of literature, but especially for younger readers who are, perhaps, learning about such events for the first time.

In section eight of his text titled *Heidegger and "the jews,"* Lyotard begins to discuss representation in the aftermath of the Holocaust and its relationship to the unpresentable.[23] Lyotard is particularly concerned with the relationship between the unpresentable and memory or forgetting. In his view, the "politics of absolute forgetting" that the SS carried out in the name of National Socialism has two faces or versions. The first face of this "politics" is the obvious: the extermination of a people. The Nazi party hoped that the world would forget the Jewish people if they ceased to exist. Thankfully, this face of forgetting was avoided despite the catastrophic loss of lives. But the second face of absolute forgetting can be caused, paradoxically, by representation. Is it possible, Lyotard asks, that in representing the "crime" (that is, the genocide itself) that we are not thereby compelled to remember it but are instead made to forget it? He states:

> It [the Holocaust] cannot be represented without being missed, being forgotten anew, since it defies images and words. Representing "Auschwitz" in images and words is a way of making us forget *this* . . . I am thinking of those very cases that, by their exactitude, their severity, are, or should be, best qualified not to let us forget.'[24]

But what is the "this" that we are made to forget? Certainly Lyotard is not suggesting that we are made to forget the Holocaust. Representation does not lead us to forget the fact that the genocide occurred. Rather, what we are made to forget, through representation, is the fact that the Holocaust defies images and words. We are made to forget that we are not capable of capturing and representing this event. Some "remainder" will always elude our representational grasp, and it is to this remainder, Lyotard argues, that we must yet attempt to bear witness.[25]

Lyotard asserts that "whenever one represents, one inscribes in memory, and this might seem a good defense against forgetting. It is, I believe, just the opposite."[26] He suggests that any attempt to represent the event of a genocide is doomed to failure. However, Lyotard does not, like philosopher Theodor Adorno, find post-genocide representations shameful or distasteful.[27] Immediately after he states that representation is not a guarantee for memory, Lyotard argues that, nevertheless, "one must, certainly, inscribe in words, in images. One cannot escape the necessity of representing."[28] The creation of a collective or public memory of the genocide requires representations in some shape or form. Lyotard further argues against his own initial pessimism; he writes, "What art can do is bear witness not to the sublime [the event, the genocide], but to this aporia of art and to its pain. It does not say the unsayable, but says that it cannot say it."[29] This statement echoes the story that precedes the first chapter of Elie Wiesel's novel *The Gates of the Forest*, which tells of a progressive forgetting by three rabbis and one disciple. Each successive rabbi forgets aspects of an apotropaic ritual and special prayer until every element is lost. The final rabbi concludes the story by speaking to God: " 'I am unable to light the fire and I do not know the prayer; I cannot even find the place in the forest. All I can do is to tell the story, and this must be sufficient.' *And it was sufficient.*"[30] Despite their incapacity—indeed, because of this very incapacity—the rabbis, and those who represent the events of the genocide are, for Lyotard, capable. They are able to "bear negative witness to the fact that . . . to bear witness to this impossibility remains possible."[31] These post-genocide representations, even as they give us glimpses into the events of the genocide, can also indicate what they are unable to represent to us.

Lyotard's account of post-genocide representation asserts that, while we may never be able to represent a genocide fully, we can multiply the perspectives of the event and our ways of approaching it. We can always create and identify more pieces of the puzzle, even if it will remain impossible to put them together into a whole. This does not, of course, mean that all representations of genocide are equal. For example, the popular film *Hotel Rwanda* perpetuates the image of hotel manager Paul Rusesabagina as a hero, when in reality numerous individuals who sheltered at the Milles Collines have accused him of stealing money from refugees, charging them for food from humanitarian organizations that should have been free, cutting phone lines, and threatening to turn individuals who did not obey him over to the genocidaires.[32] Lyotard does not suggest that *any* representation is necessarily a *good* representation. We should view Lyotard's work on representation as revealing the need for *more* representations, more attempts to testify to that which remains unpresentable, and more attempts to remember that there is the remainder. While perfect depiction is impossible, representations should be as faithful to history as possible.[33] We should be open to new, innovative ways of encountering that remainder with which Lyotard was so concerned. And if we cannot "say it [the remainder]" (or represent it), then at least we can testify to the fact that we are unable to say it, unable to represent it completely. By multiplying the representations, we do not hope for a whole to emerge; we do not believe that we will someday acquire all the pieces of the whole and thus possess a unified representation of the event of a genocide. Rather, the varied representations that must be allowed to come forth reveal that our work of remembrance is never done. This work is never complete; it is active, ongoing, and treacherous.[34]

Deogratias and the Unpresentable: The Importance of Difficulty in Young Adult Literature

Where, then, is the unpresentable in *Deogratias*? In what way does this graphic novel say or show that which it cannot say or show, that which must remain unpresentable? And in what way is this concept important for young readers? *Deogratias* illustrates the concept of the unpresentable most clearly at the moments when Deogratias becomes (or believes that he is becoming) a dog, as well as through the lack of closure at the ending. Deogratias is depicted as a dog when his memories burst forth and overwhelm him to such an extent that his speech becomes incoherent; his mind is tormented by his memories, but he is unable to articulate his suffering in any kind of clear or logical fashion.

There are six separate instances in the graphic novel in which Deogratias is depicted in the graphic panels as a dog (there are other occasions where he is illustrated with human features but is treated like an animal or is called a dog by other characters). Initially, Deogratias's "transformation" into a dog only seems to occur at night, when he is unable to find enough *urwagwa* to drink away his memories.[35] However, by the third occurrence of Deogratias's transformation, the reader sees that now he is not safe even in the sunlight. Unable to find *urwagwa* in the daytime, he mumbles to himself,

> Night-time . . . but it's day . . . It's at night that I'm scared . . .
> What's happening to me? I'm not afraid of the day . . . But my

head is spilling out, it's spilling out in the day! The sun isn't watching over me anymore. There are no dogs . . . But the stars are melting . . .[36]

The phrase "my head is spilling out" is repeated during a couple of the transformations; it seems to indicate the moments when Deogratias's memories overwhelm him completely. The fourth instance of Deogratias as a dog is very brief and shows only a tormented Deogratias in dog form at night, unable to sleep, but the fifth and six instances also take place during the day.[37] The reader sees Deogratias wandering the streets as a dog, but he is brought back to himself by Brother Philip, who left Rwanda during the genocide but has recently returned. He gives Deogratias a beer, and Deogratias confesses to him his complicity in the deaths of Benina, Apollinaria, Venetia (the mother of the two girls), and Augustine (a Twa character); he also admits that he has been poisoning all those who knew about his activities during the genocide, and then tells Brother Philip, "Drink a beer with me, Brother Philip . . . Now it's your turn to drink the poison!"[38] It is at this moment that Deogratias is arrested for the poisonings, and as the officials carry him away, he is completely in dog form.

All of the occasions on which Deogratias is depicted as a dog occur when his memories are threating to spill over in his mind (or when he is actively overcome by them in the midst of a flashback). These are the moments in the text where the unpresentable erupts. Rather than have Deogratias try to speak or narrate the sequence of events, Stassen allows the imagery to "speak" for him and indicate that there are things that Deogratias cannot say, horrors he cannot convey. These moments also give the reader hints that the ending will likely not bring justice, closure, or reconciliation.

The pieces of Deogratias's narrative do not fit together into a perfect whole. The fabula of the story is not incomplete, but the novel does not follow a typical narrative arc culminating in a denouement and grand moment of reconciliation, either for Deogratias or the other characters of the novel. Kate Polak acknowledges that the reader does not experience a feeling of hope at the end of the novel, but is instead forced to confront the question of what hope even means in such a context.[39] As previously mentioned, the novel ends with Brother Philip remarking sadly that Deogratias "was a creature of God" as the police take him away. This is the final line of the novel, and the graphic panels conclude with the imagery of a sunset and the rising of the stars. Night has fallen for Deogratias with finality. We have no reason to suspect that the sun will rise again for him, at least not in the metaphorical sense. The text refuses our desire for either a happy ending, in which Deogratias receives help, works through his trauma and recovers, or for justice, in which his crimes during the genocide are addressed; the poisonings for which Deogratias is arrested took place in the aftermath of the genocide. He is not being arrested because of his complicity in the genocide; in fact, at one point in the novel his friend Bosco even remarks to him that "you, you poor crackpot, you're not suspected of anything in particular. Besides the jails are full, there's no more room . . ."[40] In this sense, the text is not "whole"; it refuses to comply with our expectations or hopes for justice, reconciliation, or forgiveness.

Novels like *Deogratias* make us uncomfortable. Representations without closure, completeness, and coherence make us uneasy and can attest to the ongoing nature of trauma. The impact of the Rwandan genocide on Deogratias is of such an extent that he cannot testify to the event; he goes to extremes to purge his memories both from his own mind and from the minds of others. However, he cannot erase his own memories, and they can—and do—burst forth at times, especially during the night. Deogratias can neither fully forget nor fully remember.

The indications of that which lies outside the reach of representation have an ethical import for young readers. They emphasize that everything has not yet been said—that indeed everything about or concerning a genocide *cannot* be said. As Lyotard has stated, the horror of such an event exceeds words and images. We simply do not have the means to represent it, much less to understand it. If we think that we understand something, if we believe that we can grasp it and render it knowable, make it "make sense" to us, then we run the risk of becoming complacent. This is not to say that we should not try to understand how, why, when, where genocides occur, but only to emphasize the need for humility in the face of horror. We are constantly learning more about the genocides in our global history, and this is certainly vital as a component of memorialization. But some parts of the event will remain opaque to us. Kate Polak argues that *Deogratias* implicitly questions the extent to which genocide is an object that is "knowable."[41] Furthermore, who can say that they fully understand the horror of the event itself? Surely not we who were not present. It is also not uncommon to hear genocide survivors say that they feel inadequate or incapable of testifying to their own experiences, that they do not feel capable of saying what has happened.[42] Lyotard argues "what art [representations] can do is bear witness . . . to its pain. It does not say the unsayable, but says that it cannot say it." All one can do is say that one no longer knows how to tell this story. "And this should be enough. This has to be enough."⁴³ For Lyotard, those who represent after a genocide—and in particular the survivors, even morally gray survivors such as Deogratias—are capable because of their very incapacity; "they are enough and have been enough" to bear witness to the fact that bearing witness to this impossibility (of saying or representing) remains possible.

If stories and representations like *Deogratias* show the incompleteness inherent to representation in the aftermath of genocide, then they also illustrate the ethical demand for *more* representations, even if they are "doomed" in a certain sense. We may never be able to represent a genocide fully, to give a complete, coherent, and clear picture or rendering of it to ourselves, but we can multiply the perspectives of the event, its sense and our ways of approaching it. We can always create and identify more pieces of the puzzle, even if it will remain impossible to put them together into a whole. If one agrees with Lyotard (and others like him) who argue that we have an ethical responsibility to bear witness to genocides, then it seems imperative that we continue to try to do so, that we continue to attempt, inevitably through representations, to bear witness to that which remains unsayable and unpresentable. In doing so, we "remember" because we do not forget that there is some remainder, something more that remains to be said but that we are as yet incapable of saying or rendering representable. We do not become complacent, but remain vigilant, aware that the remainder eludes the grasp of our many and various representations. The activity of remembrance is never done; it is active, ongoing, and always of necessity incomplete.

Conclusion

In the foreword to *Heidegger and "the jews,"* David Carroll asks how we can reconcile the idea that our words, images, and historical/political concepts are inadequate to the task of representing the horror of a genocide with the feeling that there is still an obligation to bear witness to those events.⁴⁴ Despite our inadequacies and inabilities, he reminds us that it is necessary that we "talk about that" (a play on a line from the film *Shoah*, in which a character says "And let's not talk about that"—"that" being the Holocaust); it is necessary that we continue to represent. And it is important that not only adults engage with these admittedly difficult representations of atrocities, but also that children and young adults do so, albeit in a different way. *Deogratias* reveals that even difficult concepts like "the unpresentable," which are often found only in scholarly works intended for adults and academics, are accessible and useful for younger readers as well. *Deogratias* highlights the way in which certain representations, though they may appear to us as tragic, incomplete, or unresolved, have the potential to reveal to us something important about all such representations—the fact that they are all "unsuccessful," that they all fail to present the event of a genocide in its entirety. *Deogratias*—both story and character—testifies to the remainder, which remains unpresentable and eludes our grasp. It testifies to the sheer horror for which we (Western readers, the novel's target audience) likely have neither sufficient word nor image. Perhaps most importantly, stories like *Deogratias* teach us something about remembrance as well, and it is this lesson that is especially valuable for young readers. As Elizabeth Baer reminds us, "no one book is sufficient unto itself as a confrontation [with the event]."[45]

Deogratias certainly has its flaws. It does not recount the decades of colonial violence that preceded the 1994 genocide and speaks only to the experiences of a Hutu boy, who was coerced but nevertheless chose to participate in the genocide as a perpetrator. And perhaps most glaringly, it was not authored by a Rwandan. Deogratias reveals only a tiny fragment of the Rwandan genocide to its readers. Deogratias himself never speaks about the genocide directly until his confession at the end of the novel (the other comments he makes are vague, ominous, and murmured to himself during the hours of darkness, in which he is a dog), but the entire story nevertheless gives the reader keen insights into the horrors he and others experienced. Deogratias gives young adult readers the chance to start a dialogue with a character whom they may never have encountered otherwise, and it forces them to confront that which exceeds the novel itself: the unpresentable, which bursts forth in moments of uneasiness and disruption. Readers may struggle to empathize with Deogratias's plight, but, as the text reminds us, uneasily, "he was," nevertheless, "a creature of God."

Notes

1. It is worth noting that the novel has not been translated into Kinyarwanda, which is the language spoken by all Rwandans. It has been very deliberately targeted at Western readers. It is important to ask why a book that deals with the Rwandan genocide has not been made accessible to all Rwandan readers, and not

just to those who speak English, French, or another of the languages into which it has been translated. Perhaps most clearly, such a choice reflects the continuing Eurocentrism of the literary world and disregard for an entire potential audience in Rwanda. This debate over *Deogratias*'s origins has been taken up in the work of Madelaine Hron and Amy Larsen (see note 32).

There are works by Rwandans that, like *Deogratias*, gesture toward the unpresentable of the genocide. "Dead Girl Walking," a short story by Benjamin Sehene, comes to mind (though this is also available in French and English—not Kinyarwanda). I have nevertheless chosen to engage with Deogratias because it forces the confrontation in a way that "Dead Girl Walking" does not: by relaying the story of a perpetrator instead of a victim.

2. Michelle Bumatay and Hannah Warman, "Illustrating *Genocidaires*, Orphans, and Child Soldiers in Central Africa," *Peace Review* 24, no. 3 (2012): 333.

3. For a quick and insightful overview of *Deogratias*, see *Critical Survey of Graphic Novels: Independents and Underground Classics*, ed. Bart Beaty and Stephen Weiner (Ipswich: Salem Press, 2012), 205–8.

4. Rick Iadonisi, "Bleeding History and Owning His [Father's] Story: 'Maus' and Collaborative Autobiography," *College English Association Critic* 57, no. 1 (1994): 45. Iadonisi posits that these irruptions of the past into the present allow Art (both author and character) to cope and survive as the child of Holocaust survivors (46). But *Deogratias* is in no way an autobiographical text, and so the disruptions are solely for the readers to encounter and experience.

5. Roger Luckhurst, *The Trauma Question* (New York: Routledge, 2008), 87–88.

6. Jesse Arseneault, "On Canicide and Concern: Species Sovereignty in Western Accounts of Rwanda's Genocide," *English Studies in Canada* 39, no. 1 (2013): 143.

7. As the novel progresses, we learn through Deogratias's flashbacks that he cared for both Benina and Apollinaria. He was initially romantically interested in Apollinaria, but after she rejects him, he pursues Benina, with whom he has more success.

8. Jean-Philippe Stassen, *Deogratias: A Tale of Rwanda*, trans. Alexis Siegel (New York: First Second Books, 2006), 18.

9. In *Season of Blood*, Keane explains that understanding the Rwandan genocide as standard tribal violence is a complete misunderstanding of the nature and history of the conflict. He states that "Rwanda's genocide was not a simple matter of mutual hatred between tribes erupting into irrational violence. Neither were the mass killings the result of a huge and sudden outpouring of rage on the part of Hutus following the murder of their president. The killings—and there is ample documentary evidence to prove this—were planned long in advance by a clique close to President Habyarimana himself" (8).

In addition, Eltringham highlights the historical-dialectical processes of racialization in Rwanda in *Accounting for Horror*. He describes the manner in which

European racist theories, imposed on Rwanda and other colonized regions, laid the groundwork for rigid "ethnic" divisions and future violence. Eltringham's work helpfully emphasizes the importance of the "colonial distortion of social distinction in Rwanda" (12) and shows the way in which myths about the Tutsi were spread by the colonizers as they attempted to understand Rwandan society through their racist framework.

10. Stassen, *Deogratias*, 22–23.

11. Stassen, *Deogratias*, 58–59.

12. As Leanna Fry notes in her article, the most graphic accounts of violence during genocide are found in literature on Rwanda, including *Deogratias*. Fry posits that this is because the violence of the Rwandan genocide was so visible that it could not be ignored, even in literature. See "'Never Again': International Children's Genocide Literature," *Bookbird* 47, no. 1 (2009): 6–9.

13. Stassen, *Deogratias*, 71. Though Deogratias admits to bearing some of the responsibility for the deaths of Benina and Apollinaria, he also tells Augustine (a Twa character who accuses him of causing their deaths) that "they forced me, don't you see?"

14. Ursula Sherman, "'Why Would a Child Want to Read About That?': The Holocaust Period in Children's Literature," *How Much Truth Should We Tell Children: The Politics of Children's Literature*, ed. Betty Macon (Minneapolis: MEP, 1988), 182.

15. Suzanne Keen, "Fast Tracks to Narrative Empathy: Anthropomorphism and Dehumanization in Graphic Narratives," *SubStance* 40, no. 1 (2011): 141.

16. Perry Nodelman, *The Hidden Adult: Defining Children's Literature* (Baltimore: Johns Hopkins University Press, 2008), 97.

17. Roberta Trites, *Disturbing the Universe: Power and Repression in Adolescent Literature* (Iowa City: University of Iowa Press, 2000), 2–3.

18. Nodelman, *The Hidden Adult*, 58.

19. Elizabeth Baer, "A New Algorithm in Evil: Children's Literature in a Post-Holocaust World," *The Lion and The Unicorn* 24 (2000): 384–85.

20. Arseneault, "On Canicide and Concern," 142.

21. Stassen, *Deogratias: A Tale of Rwanda*, 78, my emphasis.

22. See, for example, Giorgio Agamben, who argues that there is something at the center of the event to which one cannot bear witness. Agamben, *Remnants of Auschwitz: The Witness and the Archive*, trans. Daniel Heller-Roazen (New York: Zone Books, 2002), 11.

See also Dorota Glowacka, *Disappearing Traces: Holocaust Testimonials, Ethics, and Aesthetics* (Seattle: University of Washington Press, 2012); Michael Bernard-Donals, *Forgetful Memory: Representation and Remembrance in the Wake of the Holocaust* (Albany: State University of New York Press, 2009); Andreas Huyssen, "Monument and Memory in a Postmodern Age," in *The Art of Memory: Holocaust Memorials in History*, ed. James Young (New York: Prestel-Verlag, 1994), 13; Jean-François

Lyotard, *Heidegger and "the jews,"* trans. Andreas Michel (Minneapolis: University of Minnesota Press, 1990).

23. When Lyotard uses the word "representation," he is using it to describe objects such as books, movies, plays, art, etc.

24. Lyotard, *Heidegger and "the jews,"* 26, my emphasis.

25. This remainder (the unpresentable) is, of course, what Lyotard identifies as "the jews"—a term that refers "neither to a nation, nor to a political, philosophical, or religious figure or subject. It is neither a concept nor a representation of any specific people as such" (xii). Lyotard states, "I use quotation marks to avoid confusing these 'jews' with real Jews" (3). David Carroll refers to Lyotard's decision to use such a term to refer to the unpresentable "provocative," and it certainly is that, but it is also potentially problematic in that it may reinforce certain stereotypes of Jewish people (who are, after all, the ones who suffered for their identity).

26. Lyotard, *Heidegger and "the jews,"* 26.

27. Adorno famously stated that "All post-Auschwitz culture, including its urgent critique, is garbage." See Theodor Adorno, *Negative Dialectics*, trans. E. B. Ashton (New York: Continuum, 1973), 365.

28. Lyotard, *Heidegger and "the jews,"* 26.

29. Lyotard, *Heidegger and "the jews,"* 47.

30. Elie Wiesel, *The Gates of the Forest*, trans. Frances Frenaye (New York: Schocken Books, 1966), my emphasis.

31. Lyotard, *Heidegger and "the jews,"* 47.

32. For a fuller discussion of the "Hotel Rwanda" and Rusesabagina, see Edouard Kayihura and Kerry Zuku's *Inside the Hotel Rwanda: The Surprising True Story . . . And Why It Matters Today* (Dallas: BenBella Books, 2014).

33. Madelaine Hron argues that novels like *Deogratias* are misguided and misinformed representations of the Rwandan genocide and necessarily fail to convey the facts and experience of the Rwandan genocide because the author, Stassen, is not Rwandan but Belgian, and Stassen's target audience is Western French speakers (not Rwandans). See "*Itsembabwoko* 'À la Française?'—Rwanda, Fiction and the Franco-African Imaginary," *Forum for Modern Language Studies* 45, no. 2 (2009): 162–64.

Against Hron, Amy Larsen argues that, though Hron's points are worth considering, this does not mean that *Deogratias* as a novel is entirely without merit or value for readers. See Larsen, "The Duty of Memory in J. P. Stassen's *Deogratias: A Tale of Rwanda* and Rupert Bazambanza's *Smile Through the Tears*," *Literature and Values: Selected Proceedings of a Conference Held at the University of Waterloo, 3–5 June 2011* (Newcastle: Cambridge Scholars, 2012): 109–11.

34. I am thinking here of the work of James Young, who argues that we must acknowledge that the most important work of remembrance "consists in the ongoing activity of memory, in the debates surrounding these memorials"; Young, *The Changing Shape of Holocaust Memory* (New York: The American Jewish Committee,

1995), 44. Young calls this "the art of memory" and reminds us that it encompasses not only literal representations, but "also includes the activity that brought them into being, the constant give and take between memorials [representations] and viewers, and finally the responses of viewers to their own world in light of a memorialized past" (see page 20 of the same text).

35. The first depiction of Deogratias as a dog takes place on pages 26–27 of the English translation. Here he is unable to find any alcohol. The second illustration, which occurs on pages 47–49, is slightly different: though Deogratias begins to transform into a dog (his face elongates, and he is shown with a stooped posture), he is given *urwagwa* by a woman, and his face becomes human once more.

36. Stassen, *Deogratias*, 52.

37. Stassen, *Deogratias*, 57.

38. Stassen, *Deogratias*, 68–76.

39. Kate Polak, *Ethics in the Gutter: Empathy and Historical Fiction in Comics* (Columbus: Ohio State University Press, 2017), 41.

40. Stassen, *Deogratias*, 17.

41. Polak, *Ethics in the Gutter*, 44.

42. For example, in an interview, Rwandan genocide survivor Consolee Nishimwe says, "I can't find words to describe how I felt . . . I did not have words to describe what happened to me and my family." Nishimwe also states that she only tells her story now because she believes it may help others, especially women, who still feel unable to speak or find the words to describe their own experiences. See https://www.un.org/africarenewal/web-features/i-was-tested-limit-%E2%80%94-rwanda-genocide-survivor for her full interview. See also the story of Holocaust survivor Freddie Knoller, who refused to tell even part of his story for thirty-five years after being liberated: https://www.telegraph.co.uk/history/world-war-two/11370513/Holocaust-survivors-70-years-of-trauma-I-could-cry-nonstop-even-now.html.

43. Lyotard, *Heidegger and "the jews,"* 47.

44. Lyotard, *Heidegger and "the jews,"* viii.

45. Baer, "A New Algorithm in Evil," 386.

Works Cited

Adorno, Theodor. *Negative Dialectics*. Translated by E. B. Ashton. New York: Continuum, 1973.

Agamben, Giorgio. *Remnants of Auschwitz: The Witness and The Archive*. Translated by Daniel Heller-Roazen. New York: Zone Books, 2002.

Arseneault, Jesse. "On Canicide and Concern: Species Sovereignty in Western Accounts of Rwanda's Genocide." *English Studies in Canada* 39, no. 1 (March 2013): 125–47.

Baer, Elizabeth. "A New Algorithm in Evil: Children's Literature in a Post-Holocaust World." *The Lion and The Unicorn* 24 (2000): 378–401.
Beaty, Bart, and Stephen Weiner, eds. *Critical Survey of Graphic Novels: Independents and Underground Classics, volume I*. Ipswich: Salem Press, 2012.
Bernard-Donals, Michael. *Forgetful Memory: Representation and Remembrance in the Wake of the Holocaust*. Albany: State University of New York Press, 2009.
Bumatay, Michelle, and Hannah Warman. "Illustrating *Genocidaires*, Orphans, and Child Soldiers in Central Africa." *Peace Review* 24, no. 3 (2012): 332–39.
Eltringham, Nigel. *Accounting for Horror: Post-Genocide Debates in Rwanda*. London: Pluto Press, 2004.
Fry, Leanna. "'Never Again': International Children's Genocide Literature." *Bookbird* 47, no. 1 (2009): 6–9.
Glowacka, Dorota. *Disappearing Traces: Holocaust Testimonials, Ethics, and Aesthetics*. Seattle: University of Washington Press, 2012.
Goldhill, Olivia. "Holocaust Survivors' 70 Years of Trauma: 'I Could Cry Nonstop, Even Now.'" *The Telegraph*, January 26, 2015. https://www.telegraph.co.uk/history/world-war-two/11370513/Holocaust-survivors-70-years-of-trauma-I-could-cry-nonstop-even-now.html
Hron, Madelaine. "*Itsembabwoko* 'À la Française?'—Rwanda, Fiction and the Franco-African Imaginary." *Forum for Modern Language Studies* 45, no. 2 (2009): 162–75.
Huyssen, Andreas. "Monument and Memory in a Postmodern Age." In *The Art of Memory: Holocaust Memorials in History*, edited by James Young, 9–17. New York: Prestel-Verlag, 1994.
Iadonisi, Rick. "Bleeding History and Owning His [Father's] Story: 'Maus' and Collaborative Autobiography." *College English Association Critic* 57, no. 1 (1994): 41–56.
Keen, Suzanne. "Fast Tracks to Narrative Empathy: Anthropomorphism and Dehumanization in Graphic Narratives." *SubStance* 40, no. 1 (2011): 135–55.
Larsen, Amy. "The Duty of Memory in J. P. Stassen's *Deogratias: A Tale of Rwanda* and Rupert Bazambanza's *Smile Through the Tears*." In *Literature and Values: Selected Proceedings of a Conference Held at the University of Waterloo, 3–5 June 2011*, 109–25. Newcastle: Cambridge Scholars, 2012.
Luckhurst, Roger. *The Trauma Question*. New York: Routledge, 2008.
Lyotard, Jean-François. *Heidegger and "the jews."* Translated by Andreas Michel. Minneapolis: University of Minnesota Press, 1990.
Kayihura, Edouard, and Kerry Zuku. *Inside the Hotel Rwanda: The Surprising True Story . . . And Why It Matters Today*. Dallas: BenBella Books, 2014.
Keane, Fergal. *Season of Blood: A Rwandan Journey*. London: Penguin Books, 1996.
Nishimwe, Consolee. "I Was Tested to the Limit—Rwanda Genocide Survivor." Interview with The United Nations, Africa Renewal. Transcribed, https://www.

un.org/africarenewal/web-features/i-was-tested-limit-%E2%80%94-rwanda-genocide-survivor

Nodelman, Perry. *The Hidden Adult: Defining Children's Literature*. Baltimore: Johns Hopkins University Press, 2008.

Polak, Kate. *Ethics in the Gutter: Empathy and Historical Fiction in Comics*. Columbus: Ohio State University Press, 2017.

Sherman, Ursula. "Why Would a Child Want to Read About That?: The Holocaust Period in Children's Literature." In *How Much Truth Should We Tell Children: The Politics of Children's Literature*, edited by Betty Macon, 173–84. Minneapolis: MEP, 1988.

Stassen, Jean-Philippe. *Deogratias: A Tale of Rwanda*. Translated by Alexis Siegel. New York: First Second Books, 2006.

Trites, Roberta. *Disturbing the Universe: Power and Repression in Adolescent Literature*. Iowa City: University of Iowa Press, 2000.

Wiesel, Elie. *The Gates of the Forest*. Translated by Frances Frenaye. New York: Schocken Books, 1966.

Young, James. *The Changing Shape of Holocaust Memory*. New York: The American Jewish Committee, 1995.

Chapter 3

Tracing Trauma

Childhood, Innocence, and Memory in Cypriot Children's Literature since 1974

Maria Chatzianastasi

Introduction

This chapter addresses a body of Greek-Cypriot writing for the young that is underdiscussed in global terms: that which features the trauma and memory of the 1974 invasion of Cyprus, which divided the country in half. It examines how this topic has been dealt with in Cypriot children's literature over the three decades that followed the invasion by providing close readings of samples of writing published between 1976 and 2010. It also explores the way in which chronological distance between actual events and writing affects how trauma is represented in writing for the young in Cyprus as well as the role of fictional child characters in Cypriot fictions of childhood. The primary texts are discussed in relation to trauma theory and children's literary criticism, including the work of Hamida Bosmajian, Elizabeth Baer, and Kenneth Kidd. A recurring figure in this body of criticism, which plays a key role in this discussion, is the trope of the wounded child.

As I seek to demonstrate, there is significant continuity in the patterns of representation and the role of innocence in Cypriot children's literature of the invasion, although recently there have been signs that the use of fictional child characters is undergoing transformation of a kind that shows a more mature approach to writing dealing with trauma for a younger audience. The depiction of childhood in these texts from one decade to another, I argue, works to explain the causes and nature of trauma, its stages, and effects over the years and attests to Michelle Balaev's observation that the functions of trauma in literature and society can be more varied than initially thought because the values and responses arising from trauma can be influenced by a variety of individual and cultural factors that change over time.[1]

Previous discussions of Holocaust writing for the young, in particular the work of Bosmajian, have shown that describing trauma and atrocity is a demanding task. Significantly, the changes in the more recent works discussed in this chapter show that Bosmajian's conclusion that children's literature cannot also be effective trauma writing needs some adjustment. In line with previous discussions about representations of atrocity and trauma in children's literature, I suggest that the examples discussed here offer significant evidence to support the argument that authors of children's literature can and should engage with traumatic subjects effectively without traumatizing their readers.

Cypriot children's literature rarely crosses the borders of the nation that produces it, making it a minority literature. The findings of this chapter are culturally specific to the body of writing, yet significant in literary discussions of trauma. The process of uncovering history that has taken place in Cyprus has much to say to writers in the many countries where children are experiencing similar trauma as well as highlighting the potentially important work children's books can perform in helping young readers acknowledge and understand trauma.

In chronological order, the material discussed below relates to the following works: Maria Piliotou's *The Wolves and Red Riding Hood* (1976), Agni Charalambous' "In Iris's Colors" (1998), Sotiria Pyla's *Memories That Hurt* (2004), and Paraskevoula Georgiou Pitsiri's *What Does Enslavement Mean?* (2010).[2]

Before looking closer into the literary representations of childhood and trauma in these texts, it is necessary to explain a specific term employed here and offer some contextual information about the Cypriot children's literature and the focus texts by providing plot summaries for each of the stories. Even though this is not a historical study, it is necessary to first provide a brief historical review of Cyprus' recent history to offer some context for the literature examined here. Because this volume appeals to global readers, including millennial readers with little collective memory of this event and possibly little historical knowledge of it, this overview will help them acknowledge the historical situation to which this chapter refers.

Invasion in the Contemporary History of Cyprus

According to Zembylas, "Cyprus has been and remains a deeply divided (and segregated) society due to the protracted nature of conflict between Greek Cypriots (the majority, around 80 per cent) and Turkish Cypriots (the island's largest minority, around 18 per cent)."[3] Various reasons and chains of events and conditions led up to the events that are commonly known in Cyprus as the Turkish invasion.

Cyprus won its independence from the British in 1960, and, as Agathangelou and Killian put it, "the elites of the Greek and Turkish ethnic communities worked together towards consolidating their power in Cyprus."[4] Having signed an ambiguous constitution of independence, a few years later Greek-Cypriot President Makarios proposed some constitutional amendments to improve the functionality of the Cypriot State based on a unified administration and majority rule.[5] The thirteen proposed amendments to the constitution of Cyprus that Makarios submitted to his Turkish-Cypriot vice president were immediately rejected by the Turkish community and triggered the escalation of conflict and violence between Greek and Turkish Cypriots. The violence of this response to Makarios's attempt opened the way for the preparation of the invasion of 1974 that was driven by Turkey's long-standing ambitions to control Cyprus following the end of British authority on the island. The period between December 21, 1963, and August 10, 1964, has been characterized as the most violent period in contemporary Cypriot history, with casualties on both sides.[6] As a result, all Turkish Cypriot representatives in the government decided to withdraw from their posts. Turkish Cypriots, either of their own will or by force, began retreating from isolated rural areas and villages and were relocated in groups in consolidated enclaves with strong lines of defense that were considered safer for them.[7] According to Kliot and Mansfield, Turkish Cypriots completely evacuated their properties in seventy-two mixed villages and abandoned twenty-four Turkish Cypriot villages during this period. Twelve mixed villages were also wholly or partially deserted by their Greek Cypriot inhabitants because of the fighting. When these movements ended in August 1964, there were 200 Greek Cypriot refugees, compared to approximately 25,000 Turkish Cypriot refugees, registered by the United Nations Peace Keeping Force in Cyprus (UNFICYP), and forty-two Turkish-controlled territorial enclaves were formed containing 115 villages and town quarters that Greek Cypriots could not enter. Central government efforts to reintegrate the Turkish Cypriot community failed, while the desire to impose *Taksim* or partition was growing in the political circles of the Turkish Cypriot community, especially between 1967 and 1968. This situation persisted over a ten-year period to 1974.[8]

The unstable political climate from 1963 and the conflict between Greek Cypriot and Turkish Cypriot communities on the island led to further turmoil, with the Greek junta organizing a coup and Turkey invading Cyprus in 1974.[9] On July 20, 1974, after the failed coup against President Makarios organized by the Greek junta, Turkey began invading Cyprus. By violating the treaty of independence, Turkey claimed its role as guarantor for the Turkish-Cypriot minority with the assumption that the coup would ultimately lead to the annexation of Cyprus by Greece.[10] The Turkish invasion divided the island into two parts, North and South, causing the displacement of thousands of civilians from both communities. A total of 250,000 Greek Cypriots and 45,000 Turkish Cypriots were forcibly displaced as a result of the Turkish invasion and occupation of 38 percent of the total area of Cyprus. Nicosia, as Anderson notes, became a Mediterranean Berlin, divided by barbed wire and barricades.[11] Since then, the "Green Line" has been dividing the island, imposing a de facto partition of the island into two ethnically homogenous parts.[12,13] Katsonis and Kyriakides note that the events of the summer 1974 came to dominate the political, cultural, and social scene in Cyprus and still affected life in Cyprus even though there were strong expectations for a peaceful solution and reconciliation under the auspices of the United Nations that supported the peace talks between the two communities.[14] Most notably for this thesis, they argue that literature was bound to be influenced by this historical landmark, whether it addressed adults or children.

Defining the Children's Literature of Atrocity

In this chapter I use terms such as atrocity, trauma, children's literature of atrocity, and children's trauma literature. As this volume is interested in investigating the problem of atrocity in children's literature and the literature of childhood, it is necessary to explain first what children's literature of atrocity is and how the Greek-Cypriot literature of invasion fits in this discussion.

According to Kidd, writing for the young about trauma has a long history that demonstrates the management of trauma, including topics of death, war, divorce, racism, and class struggle. Children's literature of atrocity made its appearance in the 1980s and 1990s, emphasizing the main characters' experiences of pain, suffering, the profound toll of trauma on them, and the impossibility of recovery.[15] It is a form of narrative committed to the representation of the ghostly memories of such twentieth- and early twenty-first-century events as Auschwitz, Hiroshima, and the terrorist attacks of September 11, 2001.[16] To effectively address such traumatic contexts, writing for the young must take the form of "children's literature of atrocity," meaning that it should deal directly with evil, as Baer insists.[17] Kidd observes that, in Baer's terms, stories about atrocity manifest the intention that reading about atrocity is expected to be traumatizing for young readers.[18] Such stories, Anastasia Ulanowicz adds, challenge narratives of historical progress, individual reason, and utopian uses of science and technology while they also make little effort to shelter children from the horrors they describe, thus making a "dramatic departure" from the belief that young readers should be protected rather than exposed to traumatic materials.[19]

The literature of the invasion can be considered as a special case of children's literature of atrocity because it is concerned with representing and reproducing the memories of the events and atrocities of July 1974 and their long-term consequences as well as with registering the pain and suffering arising from the trauma of the invasion, refugeedom, and enclavement.[20] These stories, however, are not interested in representing their main characters' direct confrontation with the atrocities of the events or in shocking their readers to force an understanding of trauma. As will be shown, some of these stories involve the belief that what happened cannot change and that trauma is felt acutely by those who lived through the events, but they also involve a sense of hope arising from the possibility that trauma can ultimately be shared and passed on at least to some extent.

Stories about the Invasion: Introducing the Primary Texts

In Cyprus, a dramatic increase in the literary production for the young appeared in the decades following the invasion on July 20, 1974. As Petros Panaou and Frixos Michaelides note, "[i]ronically, one of the darkest moments in the modern history of Cyprus brought the booming development of its literature."[21] Specifically, the events of 1974 and the consequences of the invasion stimulated the third and most productive period of literary writing for the young in Cyprus.[22] This initially took the form of what Costas Katsonis refers to as "literature of the invasion," meaning children's literature that describes, directly or obliquely, the coup preceding the invasion, the events of the invasion, refugeedom, the missing, and the enclaved.[23] The traumatic experience arising from those events significantly affected the development of juvenile literature in Cyprus and constantly appears as a central theme in the following texts that comprise the primary material of this chapter.

Piliotou's *The Wolves and Red Riding Hood* focuses on the first days of the war. Through the story of Renoula, a young girl, the narrative offers a literary witnessing of key events, including the coup prior to the invasion and the attempted assassination of the president; the political instability and threatening atmosphere created by the national army and then the invasion; the call for men to join the army; and the burning of Pentadaktilos mountain. As shown in my analysis later in the chapter, the writing is intensely emotional, and the text features a deeply ideological construction of childhood innocence.

Charalambous's short story "In Iris's Colors" focuses on trauma as an unresolvable experience with belated repetitions. Considerably different from the previous example of writing, addressing an older, young-adult audience, it deals with the rape of its central character, Ariadne, during the invasion. The depiction of atrocity is more straightforward here, and the focus shifts from the experiences of child characters found in the previous text to the traumatic experiences of an adult character in this one. Gradually over the years, Ariadne develops symptoms of trauma related to her rape and multiple additional losses she experienced and therefore grows an intense generated hatred toward Turkish people. Therefore, a letter she receives in 1997 from her Turkish-Cypriot childhood friend Aishe, asking her to reunite becomes profoundly unsettling, bringing back her recurring flashbacks of her rape. The narrative time collapses, showing both the trauma and the character's struggle. Her past is reexperienced through flashbacks of childhood, friendship, engagement, and haunting images of invasion. Although the focus of the story is Ariadne's trauma, the largest part of the text is invested in her childhood and friendship with Aishe, working as a background story and reconstructing childhood innocence as a way of instilling hope and trust in the damaged adult character.

Childhood innocence is also central in the autobiographical novels *Memories That Hurt* by Sotiria Pyla and *What Does Enslavement Mean?* by Paraskevoula Pitsiri. Both stories emphasize the effects of the invasion on their child characters. *Memories That Hurt* deals with the writer's family life in the years before, during, and after the invasion, ending in the present time. Its description of the first moments of the invasion shows its traumatic impact on children who experienced the events and then grew up into traumatized and suffering adults. The text depicts children's traumatic responses to the frightening sight and sounds of attacking airplanes, the warning sound of sirens, and the bombings. The most important feature of the book is its conceptualization of trauma, demonstrating how it can be felt in the lives of its main characters over the years, as shown later through the analysis of the book.

Similarly, in *What Does Enslavement Mean?*, the adult self resonates with the trauma felt by young Vagelitsa during the invasion. The book details the author's childhood years in Famagusta and her flight during the war as these are focalized through her alter ego, ten-year-old Vagelitsa. Trauma is linked with a loss of childhood dreams and with the crisis invasion brings upon child characters. The analysis of these stories is underpinned by earlier discussions about the challenges and the special position of childhood in children's trauma literature. Therefore, the next section considers children's literature criticism focusing on discussions of children's trauma literature.

Challenges at the Roots of Children's Trauma Writing

Since the early 1990s, children's literature has emerged as a valuable space for the conceptualization and representation of trauma, yet it is encompassed by specific challenges. Scholarly discussions about this genre in the early 2000s began by considering "the special position of childhood in relation to trauma writing."[24] They highlighted the challenges in the representation of atrocity and trauma in children's literature, particularly because literary techniques and conventions are adapted in line with what is considered suitable for young readers.[25]

The challenges at the heart of trauma writing for the young originate both from the difficulties and sensitivities of its subject matter, which have preoccupied trauma studies following the publication of Cathy Caruth's work, as well as from the characteristics of its target audience. Focusing almost exclusively on the testimony of Holocaust survivors, Caruth considers trauma to be an unresolvable unconscious problem.[26] In *Trauma: Explorations in Memory*, Caruth calls particular attention to the difficulty of listening and responding to trauma, as well as identifying ways to express trauma beyond its pathology and the painful repetitions of suffering, meaning that there is no straightforward access to trauma.[27] Where trauma fiction addressing an adult audience has experimented with various literary techniques that register trauma's impossibility in the effort to "narrate the unnarratable,"[28] children's trauma literature has drawn critical attention to authors' representational strategies that attempted to "communicate 'difficult' or 'delicate' topics to ostensibly sensitive young readers."[29] This has involved questioning the effectiveness and suitability of children's literature to handle difficult and often traumatic subject matter.

In her study of Holocaust writing for the young, *Sparing the Child: Grief and the Unspeakable in Stories about Nazism and the Holocaust*, Bosmajian stresses the importance of writing that deals more effectively with trauma by exploring the deep traces of memory and questioning the disturbing effects of trauma in individuals and thus allows readers to work through traumatic experiences and memories. Bosmajian uses Kafka's metaphor of the "frozen sea" to refer to the memory and experience of the Holocaust in adult survivors and witnesses and highlights the important role such writing can play in adults.[30] For a book to become "the axe in the frozen sea in us," for adult readers to be able to understand trauma, Bosmajian believes, they must pass through a crisis, meaning they have to be traumatized by the story. Unlike adult narratives, such responses, she maintains, cannot be demanded from children, as writing for the young has traditionally sought to avoid confronting young readers with graphic and disturbing material.[31] Because "those who speak to children or write books for them about the disaster seek to inform, perhaps to teach, but not to shock them so severely that the young reader is lost and alienated," this attitude toward children's literature has meant that "a children's book cannot be the axe for the child reader."[32] As explained in my introduction, this conclusion needs adjustment, and this chapter offers evidence in this direction.

Where Baer and Bosmajian privilege direct confrontation with atrocity through reading, with Bosmajian concluding that children's literature cannot also be effective trauma writing, Kidd adopts a more nuanced perspective. Studying the mutually constitutive history between psychoanalysis and children's literature in the twentieth century, he proposes that some of the materials he examines cannot tackle the difficulties encompassing trauma writing for the young but rather opt for simplistic narratives.[33] He refuses, however, to give these works the last word.[34] He insists that despite such stories, there is and there should be effective trauma writing for the young that does not aim to traumatize its audience.[35] Indeed, some of the works discussed here extend and support this argument.

The Desire for Childhood Innocence Turned into a Fantasy

Cypriot writers used child figures to explore their anxieties regarding the traumatic impact of the invasion on children as well as their desire for childhood innocence. Capshaw Smith observes that the construction of children's responses in writing for the young, as either victims or survivors of trauma, arises from adults' desire for childhood innocence and is "deeply invested in allaying adult anxieties."[36] This observation is particularly useful when thinking about Cypriot trauma writing. This use of child characters in relation to trauma can be productively linked to the work of psychoanalysis through the trope of the "wounded child" and Freud's discussion of creative writing as equivalent to daydreaming and desires. The focus here is particularly on desires related to childhood innocence and the trauma of the nation rather than daydreaming. Examining a body of writing produced over a longer period of time, this chapter recognizes the passage of time as a means for allowing these desires to change, affecting how traumatic childhood is conceptualized and constructed in trauma writing.

As Tribunella explains,

> the figure of the child is central to the understanding of trauma and vice versa [. . .] This use of the child to understand trauma has created a sense in which the prototypical sufferer of trauma is the child or a sense in which childhood is or even should be the originary moment or site of trauma.[37]

Originating in Freud's *The Interpretation of Dreams*, the figure of the wounded or "burning" child has received renewed attention since the development of trauma studies and the subsequent emergence of the children's literature of atrocity.[38] Its emblematic use in American writing, discussed by Tribunella and in the children's literature of atrocity discussed by Kidd, disguises adults' fear for children's traumatic suffering and their desire for an intact childhood. In the literature of invasion, child characters are depicted to be psychically wounded, suffering the consequences of trauma. They are used as a literary device that prolongs the sense of childhood innocence even as it challenges it, especially in the earlier texts.

According to Douglas, childhood "is a recognizable synecdoche of history—a means for explaining and interpreting the past, revising and correcting the mistakes of history."[39] While Douglas refers to childhood in relation to autobiographical writing, as the discussion of texts in this chapter shows, her argument can usefully be extended to other forms of trauma writing. In the literature of the invasion, representations of childhood reveal the writing as a cultural space that reflects ideologies and desires, memories, anxieties, and opportunities for exploration and experimentation. Being ideologically and symbolically constructed, child figures in the texts discussed embody not only the writers' personal desires but also the cultural-national desire to represent and make visible specific historical instances of trauma, which, as Anne Whitehead in *Trauma Fiction* explains, is part of what inspires trauma writing in the first place.[40]

The fact that Cypriot writers continued to write about the invasion for more than four decades means that their choice to use child figures as the embodiment of national trauma and desires and as objects of collective memory had a strong impact on readers. Freud equates creative writing with fantasies and daydreaming; creative writing has such a strong impact on readers because, he notes, writers draw their sources of inspiration and emotion invested in their writing from fantasies and daydreaming, which function as the fulfillment of abandoned or unfulfilled wishes and of the human desire to alter the existing and often unsatisfactory or unpleasant real world. Although Freud refers to creative writing generally, his arguments are productive in thinking about trauma writing, especially because the desire to change unpleasant realities that may underpin the creation and production of creative writing can be particularly potent in the case of trauma writing. Consider for instance the motto "Never again" underpinning Holocaust writing or "I Don't Forget" associated with the production of the "literature of invasion." Literary works, Freud maintains, affect readers strongly; they give shape to such desires or fantasies that they share with readers, releasing a sense of pleasure in them by helping them understand that others may have similar fantasies or desires.[41] In Cypriot writing for the young, this is relevant to the understanding of trauma and emerges from the common nature of experiences and memories of the invasion shared by Cypriot people. Equally, for those who are not traumatized themselves, such pleasure can arise from the possibility for trauma resolution or working through as part of fiction. Because the "literature of the invasion" spans four decades, the type of experiences underpinning the writing has changed over the years, as has the fantasy-memory, which is satisfied by each of these works.

Childhood as Object of Memory in
The Wolves and Red-Riding Hood[42]

Piliotou's *The Wolves and Red-Riding Hood*, one of the earliest texts produced in the period following the 1974 invasion, powerfully registers the impact of trauma, both individual and collective, and expresses anxieties arising from the trauma of invasion. Featuring innocent traumatized child characters, this story works to make visible the traces of the historic instance of invasion and its traumatic consequences that followed.[43] Renoula and the other children in the book appear as the living but "wounded children" of the invasion and so of the nation. Piliotou's child characters are equally constructed as the ultimate victims and survivors of trauma, in keeping with the work of Capshaw Smith; their suffering becomes part of or even equal to the national suffering, thus awakening adult fears and anxieties. This construction of childhood in the story also attests to Anne Higonnet's assertion that childhood innocence "replaces what we have lost, or what we fear to lose. Every sweetly sunny, innocently cute [. . .] child image stows away a dark side: a threat of loss, of change, and, ultimately, of death."[44] Emphasizing the innocence of its characters and creating an innocent point of view, the story works to transform the impact of the invasion and the loss of childhood innocence into fantasy. As such, Pyliotou's story aligns with Freud's theory of creative writing, which in this case is encompassed by the desire to change the unsatisfactory or unpleasant realities of the invasion.

The innocent point of view is communicated through language. Renoula, the book's main character and narrator, observes the critical situation and reports it in ways that make her innocence and limited world experience evident to readers through first-person narration. Language choices emphasize her naive point of view; for instance, circumlocutions are used to designate ideas or terms that she does not yet possess, such as "the good king" instead of president of the government or "the wolves" meaning the paramilitary group associated with the coup and the invaders. The use of this perspective both produces a sense of childhood innocence and provides a knowingly restricted viewpoint for the reader. Although it creates an understanding of trauma from the perspective of childhood, it also results in an emotional and palpable representation of trauma.[45]

For instance, while Renoula finds refuge in her room as the invasion begins, the narrative focuses on her thoughts, once again alluding to her innocence. The writing makes overuse of diminutives to describe objects and space as a way of conveying information about her spatial and psychological point of view. As Lorna Martens explains, places and objects figure prominently in the workings of memory in literary writing that depicts childhood memories. This, Martens observes, offers ways of understanding that draw on a childlike view of the world "that is object-focused, imaginative, and emotionally intense."⁴⁶ These aspects of a childlike perception of the situation also appear in Renoula's description of her room, which is fixated on tiny objects. Because the use of objects in this text is a way of defining a childlike or innocent view associated with traumatic experience, this approach gives some insight into how trauma is experienced from the perspective of childhood but in an intensified emotional tone achieved through the specific use of language, which creates the impression of an idyll that will soon be lost.

Renoula's description reflects a wish to prolong this moment by erasing the threat of the invasion.

> I look at my room, illuminated by a *small electric lamp*. Every corner an unforgettable moment. My dolls' corner reminds me of my encounter with the good king; his hand stroking my hair; his smile. Another corner [has] my *little closet*, and in there, embroidered *petite dresses* made by my *mummy's* hands, *minute knitted sweaters, tiny skirts*; all handmade with love. Here is the corner with my toys too; all *small*, but bought with love from my father, and next to that is my *little bookcase* with my desk (emphasis added).⁴⁷

Everything appears tiny, vulnerable, and beautifully fragile; all those tiny objects, carefully assembled in that room, not only draw an ideal childhood, but also reproduce a dream or a fantasy, one that reflects and replaces the loss of this world as a result of invasion.

In this story the creation of a childlike and innocent point of view, as well as the representation of children as victims and survivors of trauma, are intensified by the troubling images of the "wounded" and suffering children appearing in the illustrations, which arise like a haunting dream from the pages of the book. As Higonnet explains, when "we look at troubling images of children, we not only see abstract meanings, but dread real consequences."⁴⁸ On page 7 of the book readers encounter a picture of the main character and her friend, who are hidden behind the fence of a luxurious hotel watching

Figure 3.1. Illustration no. 1 from the book *The Wolves and Red Riding Hood* (foreword).

a wedding party shortly after the invasion (figure 3.1). The simplicity of the drawing technique, including the absence of color, creates a focus on the characteristics of the two faces. Curiosity, anxiety, pain, and sadness are evident in the shape and size of the two pairs of eyes and lips that remain closed and lean downward, creating faces full of despair and agony.

In the specifics of the eyes and the lips, the author-illustrator constructs a fragile form of childhood, one that appears to be wrought by the experience of war. These disembodied, sad eyes, which look directly at the reader, resemble Freud's traumatic dream of the burning child. Ghostlike as they seem, they are similar to illusionary figures from a Freudian dream rather than real children; their eyes are eloquent, piercing through the reader's eyes though their lips remain silent. The traumatic reality passed on through the silence of this image reveals the inadequacy of oral language in the face of trauma as well as the impossibility to straightforwardly access trauma that has preoccupied Caruthian theory.[49] In addition, the image of the two children can potentially arouse extreme anxiety, as Higonnet also observes, but can also work as an awakening, as happens with Freud's dream.[50] In the dream, the burning child calls for help, which wakes up the father. In Piliotou's illustration, these figures communicate trauma's disturbing reality to awaken both young and adult readers and help them recognize the painful reality felt by children.

Contrary to Baer's arguments, the book reveals the painful impact of the events on its characters, especially Renoula, without depicting their direct confrontation with evil and atrocity and without seeking to upset or shock its audience. However, as argued above, the text draws upon the idea of childhood innocence, ultimately making it almost as central as the trauma to the characters' experience. The suffering characters in Pyliotou's story function in ways similar to Capshaw Smith's description of the pole of survival. Therefore, their portrayal is reflective of the cultural-national need to represent a specific historical trauma. Such work recalls Whitehead's arguments concerning the factors that encourage the writing of trauma fiction. Douglas's idea of childhood as a means of explaining and interpreting the past can be observed here as well because Pyliotou's story seems to equate the national trauma of the recent past with the trauma experienced by innocent children attributing responsibility to what happened to children to adults' mistakes and hatred.

Childhood as a Reconciatory Device in "In Iris's Colours"

Written in the late 1990s, Agni Charalambous's young adult story shares similarities with earlier writing in style and tone. The style, for instance, is similarly emotional to represent the extent of Ariadne's traumatic suffering. In this character's suffering, readers can recognize symptoms and characteristics of the traumatic experience. Trauma appears in the story as an unresolvable, unconscious problem[51] characterized by Ariadne's nightmares and hallucinations, which do not allow her to directly and fully access the most painful of her memories.[52] Unlike the previous story, this text adheres, at least to some extent, to Baer and Bosmajian's idea of the children's literature of atrocity because it depicts its main character's direct confrontation with atrocity through the scene of her rape, which is described through the narrative. What is different, however, is the protective distance the writer creates for her audience by using a young but adult character who is confronted with evil as a way of achieving balance between the level of description and the degree of readers' confrontation with atrocity so as not to shock them.

As presented earlier in the plot summary provided for this story, the figure of the child has also a central role. The depiction of a child character resembles Freud's dream, as it expresses the adult desire for a perfect and undamaged childhood. However, despite its similarities with the previous story, this book has a different orientation. Compared to previous writing in this three-decade period, "In Iris's Colors" features a different emphasis on collectivity, which accordingly conveys a different stage and understanding of trauma, one that rhymes with Balaev's observation that changing values and responses arise from trauma over time.[53] The symbolic association of the suffering child characters with the burning children of the nation is now replaced with the traumatic suffering of an individual adult woman who, like the nation, is caught between the painful memories and repetitions of trauma and the need to hack away at the pain arising from these memories. The child figure appears largely in this text too but serves a different goal. Because it carries no previous baggage of experience, does not know trauma, it conveys a reconciliatory desire. The innocent child self of Ariadne is neither a victim nor a survivor of trauma narrowly constructed by Capshaw Smith, but her appearance in the story takes the form of spiritual advice for the damaged and suffering adult. Douglas's argument of childhood as "a synecdoche of history" can be usefully extended to this fictional story as well. The writer uses the child as a means for "revising and correcting the mistakes of history" by reminding the central character of a time in which there was not hatred between Greek and Turkish Cypriots through the childhood friendship of Ariadne and Aishe.[54]

Considering Freud's arguments concerning the use of fantasies in creative writing, it seems that Charalambous's writing shifts away from the fantasy of childhood innocence as a way of preserving painful memories toward the acceptance of traumatic realities and the need to find ways forward. Unlike Piliotou's children, it works as a symbol for the future because it awakens the need to communicate suffering. Once Ariadne recollects her child self, pieces from her life story are recovered. Through the memory of her childhood, Ariadne recalls a space and time in her life before she was traumatized as an adult. As the child figure appears in the story in the form of a memory, it revisits and revises a part of history that remains unaffected by the traumatic experiences of the invasion with an emphasis on reminding readers of the friendships between Greek and Turkish Cypriots before the conflict. Consequently, it becomes a reconciliatory device that works to encourage a fresh perspective characterized by a more nuanced relation with the past.

Initially, this approach may seem to share similarities with some of the materials discussed by Kertzer, Bosmajian, and Kidd. For instance, some Holocaust writing for the young, Kertzer observes, is characterized by adults' need to provide lessons about history through children's voices, as well as by didactic and pedagogic approaches with simplistic and naive lessons. Indeed, Charalambous's story builds heavily on the cultural idea of childhood innocence. Significantly, however, the plot is set in three different narrative times, all experienced by the main character, whose trauma unsettles chronology and time, meaning that the depiction of the child figure does not overwrite the traumatic experience but reveals that the character takes refuge in the memories of her childhood and begins to acknowledge experiences and memories she has buried through years of suffering and hatred. The story does not urge young readers to hold on to the promise "Never again" or "Don't Forget"; rather, it attempts to explain the effects of trauma and the past by giving expression to experiences and memories. It reveals, in other words, how painful it can be to hold on to such promises.

This ideological construction of childhood innocence ultimately creates a sense of relief mixed with euphoria for the main character as the story draws to an end and Ariadne walks with confidence and eagerness to meet Aishe.

> She is thrilled: "A rainbow connects Cyprus together," she thinks, "certainly, there are no borders . . . People can have the power to tear down borders and fences [that separate them] . . ." Her steps that felt so heavy until this very moment, now become light again.[55]

Ariadne's joy arises from the promise that she will be reunited with her childhood friend and thus able to express her memories by telling her story. Despite Ariadne's painful experiences, the story carries the promise of a better future in which hurtful memories can find expression even after years of pain. As trauma writing for young Cypriots enters a new stage since the 2000s, the need to express and share those memories intensifies.

Childhood as a Compromised Space in *What Does Enslavement Mean?*

Compared with the previous stories, Pyla's *Memories That Hurt* and Pitsiri's *What Does Enslavement Mean?* are based on their writers' personal involvement, childhood memories, and traumatic experiences of the invasion. Significantly, however, and maybe because of this personal attachment to the events, these stories work to represent not only the experience of trauma but also working through traumatic memories.

What Does Enslavement Mean? is more emotional in its tone than *Memories That Hurt* and reflects a more affective relation with the past evident from the beginning, in which the omniscient narrator of the story begins recollecting the events of the invasion, anticipating them with intense emotion: "It was not long before the dark summer of 1974 came. The summer of war and disaster. And it would bring so much pain that Vagelitsa's heart was unable to contain. It would wound anything beautiful she dreamed of."[56] The choice of language, including expressions such as "dark summer," "wound," or the inability to contain the pain reveal once again the wounding, the "burning" of the child. For the writer, the original moment of her trauma can be found in her "wounded" childhood self. To be able to repair herself, she must return to that original moment of trauma. The child character is not depicted as a perfectly innocent child, nor does the writing reproduce the image of an ideal childhood innocence, as in the previous texts discussed here. Conversely, the writer accepts childhood as a contested and compromised space. This realization and acceptance are ultimately registered through the emotional choices in language.

By returning to the events of her childhood, the writer bears witness to a traumatic past through which she begins to accept the loss she experienced as a child. According to Dori Laub, "testimony is inherently a process of facing loss—of going through the pain of the act of witnessing [. . .] It reenacts the passage through difference in such a way, however, that it allows perhaps a certain repossession of it."[57] The third-person narration becomes the writer's testimony in coming to terms with the realization of the loss of her childhood innocence, which allows her to go through the pain of that loss, revisit, and repossess her role as a witness who can now, decades after the events, pass on her memories.

As a way of creating a literary testimony, the narrative voice focuses on the description of the first moments of the invasion and the father's announcement that he must leave for the army. The descriptions of airplanes flying low above the ground bombing the city; Vagelitsa's mother's crying eyes; the seriousness in the expression of her father; the announcement of the war and the terror, which is felt by Vagelitsa; the experience of window glass shattering, allowing the smoke of shellfire to get into the house and then horrified people running to hide in the basements; and young children and babies screaming and clinging onto their mothers, who are crying and screaming more than their children, all work to create a literary testimony. These images allow both writer and reader to bear witness to the experience of separation and loss. For the writer, they reenact the moment, allowing her to repossess her memories and claim her position as a witness, as she describes in the preface. For readers, who have no direct experience of the events, it creates mental images and emotions that can potentially help them understand what the generation of the invasion went through. Although confronted with images of destruction, loss, and confusion, readers are not left alienated and lost. Emphasizing Vagelitsa's experiences of the first moments and days of the invasion and the pain, suffering, and profound toll of trauma on her, the story highlights the difficulty of recovery, as happens in Baer's stories, but does not deny the possibility of closure. Although Vagelitsa is depicted as a child survivor of the invasion, this depiction departs from the narrow constructions of child characters that Capshaw mentions. This autobiographical text is free from ideologically constructed child figures for the sake of a specific national image, which are observed in the earlier texts discussed here, or from naive and simplistic approaches that spare children and contribute to the de-realization of history, which Kertzer, Kidd, and Bosmajian have recognized in other occasions of children's trauma literature.[58]

In discussing the earlier examples of writing about the invasion, I have pointed to analogies with the dream of the burning child and the use of fantasies in creative writing. Here the writing functions rather differently. There are indeed similarities between the traumatic suffering of the writer's childhood self and the child as the prototypical sufferer of trauma, as depicted by the literary testimony provided through Vagelitsa. The figure of the child becomes central to the understanding of trauma in this story, and as the narrative becomes a recollection of the writer's childhood years in her hometown, childhood is recognized, as Tribunella also points out, as the originary moment of trauma.[59] Significantly, however, there is a clear shift in the focus of this text. Where earlier texts employ child characters as a symbol for a "national catastrophe," embracing and reproducing national ideologies about atrocity and painful collective memories as well as adult anxieties for the damage done to children, this text conveys a more personal rather than collective form of memory. By sharing her story and her wish or "fantasy," of moving beyond trauma, Pitsiri's writing works to arouse in readers a form of pleasure arising from a sense of relief and realization that the experience of trauma can ultimately be given shape and passed on. Radically, it is the breaking free from the memory of the wounded and suffering child rather that holding on to its innocence that allows the events to be re-witnessed and the writer to express her traumatic memories. Even though there are stories that cannot tackle the difficulties encompassing trauma writing for the young but rather opt for simplistic narratives, as Kidd proposes, *What Does Enslavement Mean?* and *Memories That Hurt* work to extend his argument that there are also books that "explore difficult questions about loss and memory, trauma and survival" offering "substantive and powerful testimony and witnessing."[60]

Returning to Childhood Trauma in *Memories That Hurt*

The shift from collective to personal memories is also visible in Pyla's *Memories That Hurt*. Written thirty years after the invasion, the story shows how time allows the working through of traumatic suffering and a conscious recognition of memories' painful impact. The language of the book is simple and clear without the emotional tone of previous writing. Told in first- rather than third-person narration, it creates a sense of a closer relation between story, narrator, and readers. In its title, the book demonstrates a realization that the memories of invasion and refugeedom have been hurtful for a long period of time; they need to be accessed and given shape to bring a halt to their painful repetitions and ways forward. The story represents this process. As an autobiography of the writer's family life before and after the invasion, the story becomes a testimony that finally accesses the memories, sharing them with young readers and showing them how a conscious and reconciliatory relation can begin between the individual and the past.

Following the life experiences of the daughters of the family, the story focuses on creating images of psychic suffering as this is experienced by children, helping readers understand trauma associated with a single overwhelming event. Initially Maria, the older daughter and narrator, describes the experience of trauma as a shock that unsettles and overwhelms children. Although Maria asserts that the first moments of the invasion were experienced by everyone in the family, she focuses on her little sister's response to the sounds of airplanes and bombs. Her voice reveals that her sister's exposure to the traumatic event is overwhelming. The word "horror" with which the narrator closes the description holds the weight of this experience; she recognizes "horror" or trauma in her sister's eyes, but at the same time it appears that the view of this horror puzzles her as well.

> I saw my youngest sister lying prone on top of my father, with her hands tightly bound around his neck. [. . .] Tota could not let him go. She held him so tightly, that he was unable to move. [. . .] The horror I saw in her eyes is something that will hardly be erased from my memory.[61]

As a result, the trauma described in this quote is dual: first, the trauma of the youngest child shown through the narrative voice's description of her inability to let go, shaking, intense fear and horror; and second, the trauma experienced by the oldest daughter as a result of seeing her sister's fear. The horror the narrator sees in the eyes of the youngest is something unrecognizable and new. It represents an alteration in the child; a sign of psychic injury. Because Maria cannot "recognize" her sister anymore—she seems changed by horror—she experiences a loss in her sense of familiarity linked to the figure of her child sister, and this is registered in her memory forever, traumatizing and changing her as well.

Pyla's *Memories* also shows how this moment of trauma belatedly returns in the lives of the three sisters. Maria's narrative voice describes the traumatic repetitions of the overwhelming moments of the invasion for her younger sisters. The shapes of clouds transform from rabbits and horses running in the sky as well as dancing ballerinas into memories of the invasion erupting into consciousness as "Lily saw ballerinas that quickly turned into dragons, or she saw Turks with their guns and airplanes."[62] The transformation in the clouds is also a transformation in the characters because of their traumatic experiences. Their childhood has been altered and shaped by trauma and haunted by its return. The narrator undergoes a similar transformation, depicted as a tornado. The moment of the invasion returns and affects Maria in a flashback: "I hear gunshots and I think I see smoke and dust from the window. Like then, when the tornado came. I go outside. Sky is vividly blue. Nowhere smoke . . . Nowhere dust. . . ."[63] Both passages reflect the painful way in which ordinary images, such as those of clouds or the view from a balcony, are infected with the traumatic images of the invasion. At that stage, the characters are tormented by those memories. As rabbits and horses, ballerinas and dogs take the form of dragons and guns and airplanes, images of everyday life unconsciously and unwillingly turn into suffering and anguish.

The repetitions of the traumatic moment, narrated by the now-adult Maria, however, seem to no longer be attached to posttraumatic suffering. The simplicity of the language, dismantled by all the intense emotion, suggests that the narrator has reached a stage of acceptance, ultimately coming to terms with her past experiences. Because the children represented in the story are now adults, their representations work as a recollection of a time that was associated with trauma. As a result, the ideological constructions of the child in the story also become, as Douglas explains, a means for explaining and interpreting as well as revising the past. Similarly to the previous story, childhood in Pyla's *Memories* is also a means of facing loss and letting go of the painful repetitions of the hurtful memories. The representation of wounded children in the story departs from the desire to hold onto childhood innocence. Like the wounded child of theory, it awakens the traumatized and suffering adult but as a way of letting go and moving on.

Conclusion

This chapter addresses a body of Greek-Cypriot writing for the young featuring the trauma and memory of the 1974 invasion. It explores how Greek-Cypriot children's writers have produced writing that registers the impact of trauma and negotiates the special position of childhood in relation to that trauma. In the forty years that Greek-Cypriot writers have been producing writing for children about the invasion, the modes, motivations, and thus the kinds of stories have changed considerably, affecting the literary representations of childhood trauma. Although there are similarities between this body of writing and the texts discussed by Kidd, Bosmajian, Capshaw Smith, and others working with similar texts, my comparison of texts from a longer period of time provides significant insights about this body of literature that can be tested in other examples of children's trauma literature. Using examples from across four decades, the chapter shows that some of the most recent texts in Cypriot children's literature have begun to show signs of significant change in the way trauma is conceptualized and understood in relation to childhood over the years. This demonstrates the ways in which the representation of atrocity and subsequent trauma has changed over time. Such representations emphasize the harm caused by traumatic experiences as well as the multiple sources that inform the definitions, representations, and consequences of trauma. It therefore suggests the important role of chronological distance from the events in dealing with trauma writing for the young. Finally, the learning process evidenced in Cypriot writing, as seen through the changes and transformations in the literary representation of trauma revealed in this chapter, has challenged Bosmajian's argument that children's literature cannot deal effectively with trauma. There are already examples of children's books about trauma that deal effectively with the complexities associated with the experience of atrocity and trauma. Moving from an emotional representation of trauma toward the kind of writing that begins to deal more effectively with the traumatic experience, writing about the invasion over the years has begun to more effectively explore difficult questions about loss and memory, trauma and survival in relation to childhood. This change highlights the potentially important work children's books can do in helping young readers acknowledge and understand trauma without traumatizing them and the need for such books as Kidd also proposes.

Notes

1. Michelle Balaev, *Contemporary Approaches in Literary Trauma Theory* (New York: Palgrave Macmillan, 2014), 4.

2. All these books are written in Greek. Because none of them has ever been translated, I provide translations for key excerpts from the original texts where considered necessary.

3. Michalinos Zembylas, "Ethnic Division in Cyprus and a Policy Initiative on Promoting Peaceful Coexistence: Toward an Agonistic Democracy for Citizenship Education," *Education, Citizenship, and Social Justice* 6, no. 1 (2011): 53–67.

4. Anna Agathangelou and Kyle Kilian, "The Discourse of Refugee Trauma: Epistemologies of the Displaced, the State and Mental Health Practitioners," *Cyprus Review* 21, no. 1 (2009): 19–58.

5. Agathangelou and Kilian, *Cyprus Review*, 27 Perry Anderson, "The Divisions of Cyprus," *London Review of Books* 30, no. 8 (2008): 7–16.

6. Nurit Kliot and Yoel Mansfield, "The Political Landscape of Partition," *Political Geography* 16, no. 6 (1997): 495–521.

7. Agathangelou and Kilian, *Cyprus Review*, 27; Anderson, *London Review of Books*, n.p.; Kliot and Mansfield, *Political Geography*, 500.

8. Nurit Kliot and Yoel Mansfield, "Resettling Displaced People in North and South Cyprus: A Comparison," *Journal of Refugee Studies* 7, no. 4 (1994): 328–459; Kliot and Mansfield, *Political Geography*, 501–3.

9. Costas Katsonis and Elena Kyriakides, "Reflections of Cyprus History in Novels for Children and Young Adults" (paper presented at 31st World Congress of the International Board on Books for Young People [IBBY], Copenhagen, Denmark, September 7–10, 2008).

10. Kliot and Mansfield, *Political Geography*, 503; Anderson, *London Review of Books*, n.p.; Agathangelou and Kilian, *Cyprus Review*, 27.

11. Anderson, *London Review of Books*, n.p.

12. Anderson, *London Review of Books*, n.p.; Kliot and Mansfield, *Political Geography*, 504; Michalinos Zembylas and Zvi Bekerman, "Education and the Dangerous Memories of Historical Trauma: Narratives of Pain, Narratives of Hope," *Curriculum Inquiry* 38, no. 2 (2008): 134; Zembylas, *Education, Citizenship and Social Juctice*, 55; Michalinos Zembylas, Zvi Bekerman, Muhammad Haj-Yahia, and Nader Schaade, "The Politics of Mourning in Cyprus and Israel: Educational

Implications," *Compare: A Journal of Comparative and International Education* 40, no. 5 (2010): 564.

13. In addition, about 4,000 Greek-Cypriots lost their lives and another 12,000 were wounded, while a similar proportion of Turkish-Cypriots lost their lives too. A total of 2,000 people went missing, of whom about 1,500 were Greek-Cypriots (Anderson n.p.; Zembylas et al., 564).

14. Katsonis and Kyriakides, IBBY, n.p.

15. Kenneth Kidd, *Freud in Oz: At the Intersections of Psychoanalysis and Children's Literature* (Minneapolis: University of Minnesota Press, 2011), 182.

16. Kenneth Kidd, "'A'" is for Auschwitz: Psychoanalysis, Trauma Theory, and the "Children's Literature of Atrocity," *Children's Literature* 33 (2005): 137.

17. Elizabeth Roberts Baer, "A New Algorithm of Evil: Children's Literature in a Post-Holocaust World," *Children's Literature* 33 (2005): 384.

18. Kidd, "A" is for Auschwitz," 120; Kidd, *Freud in Oz*, 191.

19. Anastasia Ulanowicz, *Second-Generation Memory and Contemporary Children's Literature: Ghost Images* (New York: Routledge, 2013), 2.

20. For a discussion on the literary representations of enclavement in Cypriot children's literature, see Maria Chatzianastasi, "The Role of Borders in the Lives of Greek-Cypriot Enclaved Children in Hera Genakritou's *Beyond the Barbed Wire* (1997)," *Jeunesse* 11, no. 2 (2019): 177–201, and Maria Chatzianastasi, "Cultural Expression and Representation of the Quotidian Trauma of Enclavement in Literature for the Young in Cyprus," *Bookbird* 56, no. 2 (2018): 36–42.

21. Petros Panaou and Frixos Michaelides, "Greek-Cypriot Children's Literature: A Small Literature and the Challenges It Faces in the Big World of Globalized Publishing for Children" (paper presented at the 32nd International Board on Books for Young People [IBBY] World Congress, Santiago de Compostela, Spain, September 8–12, 2010).

22. Several Cypriot scholars in the field of children's literature divide the history of Cypriot children's literature into three periods: the first, characterized as "the beginnings" or "colonial period," involves the years between 1894 and 1960, the time of independence; the second, which is "the period of independence," spans the years between 1960 and 1974; and finally, the third or "forming" period begins in 1974 and continues until very recently. Some scholars divide the first period in two smaller periods, one from 1894 to 1945 and one from 1945 to 1960. Furthermore, Petros Panaou and Frixos Michaelides add one more period that begins in 2004, when Cyprus became a part of the European Union.

23. Κώστας Κατσώνης, *Νεότερες εξελίξεις στη Λογοτεχνία της Κύπρου για παιδιά και για νέους* (Λευκωσία: Πάργα, 2003), 19.

24. Katharine Capshaw Smith, "Forum: Trauma and Children's Literature," *Children's Literature* 33 (2005): 115.

25. Nicholas Tucker, "Depressive Stories for Children," *Children's Literature in Education* 37 (2006): 199–210.

26. Balaev, *Contemporary Approaches in Literary Trauma Theory*, 1.

27. Caruth, *Trauma: Explorations in Memory*, vii–viii.

28. Roger Luckhurst, *The Trauma Question* (Oxon: Routledge, 2008), 81; Anne Whitehead, *Trauma Fiction* (Edinburgh: Edinburgh University Press), 3–4.

29. Ulanowicz, *Second-Generation Memory and Contemporary Children's Literature*, 2.

30. "We need these books, which affect us as if we are overcome by a great misfortune that pains us like the death of someone we loved more than ourselves, as if we were exiled into the woods away from all humankind, as if there had been a suicide—a book must be the axe for the frozen sea in us." Hamida Bosmajian, *Sparing the Child: Grief and the Unspeakable in Youth Literature about Nazism and the Holocaust* (New York: Routledge, 2001), 247.

31. Bosmajian, *Sparing the Child*, xiv.

32. Bosmajian, *Sparing the Child*, 248.

33. Kidd, *Freud in Oz*, 185.

34. Kidd, *Freud in Oz*, 204.

35. Kidd, *Freud in Oz*, 185, 204.

36. Katharine Capshaw Smith, "Forum: Trauma and Children's Literature," 116.

37. Eric L. Tribunella, *Melancholia and Maturation: The Use of Trauma in American Children's Literature* (Knoxville: University of Tennessee Press, 2010), xii.

38. Kenneth Kidd, *Freud in Oz*, 183–84.

39. Kate Douglas, *Contesting Childhood: Autobiography, Trauma, and Memory* (New Brunswick: Rutgers University Press, 2010), 9.

40. Whitehead, *Trauma Fiction*, 3.

41. Sigmund Freud, "Creative Writers and Day-dreaming," in *The Standard Edition of the Complete Psychological Works of Sigmund Freud*, vol. 9 (London: Hogarth Press and the Institute of Psycho-Analysis, 1953–1974), 427.

42. For a longer analysis and translations of the stories discussed, including supporting passage quotes, see Maria Chatzianastasi, "Tracing and Translation Trauma: Childhood, Memory and Nationhood in Cypriot Children's Literature since 1974" (PhD diss., Newcastle University, 2017), 42–80.

43. See Whitehead above.

44. Anne Higonnet, *Pictures of Innocence: The Crisis of Ideal Childhood* (London: Thames & Hudson, 1998), 28–29.

45. See the analysis on Freud in the previous section.

46. Lorna Martens, *The Promise of Memory: Childhood Recollection and Its Objects in Literary Modernism* (Cambridge: Harvard University Press, 2011), 209.

47. Μαρία Πυλιώτου, *Οι λύκοι και η Κοκκινοσκουφίτσα* [The Wolves and Red Riding Hood] (self-pub., Λευκωσία, 1976), 26.

48. Higonnet, *Pictures of Innocence*, 11.

49. Caruth, *Trauma: Explorations in Memory*, vii–viii.

50. Higonnet, *Pictures of Innocence*, 11.
51. Balaev, *Contemporary Approaches in Literary Trauma Theory*, 1.
52. Caruth, *Trauma: Explorations in Memory*, vii–viii.
53. Balaev, *Contemporary Approaches in Literary Trauma Theory*, 4.
54. Douglas, *Contesting Childhood: Autobiography, Trauma, and Memory*, 9.
55. Αγνή Χαραλάμπους, *Στα χρώματα της ίριδας* [In Iris's Colors] (Λευκωσία: Κ.Ν. Ιωάννου, 2001), 27.
56. Γεωργίου-Πιτσιρή Παρασκευούλα, *Τι θα πει σκλαβιά;* [What Does Enslavement Mean?] (Λευκωσία: Εκδόσεις Επιφανίου, 2010), 20.
57. Dori Laub, "Truth and Testimony: The Process and the Struggle," in *Trauma: Explorations in Memory*, ed. Cathy Caruth (Baltimore: Johns Hopkins University Press, 1995), 74.
58. Adrienne Kertzer, *My Mother's Voice: Children, Literature and the Holocaust* (Canada: Broadview Press Ltd., 2002), 38; Kidd, "'A'" is for Auschwitz," 124, 133–34; Bosmajian, *Sparing the Child*, 146.
59. Tribunella, *Melancholia and Maturation*, xii.
60. Kidd, *Freud in Oz*, 185, 204.
61. Πύλα Σωτηρία, *Μνήμες που πληγώνουν* [Memories That Hurt] (self-pub., Λάρνακα, 2004), 52.
62. Σωτηρία, *Μνήμες που πληγώνουν* [Memories That Hurt], 77.
63. Σωτηρία, *Μνήμες που πληγώνουν* [Memories That Hurt], 95.

Works Cited

Γεωργίου-Πιτσιρή, Παρασκευούλα. *Τι θα πει σκλαβιά* [What Does Enslavement Mean?]. Λευκωσία: Εκδόσεις Επιφανίου, 2010.
Πύλα, Σωτηρία. *Μνήμες που πληγώνουν* [Memories that hurt]. Self-published, Λάρνακα, 2004.
Πυλιώτου, Μαρία. *Οι λύκοι και η Κοκκινοσκουφίτσα* [The Wolves and Red Riding Hood]. Self-published, Λευκωσία, 1976.
Χαραλάμπους, Αγνή. *Στα χρώματα της ίριδας* [In Iris's Colors]. Λευκωσία: Κ.Ν. Ιοάννου, 2001.
Agathangelou, Anna, and Kyle Killian. "The Discourse of Refugee Trauma: Epistemologies of the Displaced, the State and Mental Health Practitioners." *Cyprus Review* 21, no. 1 (2009): 19–58.
Anderson, Perry. "The Divisions of Cyprus." *London Review of Books* 30, no. 8 (2008): 7–16.
Baer, Elizabeth Roberts. "A New Algorithm of Evil: Children's Literature in a Post-Holocaust World." *Children's Literature* 33 (2005): 378–401.
Balaev, Michelle. *Contemporary Approaches in Literary Trauma Theory*. New York: Palgrave Macmillan, 2014.

Bosmajian, Hamida. *Sparing the Child: Grief and the Unspeakable in Youth Literature about Nazism and the Holocaust.* New York: Routledge, 2001.

Caruth, Cathy. *Trauma: Explorations in Memory.* Baltimore: Johns Hopkins University Press, 1995.

Capshaw Smith, Katharine. "Forum: Trauma and Children's Literature." *Children's Literature* 33 (2005): 115–19.

Douglas, Kate. *Contesting Childhood: Autobiography, Trauma, and Memory.* New Brunswick: Rutgers University Press, 2010.

Freud, Sigmund. "Creative Writers and Day-dreaming." In *The Standard Edition of the Complete Psychological Works of Sigmund Freud.* Vol. 9. London: Hogarth Press and the Institute of Psycho-Analysis, 1953–1974.

Hernan, Judith. *Trauma and Recovery: The Aftermath of Violence—From Domestic Abuse to Political Terror.* New York: Basic Books, 1992.

Higonnet, Anne. *Pictures of Innocence: The Crisis of Ideal Childhood.* London: Thames & Hudson, 1998.

Κατσώνης, Κώστας. *Νεότερες εξελίξεις στη Λογοτεχνία της Κύπρου για παιδιά και για νέους.* Λευκωσία: Πάργα, 2003.

Katsonis, Costas, and Elena Kyriakides. "Reflections of Cyprus History in Novels for Children and Young Adults." Paper presented at the 31st World Congress of the International Board on Books for Young People (IBBY), Copenhagen, Denmark, September 2008.

Kertzer, Adrienne. *My Mother's Voice: Children, Literature and the Holocaust.* Peterborough, ON: Broadview Press Ltd., 2002.

Kidd, Kenneth. "'A'" is for Auschwitz: Psychoanalysis, Trauma Theory, and the "Children's Literature of Atrocity." In *Under Fire: Childhood in the Shadow of War,* edited by Elizabeth Goodenough and Andrea Immel, 161–84. Detroit: Wayne State University Press, 2008.

Kidd, Kenneth. "'A'" is for Auschwitz: Psychoanalysis, Trauma Theory, and the "Children's Literature of Atrocity." *Children's Literature* 33 (2005): 120–49.

Kidd, Kenneth. *Freud in Oz: At the Intersections of Psychoanalysis and Children's Literature.* Minneapolis: University of Minnesota Press, 2011.

Kliot, Nurit, and Yoel Mansfield. "Resettling Displaced People in North and South Cyprus: A comparison." *Journal of Refugee Studies* 7, no. 4 (1994): 328–459.

Kliot, Nurit, and Yoel Mansfield. "The Political Landscape of Partition." *Political Geography* 16, no. 6 (1997): 495–521.

Laub, Dori. "Truth and Testimony: The Process and the Struggle." In *Trauma: Explorations in Memory,* edited by Cathy Caruth, 61–75. Baltimore: Johns Hopkins University Press, 1995.

Luckhurst, Roger. *The Trauma Question.* Oxon: Routledge, 2008.

Martens, Lorna. *The Promise of Memory: Childhood Recollection and Its Objects in Literary Modernism.* Cambridge: Harvard University Press, 2011.

Panaou, Petros, and Frixos Michaelides. "Greek-Cypriot Children's Literature: A Small Literature and the Challenges It Faces in the Big World of Globalized Publishing for Children." Paper presented at the 32nd World Congress of the International Board on Books for Young People (IBBY), Santiago de Compostela, Spain, September 8–12, 2010.

Tribunella, L. Eric. *Melancholia and Maturation: The Use of Trauma in American Children's Literature*. Knoxville: University of Tennessee Press, 2010.

Tucker, Nicholas. "Depressive Stories for Children." *Children's Literature in Education* 37 (2006): 199–210.

Ulanowicz, Anastasia. *Second-Generation Memory and Contemporary Children's Literature: Ghost Images*. New York: Routledge, 2013.

Whitehead, Anne. *Trauma Fiction*. Edinburgh: Edinburgh University Press, 2004.

Zembylas, Michalinos. "Ethnic Division in Cyprus and a Policy Initiative on Promoting Peaceful Coexistence: Toward an Agonistic Democracy for Citizenship Education." *Education, Citizenship, and Social Justice* 6, no. 1 (2011): 53–67.

Zembylas, Michalinos, and Zvi Bekerman. "Education and the Dangerous Memories of Historical Trauma: Narratives of Pain, Narratives of Hope. *Curriculum Inquiry* 38, no. 2 (2008): 125–54.

Zembylas, Michalinos, Zvi Bekerman, Muhammad Haj-Yahia, and Nader Schaade. "The Politics of Mourning in Cyprus and Israel: Educational Implications." *Compare: A Journal of Comparative and International Education* 40, no. 5 (2010): 561–74.

Part 2
The Holocaust

Chapter 4

Beyond the Ovens

The Changing Nature of Holocaust Children's Literature

Barbara Krasner

Teaching the Holocaust as part of school curricula has become mandatory in eleven states including California, Illinois, New Jersey, New York, Florida, Kentucky, Michigan, Connecticut, Pennsylvania, Rhode Island, and most recently, in July 2019, Oregon. In 2017, twenty states vowed to require Holocaust and genocide study. Indeed, as children's literature scholar Donnarae MacCann attests, "A move into youth culture on the part of creative artists is, among other things, a move in the direction of culture maintenance or culture change."[1] Taking into account the full breadth of the Holocaust experience represented in children's books published between 2002 and 2016, the organization of Holocaust literature into seven categories can help educators in these states make choices. These seven areas are (1) Prewar Discrimination; (2) Occupation and Ghettoization, (3) Flight, (4) Camps, (5) Resistance, (6) Rescue, and (7) Postwar/Recovery. As more and more books are published to comply with state mandates, authors are telling new stories in new geographic settings. Authors are recovering marginalized and silenced voices of the Holocaust in what Lawrence Langer has termed "literature of atrocity": the departure from a real and familiar world into a combination of historical fact and imaginative truth of unspeakable horrors.[2] Kenneth B. Kidd in *Freud in Oz: At the Intersections of Psychoanalysis and Children's Literature* reinforces Langer's definition and subsequent interpretation by Elizabeth R. Baer as the paradoxical yet dual nature of historical event and never-ending story.³ At the core, Holocaust literature for children must, by individual state mandate, be presented to children, but (as argued by Kenneth Kidd and Lydia Kokkola among others) great care must be taken to not traumatize young readers.⁴

Still, authors are writing books about the Holocaust for young readers. The importance of these voices shines through the recognition they have received. Since 2012, the Association of Jewish Libraries has awarded at least one Sydney Taylor Book Award prize to a middle-grade or teen book with fictional, nonfictional, poetic, or graphic novel Holocaust content. Holocaust stories continue to influence editorial committees and make their way to publication and awards because there are still many stories that have not yet been told. For example, in 2019, Vesper Stamper's *What the Night Sings* (2018), an illustrated novel about a teen Holocaust survivor and her recovery, earned the Sydney Taylor Book Award in the teen category. In 2018, that recognition went to Antonio Iturbe for *The Librarian of Auschwitz* (2017), a novel based on the true story of teenager, Dita Kraus, who was given the responsibility to protect books in the camp. In 2017, Gavriel Savit's *Anna and the Swallow Man* (2016) won the teen award. Left alone in Krakow in 1939 when Nazis arrest her father, Anna meets and travels with the mysterious "Swallow Man" for four years throughout Poland to escape capture. The book also garnered the Goldberg Prize for Debut Fiction from the Jewish Book Council.

Yet, despite the growing number of states mandating Holocaust and genocide curriculum in grades K–12, a survey conducted by the Conference of Jewish Material Claims against Germany found in 2020 that 63 percent of American millennials and Generation Z did not know that six million Jews were murdered, and although there were more than 40,000 camps and ghettos, 48 percent of those asked in this national survey could not name a single one. One particularly alarming study result: 11 percent believe the Jews caused the Holocaust.⁵ While awards distinguish Holocaust content, this content is not receiving optimized attention in classrooms and libraries.

Conversations take place each year at the annual Association of Jewish Libraries conference about the dominance of Holocaust books for children. According to Heidi Rabinowitz, past president of the association:

> Every conversation seems to come around to the idea that while well written and accurate Holocaust books are important, we are in dire need of a more balanced representation of the Jewish

experience. The knee jerk response is "no more Holocaust books" but after more thoughtful discussion it always ends up that people agree we need more books on other topics to balance things out, not that we need to eliminate Holocaust books.[6]

In "Enough with the Holocaust Books for Children!" influential *Tablet* critic Marjorie Ingall argues, "The cover is gray, beige, taupe, or sepia. There's a splash of red (lettering) or yellow (star). There's often barbed wire. Oh, hey, it's yet another children's book about the Holocaust. And it looks exactly like every other children's book about the Holocaust."[7] Ingall pleads for a fuller expression of the Jewish experience for children because, she claims, "the amount of real estate, both physical and emotional, that these stories hold on our bookshelves is proportionally just too high."[8] Writing in the *New York Times* in July 2021, Ingall persists in her campaign against the publication of more Holocaust books for youth. It is a campaign of fear that Holocaust books will eclipse other Jewish-themed books and equate Jewish identity only with the Holocaust. Ingall's plea can also be read as a call to move beyond the iconography of stacked bodies, barbed wire, and guard towers. The insistence on this iconography and the perception of the dominance of death camp narratives convey a certain erroneous pattern. As Lydia Kokkola warns in *Representing the Holocaust in Children's Literature*, "Individually, many of these books are historically accurate, yet the pattern that emerges from the corpus is not."[9] While Kokkola draws attention to the earlier children's literature published in German, she also calls for "representation of the complexity of the portrayal of attitudes."[10] In particular, she refers to the ambiguities that authors intentionally present. Children's Holocaust literature published in the last twenty years demonstrates this complexity that reflects reality.

Further, the numbers do not support Rabinowitz's and Ingall's claims. Between 2002 and 2016, 380 Holocaust-related titles were published in the United States and Canada in English. When compared with about 387,000 juvenile titles published in the United States between 2002 and 2013, 313 children's books featuring Holocaust content published in the same time period seems woefully inadequate.[11] In 2016, ninety-six books reflected the Jewish experience and were submitted to the Sydney Taylor Book Award Committee. The Committee accepts books in English published anywhere in the world. Nearly 18 percent of them were Holocaust related. In 2015, Holocaust titles represented 37 percent.[12] At the same time, children's Holocaust literature has already been moving in new and more complex directions such as multiple genres, a widening geographic range, and a widening of Holocaust experience representation. I argue in this chapter for a reconsideration in the way we think about Holocaust children's literature, citing examples and numerical results from Holocaustkidlit.com, a website and online, searchable database I launched in 2017.[13] I call for classifying the literature into seven categories that reflect genocidal stages that acknowledges the plurality and nuances of roles among victims, bystanders, and perpetrators. This new classification allows for improved historical contextualization. It also signals to readers, educators, librarians, and publishers that complex questions about genocide must demand complex responses.

A breakdown of published Holocaust books for children reveals a variety of responsive approaches. For example, thirty-eight books were published in 2009 alone (a 58 percent increase over 2008), presented in figure 4.1, suggesting an initial response to the 2010 introduction of Common Core

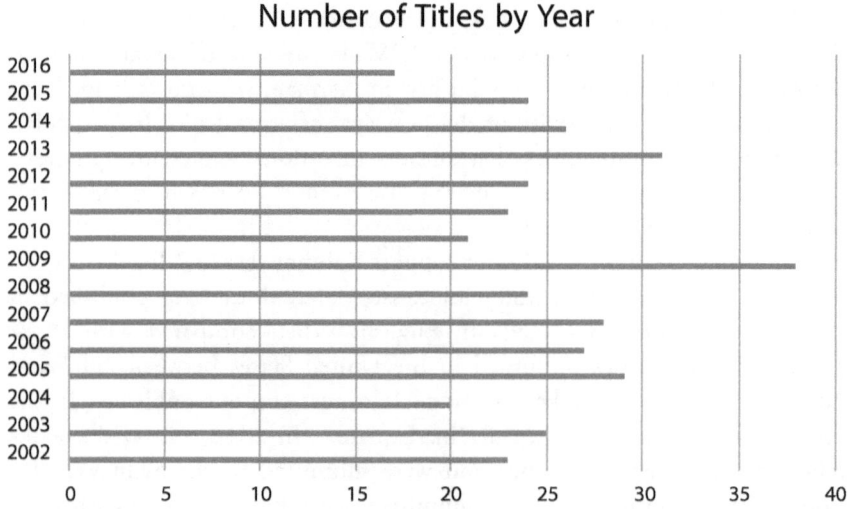

Figure 4.1. Number of Children's Holocaust Books Published in North America by Year. Source: Barbara Krasner, Holocaustkidlit.com

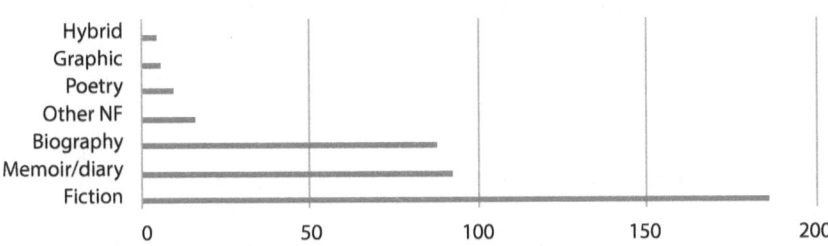

Figure 4.2. Number of Children's Holocaust Books by Genre, 2002–16. Source: Barbara Krasner, Holocaustkidlit.com

nonfiction requirements in school curricula.[14] However, as shown in figure 4.2, despite these requirements, fiction twice outweighed other genres.

Figure 4.3 indicates the dominance of middle-grade titles; they represented 56 percent of all Holocaust books published for children. A push for young adult titles appears in 2010 when the rate of publishing such books began to exceed that of middle grades.

Yet within these tabulations, nuances emerge that signal important shifts and the unique quality of individual narratives. Surveys such as the

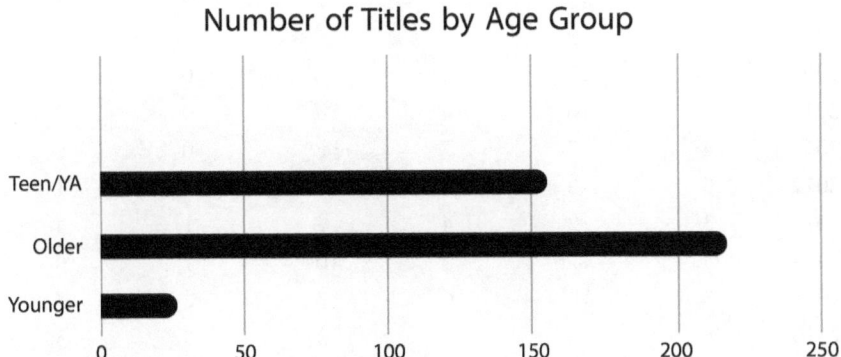

Figure 4.3. Number of Titles by Age Group, 2002–16. Source: Barbara Krasner, Holocaustkidlit.com

2020 Claims Conference assume and emphasize that Auschwitz stood at the center of the Holocaust experience. Of the six million Jews who perished, 960,000 did so at Auschwitz.[15] The need to move beyond death camps, and this death camp in particular, is acute. Young readers could benefit from exposure to the breadth of victimization and geographic experiences. While careful not to romanticize, many narratives move beyond the horrors of the camps to focus on survival and hope, sensitizing today's young readers toward contemporary refugees. Alan Gratz's *Refugee* (2017) is a prime example of this.[16] The book addresses three stories of refugee flight by sea: 1930s Joseph from Nazi Germany, 1990s Isabel from Cuba, and 2015 Mahmoud from Syria. Holocaust narratives themselves focus on refugee flight, as presented below in table 4.1.

Table 4.1. Categories by Year, 2002–16

	Resistance	Refugee/Flight	Occupation	Camps	Rescue	Recovery
2002	4	5	6	11	3	5
2003	2	8	8	6	1	1
2004	1	9	1	2	0	1
2005	4	14	6	8	1	5
2006	1	4	5	4	0	3
2007	4	15	5	7	2	5
2008	2	8	0	9	0	1
2009	2	17	12	6	0	3
2010	1	16	4	4	0	0
2011	4	7	7	8	0	0
2012	5	8	2	5	1	1
2013	3	12	4	7	1	4
2014	5	7	2	10	1	3
2015	3	13	6	3	2	7
2016	5	2	7	3	0	3
Total	46	145	75	93	12	42

Source: Barbara Krasner, Holocaustkidlit.com

Educators and Children's Holocaust Literature

While many factors exist within the realm of author's and publisher's responsibility, young readers generally encounter Holocaust texts through their teachers and classrooms. Classifying children's literature makes it easier for teachers and librarians to select appropriate titles for their classrooms and readers. Any examination of children's literature must also consider the perspectives of educators. Genocide scholar Samuel Totten rightly observes, "incorporating literature into a study of the Holocaust may be one of the most powerful and effective entry points into this complex history."[17] Yet, although he states, "Fortunately, a great quantity of outstanding Holocaust literature—including novels, short stories, poetry, and plays—exists that is ideal for use by teachers and students,"[18] he also implicitly demonstrates the serious need for Holocaust literature specifically aimed at the young adult market. A push toward the young adult market becomes evident in the period 2002–16, with 40 percent of Holocaust titles published specifically for these readers.

The introduction of Holocaust literature into the classroom brings additional benefits in the form of emotional connection. Rachel Baum poses the question: What is it that Holocaust literature teaches that history books alone do not?[19] Her response is that the literature teaches the reader to feel about the historical facts. History books rarely get to the "feet on the street" level. Through literature, young readers can begin to sympathize and even empathize with the characters they engage with.

The Importance of Categorization

Cognitive scientist George Lakoff argues, "there is nothing more basic than categorization to our thought, perception, action, and speech."[20] According to Lakoff, individuals need to classify people, objects, and events to make sense of them. The Holocaust experience, then, benefits from categorization, too. A single category of "Holocaust literature" obscures the breadth of experience. Early narratives that emerged in the 1950s might have suggested a more limited scope. For example, Claire Hutchet Bishop's chapter book, *Twenty and Ten,* appeared in 1952, relating the story of twenty French children who outwit Nazi soldiers and hide ten Jewish children in nearby caves. It marks one of the first "Holocaust" books for young readers published in the United States.[21] Earlier books were published in Germany, notably three autobiographical novels by Hans Peter Richter: *Friedrich* (1961), *I Was There* (1962/1964), and *The Time of the Young Soldiers* (1967). In the Jewish Publication Society's *Best Jewish Books for Children and Teens* (2010), librarian Linda R. Silver cites ten Holocaust books, both fiction and nonfiction, published between 1968 and the late 1970s. In the 1960s and 1970s, perhaps inspired by the televised trial of Nazi criminal Adolf Eichmann in Israel, many survivors were just beginning to share their stories.[22] The trial marked a milestone in its use of survivor testimony and elevated the status of survivor narratives. Some survivors, like Johanna Reiss (*The Upstairs Room*, 1972), chose to write about their experiences as children's books. Judith Kerr escaped Nazi Germany in 1933 with her family first to Switzerland, then to France, and ultimately to England, where they face adjustment challenges. She recalls these experiences in her classic *When Hitler Stole Pink Rabbit* (1971), the first in a children's book trilogy.

By introducing categories that are underwritten by genocidal phases and the groups of people who experienced the Holocaust, educators and librarians may gain assistance in making their selections for classroom use and for shelf acquisition. By better understanding the full scope and scale of the Holocaust experience, we can create a road map through categorization to help young readers learn.

Considerations for a New Framework from Holocaust and Genocide Scholarship

I used an interim scheme for holocaustkidlit.com. Narratives, depending on their scope, could be classified in multiple categories as shown below.

The statistics characterize broad categories that could be meaningfully modified. Existing frameworks within the canon of Holocaust scholarship can be helpful to substantiate such revision. For example, in *Perpetrators, Victims, Bystanders: The Jewish Catastrophe, 1933–1945* (1992), Holocaust scholar Raul Hilberg argues that the stakeholders of the Holocaust comprise three major groups, as the book title indicates. Victims were the most exposed at the time, and survivors have arguably received the most exposure in children's literature. However, the largest and often overlooked group in terms of story protagonists are the bystanders. This term may prove problematic to critics, but specific roles within the broad classification throughout German-occupied Europe and the so-called neutral countries can be unpacked. Hilberg refers to "bystanders" as helpers, gainers, onlookers, messengers, Jewish resisters, and churches. Helpers may have alerted unsuspecting victims of round-ups or those who offered shelter, such as families who provided shelter for Jewish children in hiding. There were also helpers who were motivated by opposition to the Nazi regime, such as Oskar Schindler. Gainers stood to profit in some way by the liquidation of the Jewish population. They do not take center stage in children's Holocaust narratives, although they may be present. Onlookers took no action. Messengers, as Hilberg has defined them, include individuals such as Jan Karski, who brought his reports of Nazi extermination of the Jews to Allied attention. No juvenile book has yet to be written about Karski or Jewish Bund leader Shmuel Zygielboim, who delivered reports of the extermination of Polish Jews and then committed suicide in both protest and despair in 1943. Messengers could also encompass the young women who served as couriers, smuggling information and materials in and out of ghettos at great personal risk. One of these heroic teens is featured in Jennifer A. Nielsen's *Resistance* (2018), a Sydney Taylor Notable Book.

Still, a gap exists when it comes to narratives of perpetrators as protagonists. In *Genocide in Contemporary Children's and Young Adult Literature: Cambodia to Darfur* (2015), education scholar Jane M. Gangi refers initially to the Holocaust but focuses on post-Holocaust genocide in chapters dedicated to Cambodia, Guatemala, Kurdish Iraq, Bosnia-Herzegovina, Kosovo, Rwanda, and Darfur. Gangi includes a useful and pioneering analysis of children's literature, organized by genre, about each of these genocides while admitting that she relies on a convenient sample of books written in English that neglects many other genocides documented in Dirk Moses's *Genocide* (2010). Most importantly, she offers a set of evaluation criteria: the representation of targeted human collectivities, the representation of the perpetrators, the representation of state-controlled bureaucracies, the representation of genocide's ideologies and technologies, the representation of atrocities beyond legitimate warfare, the representation of "us vs. them," and the representation of the defenseless.[23] While it is clear that Gangi is familiar with genocide scholarship, her criteria do not consider stages of genocide as laid out by Polish-born lawyer Raphael Lemkin and American educational psychologist David Moshman.[24] Lemkin defines two stages of genocide, the first of which concerns the destruction of the national pattern of the oppressed group and the second, the imposition on that oppressed group of the oppressor's national pattern. Moshman, on the other hand, defines genocide in terms of four overlapping stages: dichotomization, dehumanization, destruction, and denial. Gangi's criteria can be used to expand Kimmel's categories and create a more robust framework supported by Lemkin's and Moshman's definitions.

In Holocaust titles, perpetrators rarely appear as protagonists; they are mostly presented as those who carry out Nazi ideology. However, some authors present them as complex characters who wear Nazi uniforms but do not adhere to Nazi ideology.[25] In Georg Rauch's memoir, *Unlikely Warrior: A Jewish Soldier in Hitler's Army* (2016), for example, Rauch is a Viennese Jewish teen overlooked by the laws and conscripted into the German army. However, before he is drafted, he and his mother help save fellow Jews through the Viennese underground. Hermann Vinke's *Defying the Nazis: The Life of German Officer Wilm Hosenfeld* (2018) details the characteristics that enabled Hosenfeld to serve as Władysław Szpilman's rescuer in *The Pianist* (1998). Both titles demonstrate the state-controlled bureaucracy in action. Both require young readers to question the definition of a Nazi. Both allow young readers to find distinctions in human traits. The complexity shown in both books underscores the need for a framework that is both flexible and robust. Perpetrator portraits, then, become a necessary component of Holocaust literature to educate about the process of racist normalization and to point up those who resisted that ideology in a multitude of ways.

In *Sparing the Child: Grief and the Unspeakable in Youth Literature about Nazism and the Holocaust*, German literature scholar Hamida Bosmajian presents both victim and perpetrator perspectives. Her analysis begins during the Hitler period and focuses somewhat on Hitler Youth. Such texts, for the most part, were generated by those who were directly involved. She writes, "Even fifty years after the war, that silence . . . still governed family discourse about the grandparent and parent generations. Silence was thematized as a symptom that concealed something very threatening."[26] She further notes that the issue of silence and the moment when authors or narrators are compelled to tell their stories catalyze Holocaust stories for young readers. Bosmajian underscores the importance for young readers to understand the attraction Nazism offered to young people at the time. She writes, "Rarely does a narrative address the social conditions, ideological framework, or propagandistic strategies that led to Nazi power."[27] Less than a handful of titles address this attraction, but they do exist, including Anne Blankman's *Prisoner of Night and Fog* (2015). In this narrative, a teenaged girl is raised in the Nazi system and fully believes in its ideology until she meets a Jewish boy and learns that "Uncle Dolf" killed her father, who had been loyal to the Nazi party. Although it becomes a story of Resistance, it does examine

Nazi rhetoric's effect on young people. Bosmajian makes a critical point as today's readers are exposed to falsehoods and Holocaust denial.

Rather than create a unique category, however, perpetrator narratives can be classified in any of the seven categories in which the perpetrator's role contributes to the overall experience, including biographies of Hitler, Josef Mengele, Adolf Eichmann, and others. However, because the majority of titles represent victims, it would make sense to create a chronological framework more aligned with genocidal phases.

With genocidal stages as historical context, Occupation books should come first in the now sequential framework. These books take place in countries under Nazi control; occupation provides the catalyst for refugee flight, resistance, and deportation to the camps. Seventy-five books involving Occupation and Ghettoization (nearly 20 percent) were published between 2002 and 2016. They are often shared narratives with Refugee and/or Resistance. Several books tell the story of Janusz Korczak, the Warsaw ghetto doctor who refused to abandon the children in his care and accompanied them to Auschwitz, where he also perished. These include three illustrated picture books: David Adler's *A Hero and the Holocaust: The Story of Janusz Korczak and His Children* (2002), Gloria Spielman's *Janusz Korczak's Children* (2007), and Tomek Bogacki's *The Champion of Children: The Story of Janusz Korczak* (2009). In general, they portray people trying to survive as best they can within the confines of ghettos and/or loss of citizenship, rights, and property.

Books about Flight should come next following the sequence of genocidal stages. Kimmel defines them as the stories of individuals or families on the run just prior to or during World War II. They comprise the largest group of Holocaust children's literature (38 percent). They include Sonia Levitan's *Journey to America* (1971) and Judith Kerr's *When Hitler Stole Pink Rabbit* (1971). Levitan's title is the first of a three-book series. In this first volume, the Platt family escapes Nazi Germany in 1938. Their adjustment to American life continues in *Silver Days* (1989) and *Annie's Promise* (1993).

This category is broad, and the Flight experience takes many shapes, including going into hiding, Kindertransport, and permanent emigration. In *Lilli's Quest* (2015), Lila Perl writes of refugee Lilli, who journeys on a Kindertransport to England and then travels on to the United States. She returns to Europe to try to find the traces of her family. Recovery and Return represent ripe areas for additional storytelling—displaced persons resettling in Palestine/Israel, North America, Latin America, and Australia.

Narratives about hidden children form a substantial portion of books in the Flight category. These are often based on the authors' own experiences or told or researched by other authors. In *Hidden Like Anne Frank: 14 True Stories of Survival* (2014) by Marcel Prins and Peter Henk Steenhuis, hidden child survivors of the Netherlands tell their own stories. Meanwhile, *Hiding Edith* (2006) by Kathy Kacer, a daughter of Holocaust survivors, is based on interviews with Edith Schwalb Gelbard. Emphasis should continue to be placed on Flight books given today's refugee plight in global affairs. Genocide and war continue to occur, creating stateless refugees.

Resistance has tended to be bifurcated into non-Jewish and Jewish factions. However, this division is not necessary. Resistance can include intentional sabotage, smuggling of guns and explosives (as well as food and other goods), and partisan actions in cities, ghettos, and forests in Nazi-occupied territories. Nonarmed resistance, as Israeli Yehuda Bauer has compellingly argued, defining Jewish resistance during the Holocaust "as any group action consciously taken in opposition to known or surmised laws, actions, or intentions directed against the Jews by the Germans and their supporters,"[28] is classified as intentional anti-Nazi actions by non-Jews and was once thought of as only intentional sabotage and smuggling of guns and explosives by non-Jews and acts of Jewish partisans in the forests and ghettos in Nazi-occupied territories.[29] Armed and unarmed resistance have been recently highlighted in David Safier's *28 Days: A Novel of Resistance in the Warsaw Ghetto* (2020), a translation of a best-selling German young adult novel of resistance in the Warsaw Ghetto. His protagonist, Mira Weiss, at first an unarmed smuggler and saboteur, negotiates arms with the Polish Home Army and joins up with the ghetto resistance. Other titles describe the activities of organized resistance, such as the novel in verse by Flemish historian Aline Sax and illustrator Caryl Strzelecki, also about the Warsaw ghetto and the 1943 uprising in the award-winning *The War within These Walls* (2013) for teen readers. Of particular note, too, is Doreen Rappaport's nonfiction tour de force *Beyond Courage: The Untold Story of Jewish Resistance during the Holocaust* (2012). This title marks an important addition to the cadre of Holocaust children's literature because it confronts the belief that Jews were passive victims. Resistance books published between 2002 and 2016 represent forty-six titles (9 percent) of all Holocaust books for young readers. The relative lack of books describing Jewish resistance perpetuates the myth that resistance did not exist. Resistance is by no means restricted to Jews. Russell Freedman's nonfiction *We Will Not Be Silent* (2016) and Kip Wilson's novel in verse, *White Rose* (2019), both address the anti-Nazi White Rose movement led by university students and siblings Hans and Sophie Scholl, who were beheaded for their activities. Overall, the category represents an opportunity for writers and publishers to bring the stories of unsung heroes to young readers.

For the purposes of Holocaust children's literature, Rescue can be installed as its own category. Rescue then includes stories of Polish social worker Irena Sendler and Swedish diplomat Raoul Wallenberg, who saved thousands of Jews from the Warsaw Ghetto and Hungary, respectively.

Camp narratives are imperative and reflect Moshman's "destruction" phase. Such narratives, however, generate much debate about the appropriate grade level for reading and discussion. Children's author Eric Kimmel asks, ". . . is mass murder a subject for a children's novel?" Up to that point memoirs addressed the horrors of Auschwitz-Birkenau and other death camps. Kimmel adds, "Five years ago, we might have said no; ten years ago we certainly would have. Now, however, I think the appearance of a novel set in the center of the lowest circle [camps] is only a matter of time."[30]

Kimmel's prophecy bears out. The Holocaust children's literature database contains information on ninety-three books published between 2002 and 2016 in the Camp category (24 percent), nearly twenty of which combine with the Occupation category and others continuing the narrative through added categories of Rescue and/or Recovery. Auschwitz is the camp most frequently used as the setting (forty-one books), with ten taking place in Bergen-Belsen and eleven in the transit camp of Theresienstadt. Within this category, thirty-two books are fictionalized accounts, and memoir and diary comprise the majority of the fifty-four nonfiction accounts. Dividing the Camp category into individual units by camp name would not be fruitful, as the number of books dealing with camps other than Auschwitz and Theresienstadt is small.

Adding a Postwar/Recovery category fleshes out the Holocaust experience, which did not end with liberation. Although the prewar stories such as Levitan's initial volume and Kerr's may pave the way, the experiences of those families are in no way similar to those who survived the Nazi death camps, hiding, or both, and now have to deal with the aftermath of loss and renewal. The tone of Carol Matas's story of survivor Rose Rabinowitz in *Dear Canada: Pieces of the Past: The Holocaust Diary of Rose Rabinowitz, Winnipeg, Manitoba, 1948* (2013) emphasizes the postwar despair.

Still, gaps exist in the literature and represent silences that need to be voiced and brought to the forefront. For example, a young-adult narrative could detail the experiences of a Jewish-Finnish soldier fighting alongside a German one in their attempt to defeat the common Soviet enemy. Only two authors have written so far about Holocaust denial: Susan Goldman Rubin published a biography of Nazi hunter Simon Wiesenthal in *The*

Anne Frank Case: Simon Wiesenthal's Search for the Truth (2009), and David Poulsen published his young-adult novel *Numbers* (2008) about a fifteen-year-old student who finds out his awesome teacher is a Holocaust denier.

Further, although victim narratives predominate, there are victims whose voices have largely not been told. Lydia Kokkola expands on the victim definition by addressing Nazi persecution of Romani, *Mischlinge*, Catholics, Slavs, Jehovah's Witnesses, homosexuals, the disabled, and Blacks in addition to Jews. As Kokkola admits, "references to non-Jewish victims are rare in children's books."[31] This lack of representation presents yet another opportunity for authors and their publishers if these narratives can come out of the silence. Inherent in the silence is geographic location.

Expanding Geographic Settings

To date, children's Holocaust narratives primarily take place in Poland (35 percent) and Germany (28 percent), as figure 4.4 indicates.[32] Poland rep-

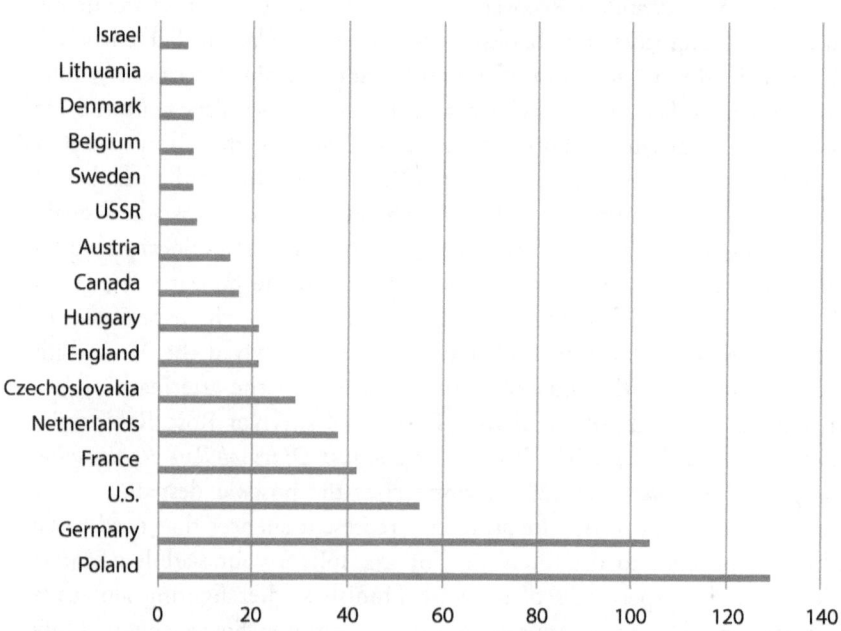

Figure 4.4. Number of Titles by Geography. Source: Barbara Krasner, Holocaustkidlit.com

resents the confluence of Jewish residence and the death camps. However, many recent texts use settings outside this area, demonstrating a broader scope of geography.

The nature of the categories also suggests a wide range of potential settings that include home country, deportation temporary and final destinations, refugee temporary and final destinations, and postwar resettlement destinations. The categories of Refugee (Flight) and Occupation (including Ghettoization), by definition, mean all those areas under Nazi control: Germany, Austria, Bohemia and Moravia lands of Czechoslovakia, Poland, France, the Netherlands, Norway, Belgium, Denmark, and Luxembourg. Possibilities also include those countries that cooperated with the Nazi regime: Slovakia, Hungary, Croatia, Rumania, Albania, and Bulgaria. Further potential includes refugee destinations such as Shanghai, the Soviet Union's Uzbekistan-Bukhara, Latin America, and North America. Transit countries such as Portugal, Spain, and Switzerland also present potential. For example, there has yet to be a book about Portuguese consul Aristides de Sousa Mendes, who helped thousands of refugees flee from France through Portugal. Between 2002 and 2016, children's Holocaust books took place in the United States (14 percent), France (11.6 percent), the Netherlands (11.3 percent), Czechoslovakia (7.6 percent, mostly Theresienstadt), England (5.8 percent), Hungary (5.5 percent), and the Soviet Union (5.5 percent, which may or may not include the Soviet-occupied Poland but does include Ukraine and the Baltics).

Lack of available and accessible source material may deter the writing and publication of narratives that take place in the Soviet Union, China, Latin America, Africa, and Oceania. However, more than fifty thousand interviews are available through the Shoah Foundation and could provide ample means for bringing an untold story to young audiences. In this way, gaps can be effectively addressed.

Even if Poland and Germany provide the settings for the majority of children's Holocaust books, the narratives may move elsewhere. In alignment with an emerging shift away from death camps, location also shifts then beyond Poland to places of both Jewish and non-Jewish resistance, rescue, and recovery and often encompasses the trek from place to place. In *The Journey That Saved Curious George: The True Wartime Escape of Margret and H. A. Rey* (2005), for example, writer Louise Borden and illustrator Allan Drummond share the experiences of Curious George creators as they flee Paris toward unoccupied southern France on bicycle, by train to Portugal, and by ship to New York. Neal Bascomb's *The Nazi Hunters* begins in Argentina with the capture of Adolf Eichmann and travels to Israel for his trial in

1960. Kathy Kacer's *Shanghai Escape* (2013) tells the story of a Viennese family who flees to Shanghai only to meet Japanese opposition. Margarita Engle's novel in verse, *Tropical Secrets: Holocaust Refugees in Cuba* (2009), is the story of a German boy, Russian émigré, and Cuban girl in Cuba after *Kristallnacht* ("The Night of Broken Glass"), the anti-Semitic two-day pogrom that led many Jewish families in Germany and Austria to emigrate.

The publication of stories in settings that reflect the Holocaust and post-Holocaust experience does not come close to its potential. While it can be understandable that only six books address China and Shanghai, five occur in Italy, four involve Cuba, and none take place in Finland or Libya, it is indeed perplexing that so few books have been published about the Soviet Union and yet it was a major site of occupation, refugees, and resistance.

What Titles and Synopses Reveal

In the current database of 380 Holocaust books for children and young adults published between 2002 and 2016 in the United States and Canada, excluding self-published and educational series titles, a content analysis of book titles and synopses reveals a set of characteristics. The most frequently used words in titles and synopses are obvious ones: story, Holocaust, Jewish, and Nazis. Forms of the word "survive" receive 64 mentions. Forms of "escape" garner 47 mentions. Resistance amounts to 33 and forms of "hide" come to a total of 33. When combined, "survive," "escape," "resistance," and "hide" all signal hope with a total of 158 mentions. "True" is used 36 times, reflecting once again the need for these narratives to have historical context. The publication of memoir, diary, and biography reinforces this point; these terms are used a combined 45 times.

But another priority emerges, too. When combined with family members—parents, mother, father, brother, daughter, son, siblings, grandmother, grandfather, granddaughter, grandson—a "family" cluster yields 158 mentions. That means that in all of its iterations, family outweighs story (123 mentions) in the content of children's Holocaust literature. It also outweighs Nazi/Nazis (119 mentions), Holocaust (103 mentions), and Jewish (97 mentions). Oddly, the term "sister" does not come up at all, although narratives certainly exist that include sisters. From a gendered perspective, "girl" receives 44 mentions and "boy" 31. Children's Holocaust literature, then, focuses on survival and family, told more often from a female point of view.

The emphasis on family aligns with the work of Elisa von Joeden-Forgey, who argues that perpetrators strategically target the family unit in what she terms life force atrocities. She defines her term in the following manner: ". . . life force atrocity is a ritualized pattern of violence that targets the life force of a group by destroying both the physical symbols of its life force as well as its most basic institutions of reproduction, especially the family unit."[33] These perpetrators inflict their violence through the small-scale institution of the family, a microcosm of the group. From a child's perspective, family members are those who matter most and where bonds are the most fragile in times of conflict.

The darker themes of extermination camps and ghettoization still garner attention. Auschwitz receives forty-one mentions. Ghetto receives forty-four. These are necessary elements of the Holocaust experience, although they are clearly not the sole components. Killing fields are an obvious silence, although accounts are available to source them.

Conclusion

By grounding a typology on Holocaust scholarship in chronological and genocidal phases, and allowing for the inclusion of victims, perpetrators, and bystanders in each, seven categories can encompass the range of Holocaust experience: (1) Prewar Discrimination; (2) Occupation and Ghettoization, (3) Flight, (4) Camps, (5) Resistance, (6) Rescue, and (7) Postwar/Recovery. Postwar narratives deserve attention because liberation from the camps or occupation did not mean automatic freedom from despair, statelessness, or aloneness. Yet many voices are still marginalized, and locations and events in the historical record are not yet represented. Books about other genocides, including Armenian, Cambodian, Rwandan, and others, can find their place using this same new sequential set of seven categories.

Analyzing title and synopsis content from a comprehensive database of children's Holocaust books reveals the priority of survival and family as themes and demonstrates the marked shift beyond the ovens. To accommodate this shift, new canonical categories need to be introduced and additional geographic settings should be explored. The database will be expanded in the near future to include all Holocaust titles published since the 1960s. Other genocidal narratives will also be included, and a regression analysis will be conducted to statistically demonstrate trends and shifts.

Notes

1. Donnarae MacCann, *White Supremacy in Children's Literature: Characterizations of African Americans, 1830–1900* (New York: Routledge, 1998).
2. Lawrence L. Langer, *The Holocaust and the Literary Imagination* (New Haven: Yale University Press, 1975), xii and 8.
3. Kenneth B. Kidd, *Freud in Oz: At the Intersections of Psychoanalysis and Children's Literature* (Minneapolis: University of Minnesota Press, 2011), 181–82.
4. Kidd, *Freud in Oz*; Lydia Kokkola, *Representing the Holocaust in Children's Literature* (New York: Routledge, 2003).
5. Conference of Jewish Material Claims against Germany, "First-Ever 50-State Survey on Holocaust Knowledge of American Millennials and Gen Z Reveals Shocking Results," http://www.claimscon.org/millennial-study/.
6. Heidi Rabinowitz, email message to author, July 9, 2019.
7. Marjorie Ingall, "Enough with the Holocaust Books for Children!," *Tablet*, April 15, 2015, https://www.tabletmag.com/jewish-life-and-religion/190231/enough-holocaust-books-for-kids. See also Marjorie Ingall, "Why Are There So Many Holocaust Books for Kids?," *New York Times*, July 8, 2021, https://www.nytimes.com/2021/07/08/books/review/-childrens-books-holocaust-jewish-experience.html.
8. Ingall.[Au: More information for this note?]
9. Kokkola, *Representing the Holocaust in Children's Literature*, 81.
10. Kokkola, *Representing the Holocaust in Children's Literature*, 81.
11. Bowker, "ISBN Output Report for 2002–2013," http://www.bowker.com/tools-resources/Bowker-Data.html. While "juvenile" is defined as pre-K–6, a separate young adult category was not created until 2009 and does not appear in this report. The data may include self-published and series titles.
12. A reasonable approximation of books published about the Jewish experience is the number of books requested by and submitted to the Association of Jewish Libraries Sydney Taylor Book Award Committee. However, not all chairs of the committee have readily available data. Ellen Tillman, email message to author, September 7, 2020.
13. To populate this database, I searched for Holocaust titles included in the Children's Literature Comprehensive Database and limited my selections to books published in English in North America between 2002 and 2016, excluding self-published and educational series titles. I specifically chose 2002 as the starting point because three academic treatments published in 2002 and 2003 addressed prior Holocaust children's books in detail. The database, contained in a WordPress plug-in application, features fields for category, genre, geography, age group, and synopsis. I use data from the application as well as the results of book title and synopsis content analysis using the NVivo qualitative analysis tool to present a new model of Holocaust children's literature categorization with twelve classifications. This model also considers Holocaust and genocidal scholarship.

14. Common Core State Standards emerged in the United States in 2010. According to the Association for Supervision and Curriculum Development, all but five states have fully adopted them. But much controversy exists about them, and some scholars believe the standards hold no value and are passé.

15. U.S. Holocaust Memorial Museum, "Auschwitz," *Holocaust Encyclopedia*, https://encyclopedia.ushmm.org/content/en/article/auschwitz.

16. In so doing, Alan Gratz's book, as do others, raises serious questions about historical accuracy and the need for it. That is, however, beyond the scope of this chapter.

17. Samuel Totten, "Incorporating Fiction and Poetry into a Study of the Holocaust at the Secondary Level," in *Teaching and Studying the Holocaust*, ed. Samuel Totten and Stephen Feinberg (Boston, MA: Allyn and Bacon, 2001), 156.

18. Totten, "Incorporating Fiction and Poetry into a Study of the Holocaust at the Secondary Level," 156.

19. Rachel Baum, " 'What I Have Learned to Feel': The Pedagogical Emotions of Holocaust Education," *College Literature* 23, no. 3 (October 1996): 44.

20. George Lakoff, *Women, Fire, and Dangerous Things: What Categories Reveal about the Mind* (Chicago: University of Chicago Press, 1987), 5.

21. Other early books include Yankev Glatshteyn's *Emil un Karl*, published by a small Yiddish press in New York in 1940 (and translated into English in 2006); Mary Berg's *Warsaw Diary* (1945); and Anne Frank's *Diary of a Young Girl* (1952). See the introduction of this volume for a historical overview of the genre.

22. Some survivors did, of course, share their experiences in print before this, most notably Primo Levi with *If This Is a Man*, first published in 1947 (published in the United States as *Survival in Auschwitz*).

23. Jane M. Gangi, *Genocide in Contemporary Children's and Young Adult Literature: Cambodia to Darfur* (New York: Routledge, 2014), 11.

24. See Raphael Lemkin, *Axis Rule in Occupied Europe: Laws of Occupation, Analysis of Government, Proposals for Redress* (Washington, DC: Carnegie Endowment for International Peace, Division of International Law, 1944), especially 79, and David Moshman, "Us and Them: Identity and Genocide," *Identity: An International Journal of Theory and Research* 7, no. 2 (2007): 115–35.

25. German books for children did explicitly position those we would call perpetrators as heroes. Notably, these include Elvira Bauer's *Trau keinem Fruch auf grüner Heid und keinem Jud bei seinem Eid* (*Trust No Fox on the Green Heath and No Jew by His Oath*, 1936).

26. Hamida Bosmajian, *Sparing the Child: Grief and the Unspeakable in Youth Literature about Nazism and the Holocaust* (New York: Routledge, 2002), 243.

27. Bosmajian, *Sparing the Child*, 243.

28. Yehuda Bauer, *The Jewish Emergence from Powerlessness* (Toronto: University of Toronto Press, 1979), 27.

29. See Kimmel, "Confronting the Ovens," 86–91.

30. Kimmel, "Confronting the Ovens," 91.
31. Kokkola, *Representing the Holocaust in Children's Literature*, 5.
32. These categories and geographic locations may be shared within a single narrative. For instance, a refugee from Vienna could first face occupation and then take flight to Shanghai. Tabulations result from an online searchable database created by the author at www.holocaustkidlit.com, launched in 2017. Conversations with Eric Kimmel in 2016 led to the inclusion of additional categories of Rescue and Recovery. The database excludes self-published titles and educational nonfiction series titles published by such houses as Rosen, Capstone, CompassPoint, etc.
33. Elisa von Joeden-Forgey, "The Devil in the Details: 'Life Force Atrocities' and the Assault on the Family in Times of Conflict," *Genocide Studies and Prevention* 5, no. 1 (2010), 2.

Works Cited

Adler, David. *A Hero and the Holocaust: The Story of Janusz Korczak and His Children*. Illustrated by Bill Farnsworth. New York: Holiday House, 2002.

Baer, Elizabeth R. "A New Algorithm in Evil: Children's Holocaust Literature in a Post-Holocaust World." *The Lion and the Unicorn* 24, no. 3 (September 2000): 378–401.

Bascomb, Neal. *The Nazi Hunters: How a Team of Spies and Survivors Captured the World's Most Notorious Nazi*. New York: Arthur A. Levine, 2013.

Baum, Rachel. "'What I Have Learned to Feel': The Pedagogical Emotions of Holocaust Education." *College Literature* 23, no. 3 (October 1996): 44–57.

Bishop, Claire Hutchet. *Twenty and Ten*. Illustrated by William Pène Du Bois. New York: Puffin, 1978. Originally published by Viking in 1952.

Blankman, Anne. *The Prisoner of Night and Fog*. New York: Balzer + Bray, 2014.

Bogacki, Tomek. *The Champion of Children: The Story of Janusz Korczak*. New York: Farrar, Straus and Giroux, 2009.

Borden, Louise. *The Journey That Saved Curious George: The True Wartime Escape of Margret and H.A. Rey*. Illustrated by Allan Drummond. New York: Houghton Mifflin, 2005.

Bosmajian, Hamida. *Sparing the Child: Grief and the Unspeakable in Youth Literature about Nazism and the Holocaust*. New York: Routledge, 2002.

Bowker. "ISBN Output Report for 2002–2013." http://www.bowker.com/tools-resources/Bowker-Data.html.

Engle, Margarita. *Tropical Secrets: Holocaust Refugees in Cuba*. New York: Holt, 2009.

Frank, Anne. *Diary of a Young Girl*. New York: Doubleday, 1952.

Freedman, Russell. *We Will Not Be Silent: The White Rose Student Resistance Movement That Defied Adolf Hitler*. New York: Clarion, 2016.

Gangi, Jane M. *Genocide in Contemporary Children's and Young Adult Literature: Cambodia to Darfur*. New York: Routledge, 2015.

Gratz, Alan. *Refugee*. New York: Scholastic, 2017.
Hilberg, Raul. *Perpetrators, Victims, Bystanders: The Jewish Catastrophe, 1933–1945*. New York: HarperPerennial, 1992.
Ingall, Marjorie. "Enough Books about the Holocaust!" Tablet, April 5, 2015. https://www.tabletmag.com/jewish-life-and-religion/190231/enough-holocaust-books-for-kids.
Iturbe, Antonio. *The Librarian of Auschwitz*. Translated by Lilit Thwaites. New York: Holt, 2017.
Kacer, Kathy. *Hiding Edith: A True Story*. Toronto: Second Story Press, 2006.
Kacer, Kathy. *Shanghai Escape*. Toronto: Second Story Press, 2013.
Kerr, Judith. *When Hitler Stole Pink Rabbit*. New York: Coward, McCann & Geoghegan, 1971.
Kidd, Kenneth B. *Freud in Oz: At the Intersections of Psychoanalysis and Children's Literature*. Minneapolis: University of Minnesota Press, 2011.
Kimmel, Eric A. "Confronting the Ovens: The Holocaust and Juvenile Fiction." *Horn Book*, February 16, 1977, 84–91.
Kokkola, Lydia. *Representing the Holocaust in Children's Literature*. New York: Routledge, 2003.
Lakoff, George. *Women, Fire, and Dangerous Things: What Categories Reveal about the Mind*. Chicago: University of Chicago Press, 1987.
Langer, Lawrence L. *The Holocaust and the Literary Imagination*. New Haven: Yale University Press, 1975.
Lemkin, Raphael. *Axis Rule in Occupied Europe: Laws of Occupation, Analysis of Government, Proposals for Redress*. Washington, DC: Carnegie Endowment for International Peace, Division of International Law, 1944.
Levitan, Sonia. *Journey to America*. Illustrated by Charles Robinson. New York: Atheneum, 1970.
Matas, Carol. *Dear Canada: Pieces of the Past: The Holocaust Diary of Rose Rabinowitz, Winnipeg, Manitoba, 1948*. Toronto: Scholastic Canada, 2013.
Moses, Dirk. *Genocide*. Abingdon, UK: Routledge, 2010.
Moshman, David. "Us and Them: Identity and Genocide." *Identity: An International Journal of Theory and Research* 7, no. 2 (2007): 115–35.
Nielsen, Jennifer A. *Resistance*. New York: Scholastic, 2018.
Perl, Lila. *Isabel's War*. Brooklyn: Lizzie Skurnick Books, 2014.
Perl, Lila. *Lilli's Quest*. Brooklyn: Lizzie Skurnick Books, 2015.
Poulson, David. *Numbers*. Toronto: Key Porter Books, 2008.
Prins, Marcel, and Peter Henk Steenhuis. *Hidden Like Anne Frank: 14 True Stories of Survival*. Translated by Laura Watkinson. New York: Arthur A. Levine, 2014.
Rappaport, Doreen. *Beyond Courage: The Untold Story of Jewish Resistance During the Holocaust*. Somerville, MA: Candlewick, 2012.
Richter, Hans Peter. *Friedrich*. Translated by Edite Kroll. New York: Holt, Rinehart, and Winston, 1970.
Richter, Hans Peter. *I Was There*. Translated by Edite Kroll. New York: Holt, 1972.

Richter, Hans Peter. *The Time of Young Soldiers.* New York: Harper, 1989.
Rothberg, Michael. *Multidirectional Memory: Remembering the Holocaust in the Age of Decolonization.* Stanford: Stanford University Press, 2009.
Rubin, Susan Goldman. *The Anne Frank Case: Simon Wiesenthal's Search for the Truth.* Illustrated by Bill Farnsworth. New York: Holiday House, 2009.
Savit, Gavriel. *Anna and the Swallow Man.* New York: Random House/Ember, 2017.
Sax, Aline. *The War within These Walls.* Illustrated by Caryl Strzelecki. Translated by Laura Watkinson. Grand Rapids: Eerdman's, 2013.
Schroeder, Peter W., and Dagmar Schroeder-Hildebrand. *Six Million Paper Clips: The Making of a Children's Holocaust Memorial.* Minneapolis: Kar-Ben, 2004.
Silver, Linda R. *JPS Guide: Best Jewish Books for Children and Teens.* Philadelphia: The Jewish Publication Society, 2010.
Spielman, Gloria. *Janusz Korczak's Children.* Illustrated by Matthew Archambault. Minneapolis: Kar-Ben Publishing, 2007.
Stamper, Vesper. *What the Night Sings.* New York: Knopf Books for Young Readers, 2018.
Totten, Samuel, and Stephen Feinberg, eds. *Teaching and Studying the Holocaust.* Boston: Allyn and Bacon, 2001.
Vinke, Hermann. *Defying the Nazis: The Life of German Officer Wilm Hosenfeld, Young Readers Edition.* Translated by H. B. Babiar. Cambridge: Star Bright Books, 2018.
Von Joeden-Forgey, Elisa. "The Devil in the Details: 'Life Force Atrocities' and the Assault on the Family in Times of Conflict." *Genocide Studies and Prevention* 5, no. 1 (2010): 1–19.
Wiesel, Elie. *Night.* Translated by Marion Wiesel. New York: Hill and Wang, 2016.

Chapter 5

Gendered Behavior in Uri Orlev's and Kathy Kacer's Literature about the Holocaust for Children

Rosemary Horowitz

Children may read historical and contemporaneous accounts of atrocities in the United States, the Caribbean, Central America, South America, Africa, the Middle East, Asia, Europe, and elsewhere. While acknowledging the vast body of literature written about atrocity for children, in this chapter I focus on literature about the Holocaust because the ideological, geographical, and demographical scope of that catastrophe is unique. From that, educators posit that teaching difficult subjects such as the Holocaust encourages readers to think about social justice, equity, diversity, and similar topics. The educator Larry Swartz lists stereotyping among these difficult topics and advocates using children's literature to address gender inequality.[1] A study of gender in Holocaust children's literature combines both perspectives.

Swartz's position coincides with the increasing application by researchers of concepts from girls' studies to a scholarly examination of children's literature. One example is Linda J. Rice's "Teaching Historically Based, Culturally Rich YA Novels with Strong Girl Protagonists."[2] She finds that while stories such Lois Lowry's *Number the Stars* are hard to read because of the difficult circumstances described, girls may gain a sense of empowerment from stories that feature female agency and learn from the strategies that girls use to overcome hardships. Attention to girls in Jewish children's literature is of particular interest as well. For instance, in her 2013 survey of Holocaust literature for children and young adult readers, one of the categories that Jeannine Ferris uses to examine the books is the gender distribution of characters. She finds that 57 percent of the protagonists in the books are female.[3] Emily Sigalow and Nicole S. Fox's 2014 study of thirty Sydney Taylor Award–winning children's books published between 1980 and 2011 is another example. The authors look at the ways in which gender and religion are depicted in the works and conclude that depictions are generally based on conservative religious traditions.[4] Still another example is the 2020 study by Rachel Leket-Mor and Fred Isaac of 102 Sydney Taylor Award–winning children's books published between 1980 and 2020. With respect to gender, their findings confirm some of Sigalow and Fox's conclusions.[5]

Alongside the growing interest in girls' studies is the proliferation of children's books. Because children's literature, as Anastasia M. Collins writes, serves to reinforce or disrupt cultural ideas,[6] one would expect that over time the growing body of children's literature would challenge traditional gendered roles. In this chapter, I apply social role theory to a content analysis of the behavior of boys and girls in eleven children's books about the Holocaust to examine that premise. In particular, my analysis considers gender and heroism in children's stories associated with that time period. In contrast to the current use of trauma as a unit of analysis, I prefer to reserve trauma for actual assault and so avoid its use as a trope. Other commonly used concepts, such as emotions, thoughts, appearance, or speech, are also not under consideration. Overall, my aim is to yield theoretical insights into the notion of gendered action and offer practical implications for classroom use of children's literature.

Incorporating biography into the classroom is one way to meet curricular objectives related to gender. With respect to the Holocaust, books about activists such as Sophie Scholl (1921–43) and Hannah Senesh (1921–44) provide accounts of young woman who defied the Nazis. Numerous biographers have traced the transformation of each girl from a privileged daughter into a member of an underground group. For instance, in 1942, while a student at the University of Munich, Sophie joined the White Rose, a clandestine organization that formed around 1941. Its members wrote, printed, and distributed anti-Nazi leaflets. At that time, her brother Hans was already part of the group. In 1943, Sophie and Hans were convicted of treason and killed. Their activities are described in *White Rose* by Kip Wilson; *We Will Not Be Silent: The White Rose Student Resistance Movement That Defied Adolf Hitler* by Russell Freedman; and *The Short Life of Sophie Scholl* by Hermann Vinke.

Senesh's life is also a story of resistance. A teenager in 1939, she left her upper middle-class life in Budapest and moved to Palestine. Then, in 1943, she volunteered with a partisan group whose mission was to help European Jews. In March 1944, she and several others parachuted into Yugoslavia with aid for anti-Nazi forces. Later that year, she was captured and executed in Hungary. Her actions are recounted in *So Young to Die: The Story of Hannah Senesh* by Candice F. Ransom; *Hannah Szenes: A Song of Light* by Maxine Rose Schur; and *In Kindling Flame: The Story of Hannah Senesh: 1921–1944* by Linda Atkinson.

In addition to biography, fiction is useful for meeting curricular objectives. Given that, this chapter explores the ways in which heroism is gendered in the historical fiction of Uri Orlev, a survivor and an award-winning Israeli writer who writes in Hebrew, and Kathy Kacer, a child of survivors and an award-winning writer from Canada who writes in English. Orlev is considered one of the most important children's writers in Israel; Kacer's many awards, such as from Yad Vashem in Jerusalem, is an indication of her importance as a writer. The methodology for selecting the two authors is in line with Sigalow and Fox's point that among sociologists "there is an established precedent for sampling award-winning books."[7] In addition, the worldwide availability of Orlev's and Kacer's works makes them influential stories. For example, *The Island on Bird Street* is available in Dutch, German, French, Russian, Danish, Polish, Spanish, Italian, Japanese, Catalan, Portuguese, Swedish, Chinese, Korean, Hungarian, and Czech. The rights to Kacer's books have been sold in Germany, China, Italy, Thailand, England, Japan, Slovenia, and other countries.[8]

From Orlev's corpus, I look at *The Island on Bird Street*; *The Man from the Other Side*; *The Lady with the Hat*; *Lydia, Queen of Palestine*; and *Run, Boy, Run*, which are among his widely translated books about the Holocaust. From Kacer's works, I analyze *The Secret of Gabi's Dresser*, *The Underground Reporters*, *Clara's War*, *The Night Spies*, *Shanghai Escape*, and *The Diary of Laura's Twin*, all published by Second Story Press as part of its Holocaust Remembrance Series for Young Readers. Middle school readers are the intended audience for these selected stories. The youngest characters in these books are Lydia, the ten-year-old girl in *Lydia, Queen of Palestine*, and Gabi, the eleven-year-old girl in *The Secret of Gabi's Dresser*; the oldest is Yurek, the seventeen-year-old boy in *The Lady with the Hat*.

Social role theory provides a framework for understanding the complexity inherent in any exploration of gender. According to the theory as espoused by Alice Eagly,[9] in industrialized Western societies the prescribed traits of masculinity are agentic. Examples are forcefulness, directness, competitiveness, competence, dominance, industriousness, heroism, and the like. The prescribed aspects of femininity in those societies are communal. Examples include kindness, helpfulness, expressiveness, consideration of others, thoughtfulness, sensitivity, and similar attributes. In general, the behavior of individuals follows the socially prescribed roles attributed to their gender. Race, class, region, and other variables shape behavior too. Simply stated, the childhood socialization process through which boys and girls acquire gender identity privileges conformity to sex-segregated roles and behaviors. Conformity is regulated on the individual and group level. Social role theory also explains the continuity and change of behavior. As a result, within constraints, men may exhibit communal traits; women may exhibit agency.

Heroism is one specific case of gendered behavior of interest. To Eagly, heroic behavior has two aspects: risk to the person and benefit to others. Thus, for Eagly and her colleagues, heroism combines agency and empathy and as a result should be considered androgynous. Eagly's study conducted with Selwyn Becker notes that "heroism is practiced by women as well as men, but that, depending on the specifics of heroic acts and their situational context, one sex may participate more than the other."[10] Eagly and Becker explore the opportunities that men and women have to exhibit heroic behavior and find that women made heroic choices as often as men, but in different domains. Eagly's research with Lindsay E. Rankin also explores the opportunities of men and women to be judged heroic; they conclude that heroism is generally defined by level of risk and so is often attributed to males.[11] One commonality in both studies is that within popular discourse, heroic acts are generally defined in terms of physical strength.

Children's Literature, Gender, and the Holocaust

To date, literature about the Holocaust for children has been examined from at least four perspectives: psychological, functional, narratological, and pedagogical. Kenneth B. Kidd, for instance, finds that trauma theory and literature have much in common and considers children's literature of atrocity a type of trauma testimony. He wants stories to deal realistically with violence and avoid infantilizing readers.[12] Kidd also believes that historical fiction has the potential of engaging readers with their own suffering.[13]

With respect to function, transmitting memory and teaching lessons are two purposes of the literature. Yael Darr has examined the ways in which the literature preserves the memory of the Holocaust, pointing to storytelling by grandparents to their grandchildren as an instance of intergenerational transmission of Holocaust information.[14] David L. Russell holds that "[s]tories of the Holocaust are like cautionary tales, warning us of the danger of complacency, reminding us of the tenuous thread on which human decency is at times suspended."[15] This is a somewhat questionable assertion because Holocaust remembrance has not stopped other genocides; nevertheless, Russell believes that beneficial lessons for young readers are inherent in the stories.

Many secondary sources discuss storytelling techniques. For instance, in his 1977 review, Eric A. Kimmel uses the schema of Dante's rings of hell to categorize literature about the Holocaust for children. On the outer rings, he places tales of resistance, of refugees, and of hiding, the content of most of the books at the time. Moving toward the inner rings, he finds one story set in a camp, but none set in a crematorium, the innermost ring.[16] Another look at storytelling is found in the work of Phyllis Lassner and Danny Cohen. Using genre analysis, Lassner and Cohen examine the ways in which the fantasy novel and the fairy tale are used to portray the Holocaust.[17] Eva Tal examines the narrative aspects of the stories by specifically discussing how framing devices conceal or reveal the historical reality of the Holocaust.[18] Adrienne Kertzer points to the double narrative structure in Jane Yolen's *Briar Rose* as a method of tempering a happy ending with historical facts.[19]

Elizabeth Roberts Baer and Lydia Kokkola focus on education. Baer has developed a taxonomy based on genre, coupled with a list of criteria to guide those who write, select, or teach Holocaust literature for children. To test the usefulness of her theory, she analyzes various books from four different genres against her criteria with the aim of offering a judicious method for teaching about the Holocaust.[20] Kokkola uses historical faithfulness as a criterion to evaluate books for young readers. An examination of several dozen books supports her overarching claim that historical inaccuracies in Holocaust literature for children are immoral.[21] She especially wants adults to guide children in their reading about the war.

Although the Holocaust has been explored from various approaches, gendered analyses of children's literature are not very common. This omission may be related to Marion Kaplan's finding that the use of gender as a unit of analysis has been criticized by various Holocaust historians and survivors.[22] One objection is that because all Jews were victims, gender distinctions are irrelevant. However, Kaplan notes that much may be learned from studying gendered experiences, including understanding the survival strategies of men and women, power imbalances between men and women, and sexual experiences of men and women, along with other topics. By extension, there is merit in differentiating between the actions of boys and girls too. For example, Anika Walke's study of the orphanages, work sites, and other locations in and around the Minsk ghetto analyzes the lives of youth and teenagers and uncovers evidence that work assignments as well as types of violence and abuse targeted women and men differently.[23]

A few studies of children's literature differentiating between boys and girls may be found. One is Kertzer's study of Ida Fink's and Carol Matas's fiction.[24] Foregrounding gender and choice, Kertzer looks at the ways in which Matas's Holocaust stories, such as *Lisa* and *Greater Than Angels*, address matters related to age, romance, religion, and speech of her female protagonists. Another is Lassner's study of boys in Holocaust literature. By focusing on Rachel Seiffert's 2017 novel *A Boy in Winter* and Pepe Danquart's 2013 film *Run Boy Run*, based on Uri Orlev's novel, Lassner looks at representations of Jewish boyhood in Holocaust fiction and film that complicate the usual coming-of-age story.[25] More studies of children's literature that look at the portrayals of girls and of boys before, during, and after the Holocaust are needed because the treatment of Jews did have a gendered aspect. Sara R. Horowitz notes that even the main historian of the Warsaw ghetto, Emanuel Ringelblum, documented the reversal of gender roles in the ghetto, consequently valuing the importance of distinguishing between the experiences of men and women.[26]

Gendered Behavior in Orlev's and Kacer's Books

Because approximately one and a half million Jewish children were killed during the Holocaust, accounts of a child's agency are extremely exceptional. Yet, while the ability of children to make choices, act freely, and exert control was virtually impossible during the Nazi era, nevertheless many authors of children's literature of atrocity feel compelled to provide some degree of hope for their young readers. Although authors recognize that both girls and boys want to be active, what children may do depends on gendered roles, as well as what is actually possible within a given situation.

While historically rare, nevertheless, in several of Orlev's and Kacer's stories, children actually challenge their enemies directly. Alex, in *The Island on Bird Street*, is extremely assertive, resourceful, and independent. Early in the novel, his father teaches him how to shoot. Later, during a round-up in the ghetto, the father and a family friend arrange for Alex to slip away from the guards and run to an abandoned building, where he will wait in hiding for the father's return. The backpack of supplies that the two men prepare for Alex includes the father's pistol. Throughout his months in hiding, Alex carries the pistol for comfort, as well as for protection. He uses the pistol twice: once he shoots and scares a man who is dragging a girl through an apartment, and at another time, he shoots and kills a German soldier who is threatening two men in the building. Although Alex feels proud of his proficiency, he is sad and lonely. The two men he protected console him when he cries after the killing.

Alex's father also taught him to fight. In another scene, when confronted by a bully, Alex plans his attack:

> I'd sock him as hard as I could in the face and again in the stomach, in the place that father called the solar plexus. It was the only way to get rid of him. Maybe it wasn't nice to do a sneaky thing like that instead of challenging him to a fair fight, but it was the same as being a gentleman with the Germans.[27]

After beating up the bully, once again, Alex is satisfied with his actions:

> At first I walked slowly. Then I heard shouts and I crossed to the other side of the street and broke into a run. Not a real run. It was more of a skip, the way you run just to show you're feeling good.[28]

Here again, Alex is proud of his actions and very pleased with himself. Skipping is a way of expressing his happiness. In the novel, either with his pistol or his fists, Alex fights back when he can without hesitation.

In the stories, while girls generally do not directly confront an enemy, their brothers or cousins may do so on their behalf. In *Clara's War*, Peter, Clara's brother, attacks the guard who is harassing her:

> "Get away from her!" Peter shouted, planting his feet firmly in front of the guard, fists up in front of his face as if he were a boxer facing his opponent in the ring. For a moment, the guard was stunned and paused, shaking his head. This was almost comical. Who was this small, Jewish brat challenging his authority? The guard's face was startled at first, then almost amused, and

finally, dark and angry. He raised his hand and slapped Peter hard across the face . . . Clara couldn't believe her little brother had taken this risk to protect her.[29]

By comparing Peter to a boxer, the story perpetuates the sport as primarily male coded. Even though younger than Clara, Peter willingly risks his own safety and puts himself in danger to fulfill expectations. Ready to fight despite his youth, Peter accepts the role of defending his sister.

One exception to the norm of girls not being involved in combat appears in *The Night Spies*, in which Gabi, Max, and Eva get the opportunity to actively help the partisans. Dominik, one of the partisans, allows the three children to join in the attack on the Nazis. In delegating their responsibilities, he says:

> "Gabi," he said. "You can help carry the radio on your back. We need to be in contact with the other partisan troops as we advance. Eva, you and Max will carry these backpacks filled with extra ammunition. The soldiers will come to you, when they need to reload their weapons. Oh, and one more thing," he said, reaching into his own back pocket, "I think this belongs to you, Max." Dominik withdrew a gun and placed it in Max's hands.[30]

While the girls are given vital tasks to carry out insofar as the radio and bullets are very crucial to the success of the mission, they are not given weapons. Theirs is a support role. So, like Alex, only the boy is allowed to be armed. Another exception is found in *The Man from the Other Side*, where Marek sees girls in the Warsaw ghetto shooting at Germans.

In the stories, aside from fighting, other actions that depend on physical skills are assigned to boys; girls usually do not rely on their physicality. In *Run, Boy, Run*, Jurek/Srulik uses his agility to escape from the soldiers pursuing him. From that scene:

> Srulik waited for them to enter the barn. Then he slipped from the storeroom, scaled the picket fence, and ran along the path leading past the potato field to the forest. . . . Srulik kept crawling toward the forest. He could see the branches of the trees without having to raise his head. He would get as close as he could and make a dash for them.[31]

By describing Jurek/Srulik's actions with a series of active verbs—slipping away from the Germans, scaling the fence, crawling through the fields, and dashing from his pursuers—the story ties the boy's escape to his physical abilities.

Jurek/Srulik is also resourceful, which helps him in the forests and fields while he is hiding from the soldiers. At first, he is with a group of Jewish boys who show him how to steal food and scavenge for food. From them, he learns to forage for mushrooms, nuts, and berries. He also uses his slingshot to hunt. He starts to understand the ways of the forest. For example, at one point, he discovers a rabbit caught in a trap and immediately understands that he has to kill the animal. He develops good outdoor skills: "Jurek became a good hunter. He bagged a small rabbit, a squirrel, and, once, after several misses, a large duck swimming in reed-encircled pond."[32] He even learns to kill birds. This image of a hunter is also male-coded.

No girls in the stories employ survival skills, namely techniques used to provide basic necessities in an emergency. Those specialized skills are only attributed to boys. Like Jurek/Srulik, Alex in *The Island on Bird Street* also demonstrates masterful competency in finding provisions and shelter within his extreme living conditions. Alex lives alone in an abandoned building for eight months while waiting for his father's return. During that time, he uses the knowledge that he has acquired from the men in the rope factory to fashion a ladder to access his hiding place on the floor of the building. He also scours the abandoned apartments for items he needs.

The Lady with the Hat provides another instance of a boy's agency. In that story, Yulek travels from a Zionist training camp in Italy, where he is living with a group of teenagers preparing to go to Palestine, to his hometown to see if any of his family members have returned. What he finds is that a Polish family has taken over his childhood house. The current owner, Pan Pilak, who is the boss of the local Communist party, answers the door brandishing a double-barreled shotgun. He tells Yulek: "Poland belongs to the Poles now, do you get it? And this house is ours. But if you sign a document that I've prepared, I'll give you some money for the road."[33] After seeing the ways in which his family house was redecorated, Yurek is so upset with the changes that he signs the documents without even reading them. He does not have the desire to bargain with the new owners. Although he is later criticized by Robert, one of the leaders of the Zionist group, for not asking for more money, Yulek just wanted to get away from his town so he left once he got his money. Recognizing the new circumstances in Poland, he decides to say goodbye to his former life and pledges to bear witness to all his losses. At that point, his pledge to the memory of the destruction of Jewish life in Poland becomes his means of challenging the enemies.

However, later in the story Yulek gets two chances to offset the earlier decision to leave his house without putting up a fight. The first is when he refuses to disembark the ship that has been sent from Haifa to Cyprus. Instead, he helps repel the tear gas canisters that the British soldiers were throwing at the Jews on board. The second occurs when he is finally settles on the kibbutz in Palestine and is given a job as a security guard on the kibbutz bus that passes Arab villages. So, by resisting the disembarkation from the enemy vessel as well as by protecting the kibbutzniks from the villagers, Yulek compensates for his earlier inaction and, in effect, gets his pride back.

Unlike Yulek, neither Lily in *Shanghai Escape* nor Frances in *The Underground Reporters* gets a second chance to assert herself. Realistically, although both girls and boys may have an urge to do something, all were in constant danger, and in that regard, adults tried to protect children from direct contact with the enemy. Given their prescribed roles, the girls in the stories tend to be sensitive to the wishes of their parents and follow parental directions. In *Shanghai Escape*, Lily and her family travel from Vienna to Shanghai in 1938, where they live in the city's Jewish quarter under harsh conditions. Lily's mother has a work pass, which allows her to earn money for the family. One day, while walking with her mother, the two are confronted by a Japanese soldier who demands to see identification papers. The soldier grows inpatient as Lily's mother fumbles for her papers:

> Without warning, he suddenly drew back his hand and slapped Mom hard across the face. She staggered backward and Lily let out a scream. Mom quickly brought her hand up to her cheek, but when she moved her hand away, there was a small line of blood oozing across her lower lip. For a moment, no one moved. And then Mom turned to Lily and screamed, "Run, Lily! Get home—now!"[34]

To save her daughter from the possibility of witnessing more attacks or perhaps an attack on the child herself, Lily's mother's commands her daughter to run. After doing so, Lily feels guilty for abandoning her mother. When

Lily apologizes for running away, her mother reminds Lily that she was commanded to go and even questions what Lily could have actually done to the soldier. Nevertheless, Lily still feels responsible for deserting her mother during the incident on the street. As a result, Lily becomes more subdued and takes fewer risks.

A similar self-regulating response by a girl is found in *The Underground Reporters*. On the way home one afternoon, Frances decides to take a shortcut through a park closed to Jews. Remembering the fun times that she and her brother had in the park in the past, and also for the sake of convenience, Frances enters the park knowing she is violating orders. As she enters the area, she has a "sense of freedom and independence."[35] She relishes that feeling but is soon reprimanded by two Nazis on patrol. They chase her away, and she runs home. Once there, she vows to her aunt to never walk alone on the streets or in the park again. In a manner similar to Lily's, Frances willingly curtails her own independent behavior after the incident in the park.

Unlike the boys in the stories, who use their physical resources when confronted with a dangerous situation, in *The Secrets of Gabi's Dresser*, Gabi relies on her inner strength. After learning that teenage girls are being selected to work in Nazi factories, Gabi's mother develops a plan to hide her daughter in a chest of drawers when the soldiers come to the house. Gabi realizes that she has no choice but to comply with her mother's plan. As she thinks to herself:

> This was my only chance for safety. At any minute the soldiers would burst through the door, and once they arrived, there would be no hope for me. I was certain to be taken away. My choice was to face the soldiers or face the darkness.[36]

Once inside the dresser, Gabi panics just as she did during an earlier practice session in the hiding place. However, after a while, she starts to feel the presence of her deceased father, which is comforting. Using her inner strength to quell fear, Gabi exhibits a degree of resilience that helps her endure the confinement in the dresser. The mother's strategy along with the girl's resilience ultimately tricks the soldiers.

Flirting, generally considered a female-coded trait, may also be a tactic for dealing with danger. In *The Secret of Gabi's Dresser*, Nina, who is prohibited by her parents from maintaining a friendship with Gabi, lures Ivan, a young Nazi guard, away from Gabi and another girl as he is about to hit the two girls. Nina calls out to him:

> "You look so much older in that uniform!" She gushed. Carefully she took his arm holding the stick and pulled it towards her.
>
> "Nina? Nina! It's good to see you," said Ivan, momentarily distracted. "Where is your brother? Is he back from training yet?"
>
> "Yes, yes, and he's been asking about you," Nina continued. Quietly but deliberately she moved to put herself between us and Ivan. "In fact, I think he may be at home now. Why don't you come with me? I'm out of school early because I have a doctor's appointment. If you come home with me, I'm sure my mother would love to feed you a big lunch." Nina chattered quickly, without pausing. Her voice was high and bright as she turned Ivan away from us.[37]

Using her charms, Nina compliments Ivan's appearance and appeals to his vanity in an effort to turn him away from the girls. With the tone of her voice, her words, her eye contact, and her body movements, Nina purposefully diverts Ivan's attention away from girls, thereby shielding them from him.

Compared with Nina, who is portrayed as conventionally female, Lydia, the main character in *Lydia, Queen in Palestine*, is portrayed as a tomboy. Although tomboys are girls who do not conform to societal conceptions of gender, Shawna McDermott finds that often the end of the plot for tomboys is that they are tamed into conventional femininity.[38] Lydia's story follows that pattern. At the start of the book, she climbs rocks, goes barefoot, talks back to her teachers, misbehaves with her nannies, threatens her neighbor, beheads her doll, lies about her mother's friend, and has temper tantrums. In other words, she is not a good girl. She even calls herself "a terror." At the same time, she is fantasizing about marrying Prince Michael of Romania. However, the rise of fascism in Romania changes Jewish life as administrative orders and pogroms are carried out in the country. The direct impact on Lydia is that she is expelled from public school, enters a Jewish school, learns that her cousin has been murdered by the Iron Guard, and finds out that her mother is secretly planning to send her to Palestine. When Lydia protests, her mother finally tells the truth about the war: "It's a matter of life and death. It's not a game this time."[39] The use of the word "game" suggests that in spite of Lydia's wildness, her mother sees the daughter's activities as play and does not take them seriously. Yet, on the way to Palestine, demonstrating a measure of resourcefulness that counters her mother's critique, Lydia uses the meatballs packed in her luggage as currency to barter for a better seat on the train, to obtain pastries, and to buy ice cream. She also uses her fountain pen to bargain for bananas. However, Lydia's personal preoccupation with her family takes precedent over the events that drive her from home. Despite all her ingenuity, she often daydreams about marrying the prince and their reigning as the king and queen of Palestine. So even though the story portrays her as rebellious, Lydia is concerned with the divorce of her parents throughout the entire tale. At the end, Lydia's parents are each remarried. While she is reconciled to these new marriages and adjusted to her new life in Palestine, she still fantasizes about her own wedding to the prince.

While in many respects literacy practices are also gendered, such as the tendency to employ public and private genres, nevertheless boys and girls may each use writing as a form of resistance to oppression. As told in *The Underground Reporters*, the story of *Klepy*, the clandestine newspaper created by teenagers in the town of Budejovice, Czechoslovakia, provides a case in point. About the newspaper, one of the boys actually says, "The paper itself is a form of resistance."[40] After Ruda, another boy in the story, complains about all the restrictive laws against the Jews, his sister Irena responds by saying that there is nothing they can do about them. That answer does not satisfy the boy: "There had to be something he could do. He was not willing to give in to these endless new laws. He didn't like it when grown-ups told him to follow unfair rules that made no sense. He had to find a way to speak out. But how?"[41] Once he gets the idea to write and edit a newspaper, he encourages his friends to contribute to the project. Those who participate in the project feel empowered by their work. Although boys coordinate the paper, girls assume important roles, such as voting on policy matters. When the writers decide to change the emphasis of the newspaper from entertainment to more meaningful topics, they discuss that major editorial shift at length. Dascha, one of the girls in the group, sides against those boys who want to keep the articles light:

> "I agree with Ruda," said the outspoken Dascha Holzer. She had already written several passionate poems for *Klepy*. "The jokes are getting tiresome. Besides, how can we continue to tell jokes when people are getting arrested? It's time to speak out."[42]

The adjective "outspoken" indicates Dascha's confidence in her own opinion as well as her willingness to call on the others to be more assertive in their writing. Dascha openly expresses a desire to fashion the newspaper as a more serious, but at the same time riskier, publication.

Similarly, the diary at the center of *The Diary of Laura's Twin* consoles its writer and inspires its reader to act. For Sara, who is living in the Warsaw ghetto, writing is a way of expressing her individuality and proclaiming her presence in the world. Years later, when Laura is given Sara's diary as part of a bat mitzvah project, reading the diary prompts Laura to confront her friend Nix. After learning that Nix knows who vandalized the Jewish cemetery in their town and refuses to tell the police, Laura thinks about Sara and concludes that not confronting Nix devalues Sara's life. Although Nix ultimately reports the incident without Laura's prompting, Laura has been changed by the diary insofar as she is willing to end the friendship with Nix and maybe even put herself in danger by challenging the vandals.

Smuggling is another activity generally associated with boys and men. While *The Man from the Other Side* relates a boy's smuggling activities, *The Diary of Laura's Twin* contains an account of a girl's. In *The Man from the Other Side*, Marek helps his stepfather bring food and other items into the Warsaw ghetto via the sewer system and observes his stepfather rescue Jewish baby girls from the ghetto. One time acting on his own, Marek leads a Jewish man into the ghetto to join the Warsaw ghetto Jewish fighters. Throughout the story, either in partnership with his father or by himself, Marek make consequential decisions and willingly takes risks.

When Sara in *The Diary of Laura's Twin* discovers that her brother is active in the ghetto underground, she tells him that she wants to be useful too. After he says no, she points to their current life in the ghetto: "If I'm old enough to be here, then I'm old enough to help. I can do whatever you do." She says to herself: "Where did I get the courage to confront David like that?"[43] Sara surprises herself by insisting that she needs something to do, and so she is pleased when, some months later, her brother asks her to deliver a letter to a contact outside the ghetto. He says that her size and agility make her a suitable courier for moving through the sewers. Although scared, she is ready to act because she wants to do something for the resistance. After she successfully returns, she thinks: "That day when I completed the mission for David and the cause, I felt freer than ever before."[44] In addition, she feels less afraid and more mature, pointing out that girls, like boys, act when given a chance. Laura's risk benefits the members of the resistance.

Taken together, the eleven stories challenge the conventional male-coded definition of heroism by proposing that there are many actions that may be considered heroic. Compared with Orlev's works, Kacer's more highly value what girls do. She highlights three distinct areas of agentic female behavior: writing, smuggling, and fighting. By expanding the definition of the hero, Kacer gives her female characters more agency. While her characters rarely rely on their physical strength, nonetheless they are portrayed as risk takers and empathetic to the needs of others, which are qualities of a hero.

Theoretical Implications

For the most part, the texts validate the idea that heroism depends on situational context, foregrounding Eagly's observation that heroism is not gender specific. The opportunity for girls in the stories to write, smuggle, and fight, all agentic actions, supports the tenet of social role theory that behavior is dynamic.[45] Coupling the stories told in the children's books with historical accounts of female writers, smugglers, and fighters in the Warsaw ghetto results in a deeper understanding of gendered behavior. Although men officially coordinated the underground documentation project in the ghetto, women such as Rachel Auerbach, Cecilia Slapokowa, and Gustav Jarecka were active, valued, and trusted members of the project. They were given important writing assignments: Auerbach interviewed Abraham Krzepicki, an escapee from Treblinka; and Cecilia Slapokowa surveyed the life of women in the ghetto.

The role of girls and women as smugglers also violates conventional social roles, as Sheryl Silver Ochayon writes: "Jewish girls—some as young as fifteen years old—and women in their late teens and early twenties . . . braved danger and death in order to serve as the lifeline between Jewish communities throughout war-torn Europe."[46] The activities of Vladka Meed, Tosia Altman, Lonka Lozibrodska, Frumka Plotnicka, Tema Schneiderman, Gola Mire, Chaika Raban Folma, Chaika Grossman, and others show that girls and women willingly took part in resistance activities. In their exposure to risk and the loss of life in the line of duty, the women were equal to other participants in the ghetto resistance.[47] Some women, for example, Livia Libetkin, also took part in armed resistance. Because boys and men were anatomically easily identified as Jewish, girls and women could more readily pass.

Even without a feminist perspective, when observing the activities of girls and women in the Warsaw ghetto, Ringleblum described their "toughness."[48] He saw that they reacted to the crisis in the ghetto with resourcefulness and courage, assuming male roles and learning new skills.[49] He also noticed that from the early days of the war, women began to assume unprecedented responsibilities. Like Ringelblum, Slapokowa noticed that women's survival strategies "violated established prewar conditions."[50] She remarked that war afforded girls and women options that were not possible in peacetime.

The agentic behavior by girls and women as found in children's literature about the Holocaust, as well as in Holocaust history, demonstrates some of the ways that behavior is moderated by situational demands. With respect to studies of literature in particular, analyses of historical fiction written for older readers, such as Jennifer Neilson's 2019 Sydney Taylor Notable Book Award Winner for Teen Readers *Resistance*, which features a sixteen-year-old girl who was a courier and a soldier for the Jewish underground during World War II, would be useful for comparing representations of gender in literature for middle and high school readers. Overall, while more interdisciplinary approaches of gender are needed, the complex interaction of behavior, context, and other variables is of interest to social psychologists, historians, and authors.

Practical Implications

Given that children's literature transmits cultural values and prescriptions for behavior, analyzing the gendered aspects of literature is important because reading influences childhood development. Ya-Lun Tsao's 2008 research shows that stereotypes in literature affect how children perceive themselves. From that, he suggests that teachers should be mindful of the books they select.[51] A decade later, Aaron David Mermelstein finds that gender stereotypes continue to persist and that changes in the stories are occurring, but slowly. Mermelstein, like Tsao, calls on teachers to select books that are less gender biased, which in turn may help break stereotypes.[52]

Because teachers make choices based on personal, ethical, historical, literary, cultural, pedagogical, and other considerations, similar to Anika Walke, whose aim is to uncover and include the stories of Soviet youth in the history of the Nazi occupation, teachers of children's literature could find accounts of the lives of girls and boys within family, educational, political, economic, and other realms before the occupation, and then in the ghettos, camps, and elsewhere, as a way to represent a range of experiences. Telling stories of actual people and events and framing those stories in a way that is not entirely negative or hopeless but that does not distort the truth using historical fiction is one way to personalize history for young readers. From that, young readers may learn that sometimes, even within the narrow boundaries of what is possible during an atrocity, there is a chance to act. Contemporary girls may learn that agency, if possible, entails knowing how and when to act. Boys will benefit from that knowledge too. Ultimately, literature may teach young readers, within the limits of their abilities and situations, to advocate for social justice and against anti-Semitism, antiracism, and related matters in their own lives and in the lives of others.

Notes

1. Larry Swartz, *Teaching Tough Topics* (Markham, ON: Pembroke Publishers Limited, 2020), 11.

2. See Linda J. Rice, "Teaching Historically Based, Culturally Rich YA Novels with Strong Girl Protagonists, in *Girls' Literacy Experiences In and Out of School: Learning and Composing Gendered Identities*, ed. Elaine O'Quinn (London: Routledge Press, 2013), 29–43.

3. Jeannie Ferriss, "Paths Through the Darkness: A Survey and Content Analysis of Holocaust Literature for Children and Young Adults," *SLIS Connecting* 2, no. 2, article 9 (2013): 33.

4. Emily Sigalow and Nicole S. Fox, "Perpetuating Stereotypes: A Study of Gender, Family, and Religious Life in Jewish Children's Books, *Journal for the Scientific Study of Religion* 53, no. 2 (2014): 429.

5. Rachel Leket-Mor and Fred Isaac, "The Sydney Taylor Book Award at Fifty: Trends in Canonized Jewish Children's Literature (1968–2020)," *Judaica Librarianship* 21 (2020): 79.

6. Stacy M. Collins, "The Cultural Doings and Undoings of the Sydney Taylor Book Award," *Judaica Librarianship* 21 (2020): 95–104.

7. Sigalow and Fox, "Perpetuating Stereotypes," 421.

8. See Uri Orlev's author page on the website of the Institute for the Translation of Hebrew Literature, http://www.ithl.org.il/. Also see Kathy Kacer's author page on the website of Second Story Press, https://secondstorypress.ca.

9. See Alice H. Eagly and Wendy Wood, "Social Role Theory," in *Handbook of Theories in Social Psychology*, ed. Paul A. M. Van Lange, Amie W. Krulanski, and E. Tory Higgins (Thousand Oaks, CA: Sage Publications, 2012), 458–76.

10. Selwyn W. Becker and Alice H. Eagly, "The Heroism of Women and Men," *American Psychologist* 59, no. 3 (2004): 167.

11. Lindsay E. Rankin and Alice H. Eagly, "Is His Heroism Hailed and Hers Hidden? Women, Men, and the Social Construction of Heroism," *Psychology of Women Quarterly* 32, no. 4 (2008): 421.

12. See Kenneth B. Kidd, "'A' is for Auschwitz: Psychoanalysis, Trauma Theory, and the 'Children's Literature of Atrocity,'" *Children's Literature* 33, no. 1 (2005): 120–49.

13. Kenneth B. Kidd, *Freud in Oz: At the Intersections of Psychoanalysis and Children's Literature* (Minneapolis: University of Minnesota Press, 2011), 193.

14. Yael Darr, "Grandparents Reveal Their Secrets: A New Holocaust Narrative for the Young 'Third Generation' in Israel," *International Research in Children's Literature* 5, no. 1 (2012): 97–110.

15. David L. Russell, "Reading the Shards and Fragments: Holocaust Literature for Young Readers," *The Lion and the Unicorn* 21, *no.* 2 (April 1997): 268.

16. See Eric A. Kimmel, "Confronting the Ovens: The Holocaust and Juvenile Fiction," *The Horn Book Magazine LII*, February 1977, 84–91.

17. See Phyllis Lassner and Danny Cohen, "Magical Transports and Transformations: The Lessons of Children's Holocaust Fiction," *Studies in American Jewish Literature* 32, no. 2 (2014): 167–85.

18. See Eva Tal, "How Much Should We Tell the Children? Representing Death and Suffering in Children's Literature about the Holocaust," 2004, https://www.yadvashem.org/yv/pdf-drupal/de/education/tal.pdf.

19. See Adrienne Kertzer, "Do You Know What Auschwitz Means? Children's Literature and the Holocaust," *The Lion and the Unicorn* 23, no. 2 (1999): 238–56.

20. See Elizabeth Roberts Baer, "A New Algorithm in Evil: Children's Literature in a Post-Holocaust World," *The Lion and the Unicorn* 24, *no.* 3 (2000): 378–401.

21. See Lydia Kokkola, *Representing the Holocaust in Children's Literature* (Hoboken, NJ: Taylor and Francis, 2013).

22. See Marion Kaplan, "Did Gender Matter During the Holocaust?," *Jewish Social Studies* 24, no. 2 (Winter 2019): 37–56.

23. See Anika Walke, "Jewish Youth in the Minsk Ghetto: How Age and Gender Mattered," *Kritika: Explorations in Russian and Eurasian History* 15, no. 3 (2014): 535–62.

24. See Adrienne Kertzer, *My Mother's Voice: Children, Literature, and the Holocaust* (Peterborough, ON: Broadview Press, 2001), 277–317.

25. See Phyllis Lassner, "Jewish Boys on the Run: The Revision of Boyhood in Holocaust Fiction and Film," in *The Palgrave Handbook of Holocaust Literature and Culture* (Cham, Switzerland: Palgrave Macmillan, 2020), 129–46.

26. Sara R. Horowitz, "Gender, Genocide, and Jewish Memory," *Prooftexts* 20, no. 1–2 (2000): 171.

27. Uri Orlev and Hillel Halkin, trans., *The Island on Bird Street* (Boston: Houghton Mifflin, 1984), 145–46.

28. Orlev and Halkin, *The Island on Bird Street*, 146.

29. Kathy Kacer, *Clara's War* (Toronto, ON: Second Story Press, 2001), 60.

30. *Kathy Kacer, The Night Spies* (Toronto, ON: Second Story Press, 2003), 135.

31. Uri Orlev and Hillel Halkin, trans., *Run, Boy, Run* (Boston: Houghton Mifflin, 2003), 62.

32. Orlev and Halkin, *Run, Boy, Run*, 91.

33. Uri Orlev and Hillel Halkin, trans., *The Lady with the Hat* (Boston: Houghton Mifflin, 1995), 9.

34. Kathy Kacer, *Shanghai Escape* (Toronto, ON: Second Story Press, 2013), 171.

35. Kathy Kacer, *The Underground Reporters* (Toronto, ON: Second Story Press, 2004), 78.

36. Kacer, *The Secret of Gabi's Dresser* (Toronto, Ontario: Second Story Press, 1999), *98*.

37. Kathy Kacer, *The Secret of Gabi's Dresser*, 70–71.

38. Shawna McDermott, "The Tomboy Tradition: Taming Adolescent Ambition from 1869 to 2018," *Children's Literature Association Quarterly* 44, no. 2 (2019): 134.

39. Uri Orlev, *Lydia, Queen in Palestine* (New York: Puffin Books, 1995), 70.

40. Orlev, *Lydia, Queen in Palestine*, 85.

41. Kacer, *The Underground Reporters*, 46.

42. Kacer, *The Underground Reporters*, 84.

43. Kathy Kacer, *The Diary of Laura's Twin* (Toronto, ON: Second Story Press, 2008), 72–73.

44. Kacer, *The Diary of Laura's Twin*, 124.

45. Alice H. Eagly, Wendy Wood, and Amanda B. Diekman, "Social Role Theory of Sex Differences and Similarities: A Current Appraisal," in *The Developmental Social Psychology of Gender*, ed. Thomas Eckes and Hanns M. Trautner (Mahwah, NJ: Lawrence Erlbaum Associates, Inc., 2000), 123–74.

46. Sheryl Silver Ochayon, "Female Couriers During the Holocaust," Yad Vashem website, yadvashem.org/articles/general/couriers.html.

47. Lenore L. Weitzman, "Kashariyot (Couriers) in the Jewish Resistance During the Holocaust," in *Jewish Women: A Comprehensive Historical Encyclopedia*, February, 27, 2009, Jewish Women's Archive, jwa.org/encyclopedia/article/kashariyot-couriers-in-jewish-resistance-during-holocaust.

48. Samuel D. Kassow, *Who Will Write Our History?* (Bloomington: Indiana University Press, 2007), 241.

49. Kassow, *Who Will Write Our History?*, 242.

50. Kassow, *Who Will Write Our History?*, 245.

51. See Ya-Lun Tsao, "Gender Issues in Young Children's Literature," *Reading Improvement* 45, no. 3 (2008): 108–14.

52. See Aaron David Mermelstein, "Gender Roles in Children's Literature and Their Influence on Learners," *MinneTESOL Journal* 34, no. 2 (Fall 2018): n.p.

Works Cited

Baer, Elizabeth Roberts. "A New Algorithm in Evil: Children's Literature in a Post-Holocaust World." *The Lion and the Unicorn* 24, no. 3 (2000): 378–401.

Becker, Selwyn W., and Alice E. Eagly. "The Heroism of Women and Men." *American Psychologist* 59, no. 3 (2004): 163–78.

Collins, Stacy M. "The Cultural Doings and Undoings of the Sydney Taylor Book Award." *Judaica Librarianship* 21 (2020): 95–104.

Darr, Yael. "Grandparents Reveal Their Secrets: A New Holocaust Narrative for the Young 'Third Generation' in Israel." *International Research in Children's Literature* 5, no. 1 (2012): 97–110.

Eagly, Alice H., and Wendy Wood. "Social Role Theory." In *Handbook of Theories in Social Psychology*, edited by Paul A. M. Van Lange, Amie W. Krulanski, and E. Tory Higgins, 458–76. Thousand Oaks, CA: Sage Publications, 2012.

Eagly, Alice H., Wendy Wood, and Amanda B. Diekman. "Social Role Theory of Sex Differences and Similarities: A Current Appraisal." In *The Developmental Social Psychology of Gender*, edited by Thomas Eckes and Hanns M. Trautner, 123–74. Mahwah, NJ: Lawrence Erlbaum Associates, Inc., 2000.

Ferriss, Jeannie. "Paths Through the Darkness: A Survey and Content Analysis of Holocaust Literature for Children and Young Adults." *SLIS Connecting* 2, no. 2, article 9 (2013): n.p.

Horowitz, Sara R. "Gender, Genocide, and Jewish Memory." *Prooftexts* 20, no. 1–2 (2000): 158–90.

Kacer, Kathy. *The Secret of Gabi's Dresser*. Toronto, ON: Second Story Press, 1999.

Kacer, Kathy. *Clara's War*. Toronto, ON: Second Story Press, 2001.

Kacer, Kathy. *The Night Spies*. Toronto, ON: Second Story Press, 2003.

Kacer, Kathy. *The Underground Reporters*. Toronto, ON: Second Story Press, 2004.

Kacer, Kathy. *The Diary of Laura's Twin*. Toronto, ON: Second Story Press, 2008.

Kacer, Kathy. *Shanghai Escape*. Toronto, ON: Second Story Press, 2013.

Kaplan, Marion. "Did Gender Matter During the Holocaust?" *Jewish Social Studies* 24, no. 2 (Winter 2019): 37–56.

Kassow, Samuel D. *Who Will Write Our History?* Bloomington: Indiana University Press, 2007.

Kertzer, Adrienne. "Do You Know What Auschwitz Means? Children's Literature and the Holocaust." *The Lion and the Unicorn* 23, no. 2 (1999): 238–56.

Kertzer, Adrienne. *My Mother's Voice: Children, Literature, and the Holocaust*. Peterborough, ON: Broadview Press, 2001.

Kidd, Kenneth B. "'A' is for Auschwitz: Psychoanalysis, Trauma Theory, and the 'Children's Literature of Atrocity.'" *Children's Literature* 33, no. 1 (2005): 120–49.

Kidd, Kenneth B. *Freud in Oz: At the Intersections of Psychoanalysis and Children's Literature*. Minneapolis: University of Minnesota Press, 2011.

Kimmel, Eric A. "Confronting the Ovens: The Holocaust and Juvenile Fiction." *The Horn Book Magazine* LII, February 16, 1977, 84–91.

Kokkola, Lydia. *Representing the Holocaust in Children's Literature*. Hoboken, NJ: Taylor and Francis, 2013.

Lassner, Phyllis, and Danny Cohen. "Magical Transports and Transformations: The Lessons of Children's Holocaust Fiction." *Studies in American Jewish Literature* 32, no. 2 (2014): 167–85.

Lassner, Phyllis. "Jewish Boys on the Run: The Revision of Boyhood in Holocaust Fiction and Film." In *The Palgrave Handbook of Holocaust Literature and Culture*, 129–46. Cham, Switzerland: Palgrave Macmillan, 2020.

Leket-Mor, Rachel, and Fred Isaac. "The Sydney Taylor Book Award at Fifty: Trends in Canonized Jewish Children's Literature (1968–2020)." *Judaica Librarianship* 21 (2020): 58–94.

McDermott, Shawna. "The Tomboy Tradition: Taming Adolescent Ambition from 1869 to 2018." *Children's Literature Association Quarterly* 44, no. 2 (2019): 134–55.

Mermelstein, Aaron David. "Gender Roles in Children's Literature and Their Influence on Learners." *MinneTESOL Journal* 34, no. 2 (Fall 2018): n.p.

Ochayon, Sheryl Silver. "Female Couriers During the Holocaust." Yad Vashem website. yadvashem.org/articles/general/couriers.html.

Orlev, Uri, and Hillel Halkin, trans. *The Island on Bird Street*. Boston: Houghton Mifflin, 1984.

Orlev, Uri, and Hillel Halkin, trans. *The Lady with the Hat*. Boston: Houghton Mifflin, 1995.

Orlev, Uri, and Hillel Harkin, trans. *Lydia, Queen in Palestine*. New York: Puffin Books, 1995.

Orlev, Uri. *The Man from the Other Side*. Translated by Hillel Halkin. Boston: Houghton Mifflin, 1991.

Orlev, Uri, and Hillel Halkin, trans. *Run, Boy, Run*. Boston: Houghton Mifflin, 2003.

Rankin, Lindsay E., and Alice H. Eagly. "Is His Heroism Hailed and Hers Hidden? Women, Men, and the Social Construction of Heroism." *Psychology of Women Quarterly* 32, no. 4 (2008): 414–22.

Rice, Linda J. "Teaching Historically Based, Culturally Rich YA Novels with Strong Girl Protagonists." In *Girls' Literacy Experiences In and Out of School: Learning and Composing Gendered Identities*, edited by Elaine O'Quinn, 29–43. London: Routledge Press, 2013.

Russell, David L. "Reading the Shards and Fragments: Holocaust Literature for Young Readers." *The Lion and the Unicorn* 21, no. 2 (April 1997): 267–80.

Sigalow, Emily, and Nicole S. Fox. "Perpetuating Stereotypes: A Study of Gender, Family, and Religious Life in Jewish Children's Books. *Journal for the Scientific Study of Religion* 53, no. 2 (2014): 416–31.

Swartz, Larry. *Teaching Tough Topics*. Markham, ON: Pembroke Publishers Limited, 2020.

Tal, Eva. "How Much Should We Tell the Children? Representing Death and Suffering in Children's Literature about the Holocaust." 2004. https://www.yadvashem.org/yv/pdf-drupal/de/education/tal.pdf.

Tsao, Ya-Lun. "Gender Issues in Young Children's Literature." *Reading Improvement* 45, no. 3 (2008): 108–14.
Walke, Anika. "Jewish Youth in the Minsk Ghetto: How Age and Gender Mattered." *Kritika: Explorations in Russian and Eurasian History* 15, no. 3 (2014): 535–62.
Weitzman, Lenore L. "Kashariyot (Couriers) in the Jewish Resistance During the Holocaust." In *Jewish Women: A Comprehensive Historical Encyclopedia*. February 27, 2009. Jewish Women's Archive. jwa.org/encyclopedia/article/kashariyot-couriers-in-jewish-resistance-during-holocaust.

Chapter 6

A Sonnet of Atrocity

A Consideration of a Poem Written by a
Child at the Terezín Concentration Camp

Mary Catherine Mueller

One of the most accomplished and fabled groups of warriors were the mighty Maasai warriors of eastern Africa. No tribe was considered to have warriors more fearsome or intelligent than the mighty Maasai. It is perhaps surprising then, to learn the traditional greeting that passed between Maasai warriors was "Kasserian Ingera?" meaning, "And how are the children?" Even warriors with no children of their own would give the traditional answer, "All the children are well," which indicated that when the priorities of protecting the young and the powerless are in place, peace and safety prevail.[1]

In the years preceding and during World War II, leaders around the world often failed to ask: "And how are the children?" This period saw systematic, state-sponsored mass murder and genocide; an attempt to annihilate the Jewish people, from the unborn to the aged. Over the course of Hitler's reign, an estimated 1.5 million children, among them around one million Jewish children, were murdered.[2] In the majority, these children died without leaving any record of their internal lives.

One fragment that remains is the collection of children's poems and art from the Terezín Camp, which were found in a suitcase years after the war. Through this discovery, some of these silenced voices can be heard, albeit in a limited manner. One such poem, which I discuss in this chapter, is titled "At Terezín" and is attributed to a young author we are given to believe was named Teddy. The surname of the author of our poem is unknown. The details of his life before the Holocaust are unknown, as is the moment of his death. The facets of "Teddy's" identity that typically might frame an interpretation of the poem are missing, denied by the genocidal Nazi regime. All that remains are the poet's words, his name, and the block where he was interned: "Teddy from Block L410."

Established by Reinhold Heydrich, the first head of Reich Security, in November 1941, the purpose of the Terezín Camp was not merely to systematically dehumanize and kill, through starvation and disease, those who were interred, but also to present a façade to the Red Cross in the form of a mock camp inhabited by children and the elderly—the two groups often immediately sent to the gas chambers upon their arrival at Auschwitz.[3] Azriel Eisenberg writes:

> Theresienstadt (originally Terezín) was built as a fortress by an Austrian emperor over two centuries ago. It was situated 60 miles from Prague and was built to house at most 10,000 inhabitants. During the Holocaust years, 60,000 and more were crowded into it; 15,000 of them were children, of whom only 100 survived. It was frequently disguised as a model camp for exhibit to visitors from the Red Cross committees and foreign observers.[4]

For a short time, children in the Terezín Camp played a role in this façade.[5] As a result, young prisoners such as "Teddy" found themselves with the material to record their experiences. "Teddy's" poem, "At Terezín," testifies to the horrors he and many other children endured.

Many of the poems written by children during the Holocaust—specifically those poems that are included in the collection *I Never Saw Another Butterfly: Children's Drawings and Poems from Terezín Concentration Camp 1942–44*, edited by Hana Volavkova—illuminate the horrors children endured in this camp. The creation of this collection was facilitated by an Austrian Jewish artist named Friedl Dicker-Brandeis, who was deported to Theresienstadt in December 1942. Dicker-Brandeis "lived in the girls' home and secretly taught more than six hundred children to draw, paint, sew, and make puppets."[6]

Scholars of the Holocaust may consider how the corpus of literary and artistic work created by children in Terezín contributes to our understanding of what children endured in the camp. In this chapter, I address the significance of "At Terezín" as a sonnet of atrocity. I argue that the perspective of a child offers an alternative and potentially more accessible framing of the Holocaust experience than the works of adult poets. The poem adopts a sophisticated design for a child writer, one that is arguably at odds with the naive content of the poem, yet it is highly effective in framing the narrative in the style of an exchange between a newcomer and a more seasoned inmate. Unlike poetry written by adult victims of the Holocaust, such as the works of Paul Celan, Nelly Sachs, Tadeusz Borowski, Miklós Radnóti, and others, which impart more ominous and sinister themes throughout their lines, "At Terezín," innocently and naively echoes hopeful desires of *return*—returning to home, family, friends, and more. This wish to return to a life before ghettos and camps reflects how some children were not yet fully aware of the horrific reality of the Nazis' annihilation of their homes, families, and, eventually, their own lives. Furthermore, through our consideration of the child's poem, we will learn about the hardships, experiences, and hopes that "Teddy" clung to in the Terezín Camp.

Children and Poetry in the Terezín Concentration Camp

In many regards, Anne Frank has become the representative child victim of the Holocaust. Her *Diary of a Young Girl*, however, is not representative. Many of the children imprisoned in ghettos and camps across Europe lacked the resources to write about their experiences and, in most cases, were forever silenced by disease, starvation, or poisoned gas.

One of the children who survived is Zuzana Justman. She wrote about the limited yet poignant diary entries of her time in this camp in an article published in *The New Yorker* on September 16, 2019, called "My Terezín Diary." In this article, Justman provides readers with context to understand to understand works like "Teddy's"; "what is most striking to me today about the diary I kept in the camp, seventy-five years ago, is what I left out."[7] She also stresses the role fear and caution played in guiding her pen to omit certain details of her daily activities in case her diary were ever confiscated:

> Because I was fearful that the diary could fall into German hands and bring harm to my family, I rarely expressed myself freely in it. I did not mention my mother's arrest. I wrote, with naïve caution, "Until the age of eight I led a normal life . . . but then a foreign nation entered my country," which I must have

imagined would be less offensive to a potential Nazi reader than saying straight out that Germany had invaded Czechoslovakia.[8]

Zuzana Justman's diary sheds light on the experiences of a young girl and her family in this camp, while "At Terezin" highlights the experiences of children without families in the camp. What the poets share, however, is an absence of details that might identify them: Justman's writing omits details of her mother's circumstances; "Teddy's" poem omits a surname, age, hometown, and nationality. We can only speculate as to why these details were omitted, but it is possible that it was an act of self-preservation, much like Justman's.

The peculiar circumstance of Justman's and "Teddy's" situation is addressed by Aaron Kramer in his article *Creative Defiance in a Death-Camp*. Kramer addresses the duality of the camp when noting:

> Terezín, the old fortress town in northerner Bohemia, was to have a new and truly distinctive function: Here would come Germany's oldest Jews and those seriously wounded in World War I, distinguished for war service. Interned here as well would be prominent German Jews with international connections, whose whereabouts might be questioned abroad. In a few months, the Potemkin village was ready to show Red Cross inspectors how benignly Germany treated its Jews. This Device counteracted the ever-increasing rumors of atrocities at such places as Auschwitz and Buchenwald.[9]

Kramer further addresses the reality behind the charade of this camp by questioning:

> How could visitors guess that behind the Hollywood set was in fact nothing more than a detention center, a way station, a staging post through which Germany's Jewish intellectuals and artists were funneled into the gas chambers of Auschwitz? How could they imagine that, behind the scenes, Terezín's inhabitants lived in the most hideous filth and disease many in huge, cold, airless attics where they perished by the thousands—33,430, to be precise, almost one fourth of the 139,606 who came here. No gas chambers were needed. Exhaustion, starvation, disease, and the whip did the job quite well. And overcrowding: a population density about 50 times as great as Berlin's before the war. But

the Red Cross did not see. The population density was solved before each of their visits.[10]

Consequently, through various systematic modes of annihilation: starvation, diseases, exhaustion, or the eventual transporting to Death Camps, of the 15,000 children who stayed or passed through Terezín, fewer than 100 would survive.

More than representing a creative outlet for their authors, the poems written by children at Terezín give a rare (albeit, as Justman suggests, curated and incomplete) glimpse of the horrific atrocity endured through the eyes and voices of the children of Terezín. The following is "At Terezín":

> When a new child comes
> Everything seems strange to him.
> What, on the ground I have to lie?
> Eat Black potatoes? No! Not I!
> I've got to stay? It's dirty here!
> The floor—why, look, it's dirt, I fear!
> And I'm supposed to sleep on it?
> I'll get all dirty!
> Here the sound of shouting, cries,
> And oh, so many flies.
> Everyone knows flies carry disease.
> Oooh, something bit me! Wasn't that a bedbug?
> Here in Terezín, life is hell
> And when I'll go home again, I can't yet tell.[11]

Before discussing the key themes woven into this particular poem, we must note the differing approaches some scholars have taken when addressing works created by children during the Holocaust. Kelly Bylica, Susan Leshnoff, and Anna Ornstein consider the role of these poems primarily through a discourse focused on the psychology and pedagogy—as a creative outlet for the children rather than as literary contributions to Holocaust literature. For instance, in Hilda R. Glazer's article *Children and Play in the Holocaust: Friedl Dicker-Brandeis—Heroic Child Therapist*, she emphasizes:

> It is difficult to identify many of the individuals who worked with children in the ghettoes and camps. Of those who are not known to have worked with children in art and play, the activities and

efforts of Friedl Dicker-Brandeis (also known as Friedl Brandeis) stand out. [. . .] Dicker-Brandeis saw the principal aim of teaching to be the liberation of concealed sources of children's creativity, the development of their fantasies and imaginations, and the possibility of authentic self-expression as well as enhancement of independent judgment and observations, which, in their sum, contribute to the consolidation of self-confidence and independence. She believed that children should be given an opportunity for self-expression in their play and in their art.[12]

Glazer further stresses how Dicker-Brandeis's "premise was that art should open children up or preserve their self-determination as a source of energy, and stimulate their fantasies and enforce their judgment and observation."[13] Glazer argues that Dicker-Brandeis took efforts and risks to momentarily enable the children in the camp to process and express their ongoing experiences. This claim is also echoed by other scholars such as Al Hurwitz and Elena Makarova.[14] The lack of literary scholarship addressing these aesthetic and literary merits of the poetic texts written by the children is palpable. For example, in *The Child's Voice: Art, Poetry and Music from the Terezín Concentration Camp for the Music Classroom*, Kelly Bylica offers a more lighthearted reading of the children's poetry from the Terezín camp.[15] Bylica states that Dicker-Brandeis "encouraged students to not only see something as it was, but what it could become, thereby urging children to use art to continue to find beauty in their own world, despite the atrocities surrounding them."[16] While this affirms the impetus propelling Dicker-Brandeis's efforts with the children, this scholarship neglects the children's own articulation of their experiences. Rather than our focusing on these works of poetry as merely indicative of a compilation of creative creations, then, I read "At Terezín" as literature of testimony, for the themes imbued in several of the poems lend themselves to being read alongside the poetry of adult victims written during the Holocaust. By reading "At Terezín" as literature of testimony, the reader comes to recognize that the children are not just writing with "hopeful minds," but rather writing as a lamentation, as a chronicling of the absence of their homes, the absence of their families, and even the absence of the beauty in nature.

The Absence of the Home

"At Terezín" is representative of the poetry written by children in this camp, as it captures the key themes woven into many of the children's poems. One such theme is the absence of home. The decrees in 1938 Reichsgesetzblatt, Part I, page 47, included the injunction that "Jews were relegated to an inferior status by the denial of common privileges and freedoms. Thus, they were denied access to certain city areas, sidewalks, transportation, places of amusement, restaurants [. . .] Their homes, bank accounts, real estate, and intangibles were expropriated."[17] On October 3, 1938, "the Decree on the Confiscation of Jewish Property regulates the transfer of assets from Jews to non-Jews in Germany" became a law, and every Jewish family found itself on the path to homelessness—a path quickly leading to compulsory ghettos and to work and death camps.[18] This systematic rending of the children as homeless is echoed in this child's poem through a yearning for a return to what was, what used to be, yet what (we, as the reader knows) will never exist for them again. This theme of the absence of the home—the dwelling place—is crucial to understanding the other themes of the absence of family relations and beauty of nature.

For the children in this camp, home was not solely their previous dwelling place, domestic sphere, or destination, but a wish for security. This desire to return to their homes, and what life once was, reflects the innocence, naiveté, or even the self-censoring—as Justman accounts of her diary—of the children. We have reason to assume that, unlike Justman, "Teddy" appears to have shown little restraint in his description of camp life—it is hard to imagine, other than naming specific guards and their crimes, how he could have been more direct in detailing his suffering. This suggests, then, that his hope (if not expectation) of a return may be genuine. This theme of the absence of home is evident in the poem considered here. The first eight lines describe the shock a child experiences upon first arriving at Terezín. The straightforward, observational tone captured through the word choice of the first two lines juxtaposes the speaker's familiarity with the camp environment with the new child's astonishment: "When a new child comes / Everything seems strange to him."[19]

The poem is written in the form of an exchange between a new child arriving at Terezín and a child who has become accustomed to the daily horrors of the camp. Relying on the rhetorical device of questions followed by adamant responses and capturing a detached matter-of-fact tone in the short, concise sentences, in the octave of this poem, the speaker introduces the reader to the seemingly typical shock and disgust a "new child" encounters upon their first arrival at this camp. Here, the poet's emphasis on the "new" child also suggests that the children who were no longer considered new had learned to adjust their expectations and were no longer shocked by the dirtiness of their environment. This acceptance of the realities of the camp is also echoed in Justman's article when she recalls, as a child, being aware of the ever-present threat of illness and death in the camp: "Although the Nazis referred to Terezín as a 'model ghetto,' nearly one of every four people confined in the camp died there. Among the prisoners were some of the best doctors from Czechoslovakia, Germany, Austria, and Holland. But, given the lack of medicines and of nutritious food, there was little they could do to combat the diseases that ravaged the place."[20] The poet builds upon the notion of the new child's shock, in the midst of line 5, when the new child's questions and observations introduce the theme of the absence of home facing all the children: "I've got to stay? It's dirty here!"[21] In this moment, the new child first utters the plea to leave. This line captures a hope, a yearning to leave—a yearning to even possibly return home—that the speaker will also affirm in the latter portion of the poem. Accompanying this brief question is the new child's observation of the filthiness of "here." The speaker ends this portion of the poem with a faltering rhyme scheme in the bluntness of the truncated final line, which breaks the rhyming pattern of the previous couplets. In this moment, the reader expects the rhyme, yet is denied the expectation of a rhyme for "it": "And I'm supposed to sleep on it? / I'll get all dirty!" This interrupted rhythm of the poem and the broken rhyme scheme seems to echo the jarring reality that the new child encountered upon entering this new dwelling space. The sophistication required to select a Petrarchan sonnet structure appropriate to this kind of exchange between children is notable given the naive and artless tone and language of the poem in the new child's declarations of shock and dismay in this new environment.

This desire to return home is not the only notion repeated throughout this poem, for the speaker repeats the ideas of the dirtiness of the new child's dwelling space in the camp, which contrasts a home environment that follows or observes the teachings of Judaism—specifically regarding the laws of cleanliness. In his memoir *Survival in Auschwitz: The Nazi Assault on Humanity*, Primo Levi relates the impossibility of cleanliness in the camps when he writes about a sign in Auschwitz hanging above the washing area, dictating how the prisoners were to wash:

> For many weeks I considered these warnings about hygiene as pure examples of the Teutonic sense of humor [. . .] In this place it is practically pointless to wash every day in the turbid water of the filthy washbasins for purposes of cleanliness and health; but it is most important as a symptom of remaining vitality,

and necessary as an instrument of moral survival. I must confess it: after only one week of prison, the instinct for cleanliness disappeared in me. [. . .] The more I think about it, the more washing one's face in our condition seems a stupid feat, even frivolous: a mechanical habit, or worse, a dismal repetition of an extinct rite.[22]

As also observed by the child in the poem, for Levi, and for millions of prisoners in the camps, the command for cleanliness collides with the impossibility for one to truly be clean in such a place as Auschwitz—a habitat of diseases and death. Philp Smith also emphasizes that in the death camps,

> the simultaneous necessity and impossibility of cleanliness is part of a larger discursive apparatus designed to support the image of the Jew as "impure." [. . .] The Jew represented all that the healthy nation was not. [. . .] Close to the ideological and affective epicentre of the Nazi imaginary was the rhetorical depiction of Jews as vermin. The prisoners were made dirty seemingly of their own volition. By being made dirty they were forced to act in accordance with the larger racial doctrine of the Nazis.[23]

This "impossibility" to be clean because of the lack of sanitation and clean water directly served as a means for the Nazis and perpetrators to further dehumanize the prisoners of the camps. The environment of the concentration camps fostered the growth of disease. Whether at Auschwitz or Terezín, the purposes of the Nazi concentration camps were to strip the prisoners of their humanity and usher them to their demise, whether through sickness, exhaustion, starvation, bullets, or gas. The speaker of the poem does not seem to be fully aware of the violence that awaits him, but he knows the impossibility of cleanliness in the camp.

The author continues unraveling the new child's disbelief through a series of observations and questions. Again, the first two lines of this poem begin with the speaker observing the shock and disgust the new child expresses toward his new home: "When a new child comes / Everything seems strange to him."[24] The next six lines capture the series of exclamatory observations that echo the shocked tone expressed in the new child's disgust with the living conditions of the camp and a desire to return home. This longing for one's home is also echoed in Primo Levi's memoir when he describes the sharing of memories:

When one works, one suffers and there is not time to think: our homes are less than a memory. But here the time is ours: from bunk to bunk, despite the prohibitions, we exchange visits and we talk and we talk. The wooden hut, crammed with suffering humanity, is full of words, memories and of another pain. "*Heimweh*" the Germans call this pain; it is a beautiful word, it means "longing for one's home."[25]

Yet, for the new child in the poem, the shock upon his arrival about the environment of his imprisonment, his newfound residence, is at the forefront of his conversation. The exclamatory statements like "No! Not I!" and "The floor—why, look, it's dirt, I fear!" or "I'll get all dirty!" paired with questions like "What, on the ground I have to lie?" or "Eat black potatoes?" or "I've got to stay?" followed by "And I'm supposed to sleep on it?" that appear in lines 3 through 8 capture the stunned tone that the new child, and likely most children taken from their families and homes, endured upon arriving in Terezín. This new child's repetitive, adamant objection to this filthy new dwelling place captures the shock that 15,000 children likely also encountered upon their arrival to Terezín: dirt as a welcome mat, rotten black potatoes for a hosted meal, floorboards for headboards.

The last six lines of the poem indicate a shift for the reader as the speaker moves away from observing the new child's reaction to his new "home" and, instead, offers the reader his own straightforward observation of this "hell" that he yearns to leave.[26] In these final lines of the poem, the speaker interweaves the five senses to capture the horrific living conditions the children were forced to endure in this "new home." This distinct shift then occurs in the last six lines, where the speaker observes the same environment by which the new child was so taken aback.

The diction and syntax used by the speaker in this sestet almost normalizes the hell-like experience he and the new child and all the other children in this camp were forced to endure. The speaker's familiarity with the inconceivable environment of the camp is captured in the word "Here" in line 9. "Here"—this camp, this room, this moment of time—is not accompanied by sounds of nature (birds singing) or laughter and chatting (families together or children playing), but rather is accompanied by "the sound of shouting, cries, / and oh, so many flies."[27] The word choice of "Everyone knows" on line 11 further captures the almost casual, almost condescending tone of the speaker—he who has assimilated to the camp.

Everyone knows "flies carry disease." The common knowledge shared among the children in this camp was not of scholastic, but of survival information. The speaker continues to unveil his knowledge of this environment through the five senses. The first sense the author uses to introduce the reader to this environment is the sensation of sound. Typically, when one thinks of children gathered together, the thought of laughter, giggles, maybe even sometimes a lullaby might come to mind. However, in Block L410 of the Terezín concentration camp that housed the poem's author, "Teddy" and other children hear "the sound of shouting, cries."[28] This threat of an insect bite also leads to the sense of taste and touch, as stated in the line: "Oooh, something bit me! Wasn't that a bedbug?"

The last two lines of this poem contrast the speaker's present dwelling place at Terezín with the desire to return to his previous dwelling place—his home: "Here in Terezín, life is hell / And when I'll go home again, I can't yet tell."[29] This couplet concludes the poem with the speaker directly linking his present experience with his yearning for home through the conjunction "and." The significance of this conjunction lies not in its placement at the beginning of the final line of the poem, but with the two ideas it links: hell and home.

Conclusion: The Absence of Names

"Teddy" and the 1.5 million other children murdered during the Holocaust did not return home, and they did not get the chance to hear loved ones call them by their names. The Nazis sought to eradicate Jewish children by first rendering them homeless, then making them orphans by separating them from their families, and finally, making them nameless by forcing them inside ghettos, cattle cars, and then gas chambers en masse while seeking to eradicate all traces of their existence. "Teddy" had a name. Reading "At Terezín," we discover a naive testimony to life in the camp captured in the fourteen lines; we also learn a name, or part of it. The inscription "Teddy . . . from L410" may offer us a glimpse of the author's identity, but the replacement of a surname with a block designation only contributes to the stripping away of humanity that laments through his naive observations, which this chapter seeks to restore to the author. Patricia Heberer's *Children During the Holocaust* addresses the extent to which the Nazis sought to murder and erase Jewish children from existing in this world. Heberer notes:

In the course of events that formed the Holocaust, the systematic murder of Jewish children marked the passing of the threshold toward genocide. In the summer of 1941, just weeks after the Third Reich commenced its war of annihilation against the Soviet Union, traces of the "Final Solution" began to appear in reports and letters written by Germans who were involved in or witnessed the wave of mass executions sweeping across the occupied area. A member of a German police battalion wrote home to his family in the Reich. "The Jews are free game. [. . .] One can only give the Jews some well-intentioned advice: bring no more children into the world. They no longer have a future.[30]

When we read poems like "At Terezín," we encounter young testimonies and glimpse their stories. We read, teach, and write in the hope of revealing what these children experienced during the Holocaust. I hope to give voice to "Teddy from Block L410," and in doing so, remember his life by acknowledging his experience. For the children of yesterday, the children of today, and the children of tomorrow, may we never again fail to ask: "*Kasserian Ingera?*" . . . "*And how are the children?*"

Notes

1. Gloria Boutte and Nathaniel Bryan, "When Will Black Children Be Well? Interrupting Anti-Black Violence in Early Childhood Classrooms and Schools," *Contemporary Issues in Early Childhood*, December 2019, https://doi.org/10.1177/1463949119890598.

2. "Children During the Holocaust," United States Holocaust Memorial Museum, https://encyclopedia.ushmm.org/content/en/article/children-during-the-holocaust.

3. Hilda R. Glazer, "Children and Play in the Holocaust: Friedl Dicker-Brandeis—Heroic Child Therapist," *Journal of Humanistic Counseling, Education & Development* 37, no. 4 (June 1999): 194.

4. Azriel Eisenberg, *The Lost Generation: Children in the Holocaust* (New York: Pilgrim Press, 1982), 42.

5. Eyewitness accounts, as well as memoirs written by survivors, such as those by Elie Wiesel and Sara Nomberg-Przytyk, attest to the role of Terezín. Azriel Eisenberg's work *The Lost Generation: Children in the Holocaust* also attests to the unique role the Terezín Concentration Camp played in the Third Reich. See Elie Wiesel, *Night*, trans. Marion Wiesel (New York: Hill and Wang, 2006), 30–32; Sara Nomberg-Przytyk, *Auschwitz: True Tales from a Grotesque Land*, trans. Roslyn Hirsch,

David Hirsch, and Elie Pfefferkorn (Chapel Hill: University of North Carolina Press, 1985), 81–84; Eisenberg, *The Lost Generation*, 42.

    6. Ruth Thomson, *Terezín: Voices from the Holocaust* (Somerville, MA: Candlewick Press, 2013), 40.

    7. Zuzana Justman, "My Terezín Diary," *The New Yorker*, September 9, 2019, https://www.newyorker.com/magazine/2019/09/16/my-terezin-diary.

    8. Justman, "My Terezín Diary."

    9. Aaron Kramer, "Creative Defiance in a Death-Camp," *Journal of Humanistic Psychology* 38, no. 1 (Winter 1998): 14.

    10. Kramer, "Creative Defiance in a Death-Camp," 14.

    11. Teddy, "At Terezín," in *I Never Saw Another Butterfly: Children's Drawings and Poems from Terezín Concentration Camp 1942–44*, ed. Hana Volavkova (New York: Schocken Books, 1993), 3.

    12. Glazer, "Children and Play in the Holocaust," 197–98.

    13. Glazer, "Children and Play in the Holocaust," 198.

    14. Al Hurwitz, "Friedl Dicker-Brandeis: The Art Educator as Hero," in *Seeing through "Paradise": Artist and the Terezín Concentration Camp*, ed. Massachusetts College of Art (Boston: Massachusetts College of Art, 1991); Elena Makarova, *From Bauhaus to Terezín: Friedl Dicker-Brandeis and Her Pupils* (Jerusalem, Israel: Holocaust Martyrs' and Heroes' Remembrance Authority, The Art Museum, 1990).

    15. Kelly Bylica, "The Child's Voice: Art, Poetry and Music from the Terezín Concentration Camp for the Music Classroom" (*Canadian Music Educator/Musicien Educateur Au Canada* 56, no. 3 (Spring 2015): 24.

    16. Bylica, "The Child's Voice," 24.

    17. "Nazi Conspiracy and Aggression Volume 2 Chapter XVI Part 2," Avalon Project: Nazi Conspiracy and Aggression—Volume 2 Chapter XVI Part 2, http://avalon.law.yale.edu/imt/chap16_part02.asp; "Nazi Conspiracy and Aggression Volume 1 Chapter XII—The Persecution of the Jews," Avalon Project: Nazi Conspiracy and Aggression—Volume 1 Chapter XII—The Persecution of the Jews, https://avalon.law.yale.edu/imt/chap_12.asp.

    18. "Antisemitic Legislation 1933–1939," United States Holocaust Memorial Museum, https://encyclopedia.ushmm.org/content/en/article/antisemitic-legislation-1933-1939.

    19. Teddy, "At Terezín," 3.

    20. Justman, "My Terezín Diary."

    21. Teddy, "At Terezín," 3.

    22. Primo Levi, *Survival in Auschwitz, The Nazi Assault on Humanity*, First Collier books edition (New York: Collier, 1961), 40.

    23. Philip Smith, *Reading Art Spiegelman* (New York: Routledge, 2016), 87.

    24. Teddy, "At Terezín," 3.

    25. Levi, *Survival in Auschwitz*, 55.

    26. Levi, *Survival in Auschwitz*, 3.

27. Levi, *Survival in Auschwitz*, 3.
28. Levi, *Survival in Auschwitz*, 3.
29. Levi, *Survival in Auschwitz*, 3.
30. Patricia Heberer, *Children During the Holocaust* (Lanham, MD: Rowman & Littlefield, 2015), xxii.

Works Cited

"Antisemitic Legislation 1933–1939." United States Holocaust Memorial Museum. https://encyclopedia.ushmm.org/content/en/article/antisemitic-legislation-1933-1939.

Bylica, Kelly. "The Child's Voice: Art, Poetry and Music from the Terezín Concentration Camp for the Music Classroom." *Canadian Music Educator/Musicien Educateur Au Canada* 56, no. 3 (Spring 2015): 24–27.

Charney, Leon H., and Sha'ul Maizlish. *The Mystery of the Kaddish: Its Profound Influence on Judaism*. Fort Lee, NJ: Barricade Books, 2008.

"Children During the Holocaust." United States Holocaust Memorial Museum. https://encyclopedia.ushmm.org/content/en/article/children-during-the-holocaust.

Eisenberg, Azriel Louis. *The Lost Generation: Children in the Holocaust*. New York: Pilgrim Press, 1982.

Friedemann, Pavel. "The Butterfly." In *I Never Saw Another Butterfly: Children's Drawings and Poems from Terezín Concentration Camp 1942–44*, edited by Hana Volavkova, 39. New York: Schocken Books, 1993.

Glazer, Hilda R. "Children and Play in the Holocaust: Friedl Dicker-Brandeis—Heroic Child Therapist." *Journal of Humanistic Counseling, Education & Development* 37, no. 4 (June 1999): 194–200.

Green, Gerald. *The Artists of Terezín*. New York: Hawthorn Books, 1969.

Heberer, Patricia. *Children During the Holocaust*. Lanham, MD: Rowman & Littlefield, 2015.

Horowitz, Sara R. "Kaddish—: The Final Frontier." *Studies in American Jewish Literature* 29, no. 1 (2010): 49–67.

Hurwitz, Al. "Friedl Dicker-Brandeis: The Art Educator as Hero." In *Seeing through "Paradise": Artist and the Terezín Concentration Camp*, ed. Massachusetts College of Art. Boston: Massachusetts College of Art, 1991.

Justman, Zuzana. "My Terezín Diary." *The New Yorker*, September 9, 2019, https://www.newyorker.com/magazine/2019/09/16/my-terezin-diary.

Kramer, Aaron. "Creative Defiance in a Death-Camp." *Journal of Humanistic Psychology* 38, no. 1 (Winter 1998): 12–25.

Leshnoff, Susan K. "Friedl Dicker-Brandeis, Art of Holocaust Children, and the Progressive Movement in Education." *Visual Arts Research* 32, no. 1 (2006): 92–100.

Levi, Primo. *Survival in Auschwitz, The Nazi Assault on Humanity*. First Collier books edition. New York: Collier, 1961.

Makarova, Elena. *From Bauhaus to Terezín: Friedl Dicker-Brandeis and Her Pupils*. Jerusalem, Israel: Holocaust Martyrs' and Heroes' Remembrance Authority, The Art Museum, 1990.

"Nazi Conspiracy and Aggression Volume 1 Chapter XII—The Persecution of the Jews." Avalon Project: Nazi Conspiracy and Aggression—Volume 1 Chapter XII—The Persecution of the Jews. https://avalon.law.yale.edu/imt/chap_12.asp.

"Nazi Conspiracy and Aggression Volume 2 Chapter XVI Part 2." Avalon Project: Nazi Conspiracy and Aggression—Volume 2 Chapter XVI Part 2. http://avalon.law.yale.edu/imt/chap16_part02.asp.

Nomberg-Przytyk, Sara. *Auschwitz: True Tales from a Grotesque Land*. Translated by Roslyn Hirsch, David Hirsch, and Elie Pfefferkorn. Chapel Hill, NC: University of North Carolina Press, 1985.

Ornstein, Anna. "Artistic Creativity and the Healing Process." *Psychoanalytic Inquiry* 26, no. 3 (June 2006): 386–406.

P., Edith. "Holocaust Testimony (HVT-107)." Fortunoff Video Archive for Holocaust Testimonies, Yale University Library 1996. http://www.library.yale.edu/testimonies/.

Reiter, Andrea Ilse Maria. *Children of the Holocaust*. London: Vallentine Mitchell, 2006.

Teddy. "At Terezín," In *I Never Saw Another Butterfly: Children's Drawings and Poems from Terezín Concentration Camp 1942–44*, edited by Hana Volavkova, 3. New York: Schocken Books, 1993.

Schonfield, Jeremy. *Undercurrents of Jewish Prayer*. Oxford: Littman Library of Jewish Civilization, 2008.

Smith, Philip. *Reading Art Spiegelman*. New York: Routledge, 2016.

Thomson, Ruth. *Terezín: Voices from the Holocaust*. Somerville, MA: Candlewick Press, 2013.

Volavkova, Hana. *I Never Saw Another Butterfly: Children's Drawings and Poems from Terezín Concentration Camp 1942–44*. New York: Schocken Books, 1993.

Weisman, Karen A. *The Oxford Handbook of the Elegy*. Oxford: Oxford University Press, 2012.

Wiesel, Elie, *Night*. 1st ed. Translated by Marion Wiesel. New York: Hill and Wang, 2006.

Wieseltier, Leon. *Kaddish*. New York: Alfred A. Knopf, 1998.

Part 3
Dictatorships

Chapter 7

Communism for Children

Fiction Mediation and Representations of Past Wrongdoings

Simona Mitroiu

The Communist regimes scarred the history of both Central-Eastern Europe and Russia, affecting millions of people's lives. The Soviet system in Russia and the Communist regimes in Central-Eastern Europe limited their citizens' rights and freedom; the abuses ranged from starvation, imprisonment, and killing of those who opposed intellectual censorship and reshaped family units.[1] Nevertheless, the last decade of the Communist regimes in Central-Eastern Europe was marked by the regimes' loosening grip on power.[2] This chapter seeks to engage with two representations of Communist regimes in international children's literature, aiming to provide an overview of the literary mechanisms used to address the trauma and the atrocities of the past and the experience of everyday life during under Communist regimes. In doing so, I seek to question the capacity of children's literature to mediate and remediate past wrongdoings and to enable a memory discourse shaped for young readers. Second, the chapter explores the relation between adult intervention and children's capacity to apprehend social reality with or without adult guidance. Discussing the adaptation of the language to the readers' profile, this chapter explores two different cases: the graphic novel *Marzi: A Memoir* by the Polish author Marzena Sowa, translated into English in 2011, and the novel *Breaking Stalin's Nose* (2011) by the Russian émigré author Eugene Yelchin. The two novels analyzed here focus on different phases of the authoritarian regimes' development and on different regional settings, with narratives targeting both Stalin's repression and the resistance movements.

Dealing with the Past in Children's Literature

Different instruments, policies, and actions have been used in exploring and dealing with the Communist past in Central and Eastern Europe, ranging from lustration and transitional justice to public commemorations of the victims and elaborated areas of research and publishing of the victims' testimonials.[3] However, the borderlines between past wrongdoings and the post-Soviet framework proved difficult to define. Alexander Etkind writes that by historical standards, the memory of the "Soviet catastrophe" is "fresh," "conflating subject and object in a stereotypically Russian manner," and that without lists of victims and lists of executioners, without public apologies, and without adequate museums and monuments, no consensus of what occurred can be reached.[4]

Literature has a significant role in the process of coming to terms with the past at the testimonial level—autobiographies and memoirs that describe past events and their effects on the personal and social structure—and by means of the literary configuration and reconfiguration of the past, seen as mediation mechanisms of an abusive past.[5] This chapter engages with two different forms of atrocity remediated in the children's literature: crimes against humanity and war crimes (specifically the Katyn massacre). The physical and mental violence repeatedly practiced by the Soviet regimes in Russia and Eastern Europe against their citizens to instill terror and gain control is defined by its large-scale, predetermined character and its capacity to affect the core dignity of human beings. Jay David Bolter and Richard Grusin define remediation as a movement during which the content of one medium is converted into another.[6] In the process of remembering, based on the mediation and remediation power of literary expression, writers make the content of past events visible to the readers. The result is a memory discourse adapted to the readers' level of understanding. Children's literature remediates atrocities by developing narratives that gradually introduce the reader to shocking events from the past. Hamida Bosmajian describes children's literature as "a medium that spares both the author and the child reader as the official text of the story sublimates and disguises a personally or socially complicated subtext," pointing out the problematic nature of this "protective censoring and intentional limiting of the reader's understanding."⁷ To address the social function of children's literature is to discuss the educational aspect and the creators' aim to teach others about historical realities and traumas. Fiction and literary narratives may be seen in this case as complementary to historical studies, rendering historical facts more accessible and increasing the empathic approach of past events and personal histories. Adult intervention is considered in this case not only in direct relationship with the accessibility of the historical information included in the fictional narratives that can leave "productive gaps," thus impelling the children to find out more under the adult guidance, but also in terms of the adult authors' intervention in their narratives, grounding the historical facts and, in some cases, mainly in autobiographical narratives, revealing the author's reassessment of the past events.⁸

Children's literature was used as a political tool by the Soviet regimes, shaping the ways in which young people understood the world and molding their ideals and opinions. Marja Sorvari argues that the utopian project of building a new society and new humans directed the Soviet system's attention toward children, whom they regarded as future Soviet model citizens. Larissa Rudova describes the privileged position occupied by children's literature in the Soviet Union as "one of the important assets in forming Soviet identity."⁹ The Stalinist child-hero was one of the most prominent features of the Soviet literature: "Children's literature was a prime field for expounding this concept and produced a great number of positive heroes whose examples Soviet children were expected to emulate."¹⁰ Rudova argues that after Stalin's death, the model of heroic-child started to fade away in favor of more "believable characters growing up in a non-heroic social environment," and that previous action topics dominated by heroism and sacrifice were replaced by questions related to everyday life, school, and human relationships.¹¹ The collapse of the former Soviet Union and of the Communist regimes in Central-Eastern Europe as well as the subsequent social and political changes reshaped the ideals and typologies used by children's literature. Themes and genres that were popular during different stages of the Communist regimes lost their influence or were completely abandoned or renewed.¹² On the other hand, as Etkind points out, in contemporary Russia the topic of Russian memory of the Soviet terror was not fully addressed: "there is no consensus on the crucial issues of historical memory."¹³ Consequently, many researchers who focus on children's literature and education indicate the visible intergenerational gap and the lack of knowledge of the Soviet period.¹⁴

Novels such as *Breaking Stalin's Nose*, or *Marzi: A Memoir* render accessible to children and young readers the major events and the everyday life during Communist regimes in Russia and Central-Eastern Europe. They provide significant insights into common people's lives, revealing the structures of everyday existence under the Communist regimes: the duplicity of life and public discourse, the loss of privacy and individual independence, the destruction of social bonds, the impact that the state had on the children's education. Blending personal and social trauma, they mediate historical accounts of atrocity.

Beyond Formal Education: *Breaking Stalin's Nose*

Breaking Stalin's Nose is a novel written by the Russian émigré author Eugene Yelchin, who drew from his childhood experiences and knowledge of people's lives during the Stalinist dictatorial regime. Marek Oziewicz makes a compelling analysis of this novel as representative of "Bloodlands fiction," defined as young adult historical fiction engaging with the suppressed memory of the Soviet atrocities. The term "Bloodlands" is used to define the Eastern European population affected by both Nazi and Soviet regimes. His analysis focuses on collective and historical trauma caused by the Stalinist regime atrocities.[15] Following Oziewicz's analysis, in this section I argue that the author uses the intricate connections between personal and social traumas to gradually reveal the impact of the Soviet regime on the Russian society and individual lives.

Yelchin uses black-and-white illustrations alongside the prose narrative.[16] The adult intervention is visible as an educational act in the form of the author's note at the end of the novel, which tells the story of Yelchin's personal encounter with a Soviet secret policeman who tried to recruit him as an informer. Through this encounter, he offers glimpses of his life under the Soviet regime. The author provides brief information about Stalin's absolute power and the terror inflicted on citizens, making further references to the current reality of those persecuted for their ideas. Another historical intervention used to situate the story in life during the Soviet regime is that of the short explanatory notes about Sasha's town and personal life. These offer some background for the main lines of the story. They include interstitial notes on the Kremlin, communal apartments, awards, secret police, Pioneer ceremony, informers, and Lubyanka. These explanatory notes maintain the fictional narrative lines, mixing the characters' stories with the realities of life under Soviet rule, yet they firmly ground the novel's historical basis.

The novel follows the young boy Sasha—initially a devoted young Communist in Stalinist Russia—and his disillusionment with the Soviet regime. He discovers the terror, lies, and abuses of those in power and the devastating effects their actions have on the common people, including Sasha's family. At the beginning of the text, Sasha's dream is to be accepted in the Young Soviet Pioneers' organization that turns its young members into Soviet citizens. He is trained in the "Stalinist spirit," always "to be vigilant," in a permanent state of observation to report any suspicious behavior. His father works for the secret police, the State security, located in Lubyanka Square, "to unmask the disguised enemies infiltrating our borders."[17] Sasha's father is arrested following a report made by one of their neighbors. The neighbor, it transpires, made the report because he wanted a bigger room for his family. The neighbor collects his reward, leaving Sasha without a place to live. A simple denouncement was sufficient for an arrest and incarceration without trial. Sasha's world is completely shaken by the arrest. His father turns from the Soviet hero into an "enemy of the people."

The arrest triggers a series of events that determine Sasha's direct contact with both the Soviet ideology and his family tragedy. What follows is a complex journey of self-discovery dominated by his father's last words, which describe his philosophy of surviving in Soviet times: "It's more important to join the Pioneer than to have a father."[18] All the novel's encounters and events are subsumed to this forced dichotomy: family and relatives—the level of individuality and privacy, and the Soviet regime and the reign of the equal, anonymous, and obedient "we." Sasha's aunt Larisa and her family refuse to have anything to do with him following the event. In the eyes of the regime, Sasha also became, by association, an enemy of the people. Sasha is subsequently involved in a series of events that tear up his previously known world and its stability. His experiences mirror the brutal interventions of the regime at the social level. His father promised to attend the Young Pioneer ceremony as a guest of honor, and Sasha innocently hopes to see him. When he arrives at school, he has no doubt that he will become a Pioneer. While imagining different encounters with Stalin, Sasha's pride of becoming a Pioneer is mixed with a feeling of justice, and he imagines Stalin's fury and rage when he finds out about the injustice suffered by his father.[19] When handling the banner used for the Pioneer ceremony—an activity invested with great honor—Sasha chips the nose of the Stalin statue from the school hallway. Scared by his mistake, he hopes that no one saw him and avoids confessing his act, sure that his place in the Pioneer organization will be lost for good. Trying to avoid the consequences of his own actions and his father's arrest, Sasha also learns more about the stories of the other two boys, Borka Finkelstein and Vovka Sobakin, and slowly he abandons his old beliefs and in the end refuses to collaborate with the regime.

Sasha does not find out about the regime's abuses and terror from adults. Those who introduce him to the regime's cruelty are his peers who share their stories. Confronted with their experiences, Sasha is also able to look into his own personal tragedy: the loss of his mother and his father's role in denouncing his own wife. The mother figure first appears when Sasha and his father rehearse for the Pioneer ceremony; seeing his boy wearing the red scarf, the father tells him that his mother would be proud of him. Later, without parents to look after him, Sasha becomes the property of the state, doomed to the orphanage. This is the second instance when the mother figure is brought forward; as with his father's arrest, his world is beginning to fall apart. His Soviet beliefs gradually are being crushed, in the same way his mother's story is being shaped. His relatives' rejection and the night spent in the building basements bring to the surface memories of the last time he visited his aunt, while the image of his mother provides more information about her fate: "Dad dropped me off and said he would be taking Mom to the hospital because she was ill. I stayed in Aunt Larisa's room for two days. I didn't even go to school. When Dad came back, he said Mom had died at the hospital. I started crying, and Aunt Larisa hugged me and said to my dad, 'You look guilty, not sad.' He didn't say anything, just took me home."[20]

The class preparation for the Pioneer gathering, his peers' established relationships, the teacher's interactions and manipulative tactics, and the children's desire to become Pioneers and fit in the newly built Soviet society are all elements that bring together personal and social traumas and weave the narrative structure of the three children's lives. The reader meets both boys at the same time: Borka Finkelstein, the passionate "four-eyed" reader who is bullied by the other students, and Vovka Sobakin, the disobedient former top pupil who lost his preferential status. The other students are aware that Borka is the only Jew in his class, that his parents were arrested, and that he lives with his relatives. Although Sasha knows that his "enemy of the people" label is caused by his parents' arrest, under the influence of peer pressure he hits Borka with a snowball. His discussion with Borka in front of the principal's office offers Sasha significant insights into his mother's fate: "'My mom was American. Don't tell anyone.' Borka reports

'And she was arrested and shot?' 'What do you mean? Of course not. She came from America to help us build Communism.' He nods. "They think all foreigners are spies.' "[21] Borka has lost his naivete; he regards the abusive regime as an entity that is separate from the Russian people. He confronts the tragedy of losing his parents, even if he refuses to believe that they are dead, and he imagines different ways to be reunited with them. Borka's personal tragedy helps reveal the story of Sasha's mother—the tragic core of Sasha's personal narrative. The text describes both the collective trauma of the Soviet regime and the personal trauma that surrounds the loss of the boy's parents. Their teacher also calls Vovka a criminal, punishing him by refusing to let him join the Pioneer organization. Any opposition was eradicated from a very early age; no independence and autonomy of mind would be accepted. Total obedience was the only way. For example, when Borka enters the classroom with his smashed eyeglasses, the teacher offers a comparative capitalism-communism lesson, insisting that in communism the majority is consulted for making a common decision. However, when he does not raise his hand to support the teacher's decision, she resorts to personal pressure ranging from bribes to threats: "We don't allow those who vote against the majority to handle the sacred banner," she asserts as she appeals to the boy's knowledge of Soviet rules. "You're a smart boy, Zaichik; you understand."[22]

The only child who witnesses Sasha partially destroying Stalin's statue, Vovka, is suspected of the crime. His supposed guilt is compounded by association: his father was also arrested and executed as an enemy of the people. The information makes Sasha remember the time when he and Vovka were friends, and he recalls his feelings about Vovka's father. The more he finds out about his schoolmates, the deeper he plunges into his personal narrative, questioning not only the Soviet regime, but also his beliefs about his parents' lives. In this complex process of gradually expanding his knowledge of the Soviet regime, Sasha slowly enters the realm of his personal trauma, introducing the child-reader to the social and personal traumas experienced by the characters. Borka willingly confesses to having chipped the nose off the statue because he believes that, if arrested, he will be reunited with his parents in prison. This makes Sasha think further about the regime's brutality and its errors, revealing both his fears and his struggle to preserve his old beliefs: "Is Four-Eyes scared? He must be scared, wondering what will happen inside. Nothing will happen, of course; he's just a kid."[23] Sasha further retreats into an imaginary world as State Security officers investigate the destruction of the statue and arrest small children. These events, along with Sasha's father's arrest, represent the absurdity of the regime and the child's incapacity to process his experiences. Even the nose asks Sasha to give up his father. The story of the nose mirrors the discussion with the State Security officer who tries to recruit him. The officer tells Sasha that he had great respect for Sasha's father, who acted as a true Communist, who engaged in a personal sacrifice two years earlier when he submitted a report denouncing the anti-Communist activity of a foreigner, namely his wife, Sasha's mother. Sasha's father's involvement is finally revealed, and the reader is left wondering what motivated this act. The tension is further amplified by an image of a big hand trying to bring the fragile child closer. Threatened with arrest, Sasha agrees to carry the banner at the Pioneer rally and to collaborate, but in the end, he runs away, refusing his father's advice to be a Pioneer. He decides to try to visit his father at the Lubyanka prison.

The author uses illustrations, which in many cases seem to be drawn from photographs, to strengthen the text's message and enable the young reader's contact with the characters' experiences. The first image is the visual pattern of the novel that describes the relationship between a young boy and the Soviet regime, a relationship shaped by admiration, idealistic subjugation, fear, disappointment, and finally opposition. From the very beginning, the reader faces the image of the fragile boy seen from behind, looking at the portrait of the all-mighty Comrade Stalin. The most striking feature of the image is the comparison between the tiny boy and Stalin's massive head and sharp gaze, capable of seeing the traitors and the enemies of the people. The illustrations intensify the reader's reactions during significant emotionally intense scenes, such as the father's arrest. Other illustrations depict images of Moscow covered in snow, the giant statue of Comrade Stalin supervising the city and its citizens, black cars coming at night to snatch someone, and officers' black boots climbing the stairs of a building. Imagining Stalin's quick intervention to save his father, Sasha goes to the Red Square, to Stalin's office in the Kremlin towers. His escape from the guards includes the image of a massive guard that occupies the entire page, revealing not only the small child's perspective, but also the entire nation in relation to the regime. At the end of the novel, the image of a child (seen from behind) walking through the snow toward the prison building—a building that fills the page—with its upper limit not visible enforces the idea of a social tragedy. The magnitude of the building is surpassed only by the line formed by the prisoners' relatives. Their representations are included in the last eight pages of the volume, women, men, children, young and old people together, waiting quietly in line, the snow falling on them. As he interacts with a woman who is trying to see her son and who in the end invites him to live with her, Sasha continues to recount the story of his mother dying in the hospital. The reader already knows that Sasha no longer believes this story, especially because he immediately tells another lie, namely that he has no relatives. Are these just lies or necessary omissions of the truth? And what is their motivation? Is this about keeping a shred of childhood naivete, which is, in fact, lost forever, or is it about survival in a world in which everyone is at risk and revealing personal history can be disastrous? Sasha's old world was destroyed during his journey; he refuses his father's advice, he refuses to embrace the Soviet way, but he acknowledges that he is only a child and needs adult protection.

Worlds of Oppression: *Marzi: A Memoir*

The second work to be analyzed, *Marzi: A Memoir*, is written by Marzena Sowa, with art by Sylvain Savoia, and is one of a small number of works that deal with the memories of Communist regimes in Central-Eastern Europe from a child's perspective.[24] Marja Sorvari argues that, based on the Soviet ideology, the "preferred model for children was a politically conscious male child of proletarian origins, whereas femininity was associated with a 'backward' attachment to the cultural past (religion, home, private relationships)."[25] The feminine figures, particularly girls, occupied a marginal place in the Communist society and consequently in children's literature. Marzena Sowa and Sylvain Savoia offer through *Marzi* a visual narrative of everyday life in Communist Poland using a small girl's perspective and interactions with the Communist world. This graphic novel is characterized by the combination of "powerful written words" and "powerful drawn images" resulting in a "hypnotic form of poetry" that requires the reader's attention as much and as long as she/he wishes.[26] It is described by Hillary Chute as being not only about events but also, "explicitly, about *how* we frame them," as the narrative "punctuated by pause or absence" is constructed by the author based on her memories.[27] *Marzi* is in fact the story of Marzena Sowa (Marzi in the story), born in Poland in 1979, who spent her childhood during a decade of communism. The novel was labeled as "autographics" because of "the specific conjunctions of visual and verbal text [. . .] as well as the subject positions that narrators negotiate in and through comics [. . .]"[28] *Marzi* reveals the social trauma of living under the Communist regime and the personal trauma caused by a dysfunctional mother-daughter relationship.

The introduction written by Marzena Sowa presents the author's process of self-exploration and revelation, offering young readers information about personal experiences and the past's long-term effects on one's individual trajectory:

> In my life, I've always been a fugitive. If I don't like something, I leave. [. . .] I trample my past deliberately. [. . .] The Poland of my childhood found itself under the communist regime [. . .] Without choosing it, I was a witness to all these [. . .] A mute and insignificant witness perhaps. Children don't count for much. Like fish, they don't have voices. This is the motto I was raised with.[29]

The educational side is revealed by the author in an attempt to make others witnesses her own and ordinary Polish people's story, to render visible aspects of life once left unnoticed, namely a little girl's experiences of Communist rule. Marzi is a little girl who spent her childhood years in communist Poland, witnessing the political and social events and their effects on her family. Her father works in a factory and joins the workers' protests against the Communist regime. Her mother's behavior mirrors the regime's authoritarian power; her main expression of love is limited to providing food and other essentials for raising a well-behaved child, without assessing and supporting Marzi's emotional needs. Marzi narrates her childhood joys and games, everyday interactions, family relations and activities, together with her feelings of anxiety, which result from the problematic mother-daughter relationship in the larger context of the Communist regime and its pressure. The narrative reveals interconnected layers: the pervasive influence of the Communist regime, the privations of everyday life in Communist Poland, and the adults' suffocating dominance and incapacity to acknowledge their children's' anxieties and fears.

The text is written from the small girl's perspective, and the images are sketched using the same approach, revealing the world of adults suffocated by the misery of everyday life. The food shortages, but also her personal repulsion for food, occupy a significant place in Marzi's narrative. Her father stands in line all night to buy meat (in winter, snow, and cold). The child (and especially the adult who remembers the past and reframes past events) is well aware of the adults' struggle to provide for their families: "Just a little something to feed their families. A bit of sugar to sweeten their lives. To forget the stress of living in this country"; "The shelves are almost always empty. Except for the jars of mustard and vinegar, they're always there!"; "It's surprising how a sausage can give life meaning."[30] The state of suffocation is transferred from the adult world to that of the child, and it is caused not only by the social and political events, but also by the parents' low emotional investment in their children's education and knowledge of the Communist system. The two worlds are clearly separated by firm boundaries. Regarding their children, the parents' main concern is their material existence: feeding them and keeping them safe. This results not only in the children's "invisibility" invoked by Marzi—as her problems were considered small and insignificant compared with her parents' daily struggles—but also in their "vulnerability" in facing the social trauma caused by the Communist regime. This graphic novel repeatedly emphasizes the small, suffocating place occupied by a child in an adult's world. Extremely relevant in this respect are the images of the child who looks up at adults and sees only their nostrils, and those of Marzi riding in the back seat between old people who squash her little body, or between crates of potatoes.[31]

Marzi approaches social and political life by reference to imposed collective activities, such as the parade on the first of May. These celebrations required everybody's presence (even the children's) and demand general duplicity and false joy:

> Everyone has to be there. No one says so openly, but if you don't go, you could suffer consequences at your job. The authorities actively scrutinize everyone's behavior, even the children's. [. . .] We traverse the city . . . for several hours, singing and shouting loudly how much we love socialism and our work on this day, we have to be happy.[32]

Marzi explores childhood joys, toys, and common playtime in detail in terms of games and activities, relationships with peers, depicting a complex world where children interact with each other, finding reasons for happiness, but also revealing their parents' refusal to discuss social or political issues with their children. The children's lack of preparedness for the reality of the Communist regime is visible whenever a political event surpasses their limited level of knowledge. Confronted with social and political events, Marzi feels completely lost, unable to understand what is really happening; the adults' world seems impossible to penetrate. When the Workers' Rebellion starts, with her father as one of the active members, the events that follow are terrifying for a child whose knowledge of the social and political context is very limited: "In the kitchen, my mom is praying. I hear her murmuring the rosary. [. . .] why is she saying the rosary now? It's long and she never says it at home!"[33] Marzi has trouble understanding what is happening, while the absence of her father and the fear of not seeing him again become a personal tragedy. The political events that motivate her father's absence gradually reveal Marzi's personal trauma caused by the problematic relationship with her mother. Her father pays great attention to her emotions and actively invests in their relationship. His absence is the key element in the author's in-depth exploration of the daughter-mother relationship—and the resulting feelings of sadness and anxiety of the child. Marzi's childhood world is consumed not only by the economic and social pressure imposed by the Communist regime, but also by the family relationships that fail to offer her an emotionally secure environment. Her mother constructed a world where her only daughter felt insignificant and unworthy. The author's plunge in the memories of the past culminates with the scary and traumatic moment when, after Marzi refused to eat all the food on her plate, her mother physically restrained her and forced food into her throat. The text combines the little girl's fear and low self-esteem with the author adult's troubling self-reference.[34] Themes of emotional trauma mark the narration and shadow Marzi's account of Polish society under the Communist regime, also revealing the role of adults in mediating the understanding of social and political factors. Marzi only perceives fragments of the Polish people's struggle with the regime, and these pieces of information aggravate her efforts in dealing with what she senses as an authoritarian and emotionally indifferent mother.

On the political level, the author provides some general textual information regarding the resistance in Poland (Rezystor). However, for the reader, the most striking and compelling arguments are those appealing to Marzi's experience: the silent protest of not watching TV and turning off the lights in the evening, or putting a lit candle in the window, as the priest told them to: "It's very beautiful to see so many windows lit up by these tiny little lights."[35] The child worries, as she does not understand her life's context, and the adults consider her too little to be involved in their conversations or to discuss them with her: "Understanding what they mean requires a lot of effort. You'd need a special dictionary that would translate their worries, joys, and hysterics . . ."[36] The workers' protests continue in different stages, with pauses and attempts to return to a normal life, but Marzi's knowledge and understanding continue to remain limited, while her anxiety and fear are growing. To access the adults' world, the child decides to take her political and historical education into her own hands:

"To understand the world of adults, you have to do everything just like they do. I can't just put on dresses and my mom's high heels. I have to look at what they look at, listen to what they listen to, and read what they read."[37] Searching in the family library, Marzi—the unprepared child—faces the image of human atrocity—the Katyn massacre and its visual testimonial: "The book is chock-full of words that chill my blood: homicide, massacre, mass executions . . . there are photos of the people who have disappeared. And then the bodies that were found, or rather, their remains."[38] The historical information provided by the adult author is thus doubled by shocking images of skeletons wearing military uniforms and marks indicating the way they were killed: holes in their skulls, hands tied at the back. Marzi's understanding of the political events and of Soviet repression is doubled by the fear for her father's life: "I don't understand all of it. Frightened I put it back on the shelf, but its spine points at me to remind me what I've seen. [. . .] And my dad isn't home. [. . .] I'm imagining the worst possible scenarios in my head."[39] The image of atrocity forcibly enters the child's world, making Marzi more conscious of the perils associated with oppressive regimes. The reader also faces Marzi's apprehension of the historical events' brutality. The image of the father with his bike, surrounded by military figures in a forest, reproduces Marzi's greatest fear. Her angst continues, as she has no news about her father, and her mother seems to be overcome by the events or at least proves incapable of speaking to or reassuring her daughter about the current events and their effect on their lives: "What are they doing to him right now / I've already heard stories . . . so many people have been there . . . They club them, round them up, take them to the station, strip them, humiliate them . . ."[40] The joy of change and solidarity included in Marzi's narrative fades away when compared with the anxiety and insecurity she experienced at such an early age, even if the author is projecting her adult understanding onto her childhood experiences, taking into consideration the complexity of the social and political context: "The world of adults is beyond me. I'd like to be one so I would have a better grasp . . . But seeing them like this, powerless, exhausted, I tell myself it's beyond them too."[41]

Conclusion

Sasha and Marzi are depicted entering the world of a regime governed by terror and absurdity. They slowly grow to understand the regimes' crimes and their own personal traumas. Besides the complex blend between personal and social trauma, both novels speak about the children's vulnerable state of mind—the direct result of the adults' failure to guide and mediate the understanding of the authoritarian regimes. Through "productive gaps," children's literature can both surpass its inherent "sparing" nature, point to related interpretations and understandings, and introduce traumatic subjects without traumatizing the reader.[42] The child character mediates the understanding of the past and the encounter with atrocity. Sasha gradually perceives the brutal reality of the Soviet system and Marzi comes to apprehend, through literary and graphic mediated forms, the atrocity of war crimes. The knowledge of the past determines her position facing the events of her life. *Breaking Stalin's Nose* speaks to children about political manipulation resulting from the lack of access to information. Sasha believed in the reality of the Soviet system because this was the only level of knowledge accessible to him. This kind of protection from the adults' world is what made him vulnerable and left Marzi in the realm of anxiety and fear. The novel teaches children to get out of the system, to take a step backward, to fight in order to keep their minds free of prejudices and the manipulative strategies of ideologies. While thinking of the loss and privileges and the impact of being moved to the back of the classroom, Sasha reevaluates his place within the system: "From the back row, the classroom looks different. I'm here with other unreliables and I can see much better from here. Now I can see the whole room."[43] Sasha is not prepared to understand the world, yet he learns quickly, without any help from adults. The writer gives him unbelievable powers and keeps an optimistic tone by introducing at the end an adult figure who can offer him whatever material and emotional comforts he needs, what Adrienne Kertzer calls "our need for hope and happy endings."[44] Kenneth B. Kidd argues that the worst examples of addressing trauma in children's literature are "simplistic narratives of character empowerment adapted from self-help literature."[45] Yelchin avoids the simplification of the past by presenting different narratives, constructing a polyvocal narrative of the past where the happiness and optimism are rarely present. The novel avoids the trap of the "thematic of absolute evil and absolute innocence."[46] If *Marzi* clearly insists on the adults' role in changing the Communist system when the circumstances allowed them to fight in any way, Sasha's father's involvement in perpetuating the system and his role in the family tragedy remain to be discussed by the readers. For both children, the adults' knowledge and life experiences are to be further explored despite the fact that the two characters, along with the readers, enriched their life experiences through a journey that revealed the collective trauma, fear, and anxieties that deeply impacted their childhood worlds. The gradual understanding of the social and political context becomes a narrative strategy used by the authors to explore and present the main characters' acknowledgment of their personal traumas. The traumatic historical events are slowly introduced, and both authors use the exploration of personal trauma to gradually approach different aspects of atrocity: war crimes and repeatedly practiced terror and violence. The narrative strategies and visual triggers mediate the readers' grasp of the social and personal trauma. Nonetheless, the authors' projection over their texts stimulates readers' inquiries and discussions in confronting social and personal trauma.

Notes

1. Paul R. Gregory, *Terror by Quota: State Security from Lenin to Stalin (An Archival Study)* (New Haven: Yale University Press, 2009). See also Stephane Courtois, Nicolas Werth, Jean-Louis Panne, Andrzej Paczkowski, Karel Bartosek, and Jean-Louis Margolin, *The Black Book of Communism: Crimes, Terror, Repression* (Cambridge: Harvard University Press, 1999); Kevin McDermott and Matthew Stibbe, eds., *Stalinist Terror in Eastern Europe: Elite Purges and Mass Repression* (Manchester: Manchester University Press, 2010). See also Ben Fowkes, *Rise and Fall of Communism in Eastern Europe* (London: Palgrave Macmillan, 1995).

2. Matthew Stibbe and Kevin McDermott, eds., *Revolution and Resistance in Eastern Europe: Challenges to Communist Rule* (Oxford: Berg Publishers, 2006).

3. See, for example, Vladimir Tismăneanu and Bogdan C. Iacob, eds., *Remembrance, History and Justice: Coming to Terms with Traumatic Pasts in Democratic Societies* (Budapest: Central European University Press, 2015); Simona Mitroiu, ed., *Life Writing and the Politics of Memory in Eastern Europe* (New York: Palgrave Macmillan, 2015).

4. Alexander Etkin, "Stories of the Undead in the Land of the Unburied: Magical Historicism in Contemporary Russian Fiction," *Slavic Review* 68, no. 3 (Fall 2009): 634.

5. Astrid Erll and Ann Rigney, eds., *Mediation, Remediation, and the Dynamics of Cultural Memory* (Berlin: Walter de Gruyter, 2009).

6. Jay David Bolter and Richard Grusin, *Remediation: Understanding New Media* (Cambridge: MIT Press, 2000).

7. Hamida Bosmajian, *Sparing the Child Grief and the Unspeakable in Youth Literature about Nazism and the Holocaust* (New York: Routledge, 2002), 14.

8. Please see the introduction to the volumes.

9. Larissa Rudova, "'Favorite Bastard': The Children's 'Detektiv' in Post-Soviet Russia," *Slavic and East European Journal* 49, no. 2 (2005): 283.

10. Rudova, "Favorite Bastard," 289.
11. Rudova, "Favorite Bastard," 290.
12. Mariia Cherniak, "Children and Childhood as a Sociocultural Phenomenon: Reflections on Reading the Latest Twenty-First Century Prose," *Russian Studies in Literature* 52, no. 2 (2016): 115.
13. Etkin, "Stories of the Undead," 633.
14. Cherniak, "Children and Childhood."
15. Marek Oziewicz, "Bloodlands Fiction: Cultural Trauma Politics and the Memory of Soviet Atrocities in Breaking Stalin's Nose, A Winter's Day in 1939 and Between Shades of Gray," *International Research in Children's Literature* 9, no. 2 (2016): 149.
16. Eugene Yelchin, *Breaking Stalin's Nose* (New York: Square Fish, 2011).
17. Yelchin, *Breaking*, 10.
18. Yelchin, *Breaking*, 26.
19. Yelchin, *Breaking*, 73.
20. Yelchin, *Breaking*, 43–44.
21. Yelchin, *Breaking*, 63.
22. Yelchin, *Breaking*, 60.
23. Yelchin, *Breaking*, 93.
24. Marzena Sowa and Sylvain Savoia, *Marzi: A Memoir*, trans. Anjali Singh (New York: Vertigo, 2011).
25. Sorvari, "Narrating Childhood," 58–59.
26. Stephen E. Tabachnick, ed., *The Cambridge Companion to the Graphic Novel* (Cambridge: Cambridge University Press, 2017), 3.
27. Hillary L. Chute, *Graphic Women: Life Narrative and Contemporary Comics* (New York: Columbia University Press, 2010), 2, 4.
28. Gillian Whitlock, "Autographics: The Seeing 'I' of the Comics,'" *MFS Modern Fiction Studies* 52, no. 4 (2006): 966.
29. Sowa, *Marzi*, 1.
30. Sowa, *Marzi*, 15, 16, 93.
31. Sowa, *Marzi*, 36.
32. Sowa, *Marzi*, 111.
33. Sowa, *Marzi*, 126.
34. Sowa, *Marzi*, 160.
35. Sowa, *Marzi*, 137.
36. Sowa, *Marzi*, 139.
37. Sowa, *Marzi*, 145.
38. A series of mass execution in 1940 of the Polish military officers conducted by NKVD and approved by Joseph Stalin. Sowa, Savoia, *Marzi*, 146.
39. Sowa, *Marzi*, 146–47.
40. Sowa, *Marzi*, 149. More on Solidarity in Andrzej Paczkowski, "Twenty-Five Years 'After'—the Ambivalence of Settling Accounts with Communism: The Polish

Case," in *Remembrance, History and Justice: Coming to Terms with Traumatic Pasts in Democratic Societies*, ed. Vladimir Tismăneanu and Bogdan C. Iacob (Budapest: Central European University Press, 2015), 239–55.

41. Sowa, *Marzi*, 184.

42. Kenneth B. Kidd, *Freud in Oz: At the Intersection of Psychoanalysis and Children's Literature* (Minneapolis: University of Minnesota Press, 2011).

43. Yelchin, *Breaking*, 122.

44. Adrienne Kertzer, *My Mother's Voice. Children, Literature, and the Holocaust* (Ontario: Broadview Press, 2002), 75.

45. Kidd, *Freud in Oz*, 185.

46. Kenneth B. Kidd, "'A' is for Auschwitz: Psychoanalysis, Trauma Theory, and the Children's Literature of Atrocity," *Children's Literature* 33 (2005): 140.

Works Cited

Bolter, Jay David, and Richard Grusin. *Remediation: Understanding New Media*. Cambridge: MIT Press, 2000.

Bosmajian, Hamida. *Sparing the Child: Grief and the Unspeakable in Youth Literature about Nazism and the Holocaust*. New York: Routledge, 2002.

Cherniak, Mariia. "Children and Childhood as a Sociocultural Phenomenon: Reflections on Reading the Latest Twenty-First Century Prose." *Russian Studies in Literature* 52, no. 2 (2016): 114–29.

Chute, Hillary L. *Graphic Women: Life Narrative and Contemporary Comics*. New York: Columbia University Press, 2010.

Courtois, Stephane, Nicolas Werth, Jean-Louis Panne, Andrzej Paczkowski, Karel Bartosek, and Jean-Louis Margolin. *The Black Book of Communism: Crimes, Terror, Repression*. Cambridge: Harvard University Press, 1999.

Erll, Astrid, and Ann Rigney, eds. *Mediation, Remediation, and the Dynamics of Cultural Memory*. Berlin: Walter de Gruyter, 2009.

Etkin, Alexander. "Stories of the Undead in the Land of the Unburied: Magical Historicism in Contemporary Russian Fiction." *Slavic Review* 68, no. 3 (Fall 2009): 631–58.

Fowkes, Ben. *Rise and Fall of Communism in Eastern Europe*. London: Palgrave Macmillan, 1995.

Gregory, Paul R. *Terror by Quota: State Security from Lenin to Stalin (An Archival Study)*. New Haven: Yale University Press, 2009.

Kertzer, Adrienne. *My Mother's Voice: Children, Literature, and the Holocaust*. Ontario: Broadview Press, 2002.

Kidd, Kenneth B. "'A' is for Auschwitz: Psychoanalysis, Trauma Theory, and the Children's Literature of Atrocity." *Children's Literature* 33 (2005): 120–49.

Kidd, Kenneth B. *Freud in Oz: At the intersection of Psychoanalysis and Children's Literature*. Minneapolis: University of Minnesota Press, 2011.
McDermott, Kevin, and Matthew Stibbe, eds. *Stalinist Terror in Eastern Europe: Elite Purges and Mass Repression*. Manchester: Manchester University Press, 2010.
Oziewicz, Marek. "Bloodlands Fiction: Cultural Trauma Politics and the Memory of Soviet Atrocities in Breaking Stalin's Nose, A Winter's Day in 1939 and Between Shades of Gray." *International Research in Children's Literature* 9, no. 2 (2016): 146–61.
Paczkowski, Andrzej. "Twenty-Five Years 'After'—the Ambivalence of Settling Accounts with Communism: The Polish Case." In *Remembrance, History and Justice: Coming to Terms with Traumatic Pasts in Democratic Societies*, edited by Vladimir Tismăneanu and Bogdan C. Iacob, 239–55. Budapest: Central European University Press, 2015.
Rudova, Larissa. " 'Favorite Bastard': The Children's 'Detektiv' in Post-Soviet Russia." *The Slavic and East European Journal* 49, no. 2 (2005): 282–303.
Sowa, Marzena, and Sylvain Savoia, *Marzi: A Memoir*. Translated by Anjali Singh. New York: Vertigo, 2011.
Stibbe, Matthew, and Kevin McDermott, eds. *Revolution and Resistance in Eastern Europe: Challenges to Communist Rule*. Oxford: Berg Publishers, 2006.
Tabachnick, Stephen E., ed. *The Cambridge Companion to the Graphic Novel*. Cambridge: Cambridge University Press, 2017.
Tismăneanu, Vladimir, and Bogdan C. Iacob, eds. *Remembrance, History and Justice: Coming to Terms with Traumatic Pasts in Democratic Societies*. Budapest: Central European University Press, 2015.
Whitlock, Gillian. "Autographics: The Seeing 'I' of the Comics." *MFS Modern Fiction Studies* 52, no. 4 (2006): 965–79.
Yelchin, Eugene. *Breaking Stalin's Nose*. New York: Square Fish, 2011.

Chapter 8

The Uses of Allegory to Tell Youth Disappearance and Mortality under Spain's Dictatorship in Ana María Matute's 1956 *Los niños tontos* (*The Foolish Children*)

Lora L. Looney

The historical memory of Spain's Civil War (1936–39) and its postwar dictatorship (1939–75) is marked by silence and amnesia due to censorship during Franco's government and to the constitutional pact of amnesty that informed Spain's transition to democracy after 1975. In the twenty-first century, groups and individuals have worked toward recovering Spain's past. The 2007 Law of Historical Memory supports this work and offers certain retributions and reparations to the victims of the dictatorship without modifying the law of amnesty. Discoveries about youths' lives under the totalitarian rule have been critical; they show the contradiction between the national puericulture, which generated an image of morally and physically robust minors, and the horrors of juvenile life under state custody. Ana María Matute's 1956 collection of twenty-one short stories, *The Foolish Children*, is an early indicator through fictional representations of atrocity, youth disappearance, and mortality under Franco's regime.[1]

The central atrocity addressed in this chapter is the systematic extermination and forced reidentification of Spanish youth. Following Spain's civil conflict, Franco waged war on his own people by targeting the group that lost the war. To punish the Republicans, their "degenerate" offspring were forcibly institutionalized to be "regenerated," and infants born to Republican women were forcibly adopted by Nationalist families. The denial of this centralized, genocidal practice, during and after its implementation in Spain, is essential to my understanding of atrocity because what makes this loss catastrophic is "that it [. . .] was] denied in the very moment when it happen[ed]."[2] The means of denying the atrocities to which these young people were subjected included regime propaganda depicting fallaciously positive conditions in the reformatories where youth were housed, the silence of the Catholic clergy administering the reeducation homes, and the lack of prosecution of those responsible for this atrocity after 1975.

The Foolish Children contains twenty-one short stories, nineteen of which are brief in length, and fifteen of which use titles that convey the identity of the child protagonist, but never with a given name. Four of the other six titles, "Coal Dust, "The Fire," "The Tree," and "Sea," refer to natural phenomena; and two titles, "The Merry-Go-Round" and "The Pastry Shop Window," denote man-made structures.[3] The stories' content provides detailed settings and concise descriptions of the juvenile main characters as well as animals that are characters. Adults are largely absent. The work's basic plotlines correspond to readers' expectations for allegory through representations of a conflict or journey. In fact, the stories read as fables and may be didactic; however, not a single tale includes an explicit moral lesson. That the protagonist vanishes or dies is inferred through ambiguous endings (or, in three tales, beginnings). These open endings engage us in active interpretation, as does the text's construction itself, which uses simple language to create fantastic imagery to merge real and unreal worlds. While the titles, nameless protagonists, and open endings universalize the theme of youth disappearance and death in the book, each story makes highly concrete through metonymic devices this juvenile experience of atrocity.

While each story concretely individualizes the experience of atrocity, and while the representation of this atrocity is figurative, the effect, through the accumulation of minute details, is a coherent picture of genocide of youth under Spain's totalitarian puericulture. Moreover, *The Foolish Children* represents the genocidal practices inflicted on youth, and their damaging effects, in Matute's decision to not name a single character in her book. This namelessness has three impacts: 1) universalized, and not anonymized, each nameless character stands in for the larger group; 2) the characters have no "official" Christian name or surname, suggesting that their identities were reassigned; 3) stripped of their original identity, the characters may have lost the voice to speak for themselves. In fact, the child protagonists seldom utter a word. In seven of the twenty-one stories, there is no human speech at all. To theorize using Judith Butler's philosophies on genocide and memory, if there are no identifiable faces, in this case names, this feature of Matute's book signals the failure of language to speak of the violence done to others.[4] Indeed, by not naming her characters, Matute does not repeat the genocide of reidentifying youth; rather, she composes allegorical stories that give the reader the opportunity to decode the atrocities inflicted on this group. Furthermore, through the process of filling the productive gaps left open by Matute, we may participate in reconstructing the identities of the speechless and nameless juvenile protagonists whose official identity has been lost. This reader participation does not reverse the genocide, but the act of identity reconstruction by the reader may serve to counter the denial of atrocity.

The Foolish Children as Allegory

A 1957 book review in *ABC*, Spain's national newspaper, calls the tales "pure metaphor" without delving into what they represent.[5] As I seek to demonstrate, Matute uses allegory to figuratively show the harm and neglect inflicted on children under Spain's dictatorship in the 1940s, a decade of severe postwar hardship worsened by the systematic, centralized repression and control of Spanish citizens, including minors. In her book, nature is an allegory for the rigid, unforgiving totalitarian state whose ideological goals were physical asceticism and obedience to the nation, church, and family. Rather than depict the regime itself, Matute paints nature as the authority: water drowns, fire burns, cold freezes, and hunger extinguishes the individual. Fifteen of the stories end with the protagonist vanished or dead. This literary focus on the child's body points to genocidal practices while allegorical devices, including the fable and the fairy tale, universalize the tragedies thereby providing access to them. In concert with her young protagonists who actively disobey nature, Matute counters the dictatorship by writing open-ended texts to invite the reader's participation in the construction of meaning. This reader participation directly resists the overt didacticism inherent in propaganda of the day which relied on allegorical strategies to inculcate minors in political ideology and Catholic religion. To depoliticize the past, Matute's figurative and nature-based representations of postwar Spain cloak the stories in ambiguity to universalize the human experience, and thereby remember the children lost.

Following the established norm that *The Foolish Children* was not written for juvenile readers, after Matute's death in 2012, two new scholarly editions have appeared inside Spain. Prior to her passing, however, Media

Vaca Libros of Valencia, Spain, published a newly illustrated edition for children in 2000 which is a school resource inside Spain. The inner flap of this book's cover reads, "This is not a book for children!"[6] In electronic correspondence with me, the publisher, Vicente Ferrer, related what Matute herself stated about readership of *The Foolish Children*, "the book is about children, not for children."[7] Interestingly, these words repeat what the text's second censor wrote upon approving the book for adult readers in 1956, "poems that, although they are about children, are not for children."[8] To explain that she does not consider foolish the child protagonists in her book, despite its title, Matute herself described *The Foolish Children* as an example of her worry about the damage done to childhood.[9]

Within my own research and teaching, I argue that Spain's postwar literary and cinematic canon, dating to today, is marked by numerous works featuring a juvenile protagonist. Like Matute's *The Foolish Children*, these works have two common qualities: they were made for mature audiences, and they do not glorify youth roles in war-torn and totalitarian Spain. In fact, these works may be apolitical: they provide a channel for adults to remember the past without entering into the ideological conflicts that defined the war itself. As I have argued elsewhere, in Spain's Civil War and postwar film canon, the juvenile protagonist is a ubiquitous means for accessing historical memory because the youth's subjective point of view may depoliticize the past.[10] Matute wrote a number of books on children for adults, some of which could be called memoirs. In a metafictional essay inside the 1963 story collection *El tiempo*, she characterizes the short story's many faces: picaresque, innocent, cruel, happy, or sad. Matute personifies the short story genre as a vagabond traveler who always enters and leaves town at night, making this conclusion about the genre's function to recover memory, "Constantly stealing away our feelings of nostalgia, with its abiding, vagabond heart."[11] I do not contend that Matute's writing politicizes this recovery process; nonetheless, *The Foolish Children* may recover a space for national grief. To achieve this end, *The Foolish Children* illustrates unforgivingly what happened to children, and textual lacunae engage us in ascribing meaning to the stark, narrative illustrations of atrocity. In this way, Matute's book may constitute an act of political condemnation, but, more significantly, *The Foolish Children* is an act of civil disobedience. It purposefully subverts the code of denial and silence by actively engaging the reader in decoding allegories.

With particular attention to the theme of disobedience in the context of atrocity, I propose to analyze twelve of the twenty-one stories in *The Foolish*

Children with a focus on the uses of allegory to relate what happened to children during Spain's dictatorship. To offer a condensed definition of allegory, it requires a narrative structure; relates a transformation of the protagonist, even if this transformation is cast as immobility; mirrors conflict in the outer world; and may aid or frustrate a sense of order. Where nouns tend to predominate, allegorical texts depend on the symbolic value of language. In *The Foolish Children*, there is a doubling effect to the representations of characters, personified animals, and natural forces that allude to the social hierarchies of the day. Mimetic realism may appear as a primary device for Matute's storytelling because the nouns themselves are straightforwardly understandable, but the contiguity of these symbolic elements produces a fantastic tale. As in children's literature, the great building up of abstract symbols, despite their individual concreteness, universalizes each story's ideas and the work's major theme of the loss of minors in *The Foolish Children*.[12]

The Civil War in "Oven Boy" and "The Fire"

Matute signals the Civil War and its aftermath as the central topic in "Oven Boy."[13] This story, which belongs to a subgroup that narrates peer cruelty in *The Foolish Children*, most openly allegorizes the fratricide of Spain's Civil War. A sibling becomes jealous of his baby brother and roasts him in the home's clay oven. For this heinous crime, the text offers no moral lesson. While the clay oven the protagonist lights is described as his "dear little oven," the victim of the murder is described as "a skinned rabbit."[14] This moral inversion of animate and inanimate objects, specifically the non-human reference to a baby brother as a dead, mutilated animal, captures how civil violence relies on processes of dehumanization. Furthermore, this tale's thematic underscoring of demonization of the other to justify atrocity represents the war the Spanish state waged against its citizens after the Nationals claimed victory on April 1, 1939.

To consolidate power through terror following Spain's Civil War, the nationalist government rounded up and imprisoned the defeated Republicans. Martial law retroactive to the date of the coup, July 17, 1936, justified the imprisonment of people who allegedly committed crimes against the state from this date until 1948 when the law was rescinded (in other words, the Second Republic was not the legitimate government from the perspective of the nationals who instigated the coup that started the Civil War).[15] Helen Graham estimates that, to be "reeducated," a million Spaniards were held in prisons, work camps, forced labor battalions, and reformatories during the first postwar decade.[16] Infants and children of all ages were imprisoned with their mothers, and women gave birth in prison.

One narrative strategy used to allegorize ideological conflict in *The Foolish Children* is the symmetrical layering of colors. In "The Fire," the whitewashed corner of a boy's house is the scene of tragedy. He takes his orange, yellow, blue, and red pencils and lights them on fire. The green shutters catch fire, and the boy perishes under a rain of hot ash. The boy's motive for this act of disobedience is the white wall blazing in the hot sun "slicing his vision like knife blades."[17] Here the color white is linked with the violence of the knife and may indicate the repressive indoctrination of Spain's government-sponsored charities, such as the white bread campaign. As early as April 1939, the nationals celebrated their victory by distributing white bread loaves in brown-paper wrapping lettered with Falangist propaganda in red and yellow. In one poster from the era, white bread promotes the image of a charitable regime with the slogan "Franco's Spain has arrived!" In this Fascist allegory, a defeated, burning town in the poster's background represents the Republicans whose contaminated, anti-Spain character Franco's pure, white bread is designed to redeem.[18]

To send a countermessage that the nation belongs to the country's youth, not its dictator, the longest yellow pencil in "The Fire," the predominant color of Spain's flag, ignites the building corner, and the boy vandalizes the white wall. Allegorically, this story may question Spain's nationalization of puericulture. The Social Aid (Auxilio Social), which had begun in 1937 as a rearguard charity charged with fighting hunger, cold, and misery, was officialized in May 1940 and created scores of pronatality, socioscientific, and psychomedical programs for mothers and children.[14] This nationalization of centers and services for children responded to the disaster of high miscarriage and infant mortality rates and the fear of unsupervised youth. The Falangist project of regenerating society by reeducating minors conflated medical, ideological, and Catholic-based spiritual approaches. As Louie Dean Valencia-García asserts, "under fascism, youth was a site where national redemption could occur."[19]

Disappearance and Death

The Foolish Children allegorizes the disappearance and death of minors under the dictatorship's reeducation efforts. The justification for the government's actions comes from Antonio Vallejo Nájera's *Eugenics of Hispanism and*

Regeneration of the Spanish Race, Abnormal Children and Adolescents and other writings whose premise was that moral degeneration was hereditary and environmental.[20] These writings formed the ideological campaign waged at "combating the degenerative propensity of girls and boys raised in Republican environments."[21] In short, "the health of the race required that children be separated from their "red" mothers."[22] This plays out in "Coal Dust," a palette of black and white color oppositions alluding to the characterization of Republicans as morally and therefore biologically degenerate, that is, "dirty," as promoted by Vallejo Nájera, in contrast to the moral purity of New Spain (symbolized by white bread, for example). In the tale, a working-class child's mouth is filled with black dust because she lives in the coal mines. Every day she opens the faucet to see the water rush into the stone basin. She hears the moon scratching the window above the sink one night. She imagines, "If I could only wash my face with the moon, and my teeth, and my eyes."[23] The story ends with her drowning in the washbasin. The harsh conditions of this girl's life overturn Spain's idealized portrait of children living under dictatorship. Climbing into the moonlight, reflected on the surface of the washbasin, to clean herself, which results in her drowning, may also point to the massive displacement of youth to reformatories in 1940s Spain.

Spain's puericulture, under the guise of protecting orphans, was expanded and consolidated by the Law of November 23, 1940, which gave the state custody of children whose nuclear family did not meet the "moral" standards to educate them. Enrolled in Social Aid, the residential institutions caring for the minors held, "with all pertinent legal effects, the role of legal custodian."[24] Angela Cenarro cites that 75 percent of spots in these residences were reserved for orphans of the Revolution and of the War.[25] In fact, the early mission of Social Aid was to inculcate the offspring of Republican families, dubbed "children of the war" (that is, not of the revolutionary, winning side) by combining social services with Falangist indoctrination. As Ricard Vinyes, Angela Cenarro, and Susana Bardavío Estevan show, the exclusionary practice of targeting minors branded as "Reds" (rojos) for punitive discipline such as food deprivation in order to reintegrate society was in force. According to Graham, "the ingrained mindset of state personnel" held that the children of Republicans needed to "expiate the 'sins of the fathers' [. . .] yet, at the same time, the children [themselves] were irrecuperable."[26]

By 1943, 12,000 children had been relocated to homes (Hogares).[27] Moreover, of the 32,000 minors evacuated from Spain by Republican families because of the war, 20,000 were repatriated because of the Second World

War. However, of the 12,000 remaining children who were still living abroad, many were repatriated by force through clandestine operations led by Spain's Foreign Affairs Office. Although we do not know how many were returnees, Vinyes asserts that 30,000 were registered under state custody between 1944 and 1955 in addition to the 12,000 already registered in 1943.[28] A typical day in a reformatory included meals, exercise, attendance at mass, prayer recitations, group singing of patriotic hymns, talks on hygiene and culture, and school lessons or manufacturing labor, depending on the location. Whether in oral or written form, the day's activities were couched in National-Catholic discourse to redirect Spain's future by molding the next generation.

Conflict between the juvenile protagonist and nature's forces mimics tension between the individual and the state to produce the theme of repression in *The Foolish Children*. As in the fable or fairy tale, the story of the protagonist who disobeys these forces relates what is taboo in the culture. In "The First Birthday That Never Arrived," a child turning one year old with a sand bag on each foot clumsily walks out the door to look at things silhouetted in a different cast of light.[29] Extending his arms towards the light, the scream of black swifts, like ink against the sky, punctures the cast of light, and the child escapes through the hole, missing his birthday. In this depiction of the sudden removal of a toddler, the golden sand inhibiting the child's movement is the Spanish dictatorship, and the birds robed in black depict the clergy running daily operations in the reformatories. The one-year-old defies authority by walking away despite the sand bags; however, the disappeared child at the story's ending reasserts that the protagonist does not act freely. In *The Foolish Children*, the young protagonists disobey nature's authority in taboo acts of resistance such as playing with fire, climbing into the sink, and leaving home unaccompanied. Nonetheless, these juvenile characters do not overcome authority's far-reaching, targeted power to repress.

The destructive effects of nature's four elements—water, earth, air, and fire—on the body allegorize this repression. Mouths, palates, and eyes are frequent symbols of juvenile atrocity. In "Coal Dust," the inside of the girl's open mouth is a "smoked chapel" (capillita ahumada); in "Thirst and the Boy," the main character's palate is compared to an empty fountain basin; in "The Fire," the boy's eyes are irritated by the glaring surface of a recently whitewashed building corner under the hot sun.[30] The three images make double reference to institutions (church, state, and prison) that threaten or destroy the protagonist's life in order to represent the experience of youth

The Uses of Allegory to Tell Youth Disappearance and Mortality / 187

disappearance and mortality. The criticism of Spain's postwar regime is provided by the outcome of the conflict between youth and nature: the disobedient child protagonist vanishes or dies.

Three tales relate journeys, rather than battles, and may depict transportation of youth to reformatories, forced adoption practices, or covert operations to repatriate children. The Law of December 4, 1941, granted the state the power to rename children whose parents were unlocalizable.[31] Put into practice, this policy disappeared children for the cause of reeducation. It also made possible the adopting out to Francoist families babies of imprisoned and executed mothers from the losing side, usually by sequestration. These genocidal practices have been documented by Vinyes and his co-researchers in the 2002 television documentary and book *The Lost Children of Francoism*.[32]

The journey of a boy who is yellow with illness and taken to the seaside for his health in "Sea" may show child disappearance as well as the powerlessness of adults to stop it. The "high and green" (alto y verde) sea appears to him as the inside of a snail whose echo draws him into the water. Drowning, he cannot hear the voices of his stricken family on the shore. The boy's yellow skin may denote the Spanish nation and the green sea its youth. Additionally, in this story and others from the collection, as I will explain, Matute uses the amassing of discrete nouns to represent atrocity in *The Foolish Children*. Here the title, "Sea," accumulates thirteen more times. As the density of nouns conveys, despite the presence of his family, the ocean's authority over the protagonist is too great. Overwhelmed by the force, the boy does not know its dangers. The doctor's orders to go to the sea may be a veiled allusion to Spain's quasimedical theories to justify the displacement and reeducation of children.

Through the repetition of the noun "thirst" fifteen times, "Thirst and the Boy" tells the displacement, loss, and protest of the main character. To summarize, every afternoon, the thirsty boy goes to the fountain with his bread and chocolate. One afternoon there is no water to drink. The ground near the fountain is dry like his palate. "What did they do with the fountain?" he asks.[33] The boy becomes pale from thirst and finally turns to ash. When the men drag away the fountain basin and water spurts up high from the ground, no one can shut up the voice that repeats every evening, all the way to the ocean, "Who took away the basin, the dry, empty mouth of my fountain?"[34] The character's disobedience is his voice because, as Gordon Teskey argues, "without voice, the body is meat."[35] In fact, this theorist reminds us that allegory's word derivation means to speak publicly or to harangue.[36] In the story, the boy's voice defies the birds sitting in the trees "moving their black pupils from side to side" because his protest "opens a space among trees and children who eat bread and chocolate."[37] A reference to the clergy, the birds cannot silence the boy. Like Matute, who herself repeats "thirst" to point out the deprivations young people endured under state custody, the protagonist individualizes his suffering by voicing it repeatedly.

Animal Allegory

The effect of atrocity in "The Little Black Boy with Blue Eyes" depends on the accumulation of sounds, nearly all related to grief.[38] This story begins with tragedy: "they discovered that the newborn was dumb because he was not crying."[39] They leave him in a basket attended only by a cat who tortures him, stealing his blue eyes and making him blind. One day the boy raises his arms and departs through the window. He says, "Where could my blue eyes be?,"[40] then sits down to wait. At this juncture, the protagonist's blue eyes are compared to the clash of water pitchers hitting each other, a train whistle, and the cold, all of which represent journeys of exile, detention, adoption, or repatriation. Two Roma figures with a bear that is abused by these women come upon the boy. María del Carmen Luengo Santaló and Aileen Dever have associated the bear and its punctured skin with the official symbol of Spain's Republican capital, Madrid, and its defeat with the bear's injuries.[41] Historically, this tale's suballegory refers to the tens of thousands of Republicans who fled Madrid for Valencia and Alicante, in the days before the capital fell to the Fascists, in hopes of evacuation via ships. Many refugees were not evacuated because the Nationals blockaded international ships from approaching the shore. An Indo-European group known for its nomadism, the Roma figures who abuse the bear may denote Spain's battered capital and the epic, fruitless journey of exile to the beaches of Alicante where 45,000 Republicans were rounded up and transported to detention centers.[42] Overall, these nomadic Roma characters reemphasize the massive displacement of Spain's citizens, and their skin color, which may be dark like the protagonist's, depicts these characters as the other, that is, those citizens who are forced into exile by virtue of their otherness.

After his encounter with the Roma women and the bear, the boy meets a stray, friendly dog that licks him. At this stage, the protagonist is severely weak from the journey. To relate his own decline to Spain's by using the colors of the flag, Matute imagines: "All the leaves fell from the trees, and instead of shadow, the boy was bathed in colors of red and gold."[43] When the boy dies, the dog cries and digs him a grave. Twin forget-me-nots bloom on the little black boy's gravesite to represent his lost eyes. In fact, twelve references to sound describe the protagonist's journey to find his eyes; crying is mentioned six times. Although the boy, who is likely deaf or mute, does not cry, the bear and the dog do cry and whine. This tale is a synecdoche of grief: the bear that stops dancing to the Roma women's tambourine to cry, the dog's tears that ring like small bells, and the dog's clawing of the ground as it buries the protagonist are sounds of mourning.

Butler addresses mourning to argue that the human body is socially vulnerable because it is at risk of violence by virtue of its exposure to others. Writing on violence and allegory, Teskey elucidates, "To be a subject is to be vulnerable at every moment to an inscrutable violence on which the power of the state depends utterly."[44] At its core, *The Foolish Children* is a work of naturalism because Matute is deeply concerned with harmful environmental impacts on the human subject. An overall strategy in the collection is the pervasive, meticulous attention to natural forces such as the temperature and time of day, the frost of daybreak, or the heat of the sun at noon, to cite a few examples, and the bodily effects of these conditions. On the whole, the telling of youth disappearance and mortality is achieved through language that is sensorial, tactile, graphic, and concrete to underscore the physical experience of suffering. Furthermore, although the protagonist may disobey nature, the boy or girl never prevails. This recurring motif of nature's authority as inhumane points to the brutally automated repression of youth under the regime.

Under Franco's regime, children perished of thirst, hunger, disease, and exposure to cold and heat not only in the female prisons, but also in the reformatories designed for minors. Salvador Cayuela Sánchez explains that the dictatorship's project to reeducate the offspring of the losing side, because their "redemption was the first step in rejoining the national body," employed punitive systems of control from prisons and concentration camps under the guise of Social Aid.[45] "The Son of the Hunter" and "The Pastry Shop Window" may depict juvenile life in prison.[46] In the first, a son goes hunting with his father every day, counting the shots as he waits in a branch hut, then carrying the dead fowl whose sharp beaks turn the boy's knees red and black from drying blood as he walks home. One night, dreaming of rifles and dogs, the boy gets out of bed and hunts the stars, birds, and sharp wind with his father's rifle. The narrator continues, "He hunted fear, cold and darkness," stating next, "When they carried him down, at dawn, the mother saw that the early morning frost, turned red like wine, spotted the white knees of the foolish boy hunter."[47] The metonymic sequence of the character's knees in colors of red and black, then white spotted with bright red at the tale's end, signifies the boy's mortality. The circumstances of the protagonist's fatality may allude to the death of minors abandoned to harsh, ambient temperatures in detention; his disobedience is the hunting down and shooting of these official methods of repression implied by the words, "fear, cold and darkness." On a collective note, the frost hued red like wine may indicate first communion to illustrate the church's role in the disappearance of youth and to mark a stunted coming of age for the lost children of Spain.

In a story of a hungry child's refusal to eat, "The Pastry Shop Window" features a barefoot boy who dreams every night that he is inside a pastry display window. With shiny eyes of syrup and a feeling of sharp, anxious teeth in his mouth, one night he gets out of bed and goes to the pastry shop accompanied by his dog. A storekeeper appears in the door with an offer of food, to which he replies, "I'm not hungry. I'm not hungry."[48] The dogs brings him a piece of icy frost. The boys sucks it in his cold mouth while longing for candy, but it never melts. This text's ending tells mortality from hunger and cold by encoding a series of references to the boy's mouth, and his fatality is evoked by the unmelted ice in his mouth. Like the red, black, and white knees of the boy hunter, the hungry boy's mouth repeatedly spells the individual's vulnerability. The situational aspect of the shopkeeper who offers garbanzos to the child, which he refuses, may represent the inedible food conditions in prison. Like the thirsty boy, the protagonist's voice sounds dissent even after he perishes and may signify youth resistance to life in reformatory. Cenarro documents, for example, that in protest minors vomited up the rations in jail in order to be sent home.[49]

Silence and Amnesia

As Angus Fletcher explains, allegory can evoke plague-like, hellish conditions through causal relationships between images or ideas.[50] Throughout *The Foolish Children*, metonymic language constructs a fantastic world that is nevertheless realistic. The concrete, material details are naturalist, but their combination with each other produces dense allegories. In fact, in making contiguous or causal relationships between the fictional elements, the reader must track the central concepts accumulated by key words. This "rhythmic encoding" makes possible the interpretation of the text.[51] Maureen Quilligan insists on allegory's horizontal form to explain how we read allegories as they unfold, and Gay Clifford believes that the reader's freedom to interpret is granted "by the massiveness and enigma of the central concepts."[52] I would add that these devices in *The Foolish Children* universalize and depoliticize the charged environment of Spain's Civil War and its aftermath while still representing atrocities. As writers of this period experimented with textual ambiguity through densely packed narratives to elude censorship, I believe that Matute's intention was to confuse censors in order to publish *The Foolish Children* inside Spain.[53]

Yet, as Lydia Kokkola writes, Matute's approach may be to "forge an appropriate path between speech and silence."[54] Matute eludes censors while constructing a text that invites readers to decode it. In fact, the text itself may perform trauma, and the loss of language to describe it, because *The Foolish Children* "does not speak directly of the crime that generates its plot."[55] Citing Leona Toker, Kokkola might use the term "permanent suspension of information" to categorize Matute's allegories and their representation of genocide because each tale in *The Foolish Children* lacks adequate information to place the stories in the context of Spain's genocidal repression of youth.[56] Toker herself, as Kokkola explains, calls these "permanent" informational gaps "manipulative" and "inherently unethical."[57] However, earlier in the chapter on nonrepresentation and the function of silence, Kokkola asserts that the reader depends on "framed silences." I would argue that Matute's subversive uses of allegory, the suppression of moral lessons, among other gaps, signals the reader to become aware of the silences and what remains unsaid.[58]

A particularly enigmatic, obtuse tale, the "The Merry-Go-Round" depicts the national suffering of youth through the buildup of details to represent this ride at the fair. A boy without spending change walks around the fair looking at the ground, disinterested in the carnival games and rides. He criticizes the merry-go-round, saying, "It's stupid how it goes nowhere, only around and around without going anywhere."[59] One rainy day the boy finds a bottle top to use as a ride token and runs to the merry-go-round, covered by canvas because the ride is closed because of the rain. Regardless, the boy enters and rides a golden horse. Delighted, the boy rides the merry-go-round that never stops. When the sun comes out and the operator raises the canvas cover, everyone flees. The last line reads, "No kid ever wished to ride that merry-go-round again."[60]

In addition to depicting loss, Matute represents the denial of atrocity under the regime through the repetition of "nowhere" and "no one" in "The Merry-Go-Round." Silence and amnesia in Spain regarding the lost children might be explained by the fact that records do not exist for the infants and children in prison with their mothers even though the numbers of minors relocated to homes do exist. The "gap" in this record-keeping signals that these displaced children never "counted" for the state. Regarding genocide, Butler theorizes that it is denied when the lives negated through violence are already negated, that is, not counted.[61] She also theorizes that a refusal of discourse concerning human loss dehumanizes those lost.[62] In fact, the merry-go-round's closed tarpaulin cover, described twice as "so big" (tan grande, tan grande), may have a double meaning. First, it denotes Spain's centralized, insular society under dictatorship where historical memory is controlled. Second, it represents the hermetic, closed system of the allegorical text itself. This approach suggests that "The Merry-Go-Round" defies rosy government propaganda concerning the nation (evoked by the ride's golden horses) and its mission to deny the very atrocities it was perpetrating on its citizens (the protagonist drowns). While the linguistic strategies in *The Foolish Children* cannot reverse the destruction of minors, these strategies can humanize the minors by making visible and audible their loss.

The linguistic strategies that humanize loss in *The Foolish Children* simultaneously resist genre classification in order to disobey a programmatic, idealized puericulture, which depended on totalitarian, symbolic practices to shape, repress, and disappear children. Rather than prescribing and restricting one's interpretation through "naive allegory,"[63] Matute experiments with language, plot structure, and narrative endings to open the reader's imagination. For example, the absence of a moral to the story radically disrupts reader expectation in the context of state control of young minds and bodies through rhetorical propaganda. As a whole strategy in *The Foolish Children*, Matute revitalizes allegorical fiction for her own purposes to denounce censorship and brainwashing, engage the reader, and remember atrocity.

Ellipses that fragment the text may signify the space of time between loss and memory, that is, the workings of grief. In "The Tree," a sick boy feverishly obsesses about twin trees, one outside his window, the other inside a palace he sees on his way home from school; he is sure the two trees are communicating with each other. When "night [enters] the room taking everything with it," the boy is found outside in the tree branches.[64] The story ends with the repeated, enigmatic words of the mother, "Nevermind, son, nevermind."[65] Lines before, a description of "days without morning, afternoon or night," which foreshadows the final moment of life alluded to by "night," indicates the span of the character's illness.[66] In remembering atrocity, this ellipsis of time, which in its indeterminacy has a universalizing effect, may convey the time that has passed without recognition of the tragedy. Like "The Merry-Go-Round," this text may elide the disappearance itself because the details of that tragedy are too painful.[67] The concrete particulars of the child's harmful environment locate the source of loss ("tree" is used ten times in "The Tree" and "rain" three in "The Merry-Go-Round" to convey the boy's drowning), while the "nowhere" of "The Merry-Go-Round" and "The Girl Who Was Nowhere" dislocate the memory of this loss.[68] This dislocation may serve two purposes: a critique of denial of genocide and a safe passage for remembering.

In "The Girl Who Was Nowhere," the remains of a girl's life are enumerated, but the story eludes the passing of time by narrating a reverse progression in which the protagonist is old, not young, from the outset of the story. The narration takes place in a girl's bedroom where her belongings figuratively indicate mortality through illness ("camphor"), decay ("pressed flowers and ash"), coldness ("the white, cold garments of winter"), stillness, and rigidity ("the big, hard cheeks of a large doll").[69] The girl herself cannot be found. She isn't in the mirror over the dresser or in the yellow, wrinkled face looking in the mirror (the figure of the girl turned into an old woman, presumably). The ending specifies a static transformation: "The girl from that bedroom had not died, rather she was nowhere to be found," and these final words lead us back to the start, in the descriptions of her possessions, to look for the child.[70] This circular plot structure ensures that the protagonist's journey never concludes, and that transformation of the protagonist is ongoing, never complete. Fletcher explains that this "progression ad infinitum" has "no inherent 'organic' limit of magnitude."[71] As in "The Tree," "The Girl Who Was Nowhere" skips time: the protagonist's entire life span is not recounted. Distinctly, however, this last text's form repeatedly circles us back to the source of loss; this process is not unlike the retrospective act of historical memory.

Essential to the allegories in *The Foolish Children* is fragmentation, dislocation, and elision, which, to generalize, we might call a loss of language to describe atrocity. Nevertheless, atrocity is told in the stories through an "overloading" of details to characterize the protagonists and their environments. The reader's role in rehumanizing the central characters through reconstructing the texts' highly descriptive language, the density of sensorial-based nouns and adjectives which emphasize the characters' physical existence, may work to restore a sense of humanization. In Spain's totalitarian society, where there was no official communication of reality, through integrating into fictional representations what was happening in reality, Matute does not participate in the denial of the genocide. However, as we discover in the two stories just discussed, through silences and ellipses, Matute may be pointing to the incomprehensibility of the atrocity and its denial while simultaneously opening a space for grief. In sum, *The Foolish Children* has performed and continues to perform as a national elegy.

Published under censorship, and still read in the context of recovering historical memory today, *The Foolish Children* performs grief. Following Quilligan's theory that readers of allegory are on a quest, I suggest that the book invites us to reflect on children and atrocity in Spain's past. To echo Theodore Plantinga, grieving itself may be an act of disobedience given the "monopoly on remembering" the totalitarian society enforces.[72] To counter official history, Plantinga states that multiple narratives are needed to reconstruct the past because they supplement each other.[73] Butler reminds us of this collective effect of private grief: "[mourning] furnishes a sense of political community for theorizing fundamental dependency and ethical responsibility."[74] I believe that *The Foolish Children* uses allegory to depoliticize the fictional experiences of sole protagonists who vanish or die, granting us access to this memory of loss in the first place, while simultaneously announcing Spain's generation of lost children by pluralizing the book's title.

The title can be translated in a variety of ways: The Dumb Children, The Silly Children, The Annoying Children, The Impetuous Children, The Naive Children, or The Mentally Disabled Children. These versions contain admonishing, rebellious and sympathetic tones. Taken together, they all convey a sense of human fragility, a major undercurrent in the work. This collective representation of juvenile protagonists as vulnerable from the outset, and who disappear or die in the individualized narratives, calls for ethical reflection. Writing under the dictatorship, Matute was storytelling in a time and place of denial. Long-term censorship, as well as glorification of the winning side, made impossible the voicing or writing of competing truths. By adapting well-known genres in children's literature, all of which tend to humanize the past through universalization of theme, Matute's lesson to the reader is the very construction of truth in order to remember. With this purpose to open channels of memory through allegorization of Spain's history, *The Foolish Children* may be political, but it does not politicize history. Instead, the twenty-one fables depict atrocities experienced by juveniles in order to resist the denial of this genocide. There is an active role for the reader to play in the resistance of this denial. Matute explores the limits of language to describe atrocity and simultaneously provides opportunities for us to decode her text. Using metonymic substitution to identify the child protagonists, we recover their humanity. This recovery is tenuous, of course, because ultimately the loss of Spanish youth is irrecoverable. However, what is recoverable is the grievability of the lives themselves. Opening a space to grieve the loss of children in Spain may be the very purpose of *The Foolish Children*.

Notes

1. After much consideration, I have decided to use the English title, "The Foolish Children," from the 2016 bilingual edition. Using the 1994 edition by Destino, the individual story titles, plot summaries, and direct citations are my own translations. When I have translated titles and quoted materials into English, including nonfiction sources, I note the original Spanish text.

2. David Kazanjian and Marc Nichanian, "Between Genocide and Catastrophe," in *Loss: The Politics of Mourning*, ed. David Eng and David Kazanjian (Berkeley: University of California Press, 2003), 127.

3. "Polvo de carbón," "El árbol," "Mar," "El tiovivo," "El escaparate de la pastelería."

4. Judith Butler, *Precarious Life: The Powers of Mourning and Violence* (London: Verso, 2004), 139.

5. M. Fernández-Almagro, "Los niños tontos," ABC, September 29, 1957, http://hemeroteca.abc.es/nav/Navigate.exe/hemeroteca/madrid/abc/1957/09/29/017.html.

6. "¡Este no es un libro para niños!"

7. Email correspondence with Vicente Ferrer, Media Vaca Libros.

8. Susana Bardavío Estevan, "La infancia imposible: *Los niños tontos* de Ana María Matute o el fracaso de la biopolítica franquista," *Bulletin of Spanish Studies* 95, no. 8 (July 2018): 1018. "poemas que, aunque tratan de niños, no son para niños."

9. Alicia Redondo Goicoechea, *Ana María Matute (1926–)* (Madrid: Ediciones de Orto, 2000), 64. "una muestra de mi preocupación por los abusos que se cometen con la infancia."

10. Lora Looney, "Children Retell Spain's Civil War in Film," *Ojáncano: Revista de Literatura Española* 36 (2009): 3–17.

11. Matute, *El tiempo*, 259. "Siempre robando una nostalgia, con su viejo corazón de vagabundo."

12. Gary Johnson, *The Vitality of Allegory: Figural Narrative in Modern and Contemporary Fiction* (Columbus: Ohio State University Press, 2012), 130; Gay Clif-

ford, *The Transformations of Allegory* (London: Routledge & Kegan Paul, 1974), 34; Gordon Teskey, *Allegory and Violence* (Ithaca: Cornell University Press, 1996), 132; Clifford, *Transformations of Allegory*, 71; Samuel Levin, "Allegorical Language," in *Allegory, Myth and Symbol*, ed. Morton Bloomfield (Cambridge: Harvard, 1981), 25.

13. "El niño de los hornos."

14. Ana María Matute, *Los niños tontos* (Barcelona: Destino, 1994), 80. "su hornito querido." "al conejo despellejado."

15. 11. Paul Preston, *The Spanish Holocaust: Inquisition and Extermination in Twentieth Century Spain* (New York: W.W. Norton, 2012), 471.

16. Helen Graham, *The War and Its Shadow: Spain's Civil War in Europe's Long Twentieth Century* (Brighton: Sussex, 2012), 104.

17. Matute, *Niños tontos*, 25. "cortando su mirada con filos de cuchillo."

18. Angela Cenarro, *La sonrisa de Falange: Auxilio Social en la guerra civil y en la posguerra* (Barcelona: Crítica, 2006), 102.

19. Louie Dean Valencia-García, *Antiauthoritarian Youth Culture in Francoist Spain: Clashing with Fascism* (London: Bloomsbury, 2018), 15.

20. 16. "*Eugenesia de la hispanidad y regeneración de la raza.*" "*Niños y jóvenes anormales.*"

21. Ricard Vinyes, Montse Armengou, and Ricard Belis, *Los niños perdidos del franquismo*, trans. Daniel Royo (Barcelona: Plaza Janés, 2002), 58. "combatir la propensión degenerativa de los muchachos criados en ambientes republicanos."

22. Preston, *Spanish Holocaust*, 515.

23. Matute, *Niños tontos*, 16. "Si yo pudiera lavarme la cara con la luna, y los dientes, y los ojos."

24. Vinyes, *Niños perdidos*, 221. "a todos los efectos jurídicos pertinentes, el carácter de tutor legal de los mismos."

25. Angela Cenarro, "El Auxilio Social de Falange (1936–1940): entre la guerra total y el 'Nuevo Estado' franquista," *Bulletin of Spanish Studies* 91, no. 1–2 (January 2014): 57.

26. Graham, *The War and Its Shadow*, 115.

27. Vinyes, *Niños perdidos*, 59.

28. Vinyes, *Niños perdidos*, 71–77.

29. "El año que nunca llegó."

30. "La sed y el niño."

31. Vinyes, *Niños perdidos*, 63.

32. "*Los niños perdidos del franquismo.*"

33. Matute, *Niños tontos*, 67. "¿Qué se hizo del surtidor?"

34. Matute, *Niños tontos*, 69. "¿Quién se llevó el pilón de la fuente, la boca sedienta y vacía de mi fuente?"

35. Gordon Teskey, *Allegory and Violence* (Ithaca: Cornell University Press, 1996), 124.

36. Teskey, *Allegory and Violence*, 123.

The Uses of Allegory to Tell Youth Disappearance and Mortality / 197

37. Matute, *Niños tontos*, 69. "los pájaros movían a uno y otro lado sus negras pupilas." "Abríase paso, entre árboles y niños que comen pan y chocolate."
38. "El negrito de los ojos azules"
39. Matute, *Niños tontos*, 19. "supieron que era tonto porque lloraba."
40. Matute, *Niños tontos*, 20. "¿Dónde estarán mis ojos azules?"
41. María del Carmen Luengo and Aileen Dever, "Translators' Introduction," in *Los niños tontos: The Foolish Children* (Sofia: Small Stations, 2016), 26.
42. Preston, *Spanish Holocaust*, 480–81.
43. Matute, *Niños tontos*, 21. "Cayeron todas las hojas de los árboles, y, en lugar de la sombra, bañó al niño tonto el color rojo y dorado."
44. Teskey, *Allegory and Violence*, 136.
45. Salvador Cayuela Sánchez, *Por la grandeza de la patria: La biopolítica en la España de Franco (1939–1975)* (Madrid: Fondo de Cultura Económica, 2014), 124. "donde la redención era el paso previo para volver formar parte del cuerpo nacional."
46. "El niño del cazador."
47. Matute, *Niños tontos*, 66. "Cazó el miedo, el frío, la oscuridad." "Cuando le bajaron, en la aurora, la madre vio que el roció de la madrugada, vuelto rojo como vino, salpicaba las rodillas blancas del tonto niño cazador."
48. Matute, *Niños tontos*, 46. "Yo no tengo hambre. Yo no tengo hambre."
49. Cenarro, *Sonrisa de Falange*, 172.
50. Fletcher, *Theory of Symbolic Mode*, 213–14.
51. Fletcher, *Theory of Symbolic Mode*, 172.
52. Clifford, *Transformations of Allegory*, 94.
53. Many of Spain's postwar fiction writers employed a device called "tremendismo." Closely associated with social realism and naturalism, this device purposely overloads the text with detailed, and sometimes crudely expressed, descriptors to create the fictional world.
54. Lydia Kokkola, *Representing the Holocaust in Children's Literature* (New York: Routledge, 2003), 39.
55. Irene Kacandes, "Narrative Witnessing as Memory Work: Reading Gertrud Kolmar's *A Jewish Mother*," in *Acts of Memory: Cultural Recall in the Past*, edited by Mieke Bal, Jonathan Crewe, and Leo Spitzer (Hanover: University Press of New England, 1999), 65.
56. Kokkola, *Representing the Holocaust*, 82.
57. Kokkola, *Representing the Holocaust*, 57 and 72.
58. Kokkola, *Representing the Holocaust*, 56. I do pause to consider whether or not the genocide depicted in *The Foolish Children* can be allegorized by readers outside Spain. To answer, I believe that readers outside Spain will understand that children disappeared; that, together, the twenty-one stories may be an allegory for an event in Spain; but few people outside this country know of what happened in the reeducation homes during Franco's dictatorship. Nonetheless, I propose that readers, on the basis of the tragic endings (and beginnings); the nameless, speech-

less characters; and the absence of moral lessons to the allegories, will note the representation of genocide. In reading and depending on concrete, sensorial nouns and adjectives to reconstruct the atrocities depicted, in granting meaning to these metonymic gaps that we ourselves must fill, we may be restoring the humanity of the juvenile protagonists. In conclusion, the specificity of time and place regarding Spain's reeducation homes may not be obvious, but the specificity of damage inflicted on children by the event is blatantly apparent, I maintain.

    59. Matute, *Niños tontos*, 53. "Eso es una tontería que no se lleva a ninguna parte. Sólo da vueltas y vueltas, y no se lleva a ninguna parte."

    60. Matute, *Niños tontos*, 54. "Y ningún niño quiso volver a montar en aquel tiovivo."

    61. Butler, *Precarious Life*, 33.

    62. Butler, *Precarious Life*, 34.

    63. Northrop Frye, *Anatomy of Criticism: Four Essays* (Princeton: Princeton University Press, 1957), 90.

    64. Matute, *Niños tontos*, 32. "[la noche] entró en el cuarto y se lo llevó todo."

    65. Matute, *Niños tontos*, 32. "No importa niño, no importa."

    66. Matute, *Niños tontos*, 54. "los días sin mañana, sin tarde, ni noche."

    67. Mieke Bal, *Narratology. Introduction to the Theory of Narrative*, trans. Christine van Boheemen (Toronto: University of Toronto Press, 1992), 71.

    68. "La niña que no estaba en ninguna parte"

    69. Matute, *Niños tontos*, 51. "olía a alcanfor, a flores aplastadas, como ceniza en laminillas." "A ropa blanca y fría de invierno." "con mofletes abultados y duros."

    70. Matute, *Niños tontos*, 52. "La niña de aquella habitación no había muerto, mas no estaba en ninguna parte."

    71. Fletcher, *Theory of Symbolic Mode*, 174.

    72. Theodore Platinga, *How Memory Shapes Narratives: A Philosophical Essay on Redeeming the Past* (Lewinston: Mellen, 1992), 9.

    73. Platinga, *How Memory Shapes Narratives*, 149–50.

    74. Butler, *Precarious Life*, 22.

Works Cited

Bal, Mieke. *Narratology: Introduction to the Theory of Narrative*. Translated by Christine van Boheemen. Toronto: University of Toronto Press, 1992.

Bardavío Estevan, Susana. "La infancia imposible: *Los niños tontos* de Ana María Matute o el fracaso de la biopolítica franquista." *Bulletin of Spanish Studies* 95, no. 8 (July 2018): 999–1018.

Butler, Judith. *Precarious Life: The Powers of Mourning and Violence*. London: Verso, 2004.

Cayuela Sánchez, Salvador. *Por la grandeza de la patria. La biopolítica en la España de Franco (1939–1975)*. Madrid: Fondo de Cultura Económica, 2014.

Cenarro, Angela. "El Auxilio Social de Falange (1936–1940): entre la guerra total y el 'Nuevo Estado' franquista." *Bulletin of Spanish Studies* 91, no. 1–2 (January 2014): 43–49.

———. *La sonrisa de Falange: Auxilio Social en la guerra civil y en la posguerra*. Barcelona: Crítica, 2006.

Clifford, Gay. *The Transformations of Allegory*. London: Routledge & Kegan Paul, 1974.

Fletcher, Angus. *The Theory of the Symbolic Mode*. Ithaca: Cornell University Press, 1964.

Frye, Northrop. *Anatomy of Criticism: Four Essays*. Princeton: Princeton University Press, 1957.

Graham, Helen. *The War and Its Shadow. Spain's Civil War in Europe's Long Twentieth Century*. Brighton: Sussex, 2012.

Johnson, Gary. *The Vitality of Allegory: Figural Narrative in Modern and Contemporary Fiction*. Columbus: Ohio State University Press, 2012.

Kacandes, Irene. "Narrative Witnessing as Memory Work: Reading Gertrud Kolmar's *A Jewish Mother*." In *Acts of Memory: Cultural Recall in the Present*, edited by Mieke Bal, Jonathan Crewe, and Leo Spitzer, 55–71. Hanover: University Press of New England, 1999.

Kazanjian, David, and Marc Nichanian. "Between Genocide and Catastrophe." In *Loss: The Politics of Mourning*, edited by David Eng and David Kazanjian. Berkeley: University of California Press, 2003. ProQuest Ebook Central.

Kokkola, Lydia. *Representing the Holocaust in Children's Literature*. New York: Routledge, 2003. ProQuest Ebook Central.

Levin, Samuel. "Allegorical Language." In *Allegory, Myth and Symbol*, edited by Morton Bloomfield, 23–38. Cambridge: Harvard University Press, 1981.

Looney, Lora. "Children Retell Spain's Civil War in Film." *Ojáncano: Revista de Literatura Española* 36 (2009): 3–17.

Matute, Ana María. *El tiempo*. Barcelona: Destino, 1991.

———. *Los niños tontos*. Barcelona: Destino, 1994.

———. *Los niños tontos*. Illustrated by Javier Olivares. Valencia: Media Vaca, 2000.

———. *Los niños tontos*. Translated by María del Carmen Luengo and Aileen Dever. Sofia: Small Stations, 2016.

Plantinga, Theodore. *How Memory Shapes Narratives: A Philosophical Essay on Redeeming the Past*. Lewinston: Mellen, 1992.

Preston, Paul. *The Spanish Holocaust: Inquisition and Extermination in Twentieth Century Spain*. New York: W.W. Norton, 2012.

Redondo Goicoechea, Alicia. *Ana María Matute (1926–)*. Madrid: Ediciones del Orto, 2000.

Quilligan, Maureen. *The Language of Allegory*. Ithaca: Cornell University Press, 1979.

Teskey, Gordon. *Allegory and Violence*. Ithaca: Cornell University Press, 1996.
Valencia-García, Louie Dean. *Antiauthoritarian Youth Culture in Francoist Spain: Clashing with Fascism*. London: Bloomsbury, 2018.
Vinyes, Ricard, Montse Armengou, and Ricard Belis. *Los niños perdidos del franquismo*. Translated by Daniel Royo. Barcelona: Plaza Janés, 2002.

Chapter 9

Confronting Atrocity Through Geometry

Franco's First Illustrated Biography

María Porras Sánchez

> There was nothing nowhere. Nothing but silence; a wet silence that oozed, soaking to the bone; a silence that was the loss and the emptiness of the deafening brawl, already past. There was nothing, nothing above the ground . . . Underground, countless dead lay in confusion, almost ground themselves.[1]
>
> —Francisco Ayala, "Diálogo de los muertos: Elegía española" (author's translation)

This is how Spanish poet Francisco Ayala fictionalized the devastating effects of the Spanish Civil War (1936–39)—as a deathly silence and emptiness haunted by the presence of endless buried bodies. This insurmountable silence left behind by the victims remains palpable for victims' families and historians. The number of dead during the Spanish Civil War and those who were executed under Francisco Franco's dictatorship (1939–1975) has been debated by historians. According to Paul Preston, about 200,000 men and women were executed extralegally or after pseudo legal processes; 300,000 men perished in the battle fields; and roughly 20,000 Republicans were executed after the war, while the number of the civil casualties due to the bombings, the harsh living conditions, and exile remains unclear.[2]

No doubt dead bodies are a site for trauma. The victims of the Franco regime represent trauma that is central to Spain's historical memory.

This trauma is iconically represented by Valle de los Caídos [Valley of the Fallen], Franco's funerary monument that the dictator commanded to erect fifty-eight kilometers northwest of Madrid. It is one of the largest mass graves in Europe, holding the remains of 33,700 people killed in the war, most of them from the Republican side, whose bodies were transferred from cemeteries and unmarked mass graves in 1959 without the consent of their families. According to estimations of the Ministry of Justice, 114,000 bodies remain unrecovered from mass graves.

The illustrated album *Frank: La increíble historia de una dictadura olvidada* [Frank: The incredible story of a forgotten dictatorship, 2018] by Ximo Abadía (b. 1985) is the first illustrated contemporary biography of Francisco Franco. It focusses on his role in the Civil War and the instauration of the dictatorship. Overwhelmed by the presence of these mass graves, the author has emphasized his commitment to historical memory by stating that *Frank* was a "satire against collective amnesia."[3]

This chapter examines Ximo Abadía's *Frank* in the context of the graphic representations of this period in particular and of historical memory in general. It analyzes how Abadía represents the atrocities of the Civil

Figure 9.1. Abadía, Ximo, *Frank: La increíble historia de una dictadura olvidada* (Madrid: Dibbuks, 2018), front and back covers.

War and Francoism for child readers. As I demonstrate, Abadía manages to approach a traumatic sociopolitical reality deflecting death, atrocity, and violence. Despite its subject matter, the chapter argues that *Frank* does not traumatize readers because atrocities are codified using geometrical patterns, eluding a lurid effect. Finally, the chapter assesses Abadía's work as an ethical reading that enables readers to confront atrocity undramatically while recovering historical memory.

Comics, War, and Memory

Wars, their aftermaths, and their atrocities are such important source materials in comics that they constitute "the most established and most popular genre of graphic narratives."[4] Whether historical, biographic, or entirely fictional, they relate to history while fusing universal themes, such as the battle of good versus evil, the hero's quest, the futility of violence, or presenting a fictionalized canvas for heroic, redeeming, epic, or dramatic stories. The historiographic and sociocultural value of wartime comics started to be taken into account when the New Cultural History movement broadened the notion of historical source. Rather than in the construction of master narratives, "the accent in cultural history is on close examination—of texts, of pictures, and of actions—and on open-mindedness to what those examinations will reveal."[5]

Spanish comics about the Civil War show the capacity of this medium to approach subjects that master narratives and history books frequently overlook. For instance, Carlos Giménez's *Paracuellos* (1977, 1982), an autobiographical account of the plights of the children of the defeated Republicans in Francoist orphanages, is an example of how comics "can help recover marginalised and minority voices from the peripheries of representation."[6] But comics do not only have the possibility to "speak" to us as historiographic sources. When representing past events, they also display how that reality was perceived by a specific person or group at a certain moment in history. They are also the sites in which Andreas Huyssen's "present pasts" come into existence. For Huyssen, the past has become part of the present in ways that were unthinkable in the first half of the twentieth century. Huyssen situates the turning point of memory discourses in the 1980s, triggered by the public debate about the Holocaust.[7]

The interest in the Holocaust coincides with the publishing of Art Spiegelman's *Maus* (1986), a pivotal work in the medium and "the catalyst to a sea change in the commercial and critical fortunes of the alternative comic book during the mid-1980s."[8] Since then, this autobiographic work in which Spiegelman recovered his father's memory of the Holocaust has become a landmark work in Comics Studies. By using anthropomorphic characters such as mice, cats, or pigs, Spiegelman represents through visual metaphors the atrocity that could not be represented directly, because any attempt to address reality would have not been able "to match the actuality," in Spiegelman's words.[9] The use of these anthropomorphic blank "masks" allows the reader to examine the events without focusing on any specific traumatic representation. For Spiegelman, it is possible to "go through the comic into looking at the event, as opposed to trying to replace the event with the comic."[10] In fact, by exploring memory with these cartoonish characters, Spiegelman let readers fill in the blanks of atrocity. Not only did he allow readers to imagine those unimaginable events, but he also forced them to do so, perhaps for the first time.[11]

Challenging all limits of representation, *Maus* is the perfect example of the power of comics "to tell a war story from a unique vantage point and explore phenomena in ways that other media cannot."[12] While it is often used in Holocaust education,[13] its status as a work of children's literature is somewhat disputed. Spiegelman denounced parents showing his graphic novel to their kids as "child abuse." In turn, Maurice Sendak argued: "You can't protect kids, they know everything!"[14] Like Spiegelman, Abadía also resorts to visual metaphors to represent atrocity from this "vantage point," but, unlike Spiegelman's, his album is specifically and deliberately aimed at children. Abadía exposes child readers to a simplified version of atrocity through his use of geometrical motifs, sparing them from the gruesome details by avoiding mimetic representation.[15]

Spanish Civil War and Francoism in Comic Books

Michel Matly distinguishes three periods in the comic book production about the Spanish Civil War: a first stage that coincides with the fight, in which comics were used to demonize the adversary, educate soldiers, and reassure the younger population; a second stage coinciding with Francoism, when the production dwindled and it mostly praised the regime; and a third stage that coincides with democracy.[16] After the relative silence of 1990s, the 2000s mark the reemergence of Civil War and its aftermath as an important topic in the national comic production and a renovated interest in the public sphere, coinciding with the foundation of the Association for the Recovery of Historical Memory (2000) and the passing of the Historical Memory Law (2007). By the end of the decade, graphic novels and albums prevailed over short formats, and 2011 saw the peak in the national production in terms of the total number of pages published.[17] Abadía sees in this increase a side effect of decades of imposed and voluntary silence that have been breached by comics and other arts: a "scream" breaking that silence.[18]

In the last fifteen years, several generations of Spanish authors have tried to preserve family memories associated to the war and Francoism. These are frequently indirect confessional narratives with a connection between protagonists (those who experienced the war and its aftermath in the first person) and the authors (their children and grandchildren). For instance, *Dr. Uriel* (2017) by Sento Llobell is a graphic novel in three volumes based on the diaries written by the author's father-in-law, who was a young doctor when the war broke. The acclaimed *Art of Flying* (2009) by Antonio Altarriba and Kim illustrates the life of Altarriba's father, who fought for the Republican side and struggled with the coercive conditions of the early decades of Francoism, eventually committing suicide in a retirement home. The zine *Todo lo que nos contaron nuestros abuelos* [Everything our grandparents told us, 2012] by Cachete Jack illustrates how the younger generation has explored family memories of the Civil War and its aftermath. Ana Penyas, whose work has had an important influence on Abadía, has also explored her grandmothers' memories about Francoism in her award-winning *Estamos todas bien* [We are all fine, 2017].

However, there are also recent examples of graphic novels that incorporate direct testimonies of nonrelatives, such as Paco Roca's *Twists of Fate* (2013), partly based on the memories of an exiled Republican soldier, and Laura Martel and Antonia Santolaya's *Winnipeg: el barco de Neruda* [Winnipeg: Neruda's boat, 2015], the story of an exiled child. Although Martel and Santolaya interviewed survivors of the Spanish exile and contemplated the idea of creating a documentary, they finally opted for a fictionalized account made of fragments of real stories.[19] These works exemplify the power of graphic narratives to recover peripheral experiences through testimonies either directly or indirectly related to their authors: the traumatic experience of the war and its aftermath (Giménez, Martel and Santolaya, Bellver and Fanjul, Kim and Altarriba); the fight in rural areas (Altarriba and Kim); a privileged but unwilling witness to violence (Sento). These examples show how comics can endow a plurality of experiences because "they rely on exploratory, experimental, and unorthodox modes of representation to raise their readers' awareness of social, political, and historical issues, and ontological approaches to these concerns."[20] Even though many of these works include child characters and most of them can be read by young adults, none addresses children as readers like *Frank* does.

Frank's originality lies not in the content but in its ideal reader. Abadía consciously wanted to create a comic for children, not a young adult comic.[21] He soon found that a comic with a considerable amount of text would be difficult for younger readers to follow, so he opted for simplicity and created an illustrated album that uses comic devices and in which text is scarce.[22] Although comics were used for didactic purposes during the war to instruct young readers on the bounties of the respective sides and during Francoism to expose the evils of communism and republicanism, no other contemporary Spanish comic about the Civil War and the Francoism has addressed children specifically.[23]

Frank is also original in the choice of the main character. The album is both an illustrated biography of Francisco Franco and the first long graphic satire of Franco.[24] By choosing an unlikable protagonist, Abadía annuls any possible identification with him. Therefore, he averts the tendency to opt "for simplistic narratives of character empowerment adapted from self-help literature" in many picture books dealing with trauma and memory.[25] Formally, Abadía uses the double page as a canvas with no panels, what McCloud calls a "timeless space" and a "timeless presence."[26] Thematically, such space coincides with the timelessness of some children's stories. In traditional stories and folk tales, the narrative takes place in a suspended time where both wonders and horrors are possible.[27] The album bears the subtitle "La increíble historia de una dictadura olvidada" (The incredible story of a forgotten dictatorship); any Spanish-language reader would immediately associate this "incredible story" with some kind of fantastic tale for children. But *historia* also means history in Spanish, so the historic time becomes one with storytelling. The fact that the story/history of Frank/Franco takes place in this timeless space also implies that it could repeat itself, a warning for the future.

Atrocity and Ethics in the First Contemporary Graphic Narrative for Children about the Dictatorship

To the question if a Francoism-themed comic is suitable for children, critics such as Cech and Kenneth B. Kidd would say yes. Frequently, children's picture books approach sociopolitical realities without condescension. For Cech, they can be "more adult in concern and more elastic in form without losing their relevance to childhood."[28] Because of their visual power, children's picture books and comics have "greater power to shock and presumably to educate" because the genre is assumed to be innocent.[29] Like Sendak, Kidd argues that it is better to expose children to historical trauma rather than protect them.[30]

While *Frank* does present historical trauma, direct references to atrocity such as corpses, battlefields, or wounded bodies are absent. These are all simplified and codified through geometrical elements; therefore the comic educates readers without traumatizing them. The question then is not *whether* atrocity can be represented but *how* to represent it.[31] Children's literature is noteworthy for cultivating ethical awareness. In fact, when they address the Holocaust in children's literature, works are expected to fulfill a certain "moral obligation."[32] This moral obligation implies addressing history with respect and accuracy without trivializing the Holocaust. But it also invokes a commitment to the future that most memorial monuments share: an Arendtian "promise" made to ensure that atrocity would never be tolerated, that those past events would never be repeated. Only by "acting in concert," that is, by acquiring a social contract, can societies guarantee that the previous crimes will not be repeated by using "the force of mutual promise."[33] Even considering the limited effects of memorialization of the Holocaust on different sociocultural contexts, it has to be acknowledged that education and memorialization have failed to prevent genocides. Even if change has not been achieved, the expectation of change can be maintained as an ethic stance: politics of memory may be applied to educating on the past with an expectation of change as well as to honoring the dead.

According to the exhortation on the back cover, *Frank* partakes of the Arendtian promise: "Our grandparents were forced to fight. Our parents were forced to forget. It's our turn to remember the past to look at the future."[34] His exhortation and his allusion to his generation's "turn" show that the album is aimed also at adult readers. This is an example of Nodelman's "shadow text": what the author cannot say to the child explicitly but can be read between the lines.[35] By acknowledging the "present past" of the Civil War and Francoism, Abadía commits to the future. But he also invokes a social contract that was broken in the past and now can be amended through an exercise of collective memory. The same contract is a device to honor the dead, because the unopened mass graves of the Dictatorship "are not a question of politics, but a question of humanity."[36]

This social contract implies a "turn to ethics" in literary studies that also occupies a prominent position in comics studies.[37] As Hillary Chute states, "comics proposes an ethics of looking and reading intent on defamiliarizing standard or received images of history while yet aiming at communicate and circulate."[38] So it is in the very nature of comics calling into question the historic preconceptions in the gaze of the reader. In addition, children's books are there to witness, as "testimony to the unspeakable, one that recognizes the unconscious witnessing of the subject."[39] By deeming *Frank* a "satire against collective amnesia," Abadía takes an ethical stance through which he addresses a double phenomenon: the absence of allusions to the Civil War and Francoism at home when he was growing up in the 1980s and early 1990s, and the lack of depth in which these are treated in contemporary textbooks. In fact, recent studies suggest that the Civil War does not have a permanent presence in the history syllabus in primary education since LOMCE law was approved in 2013.[40] For Juan Carlos Bel and Juan Carlos Colomer, these policies might support some questionable theories in which Francoism is presented as the solution to the political upheaval in the early decades of the Spanish twentieth century.[41] With his graphic narrative, Abadía wishes to offer a "pedagogy" complementary to the history syllabus in primary education.[42]

Abadía shows Frank—Franco's graphic alter ego—as a little boy throwing a tantrum and follows him through his birth; through his youth and adult years as a soldier, general, and dictator; and finally to his death. Each double page illustrates an episode of Frank's life and beyond: the first set shows his birth in a "little town in the north,"[43] referring to El Ferrol (Galicia), where Franco was born in 1892 to a family with military bloodlines. Since the very beginning the tone is satirical, with an allusion to Franco's nickname: he was dubbed "cerillita" (literally, little matchstick) while he was in school, an allusion to the big size of his head compared to the rest of his body.[44] Abadía offers a visual translation of this dubbing, depicting the character's head as a flame. But his short stature and military cap remain a constant feature throughout the album. Another element of visual humor is found in a different double page representation of Frank in "military school," where he was "last in class."[45] There are rows of identical grown-up marching soldiers, interrupted only by a tiny figure hurrying after the last one, carrying his rifle upside-down. Through visual humor, Franco becomes a laughingstock instead of a threatening figure. This characterization prepares the reader to perceive his atrocious actions as pointless and reprehensible later in the story.

Confronting Atrocity Through Geometry / 209

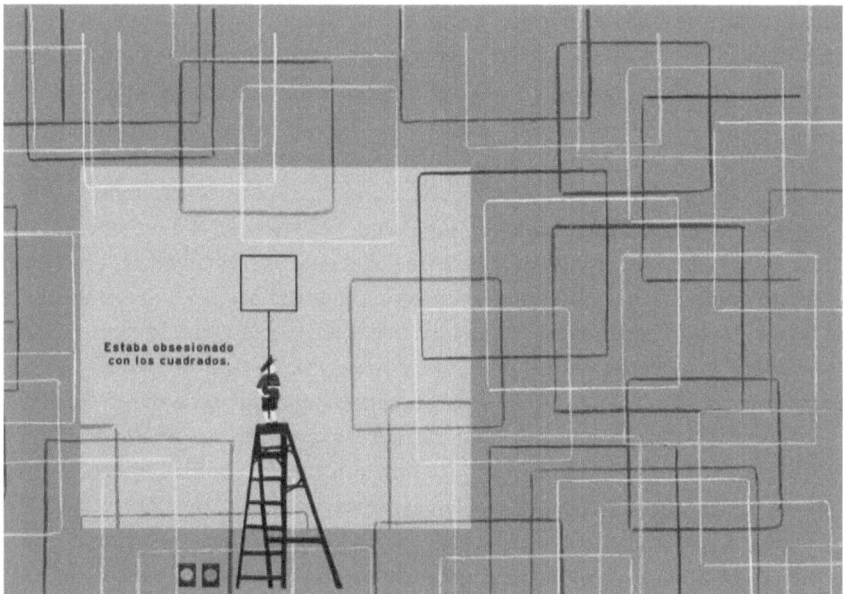

Figure 9.2. Abadía, Ximo, *Frank: La increíble historia de una dictadura olvidada* (Madrid: Dibbuks, 2018), 7–8.

The conflict becomes evident on the second double page, with Frank as a little boy "obsessed with squares" (figure 9.2).[46] This obsession is what leads him to react against other polygons. He returns "from the desert" hoisting a square—a clear allusion to Franco in Morocco, where he was stationed between 1912 and 1926 and was promoted to general.[47] Then he finds that "something had changed. There were circles everywhere," "triangles" and "rectangles."[48] Abadía fills the consecutive double pages with the outline of multiple shapes and includes Frank hoisting the square. The presence of the geometrical shapes is furtherly iterated by the background, where the author repeats the shape in different colors. By contrast, Frank's figure becomes smaller in each set, emphasizing the character's claustrophobia and powerlessness in presence of so many triangles, rectangles, and circles that he detests. Frank's anguish explodes in a page filled with a succession of concentric squares with an eye in the middle. For a grown-up reader, the eye within the square evokes the eye within the triangle that represents the Eye of Providence in Christian iconography and Orwell's Big Brother in *1984*. This eye becomes a metaphor for the square obsession that haunts Frank, but it also foreshadows Francoist repression. Angry at this plurality, Frank resolves to "break all the circles, triangles and rectangles" with a square on a chaotic double page full of broken lines of different colors.[49]

Abadía states that Frank's obsession was a means to highlight "the square, old mindset of the dictator. A mindset that, for the author, Spanish people drag with them even today: 'homeland, Catholicism and family.' I use shapes so [the message] is simpler, more iconic."[50] These iconic representations are not inferior or unfaithful, because "the past is visually not accessible through realistic representation: whatever representation [one] may choose, it is bound to be 'inauthentic.' "[51] Again, it is the gaze and the imagination of the reader that reenact the history/story that is presented to him or her. In this sense, *Frank* follows Spiegelman's strategy in *Maus* of avoiding realistic representations but takes it a step further by creating a visual analogy in which human figures are reduced to the minimum expression, geometric motifs that Wassily Kandinsky called "primary forms."[52]

These basic shapes, easily recognizable for young readers, offer a powerful visual metaphor by representing those prosecuted by Franco. During

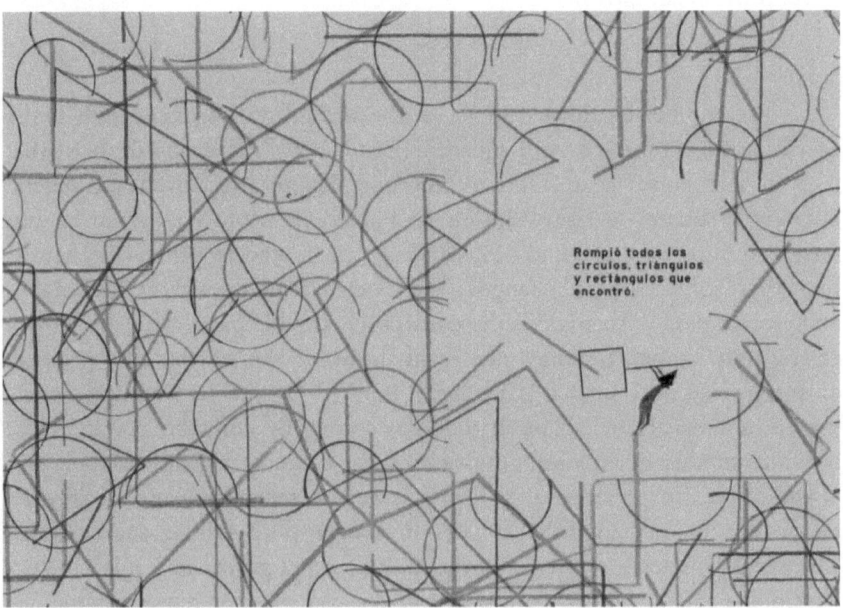

Figure 9.3. Abadía, Ximo, *Frank: La increíble historia de una dictadura olvidada* (Madrid: Dibbuks, 2018), 21–22.

the Republic, right-wing military officers and politicians started to spread a rhetoric insinuating "the racial inferiority of their left-wing and liberal enemies through the clichés of the theory of the Judeo-Masonic-Bolshevik conspiracy."[53] Since his days as a general, Franco enthusiastically embraced the circulating anti-Masonic and anti-Semitic theories. In Abadía's graphic narrative, Frank prosecutes the remaining geometrical shapes just because they are not squares. The author does not need to label each geographic shape: regardless, if they represent loyalists to the Spanish Republic, Socialists, Liberals, Communists, the Popular Front, anarchists, freethinkers, intellectuals, Freemasons, homosexuals, Roma, or nationalists from the Basque Country, Catalonia, and Galicia, all the victims of the White Terror are condensed into the geometrical motifs that populate the pages. Abadía resorts to geometric abstraction to address the ethical questions of how to present traumatic events without being explicit or simplistic. If trauma studies are a means to "reintroduce a political and ethical stake in the representation of the real without regressing to the very notions of mimetic transparency," then graphic narratives such as *Frank* might palliate the traumatic effects that photography or cinema may cause by avoiding naturalistic representation.[54] By minimizing the visual impact of these atrocities, the author highlights the absurdity and futility of the war and prosecution, educating without confusing the reader or reproducing trauma.[55]

Franco's totalitarian project is also visually supported by the presence of Fascism and Nazism. In one of the few double pages that exhibit a narrative sequence, Abadía draws Frank on the phone calling "two generals as crazy for squares as himself" to ask for their help.[56] They both answer his call on two symmetric panels on the following page. This is one of the few cases in which the author uses speech balloons to represent a dialogue, but he uses squares instead of words. Their common obsession is highlighted by the presence of squares in furniture and decorations. Both generals are easily recognizable as Hitler (because of the toothbrush moustache) and Mussolini (because of the fez). While young children may not be able to identify the dictators without their parents' guidelines, the presence of primary forms reinforces their identification with Frank. According to Kokkola, silences and narrative gaps can become an opportunity for a child and an adult to engage in productive discussion, establishing a dialogic relationship with the text, especially in the case of very young readers.[57]

There are also double pages without any word captions, such as the one in which Frank poses as a strongman in underwear while another character sculpts him, multiplying his size and nonexistent muscles. A sarcastic visual metaphor, the double image summarizes how the regime extolled Franco's figure through propaganda by lauding his success as a hunter, sportsman, statesman, family man, devout Catholic, and leader of a booming Spain. Abadía's visual metaphor works as a satire by re-creating an egomaniac figure that hid a "mediocre character."[58] At the same time, the country controlled by the dictator is presented as his playground, with Frank surrounded by toy trains, airplanes, cars, animals, a slide, and a hopscotch, while an obese figure eats the map of Spain, symbolizing Francoist ransacking and oppression. Taking this satirical stance allows Abadía to explore alternatives to historical reality and, to borrow Jill E. Twark's description, "to uncover truths overlooked or consciously elided by government and mass media discourse."[59]

Furthermore, Abadía explores the different consequences of war and repression for the Spanish population: prosecutions, summary executions, forced labor, imprisonment, and exile. A double page is used to illustrate each circumstance, although figurative characters now replace geometric shapes. The images are explicit enough to be perceived as threatening by young readers: prisoners exhibit striped uniforms or chains and military uniforms, and guns in executions are recognizable but quite schematic. The impact of images is alleviated by the fact that the faces are blank and featureless and wounds and blood are absent; therefore they do not "spare the child" to such an extent that they are misleading.[60] Cultural trauma is visually exemplified by refugees, blurred black silhouettes in the deck of a liner standing for the half-million people who fled Spain after the Civil War.[61] The blurred outlines of "those who fled far away" remind the reader of ghostly presences, re-creating the loss of the exile, caught between worlds.[62]

Abadía also uses black to represent a group of featureless silhouettes in a cage "talking" in triangles, circles, and rectangles, which stand for the silenced and repressed dissenters.[63] However, he makes use of more naturalistic characters without symbolism. Such instances include the case of a man sentenced to death before a firing squad commanded by a tiny Frank, while a fettered woman in a polka dot dress protests in vain. In the background, a man and a woman carry heavy squares. The firing squad is composed of anthropomorphic birds wearing uniforms, including a square on top of their hats (figure 9.4).[64] The absence of features and the plain colors palliate the violence of the scene, but the virulence is evident, a reminder of the 20,000 Republicans executed after the Civil War.[65] The contrast with the more symbolic scenes evidences an intention to provoke an emotional response on the reader, either adult or child.

Figure 9.4. Abadía, Ximo, *Frank: La increíble historia de una dictadura olvidada* (Madrid: Dibbuks, 2018), 35–36.

It is the same strategy of the next page (figure 9.4), showing Frank sitting in a throne too large for him while a group of prisoners works with pickaxes in a mountain in the background, crowned with squares.[66] This is an evident allusion to the approximately 500,000 forced laborers imprisoned in Francoist concentration camps.[67] The composition, with Frank in the middle and the crowning square, also foreshadows Franco's funerary monument in Valle de los Caídos, which was built by forced laborers. In the panel underneath, a lonely prisoner contemplates a bird in the window of his cell while holding a sheet of paper with a circle and written words. This is an allusion to poet Miguel Hernández (1910–42) and his short story "El gorrión y el prisionero" [The sparrow and the prisoner], a dialogue with the bird written in his cell for his son, which his death in the prison's infirmary left unfinished. The allusion, an example of Nodelman's "shadow text,"[68] is unessential to the general understanding of the plot and surely would pass unnoticed by young readers, providing an opportunity for the adult to further explain it.[69]

After this figurative attempt to reproduce Francoist repression, there is an abrupt change in the story. With the caption "Frank went away," Abadía presents a sinister nightscape where the grim reaper takes away Frank's expiring body.[70] However, the album does not end with the dictator's demise: in the next two pages, Abadía resorts again to multiple visual metaphors to explain Frank's legacy. More cryptic than the previous representations, those include the all-seeing eye, a religious authority holding two squares, two crowned figures with a clockwork mechanism throwing handfuls of banknotes, a top-hat man hoisting a flag made with one of those banknotes, and several sheep. These cryptograms are clarified by the text above: "All those who got rich with squares created a collective amnesia."[71] The author chooses not to mention the beginning of the Spanish democracy, but he graphically suggests that the Church collaborated in a collective amnesia, together with the king and businessmen, to whitewash Franco's figure. Furthermore, on the next page he uses more visual metaphors to allude to the silenced historical memory: a hand crossing out a human figure, and a toy Frank on top of a padlocked book, hinting at the attempt by some of Franco's supporters and the far-right politicians to silence the crimes committed during Francoism.[72]

But it is the last double page that is the most visually striking for the reader (figure 9.5). There is only one word, the continuation of the former

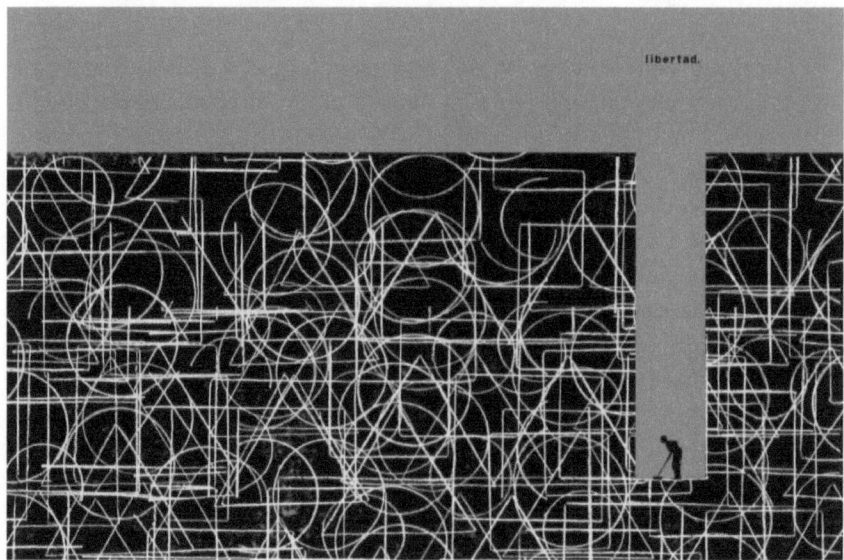

Figure 9.5. Abadía, Ximo, *Frank: La increíble historia de una dictadura olvidada* (Madrid: Dibbuks, 2018), 44–45.

sentence, "forty years after, a buried word is still heard [. . .] freedom."[73] There is a sharp contrast between this last and isolated word and what it illustrates: the double page is horizontally divided into two parts, the lower part occupying two-thirds of the page. It is entirely filled with a range of geometric shapes, painted white on top of a black background, while a lonely human silhouette digs a vertical hole in the ground. This is how Abadía choses to represent the dead bodies of those repressed by Franco that are still buried in innumerable mass graves. For Abadía, the word "freedom" is not a way of vindicating the freedom that came with democracy, but

> The freedom that is still to be won. Thousands of people are still buried in the ditches, forgotten. Those people are Spanish citizens and, regardless of their ideology, they deserve a decent burial. Their families find only difficulties to locate them and bury them. I look for that freedom and the real heroes in this story are those who work day after day trying to solve this.[74]

This bitter ending matches Huyssen's remark about Spiegelman's *Maus:* "Rather than providing us with an enlightened moral or with a happy reconciliation between high and low [. . .], trauma and memory, the aesthetic and emotional effect of *Maus* remains jarring throughout."[75] This "jarring, irritating effect" replaces the usual conciliation at the end of children's stories.

Conclusions

Is it possible to represent Ayala's countless dead bodies in a graphic format? The increasing number of comics and graphic novels about the Spanish Civil War and Francoism vouches for an affirmative answer. What is more, Abadía shows that it is feasible to represent atrocity for children by using simple geometrical motifs. For Kokkola, this would be an example of a low degree of modality because such a schematization "do not purport to represent reality, but rather to interpret it."[76] Therefore, Abadía's stylistic choice is a way of representing atrocity without resorting to mimetic representation and causing unnecessary pain.

Unintentionally, Abadía follows Spiegelman in *Maus* and lets his readers fill out the blanks of atrocity by forcing them to imagine the unimaginable: the silence of the dead bodies, the suffering of the repressed, the powerlessness of the victims' families. His strategy is to defamiliarize history through his graphic choices: a modest palette of solid colors and a formal simplicity that resembles certain graphic designs or infographics, an elementary aesthetic to engage children.[77] Abadía uses a very restricted range of colors: red, turquoise, yellow ochre, and black, which avoid the visual dichotomy associated with the Spanish Civil War of reds (Republicans) versus blues (Nationals).

Frank's characterization also seems effective, because any child can relate to the motif of a little boy throwing a tantrum. However, the main character is unlikeable and despicable, so young readers do not identify with him and the story becomes a morality tale. At the same time, its "shadow text" works as an adult satire in which Franco is a tiny brat who never grows up, that is, a mediocre, short man—he was 1.63 meters—with an enormous ego. This is a good example of Abadía's narrative strategy, a combination of sequences and codes that call the attention of the adult reader and an accessible story for children introduced in a recognizable format, the illustrated album. Even though children's narratives commonly provoke different responses in adult and young readers, the second group generally is not used to reading stories starring characters who are unempathetic or completely unredeemable.[78] *Frank*'s geometrical simplification sends a simple yet not simplistic message: the absurdity of hatred and war. By simplifying and codifying atrocity, Abadía educates without traumatizing the reader. And by establishing a visual analogy in which prisoners and corpses become geometrical figures, he creates an allegory that requires the explanations of an adult mediator. Without the additional information, the children might lack the background knowledge to even consider the comic a story about the Spanish dictatorship.[79] Nevertheless, this mediation does not undermine the educative potential of the story; it is a part of the productive exchange between child and adult to engage with historical memory.

Born to a generation that partially chose to obliterate many references to the dictatorship to spare their children their pain, Abadía's project coincides with a renewed and controversial public debate about historical memory in Spain and the denial of Francoist atrocities by the far right. The author does not enter into considerations of the numerous atrocities committed by Republicans. Nevertheless, his intention is not to present a valid graphic representation of the Civil War, but a biography of Francisco Franco and the brutal role he played during the war and the dictatorship. Abadía develops a radical exercise of synthesis, condensing almost twenty-nine years of dictatorship into fewer than fifty pages after a process of "distillation."[80] In this sense, his synthetic approach is bound to ignore numerous historical facts. However, we cannot dismiss *Frank* on the grounds of "inauthenticity" or "inaccuracy," because "the comic does not pretend to be history," but a study of how Francoism and Civil War are perceived by the generation born in the mid-1980s, grandsons and granddaughters of those who fought, died, or survived the war and suffered or tolerated Francoism.[81] It is a strategy for coping with the cultural trauma endured by the previous generations and inherited by their descendants. At the same time, it is an example of how Huyssen's "present pasts" differ from one generation to another. As Matly maintains, with cultural memory, reality is not as important as its meaning for a generation, for a group of people, or for an individual.[82] Abadía's "present past" develops a new ontological approach to Francoism combining ethics and aesthetics in which the absence of text highlights the absence of the voices of those who were forever silenced: the dead, the exiled, the repressed. *Frank* is the ethical reading of an individual citizen deeply concerned with the fact that this "collective amnesia" and all the buried bodies are hurting the democratic health of his country. In a certain way, it is an ethical contract with readers, his own re-creation of the Arendtian "promise" that ensures that atrocity would not be forgotten and obliterated from collective memory.

Notes

1. "No había nada por ninguna parte. Nada, sino silencio; un silencio húmedo que rezumaba, calaba hasta lo más hondo; un silencio que era la ausencia y el vacío de la atronadora refriega, ya pasada. No había nada, nada sobre la tierra . . . Bajo ella, muertos infinitos yacían en confusión, ahora casi tierra ya también ellos." Francisco Ayala, "Diálogo de los muertos: Elegía española," in *Los usurpadores* (Madrid: Alianza editorial, 1971), 157.

2. Paul Preston, *The Spanish Holocaust: Inquisition and Extermination in Twentieth-century Spain* (London: Harper, 2012), xi.

3. Qtd. in Fernando Bernal. "Así es el primer cómic sobre Franco," *El País*, February 7, 2018 (author's translation).

4. Tatiana Prorokova and Nimrod Tal, eds., *Cultures of War in Graphic Novels: Violence, Trauma, and Memory* (New Brunswick, NJ: Rutgers University Press, 2018), 6.

5. Lynn Hunt, *The New Cultural History* (Berkeley: University of California Press, 1989), 22.

6. Golnar Nabizadeh, ed., *Representation and Memory in Graphic Novels* (Abingdon, Oxon: Routledge, 2019), 19.

7. See Andreas Huyssen, *Present Pasts: Urban Palimpsests and the Politics of Memory* (Stanford, CA: Stanford University Press, 2003), 12; and "Present Pasts: Media, Politics, Amnesia," *Public Culture* 12, no. 1 (2000): 22–23.

8. Philip Smith, "Spiegelman Studies Part 1 of 2: *Maus*," *Literature Compass* 12, no. 10 (2015): 499.

9. Qtd. in Roger Sabin, "Interview with Art Spiegelman," in *Art Spiegelman: Conversations*, ed. Joseph Witek (Jackson: University Press of Mississippi, 2007), 108.

10. Qtd. in Sabin, "Interview with Art Spiegelman," 108.

11. Santiago García, *La novela gráfica* (Bilbao: Astiberri, 2014), 201.

12. Prorokova and Tal, *Cultures of War in Graphic Novels: Violence, Trauma, and Memory*, 9.

13. See Philip Smith, "*Maus* in the Indonesian Classroom," *Comics Forum*, February 18, 2014; and Glen Downey, "Comics in Education Presents: Resources for Teaching Art Spiegelman's *Maus*," *Comics in Education*, May 22, 2014.

14. Art Spiegelman and Maurice Sendak, "In the Dumps," *The New Yorker*, September 27, 1993, 80.

15. Cf. Kenneth B. Kidd, *Freud in Oz: At the Intersections of Psychoanalysis and Children's Literature* (Minneapolis: University of Minnesota Press, 2011), 196; and Lydia Kokkola, *Representing the Holocaust in Children's Literature* (Abingdon, Oxon: Routledge, 2003), 32, 128, 305.

16. Michel Matly, *El cómic sobre la Guerra Civil* (Madrid: Ediciones Cátedra, 2018), 9.

17. Matly, *El cómic sobre la Guerra Civil*, 161, 175.

18. Ximo Abadía, "RE: Artículo académico sobre Frank," email to María Porras Sánchez, June 25, 2019.

19. Laura Martel, "Cazarabet conversa con . . . Laura Martel, autora del texto de 'Winnipeg, El barco de Neruda,'" Cazarabet, 2015.

20. Nabizadeh, *Representation and Memory in Graphic Novels*, 1.

21. Abadía, "RE: Artículo académico sobre Frank."

22. Qtd. in Bernal, "Así es el primer cómic sobre Franco."

23. For more information on wartime comic magazines for young readers, see Matly, *El cómic sobre la Guerra Civil*, 16–29. Many comic books about the Civil War for young adults have been published in the last fifteen years. See Isabelle Gräfin Deym, "La Memoria de la Guerra Civil Española en la literatura infantil y juvenil," *Studia historica: Historia contemporánea* 25 (2007): 183–84.

24. Another biography, *Soldado invicto* [Undefeated Soldier, 1969], a collective work by Art Studium, presents Franco as a brave soldier who wanted to avoid the war at all costs. Rather than considering it a piece of propaganda, Matly suggests that it was an example of the reigning conformity of the Francoist regime (see Matly, *El cómic sobre la Guerra Civil*, 48).

25. Kidd, *Freud in Oz*, 189.

26. Scott McCloud, *Understanding Comics: The Invisible Art* (New York: HarperPerennial, 1993), 103.
27. See John Ronald Reuel Tolkien, *On Fairy Stories* (Oxford: Oxford University Press, 1947), 27.
28. Qtd. in Kidd, *Freud in Oz*, 197.
29. Kidd, *Freud in Oz*, 196.
30. Kidd, *Freud in Oz*, 196.
31. Cf. Huyssen, *Present Pasts: Urban Palimpsests and the Politics of Memory*, 122.
32. Cf. Kokkola, *Representing the Holocaust in Children's Literature*, 18.
33. Arendt, *The Human Condition*, 245.
34. Ximo Abadía, *Frank: La increíble historia de una dictadura olvidada* (Madrid: Dibbuks, 2018), back cover (author's translation. The remaining quotations from *Frank* are also translated).
35. Perry Nodelman, *The Hidden Adult: Defining Children's Literature* (Baltimore: Johns Hopkins University Press, 2008), 122.
36. Abadía, "RE: Artículo académico sobre Frank" (author's translation).
37. Robert Eaglestone, "Ethical Criticism," in *The Encyclopedia of Literary and Cultural Theory* (Hoboken, NJ: John Wiley, 2010), 581.
38. Hillary L. Chute, *Disaster Drawn: Visual Witness, Comics, and Documentary Form* (Cambridge: Harvard University Press, 2016), 31.
39. Kidd, *Freud in Oz*, 185.
40. The Organic Law 8/2013, 9th December, for the improvement of the educational quality (LOMCE) is the current legal framework governing and guiding the Spanish education system. This law has been widely criticized on the grounds of being unjustified, sexist, and classist by the rest of political parties and by different collectives and associations of students, parents, and teachers.
41. Juan Carlos Bel Martínez and Juan Carlos Colomer Rubio, "Guerra Civil y franquismo en los libros de texto actuales de Educación Primaria," *Cabás* 17 (2017): 13.
42. Abadía, "RE: Artículo académico sobre Frank."
43. Abadía, *Frank*, 1.
44. Stanley G. Payne and Jesús Palacios, *Franco: A Personal and Political Biography* (Madison: University of Wisconsin Press, 2014), 11.
45. Abadía, *Frank*, 5.
46. Abadía, *Frank*, 3.
47. Abadía, *Frank*, 7.
48. Abadía, *Frank*, 10, 12, 14.
49. Abadía, *Frank*, 18.
50. "Ximo Abadía y *Frank, La increíble historia de una dictadura olvidada*: 'Han intentado borrar de un plumazo 40 años de nuestra historia. Han creado una amnesia colectiva y no podemos crecer sin saber la historia de nuestro país, crecer

normalizando una dictadura,'" Un Periodista En El Bolsillo, February 12, 2018 (author's translation).

51. Huyssen, *Present Pasts: Urban Palimpsests and the Politics of Memory*, 130.

52. Wassily Kandinsky, *Point and Line to Plane: Contribution to the Analysis of the Pictorial Elements* (New York: Solomon R. Guggenheim Foundation, 1947), 74–75.

53. Preston, *The Spanish Holocaust*, 34.

54. Frances Guerin and Roger Hallas, *The Image and the Witness: Trauma, Memory and Visual Culture* (New York: Wallflower Press, 2007), 4.

55. Kokkola, *Representing the Holocaust in Children's Literature*, 59–60.

56. Abadía, *Frank*, 21.

57. Kokkola, *Representing the Holocaust in Children's Literature*, 60, 80, 85.

58. Qtd. in Bernal. "Así es el primer cómic sobre Franco."

59. Jill E. Twark, "Approaching History as Cultural Memory Through Humour, Satire, Comics and Graphic Novels," *Contemporary European History* 26, no. 1 (2016): 176.

60. Kokkola, *Representing the Holocaust in Children's Literature*, 305.

61. Abadía, *Frank*, 33–34; Preston, *The Spanish Holocaust*, ix.

62. Abadía, *Frank*, 34.

63. Abadía, *Frank*, 29.

64. Abadía, *Frank*, 35.

65. Preston, *The Spanish Holocaust*, ix.

66. Abadía, *Frank*, 36.

67. Javier Rodrigo, *Hasta la raíz: violencia durante la Guerra Civil y la dictadura franquista* (Madrid: Alianza Editorial, 2008), 112.

68. Nodelman, *The Hidden Adult*, 8, 204–5.

69. Kokkola, *Representing the Holocaust in Children's Literature*, 78–79.

70. Abadía, *Frank*, 41.

71. Abadía, *Frank*, 43.

72. Abadía, *Frank*, 44.

73. Abadía, *Frank*, 44–45.

74. Qtd. in Bernal, "Así es el primer cómic sobre Franco" (author's translation).

75. Huyssen, *Present Pasts: Urban Palimpsests and the Politics of Memory*, 125.

76. Kokkola, *Representing the Holocaust in Children's Literature*, 124.

77. Abadía, "RE: Artículo académico sobre Frank."

78. Kokkola has argued that Nazi characters re-create contemporary Bogeymen toward whom children can express hatred and disgust while at the same time receiving parental approval (*Representing the Holocaust in Children's Literature*, 248).

79. Kokkola, *Representing the Holocaust in Children's Literature*, 85.

80. Abadía, "RE: Artículo académico sobre Frank."

81. Huyssen, *Present Pasts: Urban Palimpsests and the Politics of Memory*, 129.

82. Matly, *El cómic sobre la Guerra Civil*, 394.

Works Cited

Abadía, Ximo. *Frank: La increíble historia de una dictadura olvidada*. Madrid: Dibbuks, 2018.
Abadía, Ximo. "RE: Artículo académico sobre Frank." Email to María Porras Sánchez, June 25, 2019.
Alexander, Jeffrey C. *Trauma: A Social Theory*. Cambridge: Polity Press, 2012.
Arendt, Hannah. *The Human Condition*. Chicago: University of Chicago Press, 1958.
Ayala, Francisco. "Diálogo de los muertos: Elegía española." In *Los usurpadores*, by Francisco Ayala. Madrid: Alianza editorial, 1971.
Bel Martínez, Juan Carlos, and Juan Carlos Colomer Rubio. "Guerra Civil y franquismo en los libros de texto actuales de Educación Primaria." *Cabás* 17 (2017): 1–17. http://revista.muesca.es/articulos17/392-juan-carlos-bel-martinez-y-juan-carlos-colomer-rubio.
Bernal, Fernando. "Así es el primer cómic sobre Franco." *El País*, February 7, 2018. https://elpais.com/elpais/2018/02/06/tentaciones/1517914567_072922.html.
"Cazarabet conversa con . . . Laura Martel, autora del texto de 'Winnipeg, El barco de Neruda." *Cazarabet*, 2015. http://www.cazarabet.com/conversacon/fichas/fichas1/martel.htm.
Chapman, Jane L., et al. *Comics and the World Wars: A Cultural Record*. London: Palgrave Macmillan UK, 2015.
Chute, Hillary L. *Disaster Drawn: Visual Witness, Comics, and Documentary Form*. Cambridge: Harvard University Press, 2016.
Dawes, James. "Human Rights in Literary Studies." *Human Rights Quarterly* 31, no. 2 (2009): 394–409.
Downey, Glen. "Comics in Education Presents: Resources for Teaching Art Spiegelman's *Maus*," *Comics in Education*, May 22, 2014. https://www.comicsineducation.com/home/comics-in-education-presents-resources-for-teaching-art-spiegelmans-maus.
Eaglestone, Robert. "Ethical Criticism." *The Encyclopedia of Literary and Cultural Theory*. Hoboken, NJ: John Wiley, 2010.
García, Santiago. *La novela gráfica*. Bilbao: Astiberri, 2014.
Gräfin Deym, Isabelle. "La Memoria de la Guerra Civil Española en la literatura infantil y juvenil." *Studia historica. Historia contemporánea* 25 (2007): 181–90. http://campus.usal.es/~revistas_trabajo/index.php/0213-2087/article/viewFile/2045/2100.
Guerin, Frances, and Roger Hallas. *The Image and the Witness: Trauma, Memory and Visual Culture*. New York: Wallflower Press, 2007.
Hunt, Lynn. *The New Cultural History*. Berkeley: University of California Press, 1989.
Huyssen, Andreas. *Present Pasts: Urban Palimpsests and the Politics of Memory*. Stanford, CA: Stanford University Press, 2003.

Huyssen, Andreas. "Present Pasts: Media, Politics, Amnesia." *Public Culture* 12, no. 1 (2000): 21–38.

Kandinsky, Wassily. *Point and Line to Plane: Contribution to the Analysis of the Pictorial Elements*. New York: Solomon R. Guggenheim Foundation, 1947.

Kidd, Kenneth B. *Freud in Oz: At the Intersections of Psychoanalysis and Children's Literature*. Minneapolis: University of Minnesota Press, 2011.

Kokkola, Lydia. *Representing the Holocaust in Children's Literature*. Abingdon, Oxon: Routledge, 2003.

Map of Graves Application. Ministerio de Justicia. https://mapadefosas.mjusticia.es/.

Matly, Michel. *El cómic sobre la Guerra Civil*. Madrid: Ediciones Cátedra, 2018.

McCloud, Scott. *Understanding Comics: The Invisible Art*. New York: HarperPerennial, 1993.

Nabizadeh, Golnar, ed. *Representation and Memory in Graphic Novels*. Abingdon, Oxon: Routledge, 2019.

Ortega, José Antonio, and Javier Silvestre. "Las consecuencias demográficas." In *La economía de la Guerra Civil*, edited by Pablo Martínez Aceña and Elena Martínez Ruiz, 53–106. Madrid: Marcial Pons, 2006.

Payne, Stanley G., and Jesús Palacios. *Franco: A Personal and Political Biography*. Madison: University of Wisconsin Press, 2014.

Preston, Paul. *The Spanish Holocaust: Inquisition and Extermination in Twentieth-century Spain*. London: Harper, 2012.

Prorokova, Tatiana, and Nimrod Tal, eds. *Cultures of War in Graphic Novels: Violence, Trauma, and Memory*. New Brunswick, NJ: Rutgers University Press, 2018.

Rodrigo, Javier. *Hasta la raíz: violencia durante la Guerra Civil y la dictadura franquista*. Madrid: Alianza Editorial, 2008.

Sabin, Roger. "Interview with Art Spiegelman." In *Art Spiegelman: Conversations*, edited by Joseph Witek, 95–121. Jackson: University Press of Mississippi, 2007.

Smith, Philip. "Spiegelman Studies Part 1 of 2: *Maus*." *Literature Compass* 12, no. 10 (2015): 499–508.

Smith, Philip. "*Maus* in the Indonesian Classroom." *Comics Forum*, February 18, 2014. https://comicsforum.org/2014/02/18/maus-in-the-indonesian-classroom-by-philip-smith/.

Spiegelman, Art, and Maurice Sendak. "In the Dumps." *The New Yorker*, September 27, 1993, 80.

Tolkien, John Ronald Reuel. *On Fairy Stories*. Oxford: Oxford University Press, 1947.

Twark, Jill E. "Approaching History as Cultural Memory Through Humour, Satire, Comics and Graphic Novels." *Contemporary European History* 26, no. 1 (2016): 175–87.

"Ximo Abadía y *Frank. La increíble historia de una dictadura olvidada*." Un Periodista En El Bolsillo. February 12, 2018. http://www.unperiodistaenelbolsillo.com/ximo-abadia-frank/.

Part 4
Institutions and Domestic Structures

Chapter 10

Picture Books and Parrhesia

The Role of Multimodal Texts in
Examining Canada's Colonial Violence

CAROLINE BAGELMAN

Canadian Residential Schools and Answering the TRC's Calls to Action

Canada's Truth and Reconciliation Commission (TRC) was established in 2008 to document and address wrongdoings of its residential school system, which involved removing Indigenous children (often forcibly) from their homes and placing them in institutions, where they were denied access to their family and community, denied the right to their cultural, spiritual, linguistic, and other practices; and often abused physically, sexually, and or emotionally.[1] The mandate of these schools was clear: to "kill the Indian in the child."[2] Testimony from Indigenous residential school survivors was carefully collected during the TRC to not only build an essential record of this atrocity, but also to generate calls for action and address ongoing suffering of survivors and persistent inequalities faced by Indigenous peoples. Importantly, findings from the TRC concluded that these schools were a form of "cultural genocide."[3] The commission stated in no uncertain terms: "That policy was dedicated to eliminating Aboriginal peoples as distinct political and cultural entities and must be described for what it was: a policy of cultural genocide."[4] As Scott Murray writes, the "TRC report [. . .] unambiguously identifies the effects of Canada's genocidal legacy on both

Aboriginal and non-Aboriginal peoples, and situates the atrocities of the residential school system within an explicit historical framework intended to resist evasion and forgetfulness."[5] Within this chapter, the term atrocity is used to describe colonial policies and practices in Canada such as the residential school system, eugenics, and starvation policies, and this usage is in keeping with Claudia Card's atrocity paradigm.[6] She suggests that events can be regarded as atrocities when they do not simply happen, but rather are perpetuated and suffered.[7] There are, in this sense, two basic elements of atrocity: wrongdoing and harm. Atrocities, she writes, are "1) controversially evil [. . .]" "2) they deserve priority of attention [. . .]" and "3) the core features of evil tend to be writ large in the case of atrocities making them easier to identify and appreciate."[8]

Central to the TRC's "Calls for Action" was the role of education in ensuring awareness of atrocity and addressing epistemic violence. They underscored the need for educational efforts both to address the wrongdoings of the Canadian state in relation to residential schools and colonization more broadly (including the intergenerational traumas and inequalities that resulted) and to celebrate the histories, thought, and cultures of Indigenous peoples in Canada today.[9] This chapter considers how children's literature, and picture books in particular, might trouble the pedagogy of retreat from atrocity I saw modeled by my schooling and government as a settler Canadian and instead reflect a commitment to addressing atrocity and building just relations.[10] In particular, this chapter considers the unique qualities of the picture book, which are generative of critical engagement on atrocity, as illustrated in the final section of this work by the engagement of young Indigenous peoples and their non-Indigenous neighbors in Alert Bay, Canada, who participated in a hands-on picture-book project. Throughout this project, participants addressed the atrocity of residential schools in their reader responses to particular picture books on colonization we explored, then focused on Indigenous food systems, food cultures, and food sovereignty (and the ways in which they relate to colonial atrocities) in creating their own double-paged spread.

While children's literature has often been understood as a depoliticized or apolitical "stepping stone to literacy"[11] for a young audience presumed to be apolitical themselves,[12] this paper suggests postmodern or critical picture books scaffolded with critical pedagogy can invite authors and readers alike to speak truth to power.[13] How, it asks, might picture books in particular both embody and provoke "parrhesia" while addressing atrocity?[14] Foucault's articulation of parrhesia is a helpful framing to consider children's literatures' (and in particular picture books') handling of atrocity and how young readers then navigate parrhesia themselves. This is the case because parrhesia highlights both the power dynamics at play in such discussions on atrocity and what is at stake in speaking truth to power.[15] Addressing atrocity, I maintain, generally involves a level of parrhesia, but I emphasize that this is especially the case when addressing domestic wrongdoings (for instance, Indigenous peoples speaking to colonization in Canada). Kenneth Kidd writes on the ubiquity of discussions and literatures on the Holocaust; however, I feel there is now little risk in these within the Canadian context (as it involves speaking truth to power elsewhere, and in another time, from which North Americans generally feel a remove).[16] In an interesting turn, there is, as Kidd indicates, likely more risk for liberal states in *not* engaging with the Holocaust (discourse that has come to reflect a stand against evil and a commitment to tolerance and democracy). Speaking truth to power presiding in the Canadian parliament or church (both past and present) and their attendant institutions, however, does reflect the high stakes Foucault discusses.

In his series of lectures on the subject, Foucault explores a number of important shifts in the use and meaning of parrhesia. Foucault traces the theory and practice of truth telling from ancient Greece through to its modern iteration, ranging from political truth telling and philosophical parrhesia "directed both as advice to the ruler (the Socratic Platonic mode) or as condemnation of their folly (the Cynic mode)" to the adoption of parrhesia within Christianity (involving telling or confessing the truth about oneself).[17] He unpacks, for instance, how these modalities have been conceived of and used differently as a means for self-understanding: Foucault "distinguishes [truth telling as] ethical self-mastery of the Stoics based on askesis (a kind of training or exercise) from the [truth telling] as self-renunciation of the early Christians [. . .] leading to salvation through confession, penance, and obedience."[18] As is the case in a growing body of postcolonial scholarship, such as Andreotti's work exploring Quechua truth telling as a possible response to "systemic harm" in education, Ewen's work on Indigenous parrhesiates in the Australian medical field, and Davidson-Harden's work on Indigenous and Black or Canadian responses to policing and addressing other social inequalities, the usage of parrhesia in this chapter employs Foucault's discussion of the philosophical or public form of parrhesia from the eighteenth century.[19] Consider that this form of parrhesia involves confronting or challenging those in positions of power on their wrongdoings, which Foucault emphasizes involves risk taking and courage[20]: "one needs the courage to oppose a community of which the parrhesiastes ("truth teller") is a member."[21] In the Greek iteration, which

Foucault stresses has renewed importance, Euripides's references to *parrhesia* are "mostly framed as the problem of citizenship. Who is a citizen, why it is vital to be one, what is the relationship between citizenship and being able to speak one's mind?"[22] This citizenship is not inherently nationalistic, as we might commonly understand it today, but is characterized by a certain participation in public discourse that involves, he suggests, truth telling.

In postcolonial praxis, the relationship between citizenship and philosophical or political truth telling is intimately connected.[23] This truth telling, or bearing witness, is considered a duty according to Indigenous storytelling methodologies or practices and is also a responsibility of the settler witness.[24] This truth telling involves what Indigenous scholar Linda Smith calls "retrieving," which requires "researching back, writing back, [and] talking back" to reveal truths of the colonial atrocities as well as subjugated knowledge that has been obscured, which can give way to "remaking" cultures, bodies of thought, and relations in line with Indigenous methods.[25] This postcolonial parrhesia involves considerable risk, often resulting in what Edward Said identified in "Representations of the Intellectual" as forms of social exile[26] or what Indigenous scholar Robin Wall Kimmerer's work "Braiding Sweetgrass" describes as attacks on one's credibility and further marginalization.[27]

Parrhesia involves a duty to engage with this speech activity—one that I suggest is often shirked by authors and educators, and one that is typically not expected of children, but is actively taken up by some postmodern or critical picture books and can be supported through a critical pedagogy of picture books.[28] This chapter begins with the claim that the unique form of the picture book provides rich terrain for addressing challenging subjects, such as the atrocity of cultural genocide in Canada, making them ripe for both embodying and inviting parrhesia. The chapter then explores a tangible example of young people speaking truth to power. Through analyzing picture book form with children from the Indigenous community of Alert Bay, British Columbia, exploring critical picture book examples together and creating their own visual narratives, they addressed the ongoing atrocities associated with colonization of their lands.

Affordances of Picture Books for Parrhesia

In her work "A New Algorithm in Evil: Children's Literature in a Post-Holocaust World," Elizabeth Baer considers criteria for effective children's literature on the atrocity of the Holocaust that I believe also reflect Foucault's articulation, in "The Courage of Truth," of what parrhesia requires: "It is necessary to speak with parrhesia, without holding back at anything without concealing anything."[29] Baer claims:

1. The book must *grapple directly with the evil of the Holocaust* [. . . and provide] the most direct confrontation available.

2. The book should not provide simplistic explanations, but rather it should present *the Holocaust in its proper context of complexity*.

3. The book must convey—through the use of facts, emotions, and/or memory—*a warning about the dangers of racism and anti-Semitism, and of complacency.*

4. To borrow again from Langer, the book should give the reader "*a framework for response.*"[30]

I hold that these criteria can be extended to children's literature dealing with other atrocities such as cultural genocide in Canada, and I suggest that the medium of the picture book in particular can support such goals. In this section, I put forth four transformative affordances of the picture book as a form that can support this direct and complex discourse on atrocity: 1) its break with literary traditions, 2) the accessible nature of composite texts, 3) "textual gaps" permitting co-authorship and critique, and 4) its dialogical nature. These traits, I submit, create the conditions for parrhesia to flourish. The last section of this chapter on employing picture books with young children in an Indigenous community to illustrate how this flourishing takes shape in real learning environments focuses on Baer's fourth criterion: the way in which literature can provide a framework for response (or parrhesia).

Beyond a Genre: Breaking with Literary Tradition

Perhaps the most promising feature of the picture-book genre is that it is not really a genre. This flexibility in picture books makes them an excellent platform for addressing challenging topics. Perry Nodelman writes, "rather than confining itself to exploring the byways of one particular type of text, verbal or pictorial, it exploits genres."[31] This is not only because the picture book embodies many genres (e.g., fiction and nonfiction; fantasy, fairy tales, poetry, mystery, historical narrative, wordless stories), but also because the way in which it presents these different narratives varies widely (e.g., graphic novel formats, pop-up style books, board books, mixed media texts, linear and alinear illustrated stories). Again, in Nodelman's words: "pictures and words can now be combined in more or less any way that a book's designer might wish and that in turn raises all sorts of possibilities and challenges for the reader."[32] Less shrouded in tradition than strictly word-based texts or more traditional or linear picture books, contemporary picture books in particular are able to "bend, stretch or break the rules and in this play with conventions, a space between the "real" world and other possible worlds is opened up."[33] In breaking with the conventional role of children's literature to deliver fanciful and pleasing stories, for instance, postmodern picture books enables Baer's call for a direct and complex handling of atrocity.[34] Far from being neutral, established literary conventions reflect specific epistemologies, those of dominant cultures in particular.[35] Texts such as postmodern picture books that break from convention reflect a critical stance on dominant and accepted ways of storytelling and are in this sense methodologically fit for conveying parrhesia (which Foucault notes is a form of criticism). This openness is especially important in postcolonial work such as the picture book workshops in Alert Bay, which are explored in this chapter. Indigenous storytelling is at the heart of relational politics, governance, law, and pedagogy in Indigenous communities, yet, as it stands outside dominant ways of storytelling, it often has been disavowed and dismissed.[36]

Children, who are less accustomed to specific literary conventions and reading practices and who have less rigid understandings of what a book is meant to look like, are receptive to this flexibility. Nodelman states: "The picture book is thus ideally suited to the task of absorbing, reinterpreting and representing the world to an audience for whom negotiating newness is a daily task."[37] The picture book's lack of commitment to any one convention reflects the aims of postmodern thinking: to acknowledge and possibly even celebrate ambiguity that arises out of our complex world(s). It holds that because our reality is amorphous, so too should be the media reflecting it. The way in which critical picture books demand "a multi-constructed reading stance," as Margaret Mackey puts it, can help create a "plasticity of mind."[38] This plasticity of mind engendered by the picture book's flexible form, I would add, also lends itself to a plasticity of mind in terms of navigating social issues or complex problems presented in its content, hence positioning the picture book as a valuable and empowering discursive tool for broaching atrocity. As the last section of this chapter illustrates, this has been put to the test in a series of picture-book workshops with Indigenous and non-Indigenous children in Canada. Due, in large part, to the open form of the picture book discussed above, and the affordances explored below, participants were able to engage in complex discussion of cultural appropriation, and other harmful aspects of colonization, and to create double-page spreads reflecting their own narratives.

Accessibility of Composite Texts

The picture book, it can be argued, was born out of a desire to transform its readers. That is, in some of its earliest most hermeneutically sealed iterations (taking the form of strict catechisms, for instance), the medium of the picture book was considered a powerful vehicle to convert (or transform) heathens to Christians. It was an effective tool because of its capacity for rather universal access: "The vast majority of new converts were illiterate. Visual images in sacred books allowed a universal reading of the Christian message."[39] Despite the fact that this chapter focuses on a very different type of transformative potential offered by the picture book (namely its capacity to incite critical social engagement and parrhesia on atrocity) than these traditions did, both recognize the power of narrative and image functioning to effect change synergistically. The ability of a picture book to reach readers of varying literacy abilities, educational backgrounds, languages, learning styles, disabilities, and so forth makes it a potent site for engagement.[40]

While there are layers of meaning to be taken from an image, which requires visual literacy abilities as well as specific cultural frames of reference, the basic ability to regard the image and derive some degree of meaning from it is a universal trait of the visually abled, Lewis explains.[41] As Roland Barthes suggests: "The message's unity occurs on the level of the story," and as the picture book (with its combination of semiotic systems) is in a sense a "twice-told tale," its stories can offer themselves up in rich ways.[42] While discussions of atrocity may often be deemed too mature for children, postmodern picture book authors such as Jewell Parker Rhodes, who addresses police brutality and lynching in the United States in *Ghost Boys*, reveal that topics do not come with age limits; rather, it is the presentation of that topic that makes the text age-appropriate.[43] As Minslow writes: "Whereas Romantic notions of childhood would have adults protect children from the unjust and often brutal aspects of life, many twenty-first-century authors of children's literature have found interesting ways to represent atrocities to children without traumatizing readers in the process of educating and socializing them."[44] Shedding a Romantic view of the child by opening discussions of atrocity to children, and children of different ability, through accessible texts may provide avenues for children to speak truth to power. As the discussion of picture book workshops demonstrates, children were very able to address complex themes of cultural genocide and food insecurity linked to colonialism in both their oral responses to picture books and their written and illustrated work that employed picture book techniques. Such expressions of truth are tied to the form of citizenship articulated in the Greek conception of political or philosophical parrhesia that Foucault traces: they refuse an apolitical status in identifying abuses of power they see unfolding in their worlds.[45]

Textual Gaps: A Space for Critical Engagement

Reading a word-based text involves an interpretive process, in which meaning is deciphered and created.[46] Visual literacy, too, requires referential as well as inferential processing of the "information" that is given and that which literally or figuratively falls out of frame.[47] It can be said, then, that each semiotic system—the word and the image—necessarily leaves gaps with which the reader must contend. These spaces afforded by a text are often referred to as textual gaps or readerly gaps.[48] Picture books (with the important exception of wordless picture books) combine both semiotic systems: "two forms of representation [. . .] enter into the construction of the story together."[49] In most cases, this means that the possibility for textual gaps is doubled and perhaps tripled if one considers the gaps not just between or within the words or the gaps within the images, but also the gaps that form between the words and images operating together, often on the same page, to create narratives. Lewis suggests that "the words and pictures together [are] truly transforming each other and in the process, transforming our understanding of what we see and read, sometimes to the point where the meaning resonates through two or three levels."[50] In the case of postmodern or critical picture books, these gaps are both intentional and plentiful. The textual gaps afforded by the combination of two systems of signs and the varied, complex relationship that these signs have with one another make the picture book ripe for critical exploration of complex topics like colonial violence. These gaps set the stage for what Baer highlights is a "framework for response."[51] In other words, the gaps make space for the reader to engage in parrhesia. Where we explored Marsden's *The Rabbits* in the picture-book workshops (outlined below), for instance, the story of settlers colonizing lands and peoples as told through the multimodal allegory of rabbits taking over another creatures' habitat enabled children to make connections to their own lands and cultures.[52] While the story is littered with textual gaps to play in, such as the otherworldly visual representation of the animals, the ambiguous ending was particularly ripe for critical dialogue that helped to spark the truth telling in their own visual narratives.

This composite or intermedial quality of the picture book embodies one of Giroux's nine "Principles of Critical Pedagogy," which suggest that "critical pedagogy needs to create new forms of knowledge through its emphasis on breaking down disciplinary boundaries and creating new spaces where knowledge can be produced."[53] Vitally, the relationship between the word and image, becoming more nuanced and wrought with textual gaps, signals an important pedagogical shift. In didactic picture books, the image tends to reflect what is written, not leaving space for the reader to reconcile the two together or create meaning within a context. This is a perfect vehicle for imparting a straightforward moral imperative (morals that are not context based and up to the discretion or critical process of the child, but rather predetermined by the author and insufficient for dealing with complex social issues). The less straightforward relationship between word and image in postmodern picture books such as *The Rabbits*[54] or Armin Greder's *The Island*,[55] dealing with the brutality of xenophobia, relies on the reader to participate actively in meaning making based on critical inferences on context, because (again) like the Mobius there is a double orientation, or a disorientation created. "If the project of postmodern books is to reveal their own processes, the goal of the revelation is empowerment for the reader; they deliver a strong invitation and even an expectation that readers will participate in meaning making."[56] According to Freire, addressing the atrocity of different forms of oppression through dialogue or praxis depends on this critical literacy.[57] Further, for Hannah Arendt, it is through thinking (and meaning making) rather than consuming information passively that we affirm our humanity and *thwart* atrocity.[58]

In addition to the form of the picture book that combines two semiotic systems permitting textual gaps, the substantive content of many postmodern picture books (often placing a focus on parody, metafiction, overlapping narrative, and so on) exposes the inconsistency and inconclusiveness of our most familiar narratives, and in poking these holes, they leave room for readers to critically navigate contradictions and consider new possibilities for meaning. In Robyn McCallum's words: "[. . .] overt forms of parodic intertextuality can have three main effects: they can foreground the ways in which narrative fictions are constructed out of other texts and discourses; they can indicate possible interpretive positions for readers; and they can enable the representation of a plurality of voices, discourses and meanings."[59] The use of these devices has been outlined in Eliza T. Dresang's "Radical Change" characteristics.[60]

Picture Books as Dialogical

It is significant that picture books are often read aloud, either by an adult reading to a child or a child reading to an adult. This long-entrenched way of interacting with the picture book means it occupies somewhat of a liminal space: it is at once a form of written or recorded storytelling and a form of oral storytelling. Through the act of reading aloud, the written text is voiced, images are deconstructed, textual gaps are navigated dialogically, and extratextual conversation unfolds between the readers. Unlike other texts, dialogue is an almost inherent component of the picture book. This is notable because of the widely recognized power of dialogue as a tool for social change (Foucault, for instance, identifies the verbal nature of parrhesia).[61] Parrhesia reflects the empowering nature of dialogue—it allows for silenced voices to be heard and for subjugated knowledge to find expression. Others like Paulo Freire underscore the value of dialogue for deepening empathy, for intra- and intercultural understanding, problem posing, and collaborative problem solving. Dialogue is defined by Freire as "the encounter between [people], mediated by the world, in order to name the world."[62] As is the case with parrhesia, in which people assert themselves as citizens through their participation in dialogue, Freire suggests dialogue is an "existential necessity," central to a process of becoming, in which one defines the self in relation to a community. He states, "[i]f it is in speaking their word that people, by naming the world, transform it, dialogue imposes itself as the way by which they achieve significance as human beings."[63] If dialogue is, as Freire states, a key condition of "being human," and parrhesia a key to citizenship as Foucault notes, it is vital that children are integrated into these dialogues.

The picture book (while not always used as a serious transformative vehicle) is already established as dialogue-stimulating medium—one that tends to be cross-generational because of the way it is read (typically guardians, teachers, older friends, and relatives reading with children). Linking closely to what Freire says of dialogue and ontology, Coates writes: "I want to suggest that children's interactions with postmodern picture books provide a key entry point into the project of self-fashioning in contemporary society."[64] Dialogue, Freire also insists, must be an act based on respect—a respect for different knowledge(s), different literacies, and different social positions, so that what unfolds is not one person speaking with authority or acting on another, but a community working together. This form of dialogue must set itself against what he famously terms "banking education" that takes place in schools, whereby teachers "deposit" knowledge in the student without any negotiation of meaning or truth with the pupils.[65] In addressing atrocity, picture books might speak truth to power, but they should also invite readers to do the same.[66]

Parrhesia in Practice: Generating Dialogue with Indigenous Children on Colonial Violence and on More-Just Futures

While the discussion above considers how the form of the picture book lends itself to embodying parrhesia in relation to atrocity, to move beyond the theoretical, the following discussion considers how this takes shape in real-world engagements with children and picture books. It seeks to demonstrate the pedagogical practices that can support the use of critical picture books and the dialogue that can result from such work. Specifically, this section explores the ways in which teaching young readers to first identify (through close reading and discussion) and then *use* these affordances (through creating visual narratives) can enable them to act as parrhesiates themselves.

This practical application of picture books to support critical engagement with atrocity unfolded through a number of picture-book workshops I initiated with children aged six to twelve at the local library. These took place in Alert Bay, an island community made up of the Kwakwaka'wakw first peoples, other Indigenous peoples, and their non-native neighbors (with roughly 1,200 permanent residents). As the location for one of the longest-standing residential schools, a site of potlatch bans, and persistent social inequalities, Alert Bay cannot ignore atrocity.[67] The workshops narrowed in on a particular facet of the colonial legacy experienced by its residents: food insecurity. In discussions, we considered the cultural and economic significance of food to Indigenous ways of life and what harms the dispossession of these food systems and food practices in residential schools and potlatch bans have caused.[68] Further, we connected this to the island's current foodscape: survivors of residential schools are trying to recover traditional food knowledge that they were denied, and most people rely on imported food. In this sense, our discussions looked at the ripple effect of the atrocity of residential schools: the less-visible atrocity of contemporary food insecurity that is disproportionately experienced by Indigenous peoples as a result.[69] While we read picture book examples like *Fatty Legs*,[70] *The Rabbits*,[71] and *The Island* to stimulate this discussion, the focus was on *using tools from picture books to enable the participants to tell their own stories* as a way of engaging with colonial violence and truth telling.[72] This unfolded in a few stages, outlined here, which offer a specific example of how employing picture books for critical consciousness on atrocity and parrhesia can be pedagogically approached.

Foucault emphasizes that parrhesiastes are "always less powerful than the one with whom he or she speaks,"[73] which is descriptive of the young participants in these workshops. Children are not only placed in positions of limited agency and power by adult society, but Indigenous children are disproportionately impacted and disempowered by colonial policies and practices: they are the most underserved by Canada's education system, most at risk of displacement by way of family removals by social services, and most food insecure in the country.[74][75] In his work on unequal treatment in the Australian medical system, Shaun Ewen illustrates the ways in which Indigenous peoples can act as parrhesiastes (in his case, speaking truth on inequalities in Indigenous health care to the very institutions that produce doctors [medical schools]).[76] In this case, the children speak to educators (in bringing their visual narratives into the classroom) and settler society (in displaying their work at the local library) about the importance of Indigenous food systems and food security that have been threatened. The risk in challenging accepted settler wisdom about food production and diet and calling for government accountability for damage to the food systems at this scale may seem minute, but opening oneself and one's culture to being discredited and discounted (adding to the long history of such dismissal) certainly does carry with it the risk of further marginalization.[77]

When designing the workshops, I imagined a few fictitious conversations about picture books that I might have with young readers based on prior reader response work.[78] Where I sensed there might be a need for explanation, interjection, questions, and room for play in this imagined conversation, I created an activity that would allow us to dwell in that space and continue the conversation and provided a few new tools (these are briefly discussed below). I provided only general or open-ended prompts such as "what do you notice about the letters on these pages?" as a light mediation of the reader response discussions.[79] Here, I will outline of how these sessions took shape.

Critical Literacy and Constructing Narrative

We began a discussion about different ways to tell stories with the aim of teaching participants how to create composite texts, textual gaps, accessible texts, and dialogue in their own final projects. They brainstormed and came up with stories told through writing, illustration or other visual art, song, dance, film, oral presentations, video games, and theater. Holding up a copy of *Who's Afraid of the Big Bad Book*, I indicated that picture books combine illustration or other visual media with words to tell stories. I asked participants, "How do authors make these two [visual and textual] ways of storytelling work together in a picture book?"[80]

To respond to these questions, participants completed annotations of picture books I provided on their tables using Post-It notes on the pages to flag interesting cases in which the author/illustrator made the two media work together. On the Post-Its, participants drew and wrote their responses and questions, which were then shared in discussion. Most participants seemed to focus on the positioning of images and text. They noticed text wrapped around an image, text at the bottom of the page, text at the top, and text integrated into the image. Others noticed the way the two modes communicated with one another: minimal text to highlight and make a strong statement about the image, a lot of text to highlight the written narrative and to give important details that were not showing in images, text that adds new details to what is in the image, and text that adds conflicting information to the image. In particular, we considered how the composite nature of the picture book can tell serious stories. We did a close reading of *The Rabbits* and explored its key themes: violence, loss of land, and harm to the environment. Here we considered, through annotation exercises and subsequent group discussions, what the words told us, what the pictures told us, and what they left for us to wonder about or interpret (within the textual gaps). Parallels were drawn by some older participants between the rabbits and settlers in Canada; they gave examples of the residential school that operated in Alert Bay and nearby old-growth forests that had been logged. Many examined the fear that the colonized creatures experienced in the book, which they spotted in its compositional elements: dark and dull color, sharp or erratic lines, or use of space on the page. This was again connected to local history and atrocity by the participants: the fear Alert Bay residents once had of being imprisoned for celebrating potlatches or of family separation.

Moving to Anthony Browne's *Voices in the Park*,[81] we shifted into a more detailed discussion of compositional elements key to storytelling in picture books. In particular, we focused on typography. We first explored the word's meaning and then found and again annotated examples in the picture book. I next asked participants to find ways of writing the words *tall, short, dark, light, angry, sad, happy,* and *scared* in such a way that the shape, color, texture, size, and boldness of the lettering reflected the meaning of the words. This offers a concrete way of thinking about and practicing typography. Participants were invited to identify interesting examples of typography and draw or write their reflections on adhesive notes surrounding the example on the page (or to annotate the text). Older participants offered their help to younger participants to complete this activity, and we then shared our findings with the group. Developing an eye and language for picture-book composition enabled students to both engage more critically with the texts and become more critical producers of visual narratives (during the final double-page spread activity) enabling a full expression of their truths.

Following the examination of themes and other compositional elements of a number of picture books, such as *Zoom*,[82] *Black and White*,[83] and *Mirror*[84] (completed through a series of mediated reader response discussions), I highlighted to the group that a popular way of telling stories to children is to make animals and other objects look and act like people, and I asked them if they could think of any examples. Some provided examples from 'Namgis First Nations mythology, like stories of Raven. We discussed why this has become a common way of telling stories, with a range of explanations coming from the group: it's funny, it's imaginative, it's more interesting than stories about people, it helps us care for animals, and it helps us relate to animals. I wrote "Anthropomorphise" on the flip chart and explained that this is a vocabulary word that means "making non-humans look and act like humans," like we just discussed. Students recorded the word and drew or wrote their own definition for the term, and we spent some time finding examples in the picture books I supplied, such as *Yertle the Turtle*,[85] *Duck, Death and the Tulip*,[86] *The Three Pigs*,[87] and *Wolves*.[88]

To support critical literacy on colonization and food security, I took bunches of bananas and a number of salmon illustrations cut out of cardboard and placed them on the tables, suggesting that we all try to anthropomorphize these food items by thinking about what their human names, jobs, personalities, and hobbies would be like, considering the places from which the food came. They were keenly aware that the salmon came from the waters around Alert Bay, but they were less certain of the banana's origins. I asked students to investigate using the produce stickers on the bananas for some information. With the origin discovered (Ecuador), I encouraged students to search the internet on my computer; some older participants found that Ecuador is 6,493 miles away from Alert Bay. I added these food miles details onto a chart I had prepared as a teaching tool. We discussed the meaning of "food miles" in simple terms (the distance from foods' origin to its destination where it will be sold and the energy it takes to transport it there). Many participants expressed both pride about their local salmon and shock that the commonplace banana traveled such a long distance to reach their tables.

Anthropomorphizing salmon was a seamless and joyful task: local food proved to be an excellent generative theme. It quickly became evident that my salmon knowledge was not nearly as deep as the children's. Some participants used Kwak'wala names for their salmon character or employed the name of friend; some used traditional salmon mythology to develop its characteristics. Many participants could provide colorful detail of the salmon's homes (e.g., the Nimpkish River that flowed right outside our workshop space) and added funny fictional elements (one participant wrote: "I live in a mansion made of kelp and get around on my Orca Whale limo"). Some participants also used scientific terms (e.g., I am a fry [baby] or smolt [teenager]) to reflect their salmon character's age. The group found it challenging to do the same for the imported banana, as they were not aware what kind of terrain, climate, or language is common in Ecuador or even how bananas grow. Some of the older students crowded around my laptop to look over a Wikipedia article about Ecuador and shared this research with the others. Every participant filled the gaps imaginatively. Most of the hilarity in this brainstorming unfolded as students dreamed up plots in which the banana and salmon met. While some had them meeting on grocery store stocking shelves, another had a banana falling off a shipping boat and getting saved by a heroic salmon while it fell to the ocean floor. Others yet had them competing at a bowling alley or over a bingo game (both popular in Alert Bay).

Participants were then offered a selection of art supplies, and we drafted double-page spreads using notes from the brainstorming. Particularly for the younger participants, illustration allowed for more open expression, reinforcing what Salisbury and Styles assert: "what children can't always express in words, they can often demonstrate in their visual work."[89] The use of images make for particularly powerful mediums to relate concepts and meaning to young people.[90] Participants used these drafts while making their final double-page spreads. As this first workshop concluded, we discussed how we can continue to develop of our food narratives and characters. "How will we tell our stories, keeping in mind what we learned about how picture books are made?" I asked. I also recommended that when we were at the grocery store, we could keep looking at the stickers on the fruit and vegetables to learn about their food miles.

A simple but useful approach to engaging participants in an embodied way was making the bananas we examined in the first workshop into banana bread, which we ate the next day while creating our food narratives. Eating while thinking about food allowed participants to experience the direct impact of food on their lives. As Margorie O'Loughlin suggests, "introducing other senses into the learning environment emphasizes the role of the body in learning, which is more meaningful, as every learner has and is a body."[91] As I portioned out the loaves, a particularly keen participant, Brennen (eleven years) mentioned what he noticed in the grocery store before I had even remembered to raise the subject. He showed us a piece of paper on which he had affixed several produce stickers above a drawing of the fruit or vegetable they came from. One mango sticker indicated the fruit had traveled from Pakistan, which seemed especially dramatic given our position on a remote island on the northwest coast of Canada. The students gathered around Brennen's work, which stimulated an exciting discussion through crumbling mouthfuls of banana bread. Others added what they had found at the grocery store: produce from Mexico, India, China, and Spain. Carmen (six years), Brennen's younger sister, mentioned that her favorite fruits (blackberries, salmonberries, and huckleberries) are free and have no food miles because they grow around her home. Collecting berries is something families have done together long before mangos and bananas made an appearance in Alert Bay. To debrief, participants made illustrations of the island. These were "heat maps" indicating where their families collected or caught food, and participants used text around the image (reflecting picture-book narrative structure explored in the first sessions) to tell this story.

In the culminating activity, we used white paper folded in half (to serve as the "gutter" of the picture book), and participants created their double-paged spreads using the picture-book "tools" they had acquired.

The youngest participants chose to use the salmons cutouts and images of bananas on their spreads rather than drawing and to embellish them with craft supplies. Other older participants created their own illustrations and used text or dialogue. Many looked at picture books while creating to get ideas for layout and compositional elements we had discussed (like typography and use of line).

What resulted were vibrant visual narratives. Anthropomorphizing in this double-paged spread allowed children to make sense of the journey that the food had taken to arrive at the store rather than simply identifying the food as "imported" and also connect in critical ways the ordinary experience of eating with a larger legacy of colonial violence. It was my intention to "teach" the concept of food miles, but the grocery store exercise was an excellent way for participants to teach themselves about food miles and the differences between local and imported food. I found this to be consistent with Illich's sentiments that the most profound learning happens outside the classroom when one take responsibility over his or her own learning.[92] This is an important practice of autonomy and freedom, he emphasizes. Going to the grocery store with a heightened attention to these often-overlooked details—or a critical outlook on a routine task—was a small but powerful example of unsettling common practices. This unsettling, it seems, is the basis of transformative learning and addressing atrocity—moving away from simplistic stories to more complex ones, as Baer advocates. In a place like Alert Bay specifically, which has been aggressively settled by outside forces, "unsettling" reflects an important double entendre. Anthropomorphizing in the double-page spread was fruitful not only for facilitating an understanding of food politics and local identity but also for encouraging participants' self-expression while making their narratives and reflecting, in their own ways, parrhesia. It allowed, as children's literature often does, participants to weave factual and imaginative details: because the process of food miles is generally veiled and procuring exotic produce from the shop has become naturalized, we often need to fill in the gaps of knowledge. Participants presented copies of their work to their teachers, and the double-paged spreads were displayed at the local library for Indigenous and settler communities to consider. One primary school teacher who had been teaching units on nutrition drawing on standard (allopathic) texts on health and digestion responded to the students' work that she would start to include an exploration of food from the local Indigenous food system in this unit and Indigenous knowledge on nutrition.

What may seem like a light or even absurd activity—putting a salmon and banana into conversation through visual narrative—in practice excited meaningful dialogue on food sovereignty. It underscored for the participants the connection between Indigenous food systems and well-being or identity, bringing into sharper focus the harm that dispossession of land and culture (through colonial atrocities) has on a people. In conversation, participants began to imagine what their island was like when all food was local, how potlatch bans and residential schools and ongoing events changed that, what that change means for their family, and what it would take to eat more local food again. This imaginative work is useful for not only thinking about atrocity but also thinking about more just futures and the parrhesia this requires. Pierre Bourdieu writes: "Only in imaginary experience (in the folk tale, for example), which neutralizes the sense of social realities, does the social world take the form of a universe of possibilities equally possible for any possible subject."[93] I hold that a goal for such work is to develop tools and exchange knowledge so that members of communities like Alert Bay are the writers and illustrators of their own histories on both atrocity *and* resilience, as Linda Smith's "Decolonizing Methodologies" pointedly advocates.[94]

Concluding Thoughts

I have suggested that the exclusion of children from social discourse on atrocity often remains unchallenged within public life, schooling, and mainstream children's literature. If, as Freire insists, "it is in speaking their word that people [. . .] transform it, [and] dialogue imposes itself as the way by which they achieve significance as human beings," it is vital that young people are included in conversation about social issues and atrocity and able to engage in parrhesia.[95] Further, there is a duty of authors and educators to speak truth to power. This chapter explored ways in which the picture book can be used as a powerful medium to both present (from the author and illustrator) parrhesia in regard to atrocity and provide a platform for children to speak truth to power (both as readers and makers of picture books). I have highlighted four elements of the picture book that lend to awareness of and truth telling on atrocity: a flexibility of the picture-book form; the accessibility arising from a combination of two semiotic systems; the textual gaps permitted by the complex relationships between word and image; and its dialogical nature. Outlining the workshops here was a way of illustrating how engaging with picture books (and, in particular, unpacking how they are made) and using these tools to create visual narratives with children can support critical literacy on atrocity and truth telling.

While Canada is seeing a slow change in its educational approaches to colonial violence following the TRC, with the now mandatory curriculum from kindergarten to twelfth grade in residential schools, there remains a problematic taboo regarding colonial atrocities (such as eugenics programs and government-run starvation policies inflicted on Indigenous peoples and ongoing injustices of unfit living conditions on reservations).[96] This chapter holds that the picture book is a potentially transformative medium that can unsettle this problematic taboo and "pedagogy of retreat."[97] As Indigenous scholar Dwayne Donald suggests: "If colonialism is indeed a shared condition, then decolonizing needs to be a shared endeavor."[98] Parrhesia, after all, is a commitment—it fundamentally requires one to speak the truth and take ownership of what is said in this "speech activity."[99] This chapter reflects a desire to "share" this endeavor of decolonization by employing picture books to reflect examples of truth telling on atrocity and invite young people to act as parrhesiates themselves.

Notes

1. In a formal apology, former Prime Minister Stephen Harper summarized the residential school system: "Two primary objectives of the Residential Schools system were to remove and isolate children from the influence of their homes, families, traditions and cultures, and to assimilate them into the dominant culture" (Truth and Reconciliation Commission (TRC) of Canada, *Calls to Action*, Ottawa, 2015).

2. TRC, *Calls to Action*, 138.

3. TRC, *Calls to Action*, 138.

4. TRC, *Calls to Action*, 141.

5. Scott W. Murray, *Understanding Atrocities: Remembering, Representing and Teaching Genocide* (Calgary: University of Calgary Press, 2017), 7.

6. Claudia Card, *The Atrocity Paradigm: A Theory of Evil* (Oxford: Oxford University Press, 2002).

7. Card, *The Atrocity Paradigm*.

8. Card, *The Atrocity Paradigm*.

9. TRC, *Calls to Action*.

10. While working as a researcher, writer, and illustrator for The Critical Thinking Consortium, a Vancouver-based NGO that generates multimodal educational resources focusing on social justice issues, I undertook a contract for Alberta Heritage (a branch of the ministry of Alberta Culture and Tourism). This ministry

requested material to critically explore the history of the province for use in its elementary schools. As the province that was home to the greatest number of residential schools in Canada, it felt not only apt but also necessary to develop a resource that considered the experiences of Indigenous children in Alberta's residential schools. At this time (2010), there was no statutory curriculum on residential schools in Canada. Alberta Heritage ultimately refused this resource we developed, deeming it "too mature" for primary school students.

11. Gunther Kress and Theo Van Leeuwen, "Visual Interaction," in *The Discourse Reader*, 2nd ed., ed. Adam Jaworski and Nikolas Coupland (New York: Routledge, 2006), 15.

12. Karin Murris, *The Posthuman Child: Educational Transformation through Philosophy with Picturebooks* (London: Routledge: 2016), 72.

13. Laurence Sipe and Sylvia Pantaleo, *Postmodern Picturebooks: Play, Parody, and Self Referentiality* (New York: Taylor & Francis, 2008), 10.

14. Michel Foucault, *The Meaning and Evolution of the Word Parrhesia*. Lecture presented at the University of California at Berkeley, October–November 1983.

15. Though Foucault's lectures such as "Fearless Speech" (2001) make clear that parrhesia is a "verbal activity," this chapter proposes that it is also a useful term for capturing the truth telling that unfolds in texts.

16. Kenneth B. Kidd, "'A' is for Auschwitz: Psychoanalysis, Trauma Theory, and the Children's Literature of Atrocity," *Children's Literature* 33, no. 1 (2005): 120–49.

17. Stephen Legg, "Colonial and Nationalist Truth Regimes: Empire, Europe and the Latter Foucault," in *South Asian Governmentalities: Michel Foucault and the Question of Postcolonial Orderings*, ed. Stephen Legg and Deana Heath (Cambridge: Cambridge University Press, 2018), 106.

18. Michael Peters, "Truth-telling as an Educational Practice of the Self: Foucault, Parrhesia and the Ethics of Subjectivity," *Oxford Review of Education* 29, no. 2 (2003).

19. Vanessa de Oliveira Andreotti, "Conflicting Epistemic Demands in Poststructuralist and Postcolonial Engagements with Questions of Complicity in Systemic Harm," *Educational Studies* 50, no. 4 (2014); Shaun C. Ewen, "Unequal Treatment: The Possibilities of and Need for Indigenous Parrhesiastes in Australian Medical Education," *Journal of Immigrant and Minority Health* 13, no. 3 (2011).

20. Foucault, *The Meaning and Evolution of the Word Parrhesia*.

21. Brent Steele, "Of 'Witch's Brews' and Scholarly Communities: The Dangers and Promise of Academic Parrhesia," *Cambridge Review of International Affairs* 23, no. 1 (2010): 49–68.

22. Michael Maidan, "Michel Foucault: 'Discourse and Truth' and 'Parrhesia,'" *Phenomenological Reviews*, April 8, 2020, https://reviews.ophen.org/2020/04/08/michel-foucault-discourse-and-truth-and-parresia/.

23. Aman Sium and Eric Ritskes, "Speaking Truth to Power: Indigenous Storytelling as an Act of Living Resistance," *Decolonization: Indigeneity, Education & Society* 2, no. 1 (2013).

24. Paulette Regan, *Unsettling The Settler Within Indian Residential Schools, Truth Telling, and Reconciliation in Canada* (Vancouver: UBC Press, 2010).

25. Linda Tuhiwai Smith, *Decolonizing Methodologies: Research and Indigenous Peoples* (New York: Zed Books, 2012), 7.

26. Edward W. Said, *Representations of the Intellectual* (New York: Random House, 2012).

27. Robin Wall Kimmerer, *Braiding Sweetgrass: Indigenous Wisdom, Scientific Knowledge and the Teachings of Plants* (Minnesota: Milkweed Editions: 2013).

28. Postmodern picture books or contemporary picture books or critical picture books are terms used in academic literature on picture books to describe texts with characteristics that break with traditions such as linearity, clear resolutions, and simple visuals that merely illustrate the text (Sipe and Pantaleo, 2008).

29. Michel Foucault, *The Courage of Truth* (New York: Picador, 2012).

30. Elizabeth Roberts Baer, "A New Algorithm in Evil: Children's Literature in a Post-Holocaust World," *The Lion and the Unicorn* 24, no. 3 (2000): 378–401.

31. Perry Nodelman, *Words About Pictures: The Narrative Art of Children's Picture Books* (Atlanta: University of Georgia Press, 1988), 65.

32. Nodelman, *Words About Pictures,* 144.

33. K. Murris, "The Epistemic Challenge of Hearing Child's Voice," *Studies in Philosophy and Education* 32, no. 3 (2012): 39.

34. Murray, *Understanding Atrocities,* 200.

35. Lorraine Kasprisin, "Literature as a Way of Knowing: An Epistemological Justification for Literary Studies," *Journal of Aesthetic Education* 21, no. 3 (1987): 17–27.

36. Tuhiwai Smith, *Decolonizing Methodologies.*

37. Nodelman, *Words About Pictures,* 137.

38. M. Salisbury and M. Styles, *Children's Picturebooks: The Art of Visual Storytelling* (London: Laurence King Publishing, 2012), 91.

39. Sipe and Pantaleo, *Postmodern Picturebooks,* 13.

40. Evelyn Arizpe, Teresa Colomer, and Carmen Martínez-Roldán, *Visual Journeys Through Wordless Narratives: An International Inquiry with Immigrant Children and the Arrival* (London: A&C Black, 2014), 3.

41. David Lewis, *Reading Contemporary Picturebooks: Picturing Text* (London: Routledge, 2001), 63.

42. Sipe and Pantaleo, *Postmodern Picturebooks,* 54; Lewis, *Reading Contemporary Picturebooks,* 41.

43. Jewell Parker Rhodes, *Ghost Boys* (New York: Orion, 2018).

44. Murray, *Understanding Atrocities,* 200.

45. Maidan, "Michel Foucault: "Discourse and Truth" and "Parrhesia."

46. Louise Rosenblatt, *Making Meaning with Texts: Selected Essays* (Ontario: Pearson Education Canada, 2005).

47. Arizpe et al., *Visual Journeys,* 30, 123.

48. Lewis, *Reading Contemporary Picture Books*; Salisbury and Styles, *Children's Picturebooks*, 78.
49. Lewis, *Reading Contemporary Picturebooks*, 33.
50. Lewis, *Reading Contemporary Picturebooks*, 53.
51. Baer, "A New Algorithm in Evil."
52. John Marsden, *The Rabbits*, illus. Shaun Tan (Port Melbourne: Lothian Children's Books, 1998).
53. Henry Giroux, *Giroux's Principles of Critical Pedagogy*, 1991, 50, http://www.public.iastate.edu/-rhetoric/105H18/pedagogy/principle.
54. Marsden, *The Rabbits*.
55. Armin Greder, *The Island* (Sydney, New South Wales: Allen & Unwin, 2007).
56. Sipe and Pantaleo, *Postmodern Picturebooks*, 80.
57. Michel Foucault, *Fearless Speech* (Los Angeles: Semiotext[e]: 2001).
58. Hannah Arendt, *Hannah Arendt: Critical Essays* (Albany, NY: State University of New York Press, 1994).
59. Sipe and Pantaleo, *Postmodern Picturebooks*, 181.
60. Eliza T. Dresang, *Radical Change: Books for Youth in a Digital Age* (New York: H.W. Wilson, 1998).
61. Paulo Freire, *Pedagogy of the Oppressed* (London: Bloomsbury Publishing, 2000).
62. Paulo Freire, *Pedagogy of the Oppressed*, 69.
63. Paulo Freire, *Pedagogy of the Oppressed*, 69.
64. Sipe and Pantaleo, *Postmodern Picturebooks*, 76.
65. Freire, *Pedagogy of the Oppressed*, 71.
66. Baer, "A New Algorithm in Evil."
67. In 1921, the government of Canada enacted Section 116 of the Indian Act in an effort to stop the potlatch custom of dance, song, and wealth distribution and confiscated many precious wooden masks, copper shields, and dance regalia (umista.org). Several people decided to celebrate regardless of this law and faced imprisonment. The ban was eventually lifted during the 1970s and 1980s.
68. While undertaking participatory action research into traditional pedagogies in Alert Bay, I was invited by the Alert Bay Public Library to lead a series of picture-book workshops for children in their Art Loft. Participants were recruited through local schoolteachers distributing flyers on public notice boards and word-of-mouth.
69. "The 2012 nation-wide survey shows that Indigenous households report more than double the rate of food insecurity than is experienced by white Canadians." Caroline Bagelman, "Unsettling Food Security: The Role of Young People in Indigenous Food System Revitalization," *Children & Society* 32, no. 3 (2017): 1.
70. Jordan-Fenton, Christy, Margaret Pokiak-Fenton, and Liz Amini-Holmes, *Fatty Legs* (Toronto: Annick Press, 2010).

71. Marsden, *The Rabbits*.
72. Greder, *The Island*.
73. Shaun C. Ewen, "Unequal Treatment: The Possibilities of and Need for Indigenous Parrhesiastes in Australian Medical Education," *Journal of Immigrant and Minority Health* 13, no. 3 (2011): 609.
74. CCHS (Government of Canada), Canadian Community Health Survey, Nutrition 2012, *Government of Canada* (Ottawa, 2012).
75. D. Macdonald and D. Wilson, *Shameful Neglect* (Ottawa: Canadian Centre for Policy Alternatives, 2016).
76. Ewen, "Unequal Treatment."
77. Ewen, "Unequal Treatment."
78. Arizpe et al., *Visual Journeys*.
79. Arizpe et al., *Visual Journeys*.
80. Lauren Child, *Who's Afraid of the Big Bad Book* (Boston: Little, Brown, 2013).
81. Anthony Browne, *Voices in the Park* (New York: DK Publishing, 1999).
82. Istvan Banyai and Astvan Banyaii, *Zoom* (New York: Viking, 1995).
83. David Macaulay, *Black and White* (Boston: Houghton Mifflin, 1990).
84. Jeannie Baker, *Mirror* (Somerville, MA: Candlewick Press, 2010).
85. Theodore Geisel, *Yertle the Turtle* (New York: Redbook, 1950).
86. Wolf Erlbruch, *Duck, Death and the Tulip* (New York: Gecko Press, 2008).
87. David Wiesner, *The Three Pigs* (New York: Clarion, 2001).
88. Emily Gravett, *Wolves* (London: Macmillan, 2005).
89. Salisbury and Styles, *Children's Picturebooks*, 78.
90. Evelyn Arizpe and Morag Styles, *Children Reading Pictures: Interpreting Visual Texts* (London: Routledge, 2003).
91. Marjorie O'Loughlin, *Embodiment and Education: Exploring Creatural Existence* (Dordrecht: Springer, 2006).
92. Ivan Illich, *Deschooling Society* (London: Marion Boyars Publishing, 1995).
93. Pierre Bourdieu, *The Logic of Practice* (Stanford, CA: Stanford University Press, 1990), 64.
94. L. T. Smith, *Decolonizing Methodologies, Research and Indigenous Peoples* (London: Zed Books, 2012).
95. Freire, *Pedagogy of the Oppressed*, 69.
96. James William Daschuk, *Clearing the Plains: Disease, Politics of Starvation, and the Loss of Aboriginal Life* (Regina, Sask: University of Regina Press, 2013).
97. Dwayne Donald, "Forts, Colonial Frontier Logics, and Aboriginal-Canadian Relations," in *Decolonizing Philosophies of Education*, ed. A. A. Abdi (Rotterdam: Sense Publishers, 2011), 102.
98. Donald, *Forts, Colonial Frontier Logics*, 102.
99. Foucault, *The Meaning and Evolution of the Word Parrhesia*, 1999.

Works Cited

Arendt, Hannah. *Hannah Arendt: Critical Essays*. Albany: State University of New York Press, 1994.
Arizpe, E., and M. Styles. *Children Reading Pictures: Interpreting Visual Texts*. London: Routledge, 2003.
Arizpe, E., C. Bagelman, A. M. Devlin, M. Farrell, and J. McAdam. "Visualising Intercultural Literacy: Engaging Critically with Diversity and Migration in the Classroom through an Image-Based Approach." *Language and Intercultural Communication* (2014): 304–21.
Arizpe, Evelyn, Teresa Colomer, and Carmen Martínez-Roldán. *Visual Journeys through Wordless Narratives: An International Inquiry with Immigrant Children and the Arrival*. A&C Black, 2014.
Bourdieu, Pierre. *The Logic of Practice*. Stanford, CA: Stanford University Press, 1990.
Bagelman, Caroline. *Picturing Transformative Texts: Anti-Colonial Learning and the Picturebook*. Glasgow: University of Glasgow, 2015.
Bagelman, Caroline. "Unsettling Food Security: The Role of Young People in Indigenous Food System Revitalisation." *Children & Society* 32, no. 3 (2017): 219–32.
Baer, Elizabeth Roberts. "A New Algorithm in Evil: Children's Literature in a Post-Holocaust World." *The Lion and the Unicorn* 24, no. 3 (2000): 378–401.
Baker, Jeannie. *Mirror*. Somerville, MA: Candlewick Press, 2010.
Banyai, Istvan, and Astvan Banyai. *Zoom*. New York: Viking, 1995.
Bauer, M. *The Narrative Interview: Comments on a Technique for Qualitative Data Collection, no. 1*. London: London School of Economics and Political Science Methodology Institute, 1996.
Browne, Anthony. *Voices in the Park*. New York: DK Publishing, 1998.
Card, Claudia. *The Atrocity Paradigm: A Theory of Evil*. Oxford: Oxford University Press, 2002.
Child, Lauren. *Who's Afraid of the Big Bad Book*. Boston: Little, Brown, 2003.
CCHS (Government of Canada). Canadian Community Health Survey, Nutrition 2012. Government of Canada. Ottawa, 2012.
De Oliveira Andreotti, Vanessa. "Conflicting Epistemic Demands in Poststructuralist and Postcolonial Engagements with Questions of Complicity in Systemic Harm." *Educational Studies* 50, no. 4 (2014).
Donald, Dwayne. "Forts, Colonial Frontier Logics, and Aboriginal-Canadian Relations." In *Decolonizing Philosophies of Education*, edited by A. A. Abdi, 91–111. Rotterdam: Sense Publishers, 2011.
Donald, D. "The Curricular Problem of Indigenousness: Colonial Frontier Logics, Teacher Resistances, and the Acknowledgement of Ethical Space." In *Beyond Presentism: Re-imagining the Historical, Personal, and Social Places of Curriculum*, edited by J. Nahachewsky and I. Johnson, 23–41. Rotterdam: Sense Publishers, 2009.

Dresang, E. T. *Radical Change: Books for Youth in a Digital Age*. New York: H. W. Wilson, 1998.
Daschuk, James William. *Clearing the Plains: Disease, Politics of Starvation, and the Loss of Aboriginal Life*. Vol. 65. Regina, Sask: University of Regina Press, 2013.
Erlbruch, Wolf. *Duck, Death and the Tulip*. New York: Gecko Press, 2008.
Ewen, Shaun C. "Unequal Treatment: The Possibilities of and Need for Indigenous Parrhesiastes in Australian Medical Education." *Journal of Immigrant and Minority Health* 13, no. 3 (2011).
Foucault, Michel. *The Courage of Truth*. New York: Picador, 2012.
———. "Discourse and Truth: The Meaning of the Word Parrhesia." Lecture presented at the University of California at Berkeley, October–November 1983. Edited by J. Pearson. Compiled from tape recordings and reedited in 1999.
Freire, Paulo. *Pedagogy of the Oppressed*. London: Bloomsbury Publishing, 2000.
Geisel, Theodore. *Yertle the Turtle*. New York: Random House, 1950.
Giroux, Henry. *Giroux's Principles of Critical Pedagogy*. http://www.public.iastate.edu/-rhetoric/105H18/pedagogy/principle, 1991.
Giroux, Henry. *The Giroux Reader*. Colorado: Paradigm Publishers. 2006.
Gravett, Emily. *Wolves*. London: Macmillan, 2005.
Greder, Armin. *The Island*. Sydney, New South Wales: Allen & Unwin, 2007.
hooks, bell. *Teaching to Transgress: Education as the Practice of Freedom*. New York: Routledge, 1994.
Illich, I. *Deschooling Society*. London: Marion Boyars Publishers Ltd., 1995.
Jordan-Fenton, Christy, Margaret Pokiak-Fenton, and Liz Amini-Holmes. *Fatty Legs*. Toronto: Annick Press, 2010.
Kasprisin, Lorraine. "Literature as a Way of Knowing: An Epistemological Justification for Literary Studies." *Journal of Aesthetic Education* 21, no. 3 (1987): 17–27.
Kidd, Kenneth B. "'A' is for Auschwitz: Psychoanalysis, Trauma Theory, and the Children's Literature of Atrocity." *Children's Literature* 33, no. 1 (2005): 120–49.
Kimmerer, Robin Wall. *Braiding Sweetgrass: Indigenous Wisdom, Scientific Knowledge and the Teachings of Plants*. Minnesota: Milkweed Editions, 2013.
Kress, Gunther, and Theo Van Leeuwen. "Visual Interaction." In *The Discourse Reader*. 2nd ed., edited by Adam Jaworski and Nikolas Coupland. New York: Routledge, 2006.
Legg, Stephen. "Colonial and Nationalist Truth Regimes: Empire, Europe and the Latter Foucault." In *South Asian Governmentalities: Michel Foucault and the Question of Postcolonial Orderings*, edited by Stephen Legg and Deana Heath, 106–33. Cambridge: Cambridge University Press, 2018.
Lewis, D. *Reading Contemporary Picturebooks: Picturing Text*. London: Routledge, 2001.
Macdonald D., Wilson D. *Shameful Neglect*. Ottawa: Canadian Centre for Policy Alternatives, 2016.
Macaulay, David. *Black and White*. Boston: Houghton Mifflin, 1990.

Maidan, Michael. "Michel Foucault: 'Discourse and Truth and Parrhesia.'" *Phenomenological Reviews*, April 8, 2020. https://reviews.ophen.org/2020/04/08/michel-foucault-discourse-and-truth-and-parresia/.

Marsden, John. *The Rabbits*. Illustrated by Shaun Tan. Port Melbourne: Lothian Children's Books, 1998.

McIntosh, A. *Hell and High Water: Climate Change, Hope and the Human Condition*. Edinburgh: Birlinn Ltd., 2008.

Murray, Scott W. *Understanding Atrocities: Remembering, Representing and Teaching Genocide*. Calgary: University of Calgary Press, 2017.

Murris, Karin. *The Posthuman Child: Educational Transformation through Philosophy with Picturebooks*. London: Routledge: 2016.

Murris, Karin. "The Epistemic Challenge of Hearing Child's Voice." *Studies in Philosophy and Education* 32, no. 3 (2012).

Niezen, Ronald. *Truth and Indignation: Canada's Truth and Reconciliation Commission on Indian Residential Schools*. Toronto: University of Toronto Press, 2017.

Nodelman, Perry. *Words about Pictures: The Narrative Art of Children's Picture Books*. Atlanta: University of Georgia Press, 1988.

O'Loughlin, M. *Embodiment and Education: Exploring Creatural Existence*. Netherlands: Springer, 2006.

Peters, Michael, "Truth-telling as an Educational Practice of the Self: Foucault, Parrhesia and the ethics of subjectivity." *Oxford Review of Education* 29, no. 2 (2003).

Regan, Paulette. *Unsettling the Settler within Indian Residential Schools, Truth Telling, and Reconciliation in Canada*. Vancouver: UBC Press, 2010.

Rhodes, Jewell Parker. *Ghost Boys*. New York: Orion, 2018.

Rosenblatt, L. M. *Making Meaning with Texts: Selected Essays*. Ontario: Pearson Education Canada. 2005.

Said, Edward W. *Representations of the Intellectual*. New York: Random House, 2012.

Salisbury, M., and M. Styles. *Children's Picturebooks: The Art of Visual Storytelling*. London: Laurence King Publishing, 2012.

Sipe L. R., and S. Pantaleo. *Postmodern Picturebooks: Play, Parody, and Self Referentiality*. New York: Taylor & Francis, 2008.

Sium, Aman, and Ritskes, Eric. "Speaking Truth to Power: Indigenous Storytelling as an Act of Living Resistance." *Decolonization: Indigeneity, Education & Society* 2, no. 1 (2013).

Smith L. T. *Decolonizing Methodologies, Research and Indigenous Peoples*. 2nd ed. London: Zed Books, 2012.

Steele, Brent. "Of 'Witch's Brews' and Scholarly Communities: The Dangers and Promise of Academic Parrhesia." *Cambridge Review of International Affairs* 23, no. 1 (2010): 49–68.

Stephens, John. *Language and Ideology in Children's Fiction*. London: Longman, 1992.

Truth and Reconciliation Commission of Canada: *Calls to Action* (PDF) (Report). Truth and Reconciliation Commission of Canada, Ottowa, 2012.

Wiesner, David. *The Three Pigs*. New York: Clarion, 2001.

Chapter 11

Hidden Atrocities in Cinematic Representations of Chinese Girlhood

Chengcheng You

In early twenty-first century China, with increasingly broader access to educational opportunities, Chinese girls became engaged in ways of presenting and performing their identity across various multimedia platforms, such as popular nationwide TV singing contests, talent shows, and nostalgic coming-of-age films.[1] In these works, contemporary Chinese girlhood becomes a signifier of burgeoning pleasures, power, and possibilities in opposition to the rigidly patriarchal construction of female values of chastity, nurturance, and obedience. Despite some positive achievements, the contradictions and tensions between the omnipotent male gaze and the increasingly visible presence of teenage girls still exist in the predominantly patriarchal Chinese society. Cinema, as a mass medium, has become a quintessential site to reflect the female experience, but studies on cinematic storytelling mostly have focused on how womanhood is conceived, understood, and represented in transnational contexts.[2] Given that film narratives can be read as addressing the collective emotion and predominant issues of today's girlhood, the present study, therefore, is an attempt to review the thematics of Chinese girlhood on-screen and to interrogate the inherent power mechanism in the selected cinematic representations.

Over the past few years, an increasing number of contemporary Chinese films have attended to the constructedness of Chinese girls' identity, with frequent references to the common themes of family relations, sexual initiation, and the nostalgia of youth. The film list includes but is not limited to *Ne Zha* (*shao nv ne zha*/少女哪吒, 2014), *Our Shiny Days* (*shan guang shao nv*/閃光少女, 2017), *The Foolish Bird* (*ben niao*/笨鳥, 2017), *The Taste of Rice Flower* (*mi hua zhi wei*/米花之味, 2017), *Angels Wear White* (*jia nian hua*/嘉年華, 2017), and *Einstein and Einstein* (*gou shi san*/狗十三, produced in 2013 and released in 2018).³ These film narratives are mostly structured around conflicts, including those that are relational (e.g., child-adult, friendship, or family), physical (e.g., sexuality in adolescence versus conservative sexual attitudes), emotional (e.g., individual desires versus the inevitable reliance on family and other collective units), educational (e.g., escalating parental or peer pressure on academic performance versus limited availability of future choices), and geographical (e.g., urban versus rural, or China versus its border regions). While these conflicts shape the diverse cinematic expressions of Chinese girlhood, it is noteworthy that violent content, which may be associated with the transitional period and includes forms such as domestic violence and sexual abuse, is often only insinuated, explicitly reduced, or vetted for various purposes. A research focus on this aspect is important, as it motivates reflection on how Chinese cinematic representations of contemporary girls are symptomatic of Chinese parenting styles and gender politics in the contemporary context. Such representations also point to the problematization of unexamined conceptual apparatuses that abound in the girls' daily lives.

Hailed into a Conformist Girlhood

While many patriarchal norms are now subject to fundamental critique because of China's social and educational development, problematic notions that inform girlhood and education still exist. The most frequently used term is *dongshi* (懂事), which refers to a foremost virtue for children. Although seemingly equivalent to "sensible" in English, this term in modern Chinese is polysemous, and it designates 1) the ability to demonstrate proper etiquette in dealing with others; 2) empathy for the circumstances of one's parents (e.g., their bitter efforts in making money); and 3) the ability to understand the rules of this world to which one should eventually adapt. Despite its seemingly positive connotations, a survey found that 65.3% of 2,000 respondents felt they had been *dongshi* children from an early age, while 43.8% thought that the parental expectations of *dongshi* children resulted in their unhappy childhoods.⁴ The other term that has a similar effect is *guai* (乖), which, in itself, has undergone a dramatic development of its denotative meanings. Etymologically, *guai* suggests the deviation and rebellion of a person, but the term metamorphoses to mean the opposite, which is synonymous with obedience without making any trouble, and seen as a praiseworthy quality in children. When children are considered well behaved, listening without retortion or interruption and showing sheer respect for age and hierarchy, they will be praised as "*guai haizi*" (good children).

Of course, these two terms can be applied in a variety of scenarios. Here I mainly refer to their use in a parental setting in which adults talk to children in a patronizing and, quite often, condescending manner. Drawing on the aforementioned survey, the eventual ambiguous or derogative implications of both terms most likely can be attributed to their subtext, or the approximate equation of children's sensibility and intelligence with their ability to accept adults' moral instructions and behavioral practices. As the two terms are used so pervasively that they are taken for granted, they have even become imperative expressions of parental figures whenever they want to discipline children. However, a question worth asking is whether it is possible for child figures to enact their constructive agency when these expressions enforce an overtone of children's pessimistic resignation and conformity to adult expectations.

In an account of interpellation, Louis Althusser describes a situation in which a policeman in the street shouts, "Hey, you there!" The hailed individual will immediately turn around. According to Althusser, "By this mere one-hundred-and-eighty-degree physical conversion, he becomes a subject. Why? Because he has recognized that the hail was 'really' addressed to him."[5] The very moment of hailing is inescapable and inaugural, initiating a form of social discipline as well as an ongoing process in which the individual, when recognized, is made to take on his or her social role as subject. *Guai* or *dongshi* is a way of ideological interpellation by which we find that girls are, by definition, unwittingly "hailed" by the call of ideology into their subject positions in performing sensible and obedient roles. In other words, these girls are hailed into standardized or disciplined behavioral codes, and, through instantiating the implicit patriarchal ideology of hailing, they nullify their agency.

One may argue that there is always an option to resist being hailed and instead call upon an alternative approach to subjectively positioning oneself in a more empowered manner. It is necessary, first and foremost, to draw a realistic portrait of Chinese girls. Many of them face intense pressure to enroll in a prestigious university, and they are generally described as "stressed and lonely."[6] To wedge themselves into the collective view of growth as a prequel to an adult success story, girls shall behave as *dongshi* to adapt to the centralized education system, which, in general, aims to train children "to follow rules and instructions, and maintain social order as they learn how to be useful people."[7] Conversely, their failure to conform to the expectations of the adults around them, especially in terms of academic success, is likely to result in guilt or unfilial feelings for their parents or other caretakers.

These notions, if applied uncritically, inevitably perpetuate the child-adult power relations that lie at the heart of children's culture. They also produce what Primo Levi calls a morally ambiguous gray zone, which, symbolically, is where "the network of human relations . . . could not be reduced to the two blocs of victims and persecutors."[8] Despite the differences of the contexts, it could be suggested that the initiation into a conformist girlhood similarly exemplifies the complicit oppression and communal destruction of agency by hailing children to obey the orders of the authoritative figures, and particularly the paternal authorities. In China, *dongshi* is so ubiquitously prescribed as a virtuous model for children's behavior that children are likely to recalibrate themselves to the collectivist interests within their social associations at various levels (i.e., families, communities, or the nation). Some can, at their best, "uncannily intuit the situation and do things without being told" and, for example, "pour tea for others before themselves, fetch things for adults, and do things voluntarily before grown-ups even realize they need doing."[9] These examples show that the expectation from a *dongshi* child radiates an odd mixture of authority, praise, and sanction. On the one hand, it naturalizes the doctrine of authoritative parenting without much parent-child negotiation. On the other hand, children, being complimented, are unknowingly cast in a role relegated to a position of obedience. This cycle thus perpetuates a form of normalization designed to prioritize collectivist recognition over individual fulfillment. This power relation is so strongly marked in the field of international children's literature and culture that the voices with which those others speak are always adults' voices—voices of a time, place, and position in an adult-governed social structure.[10] However, if the adult criteria of how children should behave assume that the hegemonic power is self-evident and hence unquestionable, then in the case of children's education, the imposition of a socially constructed subjectivity must be more powerfully in play.

Using a contemporary Chinese reality TV show that features father-son relations as an example, Sin Wen Lau and Shih-Wen Sue Chen consider *guai* children "as active agents learning to fulfill their social obligations."[11] They continue to defend the moral advantage of *dongshi* children "because they understand how society works, possess the moral capacity to evaluate their places within it, and are capable of selecting and acting on appropriate strategies for contribution to collective interests."[12] Their view is, however, deeply contingent on the assumption of trustworthy and supportive parental love, with which children can enact the idealized models to facilitate their fitting into the social pattern. Without such a premise, the blind acceptance of being *dongshi* or *guai* will cause potential and even profound infliction on the children. Given the popular and unexamined acknowledgment of these terms in contemporary China, I further consider how *dongshi* or *guai* have institutionalized a paradigm of hidden evils on Chinese girls.

Dongshi and a Paradigm of Hidden Evils

> Many wrongs suffered by the relatively powerless, which are identified publicly as inequalities are, more importantly, evils. Perhaps they are commonly identified as inequalities because it is easier to accuse those in power of discrimination than to accuse them of evildoing. "Unfair" is a less harsh judgment than "evil."
>
> —Claudia Card, *The Atrocity Paradigm*[13]

Card's atrocity paradigm, later modified in her 2010 monograph *Confronting Evils: Terrorism, Torture, Genocide*, provides a lens through which *dongshi* can be further scrutinized. According to her paradigm, a more subtle account of evils should include "1) that evils are inexcusable, not just culpable, 2) that evils need not be extraordinary (probably most are not), and 3) that not all institutional evil implies individual culpability."[14] The paradigm challenges the definition of atrocities commonly recognized as "'extraordinary international crimes' that include crimes against humanity (an appellation that neatly embodies our shared victimization), genocide, and war crimes in essence."[15] Historical events such as the Holocaust and large-scale incidences of rape and sexual assault generally exemplify the very ruthlessness and culpable wrongdoing that characterize atrocities. In contrast, Card's paradigm extends the characterization of these events to include structural evil that begets "low-profile terrorism and torture that are routine under oppressive regimes, in racist environments, and in families devastated by domestic violence."[16] Many of these evils are collective inexcusable wrongs that need not be "extraordinary" as "out of the ordinary, unusual, rare, and worthy of note," but they may still produce intolerable harms in a way that is "reasonably foreseeable," for which complicit individuals, as participants in the social structure, may not be held accountable.[17]

Drawing on Card's paradigm, it is my claim that the behavioral model of *dongshi*, particularly in the situations of male-female, parent-adolescent relations, perpetrates foreseeable harm on female children. Explicating power relations is of the utmost importance to this inquiry because power is a prerequisite for perpetrators to be able to justify their evil wrongdoing, irrespective of how such evil will affect the victims. Here, a brief note on how the Confucian family ethics guide Chinese parent-child relations will help to elucidate the moral implications of these notions. Specifically, hailing children to be filial toward their parents and respectful of their older brothers is valued as the "roots of humaneness," as Confucius states in *Analects*:

> A person who is filial to his parents and respectful of his elder brother is rarely the kind of person who is inclined to go against his superiors, and there has never been a case of one who is disinclined to go against his superiors stirring up rebellion. The cultivated person applies himself to the root. "Once the root is established, the Way will flourish."[18]

Even though the Confucian sense of filial duty does not merely involve automatic submissiveness and respect for the senior males, there is no controversy in construing its shaping force of these typically patriarchal ideas. Through this moral paradigm, the gender-specific life narrative can be easily conjured, with boys encouraged to partake in playful adventure and indulge in rhetoric and politics, and girls admonished to observe the virtues of chastity, shyness, and housekeeping ability. Accordingly, one can approach the familial education of *dongshi* and *guai* as a residual Confucian influence over how girls are expected to maintain connections and understand their gender roles in terms of stereotypical traits like passivity and docility.

To extend Card's paradigm of atrocity, Jill Graper Hernandez proposes that patriarchy be understood as a "systemic evil" that "typically and predictably produces atrocious harm—even if those who suffer as a result of it sometimes need to learn that their suffering is not natural and is in fact the result of an immoral act."[19] As in the case of *dongshi* and *guai*, the hailing power is, by all means, irresistible when female children are educated to accept the patronizing attitudes of their male counterparts and submerge their own inner voices. Gender equality and sexual exploitation turn out to be hidden in the "naturalization" of patriarchal language. Card's analysis of the terms "unfair" and "evil" further illuminates how mitigated linguistic expressions have the "potential to reduce that impact of accusations of evil-doing, thereby making defensiveness a less natural response."[20] In a similar vein, the use of "*dongshi* girl" or "*guai* child" for the purpose of exercising the putatively feminine virtues affirmed by paternal authorities downplays the seriousness of the harm that might be generated.

Another layer of harm that often goes unnoticed and unremarked upon is the parental complicity that underscores patriarchal language. Chinese writer Zhang Dachun offers his assumption of the evolution of *guai*, which shifts from its derogatory flavor to the commendatory, by referring to the ethics of child rearing:

> The altered meaning of this word in modern times, I think, stems from the helplessness of generations of parents at the "deviation" and "rebellion" of their children. When parents lull their children to sleep, they sigh, "how *guai* (bad) it is!" Indeed, parenting is full of fatigue, complaining and helplessness. However, their children finally sleep, don't they? The nature of such complaint becomes confusing.[21]

Zhang's hypothesis unconsciously values adult or parental sensibility as a characteristic force that haunts and governs children's education. Such sensibility is grounded on the typical parental altruism in Chinese family life, and, as the oft-cited saying resounds, "The most pitiable is the heart of parents all over the world" (*Kelian tianxia fumu xin,* 可憐天下父母心). Given Chinese parents' willing sacrifices, the precepts addressed to children are intended not only to enforce the duty of love, but also to regulate filial obligations of reciprocity so as to carry on the family line and, at best, ensure intergenerational dependence. In such a social structure that endorses the patriarchal filial ethics, *dongshi* itself embodies the assumption of idealized feminine virtues that are more likely to be accepted in a patriarchal society, such as being obedient, nonthreatening, and silent. In the analysis that follows, I explore how this Chinese term is represented in these films, specifically *Einstein and Einstein* and *Angels Wear White*, as necessitating the formation of a conformist subjectivity and its eventual submission to the patriarchal discourse.

Einstein and Einstein: "Growth is a Homicide"[22]

> In our past experiences, when things happened for the first time, you think you'd reached your limit, that it couldn't be more painful. Then, for a second time, again you thought this was the end, but this time, you were even more hurt. Yes, one trauma after another, time heals all wounds. Although it takes longer and longer, still you got better, you survive. After being cured, you become a new person. There's no turning back from this road, but the road to the future, has already been chosen unconsciously. All of this is a lesson, it's all fair. But I'm not the person I used to be.
>
> —A Letter from Wang Xiaobing in *Ne Zha*

What is palpably displayed in contemporary Chinese girlhood films is the subject of a disappointing, not to say painful, transition from childish naivety to sophisticated adulthood—from craving self-expression and emotional rapport to an ambivalent attitude toward growth. The theme is well encapsulated in a letter from Wang Xiaobing, a central girl character in *Ne Zha*, who has lofty aspirations for life but has to endure her parents' discord, the pains of academic failures and demanding familial love. She exhausts all the strength to strive for intergenerational understandings but in vain. Such experience is aggravated in *Einstein and Einstein*, a film that arouses the public reminiscence of girlhood and the consensus that growth, in many similar ways, is a "homicide." Li Wan, a thirteen-year-old girl, begins living with her grandparents after her parents' divorce. As an adolescent with a lack of parental love, she longs for understanding and companionship. The film starts with a monologue of her dilemma: to join the physics club or the astronomy club. While her father is busy with his new family, including an infant son, and the pursuit of career advancement, he hopes to remedy his relationship with his estranged daughter by giving her a puppy as a gift. Wan names the dog Einstein, and she gradually builds an affectionate tie with the dog. However, the dog is accidentally lost in a market when her grandfather is buying groceries. The father, without making any effort to search for the dog, scolds Wan for having created a troublesome situation for her grandparents. To make matters worse, the dog is soon replaced with a fake Einstein that her stepmother brings her. Helpless and disillusioned, Wan gives up her search efforts and masks her disappointment. She gradually learns to act as *dongshi* as she can, for instance, by getting higher grades in school and even eating dog meat at a business dinner party to please her father. Her nonchalance, though ambiguously deliberate, culminates in the final scene, in which she catches sight of the real Einstein on the street, but refuses to admit to having done so. Running away from the spot, she happens to see one of the "Lost Dog" notices she once put up and bursts into tears.

The adults' influence on Wan's socioemotional outcomes gnaws at this coming-of-age narrative. The ways of lavishing their proclaimed love vary from one to another. The grandma, who plays the role of caretaker, knows that Wan will throw up if she drinks milk, but she still hands over a bowl of milk to her granddaughter, insisting that drinking milk is good. The grandpa loses Einstein, but he does not admit his mistake in the first instance, nor does he promise to search for the lost dog. While they claim to love their granddaughter, they nevertheless tell one lie after another and act with "good intentions" without considering Wan's feelings.

The father's love takes on a more radical form. To ensure Wan's academic success, he forces her to choose English, rather than physics or astronomy, for her interest club. When Wan feels offended, the father tries to assuage her with pocket money. Seeing that money does not work, the father starts to remonstrate:

> What? You're mad because I tried to help you? I'm busy all day, and I don't even get a chance to sleep. Your teacher wanted to talk to me the whole morning. Dad doesn't have a very easy life, does he? You wait till you grow up and you'll see for whom I did all these things.

As tensions ramp up, Wan resorts to drinking to relieve her pent-up sorrow at the loss of her dog and the crumbling family relations. Seeing her drinking a bottle of beer, her father is angered. He kicks her, pulls her by her hair, hits her, and slaps her. Scolding her at the same time, he uses one hand to point at his daughter and the other to grab her by the scruff of the neck: "You only care about yourself! Tell me, what the hell do you want? You want a planet, then I'll get a ladder. Speak! I owe you something, right? I owe you; everybody fucking owes you!" After beating his daughter, however, the father apologizes by again explaining his work-related stress and justifying his good intentions. Looking at his daughter fondly and gently caressing her hair, he says with great earnestness, "Dad hit you only because I love you. When you're older, you'll understand me. When will you finally grow up?"

Many Chinese parents attach overriding importance to academic achievement as the one and only means for their children to secure a better future. In this education system, which is also based on traditional Confucian teachings, the values of child socialization are mostly associated with obedience, perseverance, and filiality. Without competitive test scores or filial attitudes, any resistance or rebellion may prove fruitless and even detrimental to a child's future. The Chinese-style love of education, revolving around filiality and the motivation for achievement, is therefore justified in the father's disciplinary beating. As Chinese aphorisms go, "(when a parent) beats (the child's) body, the pain is in (the parent's) heart" (*da zai shen shang, teng zai xin li,* 打在身上，疼在心裡), or "Beating is (a sign of) affection, (and) cursing is (a sign of) love" (*da shi teng, ma shi ai,* 打是疼，罵是愛). Such disciplinary education, paradoxical as it is, inflicts not only physical and emotional pain on children, but also vulnerability and sufferance in parents. *Teng*, as in the proverbs cited, referring to "hurt" and "care" in the same breath, is exchangeable between the parents and the children they are beating. At best, the disciplinary approach should work as a means to "elicit children's sympathy and, consequently, submission to parental control in order to alleviate the parent's suffering" and "intensify the desirable parent-child bond, both for young children and for adult offspring."[23] Hence, the strict Chinese rearing style also coexists with its rich tradition of unconditional love of the young child. Within this culture-specific context, there always lies the difficulty of defining such a style in terms of whether it is a stringent, nonauthoritarian teaching method that encourages children to become ethical citizens of a society or a harsh, disciplinary form of education that thwarts children's personal development.[24]

Although Chinese parents and their children are bound by strong affective ties, this parenting style manifests itself more in the restraint of the girl character's personal autonomy than in the possibility of adolescent rebellion against conservative family values and, by extension, nation-promulgated gender ideology. After the father's temper outburst, the daughter is trained to accept her father's punitive measures as necessary to her growth and starts to act obediently to lessen her guilt for having deepened her father's financial and emotional burden. In this respect, the scene of being offered red wine and dog meat during her father's business dinner is the most unsettling in the whole film. Wan hesitates for a few seconds and takes both. "You make your dad so proud," says the father on their way back. Beaming with satisfaction, he completes the process of domestication: "You are a *dongshi* girl now; you have grown up." Without much doubt, the daughter also thinks that this must be the right, most reasonable, and only way to enter adulthood. She internalizes the adult norms, structurally as hard as steel, without being in any position to break them.

Another catalyst for Wan's praiseworthy "growth," or submission to adult governance, is the sudden arrival of her half-brother. Within the context of the parental preference for a son in the patriarchal system, right after Wan is compelled to recognize her half-brother, she bends submissively to the will of her family. When the father holds a birthday party for his one-year-old son, Wan pretends, rather artfully but failingly, to be unaffected by the change. However, her diminished sense of self-worth gradually manifests. Putting on a *dongshi* smile, she is soon thrust out of the circle at the party when the extended family ushers in the son to an avalanche of cheers and wishes. After the familial connection with her half-brother is established in Wan's life, she needs to sacrifice her study time to play with him, only to powerlessly witness how the father beats her new dog (also called Einstein) until its leg is broken after the dog, provoked by the son, barks fiercely. On the occasion, Wan extends her hand to pat the dog tenderly and whispers, "No fear, Einstein." The dog quiets down and lays obediently at her feet. Her eventual acceptance of and identification with the new Einstein indicates her realization that her former self, as opposed to the whole family, was a lot like this nervous and neglected dog at home. The best approach to survive, then, is to remain discreet, compliant, and irrevocably attached to the family.

Wan's susceptibility to domestication enacts what Card calls "terrorism in the home." Unlike the social institution of motherhood, which Card identifies as the spawning ground of domestic violence in the home, the paternal authority portrayed in the film enforces the habit of compliance, ranging from the father's prohibitive interventions, reprimands, and physical enforcement to occasional indulgences (with money, and later the promise of taking the daughter to her dream exhibition).[25] Though it works to secure the compliance of children, the father's so-called love and "good intentions" actually demonstrates the omnipotence of the Chinese patriarchy. The father never doubts his teachings because in a culture that is more collectivistic than individualistic, parental control is "often perceived as 'love' because it is part of the effort of the parents to make the child a useful member of the ingroup or the society."[26] A patriarchal family care ethics, however, stunts the development of the disempowered in a far-reaching way and mitigates individual culpability in its exercising the power of conformity. "Evils can be collectively perpetrated by way of social norms," as Card further reflects on the complicity in structural evils. "We do not think of ourselves as participants in a practice. If we think about it at all, we are apt to think of our behavior as spontaneous, normal, or self-interested, not as learned."[27]

By delineating a girl's personal experience that starts with her wonder at the universe and ends with her reconciliation with a hypocritical, hegemonic, and mundane adult world, this film problematizes the putative virtue of *dongshi*. In this process, the patriarchal stereotype of idealized femininity as passive and acquiescent in its relation to omnipotent masculinity comes under strident criticism. As represented in the film, the hidden evils are committed, albeit quietly and slowly, when adolescent girls are compelled to assimilate their law of survival in the patriarchal system, which is all about fitting in, achieving higher scores, and turning a blind eye to adult lies. If the atrocity in *Einstein and Einstein* is ultimately a refined and collective act of torture that would sustain a slow fire of indignation for most Chinese teenage girls, a more outrageous and harassing portrait of patriarchal domination is rendered in *Angels Wear White*, which awakens the public to the true and continuing tragedy of the twenty-first century patriarchy.

Angels Wear White: "The Most Terrible Thing"[28]

> Meng Xiaowen's father: You mean we are not suing him (the assailant Director Liu)?
>
> Zhang Xinxin's father: He was drunk that day and acted on his impulse. He is rather regretful now and hopes to do his best to compensate.
>
> Meng: What about justice?
>
> Zhang: What difference will it make if he is put to prison for a few years? He will eventually be released and have his day. But how about our children? They will suffer from the verbal slings and cold glances from others. We have to consider them.
>
> —The two fathers in *Angels Wear White*

Set in a tourist seaside town, a flashy place bustling with the desire to expand business during the off-season, the film *Angels Wear White* uncovers a problematic power-saturated context in which a case of child rape is extremely difficult to prove. Mia, about sixteen years old, works in a hotel in a scenic spot. One day while she is on duty, a man requests to book a room with two girls who appear to be primary school students. With some vague concerns,

Mia opens two rooms for them. Later, in the surveillance video, Mia sees the man push himself into the room of the two girls. Feeling uneasy, she records the scene on her mobile phone. The two girls, Xiaowen and Xinxin, later identify the assailant as Director Liu, a high-ranking commissioner of the region, and Xinxin's "deputy father." After learning about this sexual abuse, Xiaowen's mother calls the police and turns to a female lawyer for assistance. However, contrary to their wishes, a lack of evidence delays the conviction of the suspect, while the most critical evidence is kept secret by Mia, whose teenage identity remains undocumented.

The two intertwined narrative strands of the film directly point to the physical and mental assault that girls have suffered at the hands of male perpetrators. Their marginalized social status, or status of "non-agency," is easily subject to the influence of patriarchal power, particularly when they lack the care of their families or live in an unstable and harsh family environment. Thus, the dysfunctional families of Xiaowen, Mia, and Xinxin further exacerbate how these girls succumb to the traumas and tragedies that lead them to the fears, prejudices, and violence that scar their growth. In Mia's case, it is discovered that she has been living away from her abusive family and has sought to make a living on her own for the past three years. As a homeless adolescent girl, she is vulnerable to losing her job should her illegal work status be disclosed, and she is blackmailed by those who threaten to send her back to her horrid family. In Xiaowen's case, her mother habitually seeks to be affiliated with any male protector and neglects her daughter after her divorce, while her father, who is socioeconomically disadvantaged, is absent during her youth. Xinxin's father maneuvers his promotion by permitting the deputy father-daughter relationship, accepts the assailant's bribery, and seeks to cover everything with the ambiguous moral excuse that it is "all for the sake of his daughter." To the detriment of their mental growth, these parents—divorced, selfish, abusive, or socially downtrodden—create toxic family environments that impede the girl characters' growth toward self-actualization.

Xiaowen, for instance, displays dual personalities in the storyline. In the first manifestation, she is an innocent and lovely girl who is found laughing and playing with her best friend, running away from home with a jar of goldfish, and shouting through a giant loudspeaker for fun. At the same time, she is also a lonely, unlikable, and "insensible" child from the adults' perspective. She is often late for school and refuses to communicate with adults or bow to greet her teachers. However, these two sides appear in specific circumstances. If adults (e.g., her teacher, her mother, and the police officer) treat her with condescending arrogance, she appears to be willful, uncooperative, and reticent. With her peers, friends, and adults who respect her (e.g., the female lawyer and her biological father), she readily resumes a sense of security and innocence. Xiaowen's fractured experience of subjectivity indicates the thorny path of growth for any female child of little physical strength, no financial ability, and disempowered social status who needs to reconcile her resistance to and interdependence on the suppressive adult world. The same holds true in Xinxin's and Mia's vulnerable realities.

Part of what is so unbearable about the case of child rape is the surrounding culture of what Stanley Cohen has described as an "atrocity triangle" of "bystanders, perpetrators and victim" when the patriarchal crime is committed.[29] Cohen's paradigm shows a spectrum of different behaviors of onlookers, such as passive bystanders and opportunists who, to a great extent, facilitate atrocity. In the film, the passivity and inaction of the bystanders, as the director hints, make gender bullying more horrifying. Although these bystanders are not direct perpetrators, they partake in the atrocious harm inflicted on the victims. These individuals include the money-mongering hotel manager who threatens Mia to keep her silent, the corrupt police bureaucrats who accomplish nothing other than maintaining a false appearance of communal peace and prosperity, and the teen hooligan who takes advantage of female bodies for profit making. After the children are sexually assaulted, the bystanders not only become the evil force that prevents the victimized from safeguarding their rights, but they also impose secondary injuries on them. Here, the high degree of fluidity between bystanders and perpetrators characterizes patriarchy as a system of evil that proves beneficial "not only for those who can exercise their power as a result of it, but for those who experience some level of protection because of it."[30]

The harmful and complicit bystanders turn away from the blatant execution of evil, as they may believe that this case will be mired in the corrupt, patriarchal bureaucracy surrounding them. As represented in this film, the interlocking groups of business figures, bureaucrats, and doctors share corrupt exchanges among themselves to cover up each other's crimes and solidify the power in their hands. It would seem that these individual agents could change the rules, but they are merely an outward manifestation of structural evils. The anonymity of these bureaucrats, especially the sexual assailant, President Liu, remains, as if an invisible hand is starkly revealing that there is no way for the girl victims to escape from Satan's evil claws. At the culminating point of the film, Xinxin's parents, who are bribed by President Liu, exhort Xiaowen's father to give up the legal proceedings. The police officer, despite the video evidence, insists on taking Xiaowen and Xinxin for a physical checkup at the local hospital. After the checkup, the male doctor, who was bribed to produce false testimony, publicly announces that "their lower bodies are unhurt." "The most terrible thing," as the director aptly notes, "does not happen in the night of rape." The film engages the audience in a process of condemning a major case of injustice, one among many that goes masked, unnoticed, or even normalized. However, just as the story seems to be ending tragically, the case is suddenly resolved with due punishment of the male perpetrators through deux ex machina. We learn from the TV report, following Mia's eyes on TV, that all the criminals have been arrested, and their convictions are suddenly affirmed. Knowing this, Mia runs away from the room where she had almost made up her mind to be a prostitute. In a white skirt, she drives a motorbike to an uncertain future, passing the colossal statue of Marilyn Monroe that is being brought down.

The Monroe statue in the iconic flying white dress by the seaside serves as a symbolic thread that interweaves gender politics with the Chinese ethics of parent-child relationships. In the opening of the film, Mia touches the statue's polished nails, photographs the bottom of the flying skirt, and tears off the poster ads on the legs. Mia is going through the process of sexual maturity without proper adult guidance, and so is Xiaowen. Neither of them can find appropriate ways to address their sexuality other than to watch and emulate the feminine images around them. However, all the other female characters, except for the lawyer, embody traditionally modest characteristics of *dongshi*-style subordination, not knowing how to pursue their multifaceted possibilities. Xiaowen's mother frantically throws away Xiaowen's beautiful skirts and cuts off her long hair, thinking that she could have avoided rape by concealing her feminine attributes. As for Mia, it is my speculation that she will still play out a feminine role bowing to the patriarchy, like her close friend Lili who has an abortion and reconstructs her hymen after being abandoned by her lover. In these similar circumstances, we can chase the tangible fear of these girls in the shadow of domineering patriarchal power, which curbs their female imagination and consciousness.

The cruelty on Chinese girlhood in *Einstein and Einstein* and *Angels Wear White* is more psychological than physical, and it is not displayed on an extraordinary scale, but is instead demonstrated through stressful, prolonged, and even coercive experiences to which individuals and social factors collectively and complicitly contribute. As is evident in both films regarding the girls' trajectories of growth, while most people consider the family to be a private and tranquil haven, it is also a central locus that exerts chronic yet efficient discipline that accords with the state's favored gender ideology. Despite the progressive agendas for significant gender disparities, the depicted Chinese society is still infested with patriarchal notions of family and growth. These two narratives effectively illustrate how a conformist girlhood is gradually rationalized, the hidden atrocities of which further incarnate and reinforce patriarchal authority. As cinematic representations contain the power to question the cultural imposition of gender differences and leave the audience to reflect on how these inequalities take shape, it has proven difficult for Chinese girls, as realistically portrayed in the selected films, to counter the patronizing attitudes surrounding their growth. Underlying the failure to resist are multiple layers of silences—from victims and bystanders to the broader social structures–which sound louder than any words. To better illustrate how the hidden atrocities are committed, I regard the ideology of *dongshi* as a particular hailing through which girls are prone to the conformist and normalizing tendency to internalize hegemonic patriarchal standards and therefore view femininity as incapable of achieving self-autonomy.

It has to be said, though, that the purpose of this chapter is not simply to condemn the practices of many Chinese parents, but to problematize the notions that are taken for granted, and so much so that they are used to cover patriarchal evil. *Einstein and Einstein* uncovers the hidden atrocity of shaping a conformist girlhood at home, while *Angels Wear White* portrays the collectivization of male domination and female subordination on both individual and institutional levels. Both films represent how authoritarian adult figures conspire to construct a conformist girlhood by physically or mentally traumatizing girl characters in the home, school, and public spaces. Such cinematic articulations should be deemed of great significance, and not just in China. Narratives that problematize multilayered power relations that have reduced girls to the state of silence, conformity, and alterity, and that champion the potential of subverting the patriarchal evil to substantially empower them, are needed now more than ever across all national contexts.

Notes

1. Funding for this chapter was provided by University of Macau (Grant no. SRG 2019-00169-FAH).

2. See Shuqin Cui, *Women through the Lens: Gender and Nation in a Century of Chinese Cinema* (Honolulu: University of Hawai'i Press, 2003); Lisa Funnell,

Warrior Women: Gender, Race, and the Transnational Chinese Action Star (Albany: State University of New York Press, 2014); Lingzhen Wang, ed., *Chinese Women's Cinema: Transnational Contexts* (New York: Columbia University Press, 2011).

3. See the filmography.

4. Jing Chen, "*Dongshi* Child, Why Aren't You Happy?" (*dongshi de xiaohai, ni bu kuaile ma?*), *Sichuan Education* (*Sichuan Jiaoyu*), no. 10 (2016): 5.

5. Louis Althusser, *Lenin and Philosophy and Other Essays*, trans. Ben Brewster (London: New Left Books, 1971), 163.

6. Xu Zhao, *Competition and Compassion in Chinese Secondary Education* (New York: Palgrave Macmillan, 2015).

7. Shih-wen Sue Chen, Sin Wen Lau, and Lennon Yao-chung Chang, "'We Are All Useful People': Useful Children and the Notion of *Guai* in Transnational Chinese Cinema," *The Child in World Cinema*, ed. Debbie Olson (London: Lexington Books, 2018), 418.

8. Primo Levi, *The Drowned and the Saved*, trans. Raymond Rosenthal (New York: Simon & Schuster, 2017), 26.

9. Song Zhu, *The Xenophobe's Guide to the Chinese* (London: Oval Books, 2010), 62.

10. Perry Nodelman, "The Other: Orientalism, Colonialism, and Children's Literature," *Children's Literature Association Quarterly* 317, no. 1 (1992): 29–35. Echoing Nodelman's observation of hidden adults in children's literature, I consider the Chinese paradigm of *dongshi* as a culture-specific variation of this power mechanism.

11. Sin Wen Lau and Shih-Wen Sue Chen, "Children's Agency and the Notion of *Guai* in Chinese Reality Television," *Representing Agency in Popular Culture: Children and Youth on Page, Screen, and In Between* (Lanham: Lexington Books, 2019), 208.

12. Ibid., 208.

13. Claudia Card, *The Atrocity Paradigm: A Theory of Evil* (Oxford: Oxford University Press, 2002), 112.

14. Claudia Card, *Confronting Evils: Terrorism, Torture, Genocide* (Cambridge: Cambridge University Press, 2010), 4.

15. Mark A. Drumbl, *Atrocity, Punishment, and International Law* (Cambridge: Cambridge University Press, 2007), 4.

16. Card, *Confronting Evils*, 17.

17. Ibid., 27.

18. Cited and translated in Erin M. Cline, *Families of Virtue: Confucian and Western Views on Childhood Development* (New York: Columbia University Press, 2015), 8.

19. Jill Graper Hernandez, *Early Modern Women and the Problem of Evil: Atrocity & Theodicy* (New York: Routledge, 2016), 28–29.

20. Card, *The Atrocity Paradigm*, 112.

21. Translated from Zhang Dachun, *Appreciating Some Chinese Characters* (*Ren de ji ge zi*) (Taipei: Ink, 2007), 56–57.

22. Ma Xue, "*Einstein and Einstein*: 'Growth is a Homicide'" (*Gou shi san: mei yi chang cheng zhang dou shi xiong sha an*), https://3w.huanqiu.com/a/c93cce/7IyEkicrw7C?agt=209.

23. David Y. H. Wu, "Child Abuse in Taiwan," in *Child Abuse and Neglect: Cross-cultural Perspectives*, ed. Jill E. Korbin (Berkeley: University of California Press, 1983), 158.

24. Ruth K. Chao, "Beyond Parental Control and Authoritarian Parenting Style: Understanding Chinese Parenting through the Cultural Notion of Training," *Child Development* 65, no. 4 (1994): 1111–19.

25. See Ann Jones, *Next Time She'll Be Dead: Battering and How to Stop It* (Boston: Beacon, 1994), 90–91.

26. Harry C. Triandis, *Individualism & Collectivism* (New York: Routledge, 1995), 63.

27. Card, *Confronting Evils*, 65.

28. Duyaojun, "Interview with Wen Wei, the Director of *Angels Wear White*: It Is a Responsibility of the Onlookers Not to Consume Other People's Sufferings," http://baijiahao.baidu.com/s?id=1584288133179686332&wfr=spider&for=pc.

29. Stanley Cohen, *States of Denial: Knowing about Atrocities and Suffering* (Cambridge: Polity, 2001), 14.

30. Hernandez, *Early Modern Women and the Problem of Evil*, 28.

Works Cited

Althusser, Louis. *Lenin and Philosophy and Other Essays*. Translated by Ben Brewster. London: New Left Books, 1971.

Card, Claudia. *The Atrocity Paradigm: A Theory of Evil*. Oxford: Oxford University Press, 2002.

Card, Claudia. *Confronting Evils: Terrorism, Torture, Genocide*. Cambridge: Cambridge University Press, 2010.

Chao, Ruth K. "Beyond Parental Control and Authoritarian Parenting Style: Understanding Chinese Parenting through the Cultural Notion of Training." *Child Development* 65, no. 4 (1994): 1111–19.

Cohen, Stanley. *States of Denial: Knowing about Atrocities and Suffering*. Cambridge: Polity, 2001.

Chen, Jing. *dongshi de xiaohai, ni bu kuaile ma?* (*Dongshi* Child, Why Aren't You Happy?). *Sichuan Education* (*Sichuan Jiaoyu*), no. 10 (2016): 5.

Chen, Shih-wen Sue, Sin Wen Lau, and Lennon Yao-chung Chang. "'We Are All Useful People': Useful Children and the Notion of Guai in Transnational Chinese Cinema." In *The Child in World Cinema*, edited by Debbie Olson, 409–30. London: Lexington Books, 2018.

Cline, Erin M. *Families of Virtue: Confucian and Western Views on Childhood Development*. New York: Columbia University Press, 2015.

Cui, Shuqin. *Women through the Lens: Gender and Nation in a Century of Chinese Cinema*. Honolulu: University of Hawai'i Press, 2003.
Drumbl, Mark A. *Atrocity, Punishment, and International Law*. Cambridge: Cambridge University Press, 2007.
Duyaojun. "Interview with Wen Wei, the Director of *Angels Wear White*: It Is a Responsibility of the Onlookers Not to Perpetuate Other People's Sufferings." *Baidu*, November 17, 2017. http://baijiahao.baidu.com/s?id=1584288133179686332&wfr=spider&for=pc.
Funnell, Lisa. *Warrior Women: Gender, Race, and the Transnational Chinese Action Star*. New York: State University of New York Press, 2014.
Jones, Ann. *Next Time She'll Be Dead: Battering and How to Stop It*. Boston: Beacon, 1994.
Hernandez, Jill Graper. *Early Modern Women and the Problem of Evil: Atrocity & Theodicy*. New York: Routledge, 2016.
Lau, Sin Wen, and Shih-Wen Sue Chen, "Children's Agency and the Notion of *Guai* in Chinese Reality Television." In *Representing Agency in Popular Culture: Children and Youth on Page, Screen, and In Between*, edited by Ingrid E. Castro and Jessica Clark, 205–30. Lanham, MA: Lexington Books, 2019.
Levi, Primo. *The Drowned and the Saved*. Translated by Raymond Rosenthal. New York: Simon & Schuster, 2017.
Wang, Lingzhen, ed. *Chinese Women's Cinema: Transnational Contexts*. New York: Columbia University Press, 2011.
Ma, Xue. *Gou shi san: mei yi chang cheng zhang dou shi xiong sha an* (*Einstein and Einstein*: Growth is a Homicide), *Huaiqiu*, December 12, 2018, https://3w.huanqiu.com/a/c93cce/7IyEkicrw7C?agt=209.
Nodelman, Perry. "The Other: Orientalism, Colonialism, and Children's Literature." *Children's Literature Association Quarterly* 317, no. 1 (1992): 29–35.
Wu, David Y. H. "Child Abuse in Taiwan." In *Child Abuse and Neglect: Cross-cultural Perspectives*, edited by Jill E. Korbin, 139–65. Berkeley: University of California Press, 1983.
Xu, Zhao. *Competition and Compassion in Chinese Secondary Education*. New York: Palgrave Macmillan, 2015.
Zhang, Dachun. *Ren de ji ge zi* (Appreciating Some Chinese Characters). Taipei: Ink, 2007.
Zhu, Song. *The Xenophobe's Guide to the Chinese*. London: Oval Books, 2010.
Triandis, Harry C. *Individualism & Collectivism*. Routledge: New York, 1995.

Filmography

Cao, Baoping, dir. *Einstein and Einstein*. 2013.
Huang, Ji and Ryuji Otsuka, dir. *The Foolish Bird*. 2017.
Li, Xiaofeng, dir. *Ne Zha*. 2014.

Qu, Vivian, dir. *Angels Wear White*. 2017.
Song, Pengfei, dir. *The Taste of Rice Flower*. 2017.
Wang, Ryan, dir. *Our Shiny Days*. 2017.

Chapter 12

Nursery Atrocities

The Australian Children's Classic *The Magic Pudding*

Jayson Althofer and Brian Musgrove

> Theory must needs deal with cross-grained, opaque, unassimilated material, which [. . .] has outwitted the historical dynamic. This can most readily be seen in art. Children's books [. . .] contain incomparably more eloquent ciphers even of history than [high drama], concerned though it is with the official themes of tragic guilt, turning points of history, the course of the world and the individual [. . .]
>
> —Theodor Adorno[1]

The Magic Pudding: Being the Adventures of Bunyip Bluegum and His Friends Bill Barnacle and Sam Sawnoff is Australia's "classic" children's book. Written and illustrated by Norman Lindsay (1879–1969), it was published in Sydney in 1918. Centenary celebrations in 2018 included readings, exhibitions, stage shows, dress-up competitions, and opinion pieces rejoicing that Lindsay's picture book still makes readers laugh, all capped by commemorative coin and stamp releases by the Royal Australian Mint and Australia Post, and the 100th Anniversary Edition published by HarperCollins. The popular and official festivities for *The Magic Pudding*, whose plot originates in a race-war murder and provides comic cover for atrocities committed against Australia's First Nations peoples, are characteristic of the national culture's colonial, rather than postcolonial, mentality—unable to remember and also keen to forget its dependence on Aboriginal dispossession. The *Pudding's* political unconscious is haunted by Indigenocide, which, in Raymond Evans and Bill Thorpe's conceptualization, "refers to those actors (governments, military forces, economic enterprises or their agents, private individuals etc.) who carry out destructive actions, policies and practices on Indigenous/ Aboriginal individuals, families and groups *mainly because of their perceived indigeneity or 'Aboriginality.'*"[2]

This chapter amplifies Chris Eipper's reading of the *Pudding* as "an imaginary manifestation of ideological anxieties haunting the national culture to do with race, sex and property."[3] It intensifies Eipper's fine illumination of the specter of dispossession by referring to both historic incidents of atrocity and atrocious incidents of historiography that deny the actuality of dispossession. The *Pudding* is underwritten by atrocity, which is confessed and denied through its dreamwork on commonplace abominations in Australia's history, such as the rampant massacre of the First Peoples by poisoned foodstuffs. Lindsay's nursery tale encodes his thinking that *not* inuring children to atrocity contributes to "the sentimental perversion of youth."[4] Contrary to the orthodoxy repeated by Eipper that Lindsay wrote it to distract himself from the horrors of the Great War, the chapter demonstrates that an active ingredient of his oeuvre—his justification of atrocity as fundamental to imperialist hegemony and of that hegemony itself as a necessary atrocity—structures and colors his graphically violent story. As distinct from Eipper's interpretation, it engages with contemporary reviews as well as subsequent interpretations to provide an analysis, synthesis, and extension of previous secondary literature through the prism of the *Pudding*'s ciphered representation of atrocity.

Generally, the critical archive's white-nationalist nostalgia and inattentiveness to the *Pudding*'s cryptic but unapologetic depiction of atrocity reflect its aestheticization of violent deeds and imperialist doctrine. As shown in this chapter, even a present-day writer who criticizes aspects of the book nevertheless rehearses clichés that, to recall Walter Benjamin, render atrocity aesthetic. Lindsay's reputation as an antibourgeois provocateur distracts attention from the *Pudding*'s affirmation of capital's edacity in its imperialist forms. The problematics of its imperial ideology figure in historiographical absurdities and symbolic atrocities—flag-waving denials of "the killing times"—involved in Australia's ongoing "History Wars." In the mid-1960s, when he supported the American invasion of Vietnam, Lindsay remembered the Second Anglo-Boer War: "Britain's job [was] to push civilized conditions into the earth's crude spaces, and a lot of Bible-thumping farmers were only obstructing a Roman occupation of the earth's surface."[5] In 1932, he had visited the

United States and addressed an American audience in similar "civilized" terms. Lindsay told *Fortune* magazine's readers that "the average Australian is a good type": "For a century he has been forcing a place for himself in a crude and difficult land [. . .] and the War of 1914 demonstrated his tradition of toughness and endurance. [. . .] For the Australian is what all penetration into unknown lands has always been, the Roman legionary. Not the constructive Roman," Lindsay stipulated: "Always in Australia I see the hard sardonic faces of Caesar's legionaries."[6] In the *Pudding*, he projected the "average" (non-Indigenous) Australian's brio, akin to the *destructive* Roman, onto indigenous fauna that act like settlers of a new world.

The Story and Its Reception

The *Pudding* begins with the anthropomorphized koala Bunyip Bluegum setting off "to see the world."[7] Hurrying to leave home and gallivant like "a Gentleman of Leisure," he forgets to pack any food. He meets human ex-sailor Bill Barnacle and his penguin shipmate Sam Sawnoff, owners of a Magic Pudding named Albert, who offers slices of himself to hungry Bunyip. Besides being able to talk and take on any flavor desired by those who eat him, Albert is a "cut-an'-come-again" pudding, magically replenishing himself as soon as he is consumed.[8] Bill and Sam initiate Bunyip into their Noble Society of Puddin'-Owners, whose "members are required to wander along the roads, indulgin' in conversation, song, and story, eatin' at regular intervals at the Puddin'."[9] Also, they must recurrently brawl to keep control of their fabulous delicacy. In particular, they are obliged "on principle" to fight the "professional puddin'-thieves" Watkin Wombat and Possum.[10] In a show trial, the owners prosecute and judge their own case against the thieves. Then, craving to "put a stop to this Puddin'-snatchin' business for ever," Bill, Sam, and Bunyip build a treehouse with "a little Puddin' paddock." They become Gentlemen of Leisure, but anxious ones; "on account of so many people wanting to have a go at the Puddin' [. . .] at night they pull up the [treehouse] ladder in case a stray puddin'-thief happens to be prowling around"; and also on account of Albert being, to adapt Theodor Adorno's terms, "cross-grained, opaque, unassimilated material."[11] As self-willed chattel, liable to abscond, Albert is kept in a paddock. While his "owners" own him, he possesses his possessors, unsettling their dream of leisure. He symbolizes, among other things, the "crude and difficult land" that his possessors struggle to keep and exploit.

In 1918, newspaper reviews established a popular orthodoxy that the *Pudding* brims with harmless laughing matter fit for child and adult alike. According to Sydney's *Evening News*, "healthy Australian boys and girls, as well as children of a larger growth, must be hard to please if they are not thoroughly amused."[12] White Australian children and the idea of an "Australian childhood" itself were interpellated as vigorous types by dozens of journalistic mediations on the book across the country. "Norman Lindsay is amazing. He is a genius," writing tales "about and for real red-blooded harum-scarum kids"; "The book is full of clean, wholesome fun [. . .] cheerfulness and blithesome foolery"; "Here is a genial philosophy of cheerfulness [. . .] The fun is as clean and fresh as the scent of gum-leaves."[13] Reviewers commended the *Pudding* for its exhilaration at the Open Road and Great Outdoors: "It is a kind of extravaganza or fantasy of the Australian bush"; its adventures "are a wild amazing whirl, which lead nowhere in particular, but provide endless entertainment."[14] It was as if the book were meant to inspire a marching battalion of robust, young Australian *Wandervögel*—antipodean avatars of Caesar's soldiers—"forcing a place" in a country where legionary force of arms was, logically, absurd, because the British Crown had declared Australia an empty land. The idea of *terra nullius*—land allegedly devoid of civilized peoples who exercised sovereignty and could resist invasion—had allowed Britain to claim possession of New South Wales in 1770 and eventually all of Australia.

Lindsay's plot concerns the "penetration" and possession of territory. It is set in a version of *terra nullius* that is transformed into another kind of "no place": a utopia, occupied and possessed by the Noble Society of Puddin'-Owners, a place to satisfy its predatory appetites. Brenda Niall remarks that the *Pudding* "has no particular setting; it gives the impression of unlimited spaces and roads without destination."[15] However, these "unlimited" prospects are redefined, as the book's recurrent conflicts are really way stations on the journey to a purposeful, sedentary conclusion. The itinerant Puddin'-Owners come to squat on land with no legal title. They constitute a "squattocracy," defined by *The Australian National Dictionary* as a land-grabbing, upper-crust "socio-economic group," "really the aristocracy of Australia."[16] They exercise a kind of *droit de seigneur* to do nothing; a leisure-class right to idleness bought by violence.

Rather than scrutinizing the absurdist adventure's collusion in triumphalist settler-invader and nation-building narratives, the secondary literature also tends to symbolic Indigenocide—ignoring or erasing Aboriginal presence and identity. Writer-critics such as Robert Holden even appropriate indigeneity in the cause of white Australian nationalism; for him, the *Pudding* represents "indigenous literature for [white] Australian children."[17] Since 1918, the book and its nationalist interpreters have nursed "healthy Australian boys and girls" into historic atrocity welcomed as "endless entertainment." Its fantastical qualities, reputation, and canonization evoke Voltaire: "Those who can make you believe absurdities can make you commit atrocities."[18]

"The Delight with Which People Read of Atrocities"

Atrocity, at its conceptual apogee, as genocide and war crime, has been widely theorized and historicized.[19] Here, the concept of atrocity also applies, in Evans and Thorpe's words, to "abomination rendered commonplace."[20] Atrocity is manifest in banal practices of racial, class-based, economic, sexual, gendered, and religious violence, even if perpetrators and beneficiaries are not conscious of the damage done to targeted individuals, groups, or minorities. Although "microaggressions in everyday life"—characterized by Derald Wing Sue et al. as "brief and commonplace daily verbal, behavioral, or environmental indignities, whether intentional or unintentional, that communicate hostile, derogatory, or negative" slights and insults—are not always or necessarily perceived as atrocities, they can amount to atrocities involving force and trauma.[21]

Norman Lindsay was a master practitioner of "abomination rendered commonplace" through the nationwide dissemination of microaggression in his weekly cartoons for Australia's most influential newspaper, *The Bulletin*. "More than any other artist," states Bernard Smith, Lindsay "gave visual definition to *The Bulletin*'s editorial policy, particularly its nationalism and racism—Aborigines invariably figured as comics, Jews as old-clothes dealers with hooked noses."[22] The *Pudding*'s courtroom scene evidences such prejudice: the Usher has "a darker complexion" than the Judge, who calls him an "unmitigated Jew" and whacks him on the head with a glass bottle.[23] Lindsay's coinage of the portmanteau "noosepapers" in the *Pudding* confounds distinctions between force and consent and between large-scale atrocity and everyday outrages.[24] The tragicomic pun signals his recognition that mass media are a means to atrocious ends: newspapers not only inform, entertain, cajole, and indoctrinate, but also subserve a *dispositif* of disciplinary, repressive, and exterminatory practices and apparatuses. In Lindsay's Australia, "noosepapers" fed the home front's uncivil and vigilantist distemper during the Great War and its aftermath; in Albert's adage, "politeness be hanged, / Politeness be jumbled and tumbled and banged."²⁵ In Lindsay's 1920 *Bulletin* cartoon "Billy Bluegum's Christmas Tree," one of Bunyip Bluegum's relatives smiles and swaggers toward the viewer, away from a gumtree whose "Christmas" ornaments are ten lynching victims. Nine are anthropomorphized koalas, two unidentified and seven labeled: AVERAGE POLITICIAN, SECTARIANISM, BOLSHEVISM, STRIKER, fat, top-hatted PROFITEER, IKEY MO (Jewish money-lender), and GO SLOW (slogan and strategy of the Industrial Workers of the World). The tenth hanged figure is a small, black creature, horned, pigeon-toed, and labeled PRICE OF FOOD.²⁶ This alludes to class struggles over foodstuffs and to the political import of "the belly" in Lindsay's theories of social order and stability. He mulled over the potential for his mass-consumed work—"half a million Australians look for the work of Norman Lindsay every week"—to whet aggressive real-world appetites.²⁷ As he theorized in 1922:

> Barbarism is not depressed by pictures of its own barbarity. If these have any effect on it, they will only stimulate and excite it to fresh barbarism. We see this obscure effect of suggestion in the delight with which people read of atrocities and deeds of violence in the newspapers. The impulse here is one of desire towards the act, not horror against it.²⁸

A Dose of Nietzsche

Lindsay prized an ideologically naturalized aristocracy: "We owe to [Nietzsche] the knowledge that the aristocratic standard is fixed by Nature [. . .] Here for the first time was affirmed the aristocracy of Beauty, Gaiety, Uprightness."²⁹ Albert's owners, the Noble Society, who "settle down to a life of gaiety, dance and song," are allegorical figures comprising Nature's aristocracy.³⁰ As John Rickard observes, "the dandyish Bunyip, 'a fine, round, splendid fellow' can stake a claim to Beauty; the irrepressible Bill, who leads the carousing, is undoubtedly Gaiety, and it is not difficult to identify Uprightness with Sam, 'the penguin bold.'"³¹ Although this ersatz "Nietzschean" aristocracy was intended to constitute an aesthete over-class of sorts, and Bunyip is "a declassé type," Lindsay would have known that he was summoning public memory of the reversionary *bunyip aristocracy*—a derisive term for the Victorian political project of transplanting the English system of hereditary peerages onto the Australian colonies.³² As early as 1862, the term "bunyip aristocracy" was a synonym for "*imposter, pretender, humbug* and the like"; a class that, like the fabled river-monster bunyip, was a "terrible primeval lust rose up out of the deepest sludge" of the emergent imperial-nationalist mentality.[33]

Nation-building issues and strategies of imposture, of primeval lust for class power, and of primordial wealth are fundamental to the *Pudding*. National identity, especially as forged by violent conflict, was on Lindsay's mind as he wrote during the war, though the idea is not openly articulated. The *Pudding* "is a key text in the history of Australian literary consciousness and the national self-conception," Christopher Kelen argues, "despite the fact that signs of Australian nationhood must be inferred from the text." Kelen continues: "the scene is set for ambivalence by the fact that though the characters are mainly indigenous fauna, in order to make themselves readable by the audience intended, they mainly behave as settlers of a new Europe, in a recently cleared landscape of smouldering stumps."[34] The book's implied nation-defining project exemplifies Adorno's belief that children's literature contains "more eloquent ciphers even of history" than the so-called "high" genres of literature. However, the literature on Lindsay's book has only occasionally turned to consider its atrocious dimensions. Contemporary reviews celebrated the *Pudding*'s fresh-faced innocence, and the tendency to circulate benign readings has been critically durable: according to Peter Kirkpatrick, "Lindsay only used local objects for light comic purposes, as in [. . .] *The Magic Pudding*."[35] However, the book's "light" comedy is both veneer and vehicle for heavy-going cruelty: as Eleanor Witcombe writes, Lindsay's tale "bounces along from violence to violence."[36] Its heterogeneous form, David Musgrave argues, "is organised around the principles of excess and limits and their corollaries, textual and physical violence and arbitrary rule-breaking."[37] For Rickard, its content is "all about aggression . . . validated in terms of the cultural élite's right to maintain itself," and Kelen calls it "a tale of brutal fettered/unfettered exploitation."[38]

The *Pudding* anticipates and condenses the "élitist and amoral" credo of Lindsay's *Creative Effort: An Essay in Affirmation* (1920).[39] *Creative Effort* is a modernist disquisition on history and the crisis of modernity, peddling an agenda including race theory and eugenics, anti-unionism and anti-Bolshevism, anti-Semitism and anti-Christianity, anti-feminism and anti-homosexuality, poorly digested Nietzscheanism and neo-Platonic spiritualism, reactionary politics, and the prerogative of a creative class to create on the back of "a benevolent system of [industrial] slavery."[40] Stylistically and ideologically, Lindsay's treatise represents "the deepest sludge" in his oeuvre. So the *Pudding*'s real magic, Rickard affirms, is that it "rendered so palatable" ideas regurgitated later: "The message that Norman Lindsay laboured so long and so boringly to express in *Creative Effort* had already been uttered, much more wittily and spontaneously, in the innocent guise of a book for children."[41] Rickard also refers to "Lindsay's official embarrassment" at the *Pudding*'s immediate and continued success, which "stemmed from its apparent targeting of the baser instincts of the mob"—that is, pandering not only to popular and middling tastes, but also to lower, disorderly urges; or, in Mikhail Bakhtin's terminology, society's lower bodily stratum.[42] However much Lindsay scandalized the respectable public, the *Pudding* and *Creative Effort* reveal that he shared many of the prevailing values and prejudices expressed by white, middle-class Australians at the time. As Humphrey McQueen argues, Lindsay was a bourgeois ideologue, whose work was

> ideologically coherent with the most immediate requirements of the bourgeoisie which centred on three things: class dominance; imperial survival; and war. Lindsay's three tiers of mind were readily accessible to bourgeois needs for they offered a social set in which the artist (Lindsay) required that the organiser (capitalist) keep the mob (proletariat) hard at work.[43]

The *Pudding* has never been out of print; translated into several languages and nostalgically handed down from generation to generation in Australia, from grandparents to parents to children, on the misperception that it is merely a whimsical tale mostly populated by cutesy anthropomorphic characters. In Australia, the book has migrated from the realm of "literature" to "myth." It is embedded in white Australia's popular culture and national imaginary, and the phrase "Magic Pudding" is common in the political lexicon to mean the dream of bounty and limitless growth. It is symptomatic of white Australia's vaunting sense of conquest over the country's Indigenous occupants that the *Pudding* appeared in the same year as another publication portraying Australia as cornucopian continent—E. J. Brady's *Australia Unlimited* (1918). Like Lindsay, Brady contributed to *The Bulletin* and advocated the White Australia Policy. Brady's economic almanac, an exhaustive survey of the Commonwealth's primary industries, is also a fantastic manifesto for "unlimited" resource extraction and exploitation. *Australia Unlimited*, like the *Pudding* and voluminous op-ed articles on "Magic Pudding economics," always-already presumes that Australia must develop by expropriating Indigenous country, which its rightful white "owners" treat as a gargantuan cut-and-come-again commodity. Both books trade on the fantasy that capital's pleonexia, land hunger, and insatiability for nonrenewable resources are not ruinous but rather magically self-sustaining. As Bill tells Bunyip, "Me an' Sam has been eatin' away at this Puddin' for years, and there's not a mark on him."[44]

A vision of the violence that Lindsay regarded as inherent, ineradicable, and inescapable in the dark heart and rapacious belly of human social existence pervades the *Pudding*'s economic subtext. Lindsay began the manuscript in 1916, when he was contributing to the Allied Powers' war effort by producing cartoons and posters on hard Australian legionaries, Hunnish atrocities, and Europe's barbarization. Critical and popular consensus supposes that Lindsay wrote the *Pudding* as a respite from daily news of the war's horrors; "distraction" is the shorthand for his motivation. This complacent consensus elides or mitigates his complicity in those horrors. *The Official History of Australia in the War* (1921–43) acknowledges that his propaganda "of a grim and forceful appeal" gave "brilliant support" to the war effort and pro-conscription campaigns.[45] The consensus also overlooks the *Pudding*'s rehearsal of the philosophy that Lindsay elaborated in *Creative Effort* and "The Inevitable Future" (1922): horrific cycles of human depravity, the impossibility of progress, war's inevitability. A comic celebration of a violent vitalism, the "innocent" *Pudding* hails masculinist and legionary values. One early reviewer wrote, "It is a book that the boys will clamour for as they would for a catapult or a gun."[46] In the aftermath of "the greatest cataclysm of political hatred and bloodshed the world has ever seen," Lindsay ruminated: "after the smoke of this world war, amid the stink of putrefying corpses, and the memory of unmentionable deeds, the voice of the optimist is still loudest, proclaiming that the Messiah of Humanitarianism has risen at last."[47] Any promise of a more pacific, humanitarian future, Lindsay scoffed, was both delusion and mental weakness; life is an endless cycle of violence and atrocity, beyond good and evil, as Nietzsche understood:

> The sociological process of a generation dies with its generation. The small quantity of administrative intelligence that governs the vast incapable mob is a fixed quantity, sufficient for the needs of its generation, neither higher nor lower than the one that went before. There is no progress here, only, in Nietzsche's phrase, "eternal recurrence."[48]

Lindsay believed that basic appetites are quintessential to culture: "We owe to Nietzsche the understanding that the human valuation is physiological as well as psychological."⁴⁹ Existence, in this Weltanschauung, is a circle of return whereby the highest aspirations join the lowest appetites, exemplified in the masses: "the mob's baseness has this justification, that the struggle for existence gives it little choice of higher impulses. [One cannot expect] greatness of heart from those whose hearts are in their bellies."⁵⁰ This conjunction of high and low has a telos:

> the future of the lower and disorderly elements of society will be organised slavery. That is inevitable, for the worker is demanding it himself, by striving to become a menace, not merely to the more intelligent and ingenious class of society, but to the process of existence, of which he is also an element.⁵¹

Murder as a Nursery Tale

In Lindsay's philosophy, most people are "primitive," "savage," and "infantile"; children and the mob alike fixated on "the belly." This ontological crux—the gut governs the brain and its fancies—reappears in Lindsay's possibly apocryphal tale of the *Pudding*'s genesis, his anecdote of a simple wager prescribed by Nietzsche's physiologism:

> Bert Stevens and I were once discussing popularity motifs in books for children and Bert gave it as his opinion that fairies formed its most fascinating subject matter. I gave mine for food, on the theory that infantile concepts of happiness are based on the belly. In short, nice things to eat. [. . .] if a kid was offered his choice between food and fairies as delectable reading matter, I was willing to bet he would plump for food.⁵²

In the *Pudding*, nice victuals, embodied by Albert, were gotten by murder. To procure Albert, Bill and Sam killed his creator, a wizard-chef named Curry and Rice. Lindsay's narrator twice relates their primal violence; first in a flashback that occurs when Bunyip meets them, and then again in the courtroom, where Albert himself refutes Sam's humbug that the "Puddin', sir, an' me has registered vows of eternal friendship and esteem": " 'All lies,' sang out the Puddin' [. . .] 'For well you know that you and old Bill Barnacle collared me off Curry and Rice after rollin [sic] him off the iceberg.'"[53] Mention that Bill and Sam have Albert because they heaved Curry and Rice from an iceberg and left him to drown in waters off Cape Horn is rare in the secondary literature. An atypical contemporary review insinuates their atrocity: "There is a dark history attached to the way in which they acquired the delicacy."[54] That "dark history" intimates thoroughgoing race war: "If, as the cook's name and Lindsay's illustration suggest, the pudding is a creation of oriental cunning, the ensuing battle for its possession has more than a hint of race survival."[55] Bill and Sam not only survive the battle but also come out on top of the world with Bunyip; their supremacy is suggested by their "splendid house" and Albert's captivity in a fenced paddock.[56]

Lindsay's vision of vagrant murderers and an accessory after the fact becoming landlords partly follows one of his favorite writers, François Rabelais. The Noble Society's treehouse emprise alludes to Rabelais's word-picture of the denizens of Abbey Thélème in *Gargantua*: "All their life was regulated not by laws, statutes, or rules, but according to their free will and pleasure. [. . .] In their rules there was only one clause: DO WHAT YOU WILL."[57] As Lindsay declaims in *Creative Effort*: "within the trivial restrictions of social morality, the motto over the gates of birth is 'Do as you please.'"[58] The *Pudding*'s carnival of conquering and squatting "has no moral lesson. The struggle for possession of the magic pudding," Niall notices, "has nothing to do with rights."[59] Its amoral plot ends with a Cockaigne-like "national dream": "a vision of endless ease and pleasure with all needs supplied by an everlasting Puddin'."[60] In Eipper's allegorical reading, the book is "about having your cake and eating it too"—"the Pudding being, in effect, symbolic of the national cake." Eipper writes:

> this a story of the Commonwealth of Australia, or rather, the uncommon wealth of Australia [. . .] one only needs to turn to the climactic, utopian illustration in the book, which has the red ensign, then the specifically Australian version of the national flag, flying over the heroes as they abundantly enjoy their newly acquired Paradisiacal abode.[61]

That flag at the masthead of their treehouse waves to the *Pudding*'s central omission: the presence of Indigenous Australia. In this regard, it is readable as the perpetuation of atrocity: the theft of First Peoples' land, food, and children, and the devastation of their civilization through frontier warfare, pastoralism, and cultural genocide since British invasion in 1788.

The flashback to Bill and Sam killing Curry and Rice exhibits Lindsay's concern for race survival—paranoia about miscegenation, devitalization, and "Asiatic" invasion remains a staple of the white Australian imaginary. It also conjures atrocities that expropriated Indigenous Country, so-called *terra nullius*, into capital's world-system. Although Bill and Sam "come by their wealth through a kind of primitive accumulation," as Eipper remarks, their exploits are "forgiven, explained away, or mythologised—sharing as they do the sort of legitimate illegitimacy so often associated with redeemed outlaws."[62] This judgment echoes Karl Marx's exposé of "the secret of primitive accumulation." For Marx, "the tender annals" that textualize the primitive accumulation of property comprise a subspecies of children's literature that both hides and heroizes appalling truths:

> as soon as the question of property is at stake, it becomes a sacred duty to proclaim the standpoint of the nursery tale as the one thing fit for all age-groups and all stages of development. In actual history, it is a notorious fact that conquest, enslavement, robbery, murder, in short, force, play the greatest part.[63]

This describes Lindsay's representation of the property question. As Musgrave observes, "ownership of the Puddin' is defended by a set of arbitrary rules which are invariably violent."[64]

Popular-cultural responses to the *Pudding* constitute an ongoing atrocity of denial concerning Australia's violent past. As a near vacancy, its landscape implies the doctrine of *terra nullius*—a flashpoint in contemporary Australian debates over history, property, and cultural affairs. There is also what the anthropologist W. E. H. Stanner labeled "The Great Australian Silence": the reluctance to acknowledge or speak about the colonial purging of Indigenous peoples, amounting to "a cult of forgetfulness practised on a national scale."[65] Since the 1990s, Australia's history wars have pivoted on these two things. Reactionary writers and journals like Keith Windschuttle and *Quadrant* aim to minimize or even deny the reality of atrocities on the emerging nation's frontiers. As Evans and Thorpe reflect in their study of "the massacre of Aboriginal History," "Windschuttle and *Quadrant* hold to the absurd proposition that Aboriginal Australians will not be content until they have regained all the land that was forfeited under colonization." This absurdity leads to atrocious "denial, distortion and disremembering":

Where Windschuttle and others prefer to see an unsullied Union Jack proudly flying over the Australian continent, we are compelled to examine the realities of what it hides. And what we discern is a chilling glimpse of Nietzsche's "festival of cruelty." [. . .] the overwhelming sense is that of abomination rendered commonplace.[66]

The *Pudding* condenses a global history of "geographic imperialism with pastoralism as its core" and thus recalls Thomas More's Utopia, where sheep eat people.[67] As a fable of indigenous fauna domesticated, dressed-up, and "whitened," the *Pudding*'s "genial philosophy of cheerfulness" and the Puddin'-Owners' paradisiacal imposture are flavored by the "joy in cruelty" theorized by Nietzsche:

> the delicacy and even more the tartuffery of tame domestic animals (which is to say modern men, which is to say us) resists a really vivid comprehension of the degree to which *cruelty* constituted the great festival pleasure of more primitive men and was indeed an ingredient of almost every one of their pleasures.[68]

For Nietzsche, "the ever-increasing spiritualization and 'deification' of cruelty" both "permeates the entire history of higher culture" and "in a significant sense actually constitutes it."[69]

Dreamwork and "Death Pudding"

"Children's literature," Kenneth Kidd states, "has been very usefully understood as therapeutic and testimonial. Certain genres seem to function much like the dreamwork as Freud described it, at once acknowledging but distorting or screening trauma."[70] This clustering of therapy and testimony, of twisting and masking trauma generated by atrocity, cleaves to the *Pudding*, which an early reviewer recognized as "a kind of extravaganza or fantasy of the Australian bush," or a phantasmagoria "in the realms of Impossibility."[71] Its motifs and narrative patterning play with the condensation, displacement, and secondary revision of Australia's frontier history—a cruel festival engendered by what Michael Grewcock calls "the criminogenic nature of settler colonialism."[72] The *Pudding* is permeated by dreamlike signs of invader hunger, greed, and atrocity; acknowledging, but indirectly, that Australia "was established through the foundational violence inherent to settler colonialism and the processes of primitive accumulation that underpinned it."[73] It is analogous to a recurring anxiety dream. The trauma it reworks is not that suffered by Australia's dispossessed Aborigines, but rather that suppressed by the perpetrators and beneficiaries of atrocities committed against them: the trauma of direct acknowledgement of atrocity. Distortion, dismissal, and denial are white wish fulfillments.

Eipper desublimates the atrocious and traumatic extratextual grounds of the Noble Society's prepossession with strangers' designs to collar their property:

> An obsession with dispossession, of having wealth stolen from you that you stole—what for Australians does this inevitably evoke if not the confiscation of a continent from its Aboriginal inhabitants? At the time Lindsay was writing, the eventual elimination of the indigenous population seemed assured.[74]

In 1920, an administrator in the Colonial Office minuted that in Australia "the process of extermination seems likely to continue."[75] In 1927, the Royal Commission into the 1926 Forrest River massacre reported that a "conspiracy of silence" had thwarted its attempts to decipher what actually happened.[76] Yet Eipper's question is not rightly rhetorical: the *Pudding*'s reception history adduces no evidence for unsettling evocations among non-Indigenous Australians generally. Amid numerous "noosepaper" pieces written in its centenary year, Jeff Sparrow's column is, perhaps, sui generis, as he mentions Curry and Rice's murder and offers a genuine cultural critique. Sparrow notes that the book bespeaks Lindsay's racism and androcentrism: "his depiction of koalas, bandicoots and other native animals adventuring through a landscape as entirely white and exclusively male" is "a reminder of Lindsay's attachment to some of the nastier prejudices of his era." However, Sparrow's opening sentence—"Norman Lindsay's book of delightfully nasty characters and superb illustrations became a beloved children's classic"—is itself a reminder that, in public discourse and a society degraded by bourgeois hegemony, "nasty characters"—their microaggressions and atrocities—can still elicit delight, remaining canonized and mythologized if they are superbly aestheticized.[77]

Lindsay's sister-in-law and fellow writer Joan Lindsay claimed that "in the field of social and political cartoons, Lindsay has made a direct contribution to Australian national art, while in a more homely sphere his illustrated juvenile classic *The Magic Pudding* has an authentic Australian flavor."[78] Dreamwork performed by the *Pudding* upon Australia's "killing times" allows this gothic transposition of her evaluation: Lindsay's classic epitomizes a national art in the *unhomely* sphere of white Australia's haunting by the specter of its reign of terror over the nation's First Peoples. This is traceable in the uncanny correlations between the nightmare of actual history and the *Pudding*'s "clean, wholesome fun."[79] For instance, just fifty years before Lindsay started writing the *Pudding*, William Stamer recorded:

> No device by which the race [sic—Aborigines] could be exterminated had been left untried [by the 1860s]. They had been hunted and shot down like wild beasts—treacherously murdered whilst sleeping within the paddock rails, and poisoned wholesale by having arsenic or some other substance mixed with the flour given to them for food.[80]

Such "civilizing" recipes, Stamer ironized, were flaunted under "our blood-red flag."[81] Likewise, Mark Twain (who relished Lindsay's father's company in Ballarat during his 1895 lecture tour of Australia) retold "a sort of exhibition of cruelty": Rosa Praed's recollection of Aborigines slain by an arsenic-laced Christmas pudding.[82]

Historians of colonial Australia verify Stamer and Praed's accounts of poisoned foodstuffs: "The act of poisoning whole communities of Aborigines with arsenic or strychnine-laced milk or rations—the so-called "death pudding"—may be regarded from one viewpoint as the most sinister and brutal of atrocities in the 'war of the races.'" One "jovial" newspaper article reported that a squatter

> gave "the niggers [. . .] something really startling to keep them quiet" in the shape of poisoned food: "The rations contained about as much strychnine as anything else and not one of the mob escaped. When they awoke in the morning they were all dead corpses. More than a hundred Blacks were stretched out by this ruse of the owner of Long Lagoon."[83]

In some regions of Australia, massacre by poisoning was "almost a commonplace occurrence."[84] A decade before the *Pudding*'s publication, a cleric was told: "if you give the blacks phosphorous in their flour it only makes their eyes water, but if you mix arsenic with the flour, that'll stretch them out."[85]

Mass poisoning is refracted, condensed, and revised in the *Pudding*'s courtroom farce. Bunyip alerts the Pudding-eating Judge and Usher that Albert has been poisoned. "The Judge turned pale" at the thought that he has been poisoned; the Usher sings, "Through this dreadfulest of crimes, / As you've eaten seven slices / You've been poisoned seven times"; and Albert "let out a howl of terror." The Judge bounds over his bench and batters the Usher, Watkin Wombat, and Possum with a port bottle. This commotion enables Bill, Sam, and Bunyip to repossess Albert from the court officials and then set off to build their treehouse. "But what about the dreadful news of me being poisoned at ten-thirty this morning?" Albert demands to know. "You ain't poisoned, Albert," replies Bill. "That was only a mere *ruse de guerre*, as they say in the noosepapers."[86] Given the eerie nexus between the martial stratagems of real-life and fictional squatters—Long Lagoon's "owner" and Albert's "owners"—the *Pudding*'s "authentic Australian flavor" smacks of toxic, indigenocidal ingredients. Bill's accusation that Albert is "very secret, crafty," and "treacherous" is a phantasmal projection of the Puddin'-Owners' own recurrent ruses.[87]

The *Pudding*, to reprise Adorno's terms, alludes to a deal of "opaque, unassimilated material." As dreamworked testimony to atrocity, it proffers mock therapy to non-Indigenous Australian readerships, or burlesques the very need for a talking cure. It functions simultaneously as apologia for atrocity and denial that Indigenous Australians are owed so much as a place in a national narrative, let alone a national apology for massacres of their ancestors. Bill's "handsome" audacity regarding the Noble Society's squattocratic treehouse—"Rough, good-humoured fellers like us don't need apologies"—is a premonitory cipher for an official theme of Australia's History Wars: "Australians," then Prime Minister John Howard asseverated in 2007, "will never entertain an apology because they don't believe that there is anything to apologise for."[88] Now as then, the story line of racism and colonial rapacity is inflected by sexist narration, like "the realist tradition that Mark Twain introduced against the excesses of 'feminine' sentimentality."[89] The fantasy-laden *Pudding* is Lindsay's modest proposal for the realpolitik of inevitable human savagery and symbolic cannibalism. In 1916, he hinted to his publisher that his book could toughen the mentality of youthful masculinity:

> Sentimental tenderness and prettiness are strictly repudiated. [. . .] I cannot lend a hand to the sentimental perversion of youth. The grown-up world, as you are aware, is having its debauch of prettiness and false sentiment at present [. . .] but let us hope that something may be done to stiffen the younger generation to a more decent frame of mind.[90]

In this phallocentric faith, "red-blooded" white Australian boys and men need not apologize for perpetrating or benefiting from aggression, assault, and atrocity.

Conclusion: "Acceptable Terror"

"It is a nice irony," Rickard quips, that Norman Lindsay, "enemy of the gumtree tradition in cultural nationalism, should have enjoyed his greatest success with such an Australian yarn as *The Magic Pudding*."[91] His sardonic tale remains successful because it appeals to the wish for and dream of an "innocent" white Australia, civilized by a noble society of gentlemen whose violent possession of "magic" is treated as a comic picaresque. It reproduces the elisions and silences on which modern Australia was founded. Its popularity correlates to its comfortable vision of a prosperous, settled nation—a house in a gumtree, a town on the horizon, and the national flag waving above it all—and to its genial and congenial perpetuation of the myth of *terra nullius* and the cult of silence.

"It is intensely discomforting to conceive of an Australian social order where the mass murder of certain people, identifiable by their ethnicity, was a way of life," Evans and Thorpe write: "tolerated by the settler majority, and winked at by a state which, in other settings, upheld the precepts of British culture, law and justice." Nonetheless, "the context of acceptable terror was the historical truth."[92] Lindsay could not choose *not* to write about this truth, so ineradicable and irrepressible that it speaks symptomatically through the white Australian Dream embedded in his book. Poet-playwright Douglas Stewart remembered that in conversation, "the small British frontier wars in India, Africa and the Sudan [were] one of the many unexpected subjects in which Lindsay was an expert."[93] For Lindsay, however, atrocity in Australian frontier warfare was almost necessarily unthinkable and unmentionable.

Coda

Since we wrote this chapter in 2019, reading *The Magic Pudding* has continued to engender uncanny resonances. George Floyd's words "I can't breathe" have breathed new life into Indigenous Australian activism against racism and governmental impassivity toward perennial black deaths in police and prison custody. In the *Pudding*'s courtroom scene, Bill Barnacle testifies that the puddin'-thieves once stole Albert by pulling a bag over the heads of the Puddin'-Owners, "compellin' [them] to endure agonies of partial suffocation [. . .] for several hours."[94] Bill's slice of tartuffery elides Albert's fate: to be bagged, tied up, cut up, eaten alive, stolen, stolen back, rebagged, and reeaten in perpetuity. The imperative that black lives matter is a modest counterproposal to perpetuating the kind of systemic atrocity that is unspoken but encoded and endorsed by Lindsay's text.

Notes

1. Theodor Adorno, *Minima Moralia: Reflections from a Damaged Life*, trans. E. F. N. Jephcott (London and New York: Verso, 2005), 151.

2. Raymond Evans and Bill Thorpe, "'Indigenocide' and the Massacre of Aboriginal History," *Overland* 163 (2001): 34.

3. Chris Eipper, "The Magic in the *Magic Pudding*," *Australian Journal of Anthropology* 10, no. 2 (1999): 195.

4. Norman Lindsay, Letter to George Robertson, ca. September 1916, qtd. in *Dear Robertson: Letters to an Australian Publisher*, ed. A. W. Barker (Sydney: Angus & Robertson, 1982), 62–63.

5. Norman Lindsay, *Bohemians at the Bulletin* [1965] (Sydney: Angus & Robertson, 1977), 17.

6. Norman Lindsay, "Australia and Australians" (1932), in *Norman Lindsay on Art, Life and Literature*, ed. Keith Wingrove (St. Lucia: University of Queensland Press, 1990), 85–86.

7. Norman Lindsay, *The Magic Pudding: Being the Adventures of Bunyip Bluegum and His Friends Bill Barnacle and Sam Sawnoff* (Sydney: Angus & Robertson, 1918), 16.

8. Lindsay, *Magic Pudding*, 14, 23.

9. Lindsay, *Magic Pudding*, 44.

10. Lindsay, *Magic Pudding*, 30.

11. Lindsay, *Magic Pudding*, 168, 171.

12. "*The Magic Pudding*. Norman Lindsay's Latest Book," *Evening News* (Sydney), October 3, 1918.

13. "'The Magic Puddin'. Norman Lindsay in High Glee," *Sydney Stock and Station Journal*, October 4, 1918; "*The Magic Pudding*," *Queenslander* (Brisbane), November 2, 1918; "Australiana. Norman Lindsay," *Daily Telegraph* (Sydney), October 5, 1918.

14. "Literary Gossip," *Leader* (Melbourne), October 12, 1918; "*The Magic Pudding*," *The Sydney Morning Herald*, October 5, 1918.

15. Brenda Niall, assisted by Frances O'Neill, *Australia through the Looking-Glass: Children's Fiction 1830–1980* (Carlton: Melbourne University Press, 1984), 202–3.

16. W. S. Ramson, ed., *The Australian National Dictionary: A Dictionary of Australianisms on Historical Principles* (Oxford: Oxford University Press, 1988), 623, 626.

17. Robert Holden, "The Plague of Lindsays: A Family of Illustrators," in Ursula Prunster, *The Legendary Lindsays* (Sydney: The Beagle Press and The Art Gallery of New South Wales, 1995), 115.

18. Voltaire, *Questions sur les miracles* (1765), qtd. in *Oxford Essential Quotations*, ed. Susan Ratcliffe, 5th. ed. (2017 online version), https://www.oxfordreference.com.

19. To nominate only a few examples, see Colin Tatz, *Genocide in Australia*, AIATSIS Research Discussion Paper no. 8 (Sydney: Australian Institute of Aboriginal and Torres Strait Islander Studies, 1999); Claudia Card, *The Atrocity Paradigm: A Theory of Evil* (New York: Oxford University Press, 2002); Dan Stone, *History, Memory and Mass Atrocity: Essays on the Holocaust and Genocide* (London: Valentine Mitchell, 2006); Philip G. Dwyer and Lyndall Ryan, *Theatres of Violence: Massacre, Mass Killing and Atrocity throughout History* (New York: Berghahn, 2012); and Lyndall Ryan et al., *Colonial Frontier Massacres in Central and Eastern Australia 1788–1930* (The Centre for 21st Century Humanities, University of Newcastle, Australia, 2017–), https://c21ch.newcastle.edu.au/colonialmassacres/about.php.

20. Evans and Thorpe, "'Indigenocide,'" 33.

21. Derald Wing Sue et al., "Racial Microaggressions in Everyday Life: Implications for Clinical Practice," *American Psychologist* 62, no. 4 (2007), 271.

22. Bernard Smith, "Lindsay, Norman Alfred (1879–1969)," *Australian Dictionary of Biography* 10 (1986), http://adb.anu.edu.au/biography/lindsay-norman-alfred-7757.

23. Lindsay, *Magic Pudding*, 162, 164.

24. Lindsay, *Magic Pudding*, 169.

25. Lindsay, *Magic Pudding*, 20.

26. Norman Lindsay, "Billy Bluegum's Christmas Tree" (cartoon), *Bulletin* (Sydney), December 11, 1920.

27. "Percy Lindsay, Artist," *The Lone Hand* (Sydney), June 16, 1919. Australia's official population was about 5.2 million; NB. Commonwealth censuses did not count Indigenous Australians before 1967.

28. Norman Lindsay, "The Inevitable Future," *Art in Australia*, February 1 (1922): 27.

29. Norman Lindsay, *Creative Effort: An Essay in Affirmation* (Sydney: Art in Australia, 1920), 14.
30. Lindsay, *Magic Pudding*, 168.
31. John Rickard, "The Magic of the Pudding," *Meanjin* 47, no. 4 (1988): 719.
32. Eipper, "Magic," 196.
33. Ramson, *Australian National Dictionary*, 109.
34. Christopher Kelen, "*The Magic Pudding*: A Mirror of Our Fondest Wishes," *JASAL* 6 (2007): 65.
35. Peter Kirkpatrick, *The Sea Coast of Bohemia: Literary Life in Sydney's Roaring Twenties* (St. Lucia: University of Queensland Press, 1992), 69.
36. Eleanor Witcombe, "The Magic of the Pudding," in *The World of Norman Lindsay*, ed. Lin Bloomfield (South Melbourne: Macmillan, 1979), 42.
37. David Musgrave, "Aspects of Symposiastic Law in *The Magic Pudding*," *Coppertales: A Journal of Rural Arts* 6 (2000): 10.
38. Rickard, "Magic," 722; Kelen, "*Magic Pudding*," 68.
39. Rickard, "Magic," 722.
40. Lindsay, *Creative Effort*, 86.
41. Rickard, "Magic," 722.
42. Rickard, "Magic," 717.
43. Humphrey McQueen, "Norman Lindsay's *Vision*," in *Gallipoli to Petrov: Arguing with Australian History* (Sydney: George Allen & Unwin, 1984), 40.
44. Lindsay, *Magic Pudding*, 23.
45. Ernest Scott, *Australia during the War*, Vol. XI, The Official History of Australia in the War of 1914–1918, 5th ed. (Sydney: Angus and Robertson, 1939), 348.
46. "'The Magic Puddin.' Norman Lindsay in High Glee," *Sydney Stock and Station Journal*, October 4, 1918.
47. Lindsay, *Creative Effort*, 9–10.
48. Lindsay, *Creative Effort*, 10.
49. Lindsay, *Creative Effort*, 14.
50. Lindsay, *Creative Effort*, 43.
51. Lindsay, *Creative Effort*, 85–86.
52. Norman Lindsay, Letter to G. A. Ferguson, May 1952, qtd. in *The Letters of Norman Lindsay*, ed. R. G. Howarth and A. W. Barker (Sydney: Angus & Robertson, 1979), 428.
53. Lindsay, *Magic Pudding*, 160.
54. "A Norman Lindsay Fantasy," *Argus* (Melbourne), October 19, 1918.
55. Rickard, "Magic," 719.
56. Lindsay, *Magic Pudding*, 171.
57. François Rabelais, *The Histories of Gargantua and Pantagruel*, trans. J. M. Cohen (Harmondsworth: Penguin, 1955), 159.
58. Lindsay, *Creative Effort*, 85.

59. Niall, *Australia through the Looking-Glass*, 200.
60. Niall, *Australia through the Looking-Glass*, 6.
61. Eipper, "Magic," 194–95.
62. Eipper, "Magic," 207.
63. Karl Marx, *Capital: A Critique of Political Economy*, vol. 1, trans. Ben Fowkes (Harmondsworth: Penguin and New Left Review, 1990), 874.
64. Musgrave, "Aspects of Symposiastic Law," 7.
65. W. E. H. Stanner, *The Boyer Lectures 1968: After the Dreaming* (Sydney: Australian Broadcasting Commission, 1969), 25.
66. Evans and Thorpe, "'Indigenocide," 21, 29, 33.
67. Evans and Thorpe, "'Indigenocide," 34.
68. Friedrich Nietzsche, *On the Genealogy of Morals [and] Ecce Homo*, ed. Walter Kaufmann, trans. Walter Kauffmann and R. J. Hollingdale (New York: Vintage, 1969), 66.
69. Nietzsche, *On the Genealogy of Morals*, 68.
70. Kenneth Kidd, "'A' is for Auschwitz: Psychoanalysis, Trauma Theory, and the 'Children's Literature of Atrocity,'" *Children's Literature* 33 (2005): 122.
71. "Literary Gossip," *Leader* (Melbourne), October 12, 1918.
72. Michael Grewcock, "Settler-Colonial Violence, Primitive Accumulation and Australia's Genocide," *State Crime Journal* 7, no. 2 (2018): 222.
73. Grewcock, "Settler-Colonial Violence," 222.
74. Eipper, "Magic," 205.
75. Unnamed official qtd. in Raymond Evans, *A History of Queensland* (Port Melbourne: Cambridge University Press, 2007), 171.
76. Lorena Allam and Nick Evershed, "The Killing Times: The Massacres of Aboriginal People Australia Must Confront," *Guardian* (Australia edition), March 3, 2019.
77. Jeff Sparrow, "*The Magic Pudding* Can Still Make Us Laugh Even after 100 Years," *Guardian* (Australia edition), October 26, 2018.
78. Joan Lindsay, "Australian Art: Introduction and Notes to Plates," in *Masterpieces of the National Gallery of Victoria*, ed. Ursula Hoff (Melbourne: F.W. Cheshire, 1949), 183.
79. "*The Magic Pudding*," *Queenslander* (Brisbane), November 2, 1918.
80. William Stamer, *Recollections of a Life of Adventure*, vol. 2 (London: Hurst and Blackett, 1866), 97.
81. Stamer, *Recollections*, vol. 2, 99.
82. Mark Twain, *Following the Equator: A Journey around the World* (Hartford: American Publishing Co.; and New York: Doubleday & McClure Co., 1897), 211.
83. Raymond Evans, Kay Saunders, and Kathryn Cronin, *Race Relations in Colonial Queensland: A History of Exclusion, Exploitation and Extermination*, 3rd. ed. (St. Lucia: University of Queensland Press, 1993), 49.
84. Evans, Saunders, and Cronin, *Race Relations*, 50.

85. Rev. F. H. Campion qtd. in Evans, Saunders, and Cronin, *Race Relations*, 50.
86. Lindsay, *Magic Pudding*, 162, 169.
87. Lindsay, *Magic Pudding*, 30.
88. Lindsay, *Magic Pudding*, 171; "PM Must Say Sorry: Indigenous Groups," *Australian* (Sydney), October 12, 2007.
89. Kidd, "'A' is for Auschwitz," 130.
90. Norman Lindsay, Letter to George Robertson, ca. September 1916, qtd. in Barker, *Dear Robertson*, 62–63.
91. Rickard, "Magic," 722.
92. Evans and Thorpe, "Indigenocide," 29.
93. Douglas Stewart, *Norman Lindsay: A Personal Memoir* (Sydney: Angus & Robertson, 1979), 157.
94 Lindsay, *Magic Pudding*, 155.

Works Cited

Adorno, Theodor. *Minima Moralia: Reflections from a Damaged Life*. Translated by E. F. N. Jephcott. London: Verso, 2005.
"Australiana. Norman Lindsay." *Daily Telegraph* (Sydney), October 5, 1918.
Barker, A. W., ed. *Dear Robertson: Letters to an Australian Publisher*. Sydney: Angus & Robertson, 1982.
Brady, E. J. *Australia Unlimited*. Melbourne: George Robertson, [1918].
Card, Claudia. *The Atrocity Paradigm: A Theory of Evil*. New York: Oxford University Press, 2002.
Dwyer, Philip G., and Lyndall Ryan. *Theatres of Violence: Massacre, Mass Killing and Atrocity throughout History*. New York: Berghahn, 2012.
Eipper, Chris. "The Magic in the *Magic Pudding*." *Australian Journal of Anthropology* 10, no. 2 (1999): 192–212.
Evans, Raymond. *A History of Queensland*. Port Melbourne: Cambridge University Press, 2007.
Evans, Raymond, Kay Saunders, and Kathryn Cronin. *Race Relations in Colonial Queensland: A History of Exclusion, Exploitation and Extermination*. 3rd ed. St. Lucia: University of Queensland Press, 1993.
Evans, Raymond, and Bill Thorpe. "'Indigenocide' and the Massacre of Aboriginal History." *Overland* 163 (2001): 21–39.
Grewcock, Michael. "Settler-Colonial Violence, Primitive Accumulation and Australia's Genocide." *State Crime Journal* 7, no. 2 (2018): 222–50.
Holden, Robert. "The Plague of Lindsays: A Family of Illustrators." In Ursula Prunster, *The Legendary Lindsays*, 114–16. Sydney: The Beagle Press and the Art Gallery of New South Wales, 1995.
Howarth, R. G., and A. W. Barker, eds. *The Letters of Norman Lindsay*. Sydney: Angus & Robertson, 1979.

Kelen, Christopher. "*The Magic Pudding*: A Mirror of Our Fondest Wishes." *JASAL* 6 (2007): 65–78.
Kidd, Kenneth B. "'A' is for Auschwitz: Psychoanalysis, Trauma Theory, and the 'Children's Literature of Atrocity.'" *Children's Literature* 33 (2005): 120–49.
Kirkpatrick, Peter. *The Sea Coast of Bohemia: Literary Life in Sydney's Roaring Twenties.* St. Lucia: University of Queensland Press, 1992.
Lindsay, Joan. "Australian Art: Introduction and Notes to Plates." In *Masterpieces of the National Gallery of Victoria*, edited by Ursula Hoff, 179–238. Melbourne: F.W. Cheshire, 1949.
Lindsay, Norman. *The Magic Pudding: Being the Adventures of Bunyip Bluegum and His Friends Bill Barnacle and Sam Sawnoff.* Sydney: Angus & Robertson, 1918.
Lindsay, Norman. *Creative Effort: An Essay in Affirmation.* Sydney: Art in Australia, 1920.
Lindsay, Norman. "Billy Bluegum's Christmas Tree" (cartoon). *Bulletin* (Sydney), December 11, 1920.
Lindsay, Norman. "The Inevitable Future." *Art in Australia*, February 1, 1922, 22–41.
Lindsay, Norman. "Australia and Australians." 1932. Reprinted in *Norman Lindsay on Art, Life and Literature*, edited by Keith Wingrove, 83–90. St. Lucia: University of Queensland Press, 1990.
Lindsay, Norman. *Bohemians at the Bulletin.* 1965. Reprint, Sydney: Angus & Robertson, 1977.
"Literary Gossip." *Leader* (Melbourne), October 12, 1918.
"'The Magic Puddin'. Norman Lindsay in High Glee." *Sydney Stock and Station Journal*, October 4, 1918.
"*The Magic Pudding*. Norman Lindsay's Latest Book." *Evening News* (Sydney), October 3, 1918.
"*The Magic Pudding*." *Queenslander* (Brisbane), November 2, 1918.
"*The Magic Pudding*." *The Sydney Morning Herald*, October 5, 1918.
Marx, Karl. *Capital: A Critique of Political Economy.* Vol. 1. Translated by Ben Fowkes. Harmondsworth: Penguin and New Left Review, 1990.
McQueen, Humphrey. "Norman Lindsay's *Vision*" (1975). Reprinted in *Gallipoli to Petrov: Arguing with Australian History*, 35–43. Sydney: George Allen & Unwin, 1984.
Musgrave, David. "Aspects of Symposiastic Law in *The Magic Pudding*." *Coppertales: A Journal of Rural Arts* 6 (2000): 5–17.
Niall, Brenda, assisted by Frances O'Neill. *Australia through the Looking-Glass: Children's Fiction 1830–1980.* Carlton: Melbourne University Press, 1984.
Nietzsche, Friedrich. *On the Genealogy of Morals [and] Ecce Homo.* Edited by Walter Kaufmann and translated by Walter Kaufmann and R. J. Hollingdale. New York: Vintage, 1969.
Rabelais, François. *The Histories of Gargantua and Pantagruel.* Translated by J. M. Cohen. Harmondsworth: Penguin, 1955.

Ramson, W. S., ed. *The Australian National Dictionary: A Dictionary of Australianisms on Historical Principles.* Oxford: Oxford University Press, 1988.
Ratcliffe, Susan, ed. *Oxford Essential Quotations.* 5th ed. (2017 online version). https://www.oxfordreference.com.
Rickard, John. "The Magic of the Pudding." *Meanjin* 47, no. 4 (1988): 717–22.
Ryan, Lyndall, et al. *Colonial Frontier Massacres in Central and Eastern Australia 1788–1930.* The Centre for 21st Century Humanities, University of Newcastle, Australia, 2017–. https://c21ch.newcastle.edu.au/colonialmassacres/about.php.
Scott, Ernest. *Australia during the War.* Vol. XI, The Official History of Australia in the War of 1914–1918. 5th ed. Sydney: Angus and Robertson, 1939.
Smith, Bernard. "Lindsay, Norman Alfred (1879–1969)." *Australian Dictionary of Biography* 10 (1986). http://adb.anu.edu.au/biography/lindsay-norman-alfred-7757.
Stamer, William. *Recollections of a Life of Adventure.* 2 vols. London: Hurst and Blackett, 1866.
Stanner, W. E. H. *The Boyer Lectures 1968: After the Dreaming.* Sydney: Australian Broadcasting Commission, 1969.
Stewart, Douglas. *Norman Lindsay: A Personal Memoir.* Sydney: Angus & Robertson, 1979.
Stone, Dan. *History, Memory and Mass Atrocity: Essays on the Holocaust and Genocide.* London: Valentine Mitchell, 2006.
Sue, Derald Wing, Christina M. Capodilupo, Gina C. Torino, Jennifer M. Bucceri, Aisha M. B. Holder, Kevin L. Nadal, and Marta Esquilin. "Racial Microaggressions in Everyday Life: Implications for Clinical Practice." *American Psychologist* 62, no. 4 (2007): 271–86.
Tatz, Colin. *Genocide in Australia.* AIATSIS Research Discussion Paper No. 8. Sydney: Australian Institute of Aboriginal and Torres Strait Islander Studies, 1999.
Twain, Mark. *Following the Equator: A Journey around the World.* Hartford: American Publishing Co.; and New York: Doubleday & McClure Co., 1897.
Witcombe, Eleanor. "The Magic of the Pudding." In *The World of Norman Lindsay,* edited by Lin Bloomfield, 42–48. South Melbourne: Macmillan, 1979.

Chapter 13

Freedom in Fiction

Trickster Tales and Enslavement in the United States

MEGAN JEFFREYS[1]

"Welcome to the Old Plantation, a place where rabbits trick, foxes hunt, turtles race, possums play dead, bears swing upside-down, and everyone gets caught up in the laughter and music of life."[2] Written on the back of a book filled with collected tales of Brer Rabbit and his friends, this quote was meant to sell the book and entice readers, both young and old, to enter the world of these unlikely critters. It appeals to a *simpler* time, back before cars and trucks, before skyscrapers and industrialization; however, what this excerpt fails to communicate are the origins and deep-seeded meanings behind these carefree tales of a rabbit and his friends. Originating from African "trickster" folktales, the Brer Rabbit stories reflect the woes and daily hardships of enslavement. First published in 1880 by Joel Chandler Harris, the stories told by Uncle Remus provided a link to slave culture that went unnoticed for decades.[3] By 1946, when Walt Disney Studios released its adaptation of the now widely known characters in *Songs of the South*, the stories of the Brer animals became even more disconnected from their ubiquitous past. While the modern world has adapted trickster tales for entertainment, the stories of Brer Rabbit and his unlikely friends illuminate a form of education used in slave communities, in which oral tales were also used as social lessons to discreetly encourage feelings of hope, facilitate ideas of resistance, and teach fellow enslaved individuals about the expectations of social order on a plantation.[4]

Since the 1970s, historians and folklorists have pursued a better understanding of African folklore and the ways that African Americans transformed these stories to reflect their struggles in pre- and post-emancipation life.[5] In 1977, Lawrence Levine became the first historian to use African American folklore as a primary source for original historical research. In his monograph *Black Culture and Black Consciousness,* Levine argues that folklore is an expression of culture that reflects personal experiences that are indicative of the hostile world in which the creators lived.[6] In this way, the creators of these tales and stories must come to terms with their trauma, using their experiences to connect to, and in some cases protect, their audience from those same circumstances.[7] Since Levine, historians and folklorists such as Charles Joyner, Judylyn Ryan, Babacar M'Baye, Henry Louis Gates Jr., and John W. Roberts traversed the bridge between African folklore and African American culture to better understand the evolution of these trickster tales and their application to more modern artistic expressions.

So how do tales of rabbits, partridges, foxes, and wolves become an educational resource? It is a more familiar process than many realize. Much the same way that tales of enchanted frogs, glass slippers, and magical wands are a part of childhood education in the modern world, so too were the tales of animals used as education by enslaved individuals. Coupled with the inability to communicate via books and texts—because of illiteracy, lack of educational materials, or a combination of the two—trickster tales, as well as other fairy-tale and paranormal stories, provided a way to pass on life lessons and cultural norms while illuminating ways to stand up against oppressors and evil foes. As John Roberts explains, trickster tales "repeatedly portrayed the trickster as an actor in types of situations that they were very likely to encounter in the slave system."[8] These connections between fiction and reality facilitated the education of enslaved youth in numerous aspects of life. From Wilma King in 1995, who noted that "[a]nimal trickster tales . . . teach lessons of survival and self-confidence," to Rebecca Griffin, who in 2005 made connections between the tales of Brer Rabbit and courtship rituals in slavery, historians allude to these connections between folklore and reality, trickster and education.[9] Nevertheless, the growing scholarship on slavery in the United States has yet to fully explore these connections. This chapter seeks to reopen this conversation and urge historians to reassess the value of folklore in understanding enslaved life and, in particular, childhood in slavery.

The sources used in this chapter to explicate the meaning of trickster tales within the context of slavery derive from slave narratives and ex-slave interviews as well as post-emancipation publications of folktales by collectors such as Joel Chandler Harris. As such, these sources rely heavily on memory. Navigating memory is an arduous task, which is only amplified when those memories originate from an institution predicated on hostility and characterized by an imbalance in power. As B. A. Botkin remarked in his introduction to *Lay My Burdens Down*, a collection of folk history from ex-slave interviews, many of the accounts are "weakened by internal contradictions and inconsistencies; obvious errors of historical fact; vague, confused, or ambiguous statements; lapses of memory; and reliance on hearsay rather than first-hand experiences."[10] But despite their inherent imperfection, these memories illuminate ideas, events, or feelings that contribute to understandings of slavery. Through the use of Maurice Halbwachs's theory on collective memory, wherein memories are recorded through filters of collective and social memories, these sources become informative of both individual and group experiences in slavery.[11] Despite their inconsistencies, the memories of formerly enslaved individuals in slave narratives, Federal Writer's Project (FWP) interviews, and oral traditions are imperative for understanding the experiences of the enslaved, whether real or imagined.[12] What follows is an attempt to navigate those memories and shed light on instances previously dimly lit or left in the darkness of the American past.

The publications of these folktales have been the center of heated debate over the racist representations of enslaved individuals. The aforementioned film *Songs of the South* has marred the reputation of the Walt Disney Company for decades, to the point where they have worked to remove it from circulation and, in the summer of 2020, released plans to transform their "Splash Mountain" ride—which was based on the film. There is no doubt that the representations of certain individuals in Harris's work, mainly African and African-descended people, illustrate "patronizing and damaging stereotypes that romanticize the Antebellum era."[13] This chapter does not attempt to address the errors in Harris's publications. Instead, it works to return the stories to their origins: to the enslaved individuals who disseminated these tales among themselves in oral traditions as a method of education and awareness. Nevertheless, the abundance of discussion surrounding this work, as well as the cultural appropriation and misrepresentation it propagated, cannot go unnoticed. Most prominently, the works of Julius Lester to reformat the original publications articulate the growing desire to represent these tales without the harmful stereotypes that have come to be associated with Harris's work. The damaging representation of a docile Uncle Remus telling tales to a white boy not only plays into concepts of white superiority and a justification of slavery, but it also removes the tales from their social context. These tales were not created or disseminated for the entertainment of white children. As Lester explains, this social setting "leaves the reader with no sense of the important role the tales played in black life."[14] While I disagree with Lester that these stories were intended more for adults, it is indisputable that these tales were a necessary part of slave life, culture, community, memory, and survival.

By focusing on ideas of collective memory and resistance—as well as elements of literary theory—this chapter resituates trickster tales within their own reality as an expression of the conditions of slavery and a tool for educating enslaved youth.[15] Using slave narratives, ex-slave interviews, and scholarship by historians and folklorists, this study uncovers connections between folklore and education, fiction and reality, survival and defeat, strength and weakness, rabbit and fox. Through these connections, this chapter illuminates the ways that trickster tales, such as the popular Brer animal stories, represent the harsh realities of enslaved life while also revealing how such stories served to educate enslaved youth in the use of whit, trickery, and resilience as survival techniques.[16]

Tricksters as Educators

Countless trickster tales tell of the many ways that Brer Rabbit, the protagonist, and his friends tricked and stole food from Brer Wolf and Brer Fox. At the core of many of these stories is one of the principle necessities of survival: food. In one story, Brer Wolf is coming home from a great day of fishing. With his haul hoisted up on his shoulders, he gets distracted by the possibility of eating Miss Partridge's eggs and leaves his fish on the road as he goes off to hunt for her nest. While he is gone, Brer Rabbit happens by the lonely bunch of fish and takes it home to eat. Eventually, Brer Wolf comes back, after failing to find the nest, and notices that his fish are gone. He immediately realizes that it must be Brer Rabbit and decides to go kill Brer Rabbit's prize cow to even the score. When he arrives at the barn, however, Brer Wolf does not find the cow. Instead, he finds Brer Rabbit, breathing heavily next to a turned-up patch of dirt. Confronted by the wolf, Brer Rabbit spins a tale about how the ground began to swallow the cow and he did everything in his power to save her. Brer Wolf immediately begins digging, hoping that he will be able to uncover the cow and still enact his revenge. Unbeknownst to Brer Wolf, the cow has been already been slaughtered and the meat hung in Brer Rabbit's smoke house for him and his children to eat.[17] Brer Rabbit saunters away with a smile on his lips as he revels in the success of yet another trick. Through these tales of trickery and greed, enslaved children learned the importance of preparedness and temperance necessary for survival on a slave plantation.

Similar to trickster tales, food occupies a central theme in slave narratives and ex-slave interviews. In his narrative, Charles Ball—who was enslaved in Maryland and Georgia from 1780 until his escape in 1810—recounted the numerous techniques he used to hunt local game to subsidize the minimal food rations he received from his owner.[18] Harriet Jacobs, previously enslaved in North Carolina from her birth in 1813 until her escape in 1835, recalled that "[l]ittle attention was paid to the slaves' meals," and in some cases starvation was part of slave punishments.[19] In his own narrative, Frederick Douglass—who was enslaved from his birth in 1818 until he successfully escaped in 1838—berated slave holders for depriving the enslaved of "necessary food and clothing."[20] In many FWP interviews, formerly enslaved individuals discuss the scarcity of good meals and how, on many plantations, enslaved children were fed slop in food troughs that typically consisted of buttermilk and food scraps.[21] On many plantations, slave owners supplied weekly or monthly provisions to each slave cabin—or sometimes the community as a whole—that included their entire allowance of grains, vegetables, and meat.[22] With enough food to stay alive, and typically not much more, enslaved individuals constantly hunted for food in nearby forests, grew their own vegetables when time and space allowed, stole from their owner's food supply, or tricked their enslavers into giving them more food than they intended.

On August 16, 1937, Josie Jordan told an interviewer with the FWP about "one master who almost starved his slaves."[23] "Some of the slaves were so poorly thin," she remembered, "they ribs would kinder [sic] rub against each other like corn stalks a-drying in the hot wind."[24] One year, Mrs. Jordan recalled, when it was almost time to slaughter seven fat hogs the plantation master had been raising, an enslaved man came up to the house to announce that the hogs had all suddenly died overnight because of illness. The master quickly came to inspect them, but he could not understand how such healthy and fat pigs had died. When he asked what illness had taken them, one of the enslaved responded by telling him they fell victim to an illness called "Malitis." Scared of what would happen when he and his family ate the infected meat, the master gave the hog meat to those he enslaved. So what is Malitis? As Mrs. Jordan recalls, it is what happens when there are "seven fat hogs and seventy lean slaves."[25]

For the slave community, and the Brer animals, survival came down to the bare essentials: food, shelter, and water. While shelter and water were typically provided, in at least survivable conditions, the hard labor on a plantation often demanded more sustenance than typical food provisions allowed. As such, enslaved children often learned to hunt at a young age. Trickster tales, such as the one above about Brer Wolf's fish and Brer Rabbit's cow, provided several lessons that enslaved children were to use when the necessity arose. The first lesson resides in the actions of Brer Wolf. After a successful day of fishing, "wid a string er fish 'cross his shoulder," Brer Wolf gets distracted by the possibility of more food.[26] His own gluttony is his downfall. If Brer Wolf had ignored his greed and taken home the food he had rightfully caught, he would not have found himself in such a predicament as to have his food supply stolen by Brer Rabbit. Trickster tales often included lessons about the infection of greed and the chaos it could cause within the slave community.[27] The second lesson comes from the typical protagonist, Brer Rabbit. When walking home from a hard day of work, he happens across the string of perfectly good fish. With no one around to claim them, he seizes the opportunity to feed his family. While opportunities for extra food were often few and far between, enslaved children were encouraged to seize those opportunities for the good of their families and their community. When festivals warranted extra food, many of the enslaved stocked up on storable supplies for times when food was not as bountiful. As Mrs. Jordan recalled in her interview, when the opportunity and necessity were present, everyone was encouraged to obtain food to help the community survive.

Finally, when Brer Wolf figures out who stole his fish, he seeks his revenge, and the only way Brer Rabbit escapes is through the use of his clever wit. The lesson here was to always be prepared to outwit their oppressors. Take for instance, again, Mrs. Jordan's story about the hogs. The chance to acquire the extra hog meat was not one of opportunity, but of necessity. When starvation loomed overhead, a few enslaved individuals took the initiative, and risk, to trick their master out of the hog meat by appealing to their owner's sense of mortality. With plenty of food to survive, the risk to the plantation master and his family was too great, and he instead errs on the side of caution and gives the tainted meat to the enslaved. The use of wit and trickery in this instance allowed them to acquire more food for the slave community, much in the way that Brer Rabbit did for his family.

Trickery, then, was viewed as a necessity of survival. When the situation required immediate action, many of the enslaved embraced deception to avoid the ever-present reality of starvation. This correlation between realistic scenarios, like the one in Mrs. Jordan's interview, and trickster tales facilitated the education of enslaved children in the ways of survival. The lessons were simple but necessary: steer clear of greed, for it could become their downfall, and when opportunity knocks, be prepared to act and, if necessary, outwit their foes.

While trickster tales and stories of the enslaved continued to include elements of food and nourishment, they also depicted some of the more brutal realities of slavery. In one story, Brer Fox grows tired of being tricked by Brer Rabbit and decides that this time, he is going to win. To trick the cunning rabbit, Brer Fox creates a *tar baby* that looks fairly similar to Brer Rabbit and places it on the road. While he is hiding in the bush, Brer Rabbit comes down the road and greets the tar baby. When the tar baby does not reciprocate Brer Rabbit's greetings, he becomes upset and strikes the contraption. Because it was made out of tar, Brer Rabbit gets stuck in the tar and threatens to hit the tar baby again if he does not let him loose. Brer Rabbit does not get an answer from the inanimate tar baby and continues to strike the contraption until his arms, legs, and head are stuck. Out from behind the bushes, Brer Fox appears with a big grin as he happily comes to claim his prize.[28]

Within slavery, deception worked both ways. Not only did the enslaved trick their owners—as in the case of Mrs. Jordan's story about Malitis—but slave owners also resorted to tricks to maintain hierarchy and extract their version of justice from the enslaved. In an FWP interview, Neal Upson recalled one such event. One day his plantation owner realized that some of his money had been stolen. Believing the perpetrators to be one of the people he enslaved, he decided to trick them into admitting the truth, or at the very least finding someone to pay for the crime. "He put up a big rooster in a coop with his head sticking out," Upson remembered, and called over all the enslaved individuals.[29] He told them that "everyone must get in line and march around the coop and touch it. He said that when the guilty ones touched the coop the old rooster would crow."[30] Obviously, the old rooster was not equipped with the powers to perceive truth; nevertheless, the master used the trick to flush out the perpetrators by looking for those who were the most scared by the prospect of being caught.

Tricks such as this were often used by slave owners, overseers, and patrollers to force reactions from the enslaved. Similar to the trickster tale of the tar baby, these stories tell of instances where the enslaved were tricked by their owners; however, in each of these tales the enslaved—or the rabbit—were only caught because they made mistakes. In the tale of the tar baby, Brer Rabbit succumbs to his anger when the tar baby fails to return his greeting. If he had simply ignored the tar baby's rudeness and minded his own business, Brer Rabbit would have continued down the road and avoided capture. Instead, anger and arrogance get the best of him, which results in his capture. In Upson's story, two individuals were caught not because of the rooster, but because they failed to maintain their composure. Slave owners, overseers, and patrollers constantly tricked the enslaved into revealing their misdeeds with promises of anonymity, immunity, and rewards. To thwart these efforts, trickster tales—such as the tar baby story—were used to teach enslaved children a lesson: always keep composure and cautiously and deliberately choose who can be trusted.

In typical trickster fashion, however, the story does not end with a victorious fox. After Brer Fox captures Brer Rabbit by deceiving him with the tar baby, he attempts to decide how he is going to kill him. As Brer Fox starts contemplating ways to hurt him, Brer Rabbit begins to plead with him, "I don't keer w'at you do wid me, Brer Fox . . . don't fling me in dat brier-patch."[31] Unconvinced, Brer Fox thinks of several ways of killing the rabbit, including hanging, drowning, and skinning him alive. After each idea, Brer Rabbit recites the same plea. Finally, Brer Fox grabs the rabbit and tosses him right in the middle of the brier patch. He looks down, hoping to see the rabbit's torment, but instead sees him sitting cross-legged and happy. "Bred en bawn in the brier-patch," Brer Rabbit yells up to him, "Bred en bawn."[32]

According to George Womble, an ex-slave interviewed as a part of the FWP, tricks like this one were part of daily life. As cotton production increased in both sum and popularity, slave owners began weighing the product output at the end of the day. Slave owners would punish those who failed to meet production quotas, which were typically created based on age, sex, and prior productivity. In some cases, they were whipped for every pound they were short.[33] On the plantation where George Womble worked, however, they found a way to trick their owners. "To avoid this punishment," Womble remembered, "they sprinkled the white sand of the fields on the dew soaked cotton and at the time it was weighed they were credited with more pounds than they had actually picked."[34] Much like the way that Brer Rabbit tricked Brer Fox into setting him free, they found ways to avoid harsh punishments by tricking their owners into thinking they were more productive and, consequently, more valuable.

It is through this correlation between reality and fiction that education occurred. As historian Wilma King explains, "Young slaves could readily identify with weak persecuted characters such as the helpless 'Brer Rabbit' who faces danger yet endures."[35] Danger was a part of daily life for the enslaved, regardless of their owner's temperament. So how does one appeal to young children while also educating them on ways to survive their own brutal realities? For many of the enslaved, trickster tales proved the perfect medium. In the tale above, Brer Fox deceived Brer Rabbit and contemplated ways to torture and kill him. For an enslaved child this story held many educational possibilities, most prominent of which is the importance of being quick-witted, clever, and resilient. When Brer Rabbit was captured, he made Brer Fox believe that the worst thing he could do was to throw him into the bristly brier patch. Having lived in the tough environment of the brier patch his whole life, Brer Rabbit knew he would survive and manipulated Brer Fox's fear of the brier patch thorns. The same goes for those Mr. Womble discussed. To avoid punishment, they found ways to deceive their owners and resist their oppressive situations. Henry Bibb, who escaped from slavery, recalls in his narrative, "The only weapon of self-defense that I could use successfully was that of deception."[36] And what better way to teach a child the art of deception than through the tales of a rabbit and his run-in with a fox?

Trickster tales, while correlating with realistic experiences of the enslaved, also provided an escape when one was unavailable in slave reality. While the previous examples from narratives and ex-slave interviews reflect instances where the enslaved were able to trick their way out of precarious situations, this was not always the case. Slavery did not always afford opportunities of physical resistance or supply circumstances where tricks enabled their escape from torture or starvation. In the tales of Uncle Remus, Brer Rabbit finds himself in many precarious circumstances where Brer Fox or Brer Wolf attempt to capture or trick him. In many of these situations, the antagonists attempt to literally devour the rabbit in a fictional depiction of Darwin's survival of the fittest. In this "eat or be eaten" world, the rabbit, like the slave, is found at the bottom of the social food chain, continuously victimized by those with more power. However, in most of these tales, the rabbit eventually gains the upper hand, and although he must endure the fear and pain associated with these punishments, he eventually tricks his way out of death. Reality was not always so kind. In many cases, trickster tales provided a fantasy situation in which the rabbit was the victor, finding freedom and surviving on his own terms. The enslaved were not always so lucky.

J. W. Terrill was born into slavery, and like many of his peers, his mother was enslaved and his father was her owner. Terrill's owner proved exceptionally cruel, as Terrill constantly reminded him of his personal weaknesses. As such, Terrill was often the victim of extensive cruelty. Before the age of twelve, Terrill was tied to a tree and "whipped like a beast by [his] father, till [he] was unconscious, and then left strapped to the tree all night in cold and rainy weather."[37] Shortly after this night of torture, Terrill was forced to wear a handmade contraption made of steel that was strapped around his shoulders and had a bell that hung about three feet above his head. "That was my punishment," Terrill remembered, "for being born into this world the son of a white man and my mammy, a negro slave."[38] Not only did the contraption make it difficult to complete his daily tasks, but it also made it impossible to lie down on the floor. Instead, he had to sleep sitting up until he was seventeen years old, when his owner died. Terrill's punishments were extensive. While he endured the daily hardships of slavery, he was also punished for things that were out of his control, such as the circumstances of his birth. The resentment that Terrill's owner bore was not uncommon in circumstances where slave owners seemed to be haunted by their lust for the bodies of the enslaved.

Terrill's situation demonstrates one of the many circumstances in which enslaved individuals could not trick their way out of punishments and torture. With his master determined to make him pay, there was little the young boy could do. So how did the enslaved resist when tricking and escape were not possible? They survived. Through the use of trickster tales, enslaved individuals taught their children ways to escape to places within their own minds. This escape enabled them to find hope even in the direst circumstances. In the Brer animal stories, this escape was typically facilitated through the use of what is called Brer Rabbit's "laughing place." In one story, Uncle Remus—the narrator of the tales—talks with a young boy about the laughing place. Throughout their conversation, Uncle Remus and the boy remark about the details of the laughing place and how it can be a place, a person, or an idea "where you kin go an' tickle yo'self an' laugh whedder you wanter laugh er no."[39] Brer Rabbit's laughing place, then, is different from those of his fellow Brer animals. What follows this conversation is a story about how Brer Rabbit tricks Brer Fox by promising to take him to his laughing place. Brer Rabbit takes Brer Fox on a journey into sharp vines, through sticker bushes, and into an angry swarm of hornets. All the while, every time Brer Fox finds himself getting poked, or cut, or stung, Brer Rabbit laughs and laughs. Finally, Brer Rabbit tells Brer Fox that it is time to go home and leave his laughing place, but Brer Fox is confused. All they did was go through a bunch of bushes and stickers. So "Brer Fox shows his tushes, an' say, 'you said dis wuz a laughin'-place.'" Brer Rabbit smugly looks up at the fox and says, "I said 'twuz my laughin'-place . . . what you reckon I been doin' all this time?"[40] Finally, it all becomes clear. The laughing place is not necessarily a physical place. It is a place or circumstance where someone can find happiness, and in this case, Brer Rabbit's happiness came at Brer Fox's expense.

While many of the trickster tales depict scenes of psychological and physical trauma, such as Brer Fox tricking Brer Rabbit with a tar baby, they also articulate ways of dealing with anguish. Brer Rabbit's laughing place is one way that the rabbit escapes the trials and difficulties of life, finding happiness, if only for a moment. This "sure-enough place" was found out of necessity to bolster "comfort and convenience."[41] The laughing place makes several appearances throughout the tales and volumes of Uncle Remus's stories. It is a place where he can escape the severity of his situation and find happiness in a joke, a story, an image, or a laugh. The stories of the laughing place were intended to teach enslaved children a way of coping with the daily brutalities of slavery. When nothing could be done, when tricks were not an option, they could escape to their happy places to survive. The animosity between the rabbit, the fox, and even the wolf is indicative of many relationships found in United States slavery. Death continuously loomed over the enslaved, and small decisions, like talking to a fake child, harbored life-or-death situations. In Terrill's case, simply being born was enough to warrant torment and pain. For his simple act of existing, Terrill was subjected to brutally harsh beatings and placed in a steel contraption for more than five years, when only the mercy of his master's death allowed him some semblance of freedom. In the torment of such a hopeless situation, tales of the laughing place told of ways to escape the inescapable and to endure the unfathomable.

"I Been There Before."[42]

Trickster tales provided enslaved adults with a way to pass down lessons of survival to children, regardless of their situations. When food was limited and starvation threatened them, trickster tales inspired ways to deceive their owners and steal, or hunt, food for survival. When plantation masters, overseers, and patrollers tricked them, they used stories like the one about the tar baby to teach composure and the power of resilience. When death seemed immanent, Brer Rabbit found ways to trick his way out of it. The rabbit's wit was both inspirational and cautionary as enslaved adults passed down these tales to younger generations. And when all hope seemed lost—when tricks could not change their circumstances—these tales taught lessons of psychological survival and ways to mentally escape their tormented reality. Illuminating the connections between trickster and reality reveals some of the ways that enslaved individuals educated their children in ways of survival and resilience.

The correlation between real experiences and trickster tales illuminates connections between reality and fiction while also exposing the importance of oral tales in the development of survival techniques and culture. To endure the torments of slavery, survival became the backbone of African American cultural development. It became the lesson in their stories, the truth in their tales, and the link that brought communities together. For enslaved children, the stories of Brer Rabbit and his friends not only stole them away from the realities they faced, but also exposed them to survival techniques, codes of conduct, and ways to escape or avoid punishments. After scouring through hundreds of ex-slave narratives and thousands of FWP interviews from across the South, hundreds of previously enslaved individuals recalled hearing the cautionary tales of a trickster animal who found ways to persevere when times were tough and to survive when death seemed imminent.[43] Through tales similar to the modern-day Tom and Jerry cartoons, enslaved children learned the power of resilience, the importance of patience, and the necessity of deception. Nevertheless, there is undoubtedly more to discover. Future research could further elucidate these connections between survival and resistance, culture and community, psychology and resilience, adults and children, fiction and reality. These children's stories of atrocities and trickery hold countless possibilities to learn more about the lives of enslaved children in the United States and the roles that culture, community, and folklore played in their survival.

Notes

1. This chapter would not have been possible without the insight and direction I received from Dr. Edward Baptist and Dr. Sandra Greene. I must also thank my colleagues at Cornell University (Chelsea, Daniel, Emilio, and Neta) for their feedback and perspectives, as well as the amazing support and intuition provided

by my dear friend Bree'ya Brown. Finally, I must also thank Dr. Brett Mizelle at California State University, Long Beach, for helping me discover, and fostering my interest in, this intriguing topic. Thank you all for making this possible.

2. Joel Chandler Harris, *The Classic Tales of Brer Rabbit* (Philadelphia: Running Press, 2007), back cover.

3. While Harris briefly articulates the origins of the stories in the introduction—most prominently in the second book, which is cited below—the historical connections between the animal stories and enslaved life went unexplored for decades. In many cases, the animal stories were taken further away from their original meanings until historians and folklorists began digging into oral folktales as a source of history in the early twentieth century; Joel Chandler Harris, *Nights with Uncle Remus: Myths and Legends of the Old Plantation* (Boston: James R. Osgood and Company, 1883), ix–xxxvi.

4. While traditionally resistance refers to the organized opposition to a ruling power, I work with a more contemporary definition. As used in several recent works on slavery, resistance is defined as an act by an enslaved individual against the slave owners, overseers, patrollers, and the slave system as a whole—or vice versa—which can manifest as both passive and active resistance. For more clarification on resistance in slavery, please see the following works: Wilma King, *Stolen Childhood: Slave Youth in Nineteenth-Century America* (Bloomington: Indiana University Press, 1995), 19; Edward Baptist, *The Half Has Never Been Told: Slavery and the Making of American Capitalism* (New York: Basic Books, 2014), xx, 113, 139; Stallen Vinthagen and Anna Johansson, "'Everyday Resistance': Exploration of a Concept and its Theories," *Resistance Studies Magazine,* no. 1 (2013): 1–46.

5. While this study focuses on the use of these tales as educational tools, this is not meant to negate the fact that they were also used for entertainment. Thus, this chapter builds on the plethora of work on African American folktales, while focusing more on the historical and educational context of the tales.

6. Lawrence Levine, *Black Culture and Black Consciousness: Afro-American Folk Thought from Slavery to Freedom* (New York: Oxford University Press, 1977).

7. While Levine does not use Kenneth Kidd's theories surrounding children's literature in his analysis, there are clearly overlapping understandings of the role of trauma in the creation of literature or folklore. While enslaved individuals created stories that illuminated their own experiences in, or observations of, enslaved life, they still had to contend with their own trauma and the anticipated trauma of their audience. For more on trauma in children's literature and folklore, see Kenneth Kidd, *Freud in Oz: At the Intersections of Psychoanalysis and Children's Literature* (Minneapolis; The University of Minnesota Press, 2011).

8. John W. Roberts, *From Trickster to Badman: The Black Folk Hero in Slavery and Freedom* (Philadelphia: University of Pennsylvania Press, 1989), 38.

9. King, *Stolen Childhood,* 72; Rebecca Griffin, "Courtship Contests and the Meaning of Conflicts in the Folklore of Slaves," *The Journal of Southern History* 71,

no. 4 (November 2005): 769–802; See also William J. Faulkner, *The Days When the Animals Talked: Black American Folktales and How They Came To Be* (Chicago: Follet Publishers Company, 1977); Charles Joyner, *Down by the Riverside: A South Carolina Slave Community* (Urbana: University of Illinois Press, 1984); Joyner, *Remember Me: Slave Life in Coastal Georgia* (Athens: University of Georgia Press, 2011); Levine, *Black Culture and Black Consciousness*; and more recent works such as Emily Zobel Marshall, "'Nothing but Pleasant Memories of the Discipline of Slavery': The Trickster and the Dynamics of Racial Representation," *Marvels & Tales: Journal of Fairy-Tale Studies* 32, no. 1 (2018): 59–75; and Harold Scheub, *Trickster and Hero: Two Characters in the Oral and Written Traditions of the World* (Madison, Wisconsin: University of Wisconsin Press, 2012).

10. B. A. Botkin, ed., *Lay My Burdens Down: A Folk History of Slavery* (Chicago: University of Chicago Press, 1945), xi–xii.

11. Maurice Halbwachs, *On Collective Memory* (Chicago: University of Chicago Press, 1992).

12. The Federal Writer's Project was commissioned by the US government as a part of the New Deal legislation enacted to lower unemployment rates around the country. For more on this program and its interviews, please see the following: "Born into Slavery: Slave Narratives from the Federal Writer's Project, 1936–1938," *Library of Congress*, https://www.loc.gov/collections/slave-narratives-from-the-federal-writers-project-1936-to-1938/about-this-collection/.

13. Marshall, "Nothing but Pleasant Memories of the Discipline of Slavery," 59.

14. Julius Lester, *The Tales of Uncle Remus: The Adventures of Brer Rabbit* (New York: Dial Books, 1987), xv; Despite the criticism of Harris's publications and the harmful stereotypes he disseminated, I have chosen to use his original publications for this chapter. This was not a decision that was made lightly; however, the modern references Lester inserted into his reproduction of the tales of Brer Rabbit take away from the original context of the stories. It is my goal, then, to focus not on the heated debate surrounding Harris's problematic, and at times disturbing, representation of enslaved individuals, but instead on the individuals who created these folktales and the ways in which they correspond with the experiences of enslavement and worked as a source of education in an ever-oppressing institution.

15. Halbwachs, *On Collective Memory*, 34; on theorizing everyday resistance: Stallen Vinthagen and Anna Johansson, "'Everyday Resistance': Exploration of a Concept and Its Theories," *Resistance Studies Magazine*, no. 1 (2013): 1–46; on literary theory as used in African American literature: Henry Louis Gates, *The Signifying Monkey: A Theory of African-American Literary Criticism* (Oxford: Oxford University Press, 2014).

16. A quick note on universality: This study uses interviews with the formerly enslaved and narratives that discuss African American tricksters, which originated from—or derived from experiences in—almost every slave state in the South. This is not to say, however, that trickster tales were universally a part of enslaved life. While

they may appear on one plantation, they may also be unheard-of on a plantation nearby. Trickster tales also were only one element of the oral traditions of slavery, and while this chapter focuses on the trickster, it is not meant to silence other forms of oral education or to elevate the status of the trickster. Finally, this chapter focuses specifically on the ways that trickster tales were used to educate enslaved children; however, that is not to say that they did not educate the young and old alike.

17. Joel Chandler Harris, *Uncle Remus: His Songs and His Sayings* (New York: Appelton and Company, 1880), 99–104.

18. Charles Ball, *Slavery in the United States: A Narrative of the Life and Adventures of Charles Ball, a Black Man, Who Lived Forty Years in Maryland, South Carolina, and Georgia, as a Slave Under Various Masters, and Was One Year in the Navy with Commodore Barney, During the Late War* (1837; repr., Chapel Hill: University of North Carolina Press, 1999), 77, 134.

19. While Jacobs escaped from slavery in 1835, she remained hidden near her previous plantation for seven years to keep an eye on her children. In 1842, Jacobs finally made her way to freedom in the North. Harriet Jacobs, *Incidents in the Life of a Slave Girl. Written by Herself* (1860; repr., Chapel Hill: University of North Carolina Press, 2003), 19, 75.

20. Frederick Douglass, *Narrative of the Life of Frederick Douglass, an American Slave* (1845; repr., Chapel Hill: University of North Carolina Press, 1999), x, 10, 76.

21. This statement is made on the basis of numerous FWP interviews from various states and collections. For more information, please look at the following collection: "Born in Slavery: Slave Narratives from the Federal Writers' Project, 1936–1938," *Library of Congress*, https://www.loc.gov/collections/slave-narratives-from-the-federal-writers-project-1936-to-1938/about-this-collection/.

22. Provisions and the frequency with which they were disseminated varied on each plantation. For the purpose of this chapter, an average was taken based on multiple secondary sources that discuss food provisions and nourishment. For more information on nutrition and provisions, please see the following works: Ira Berlin, *Generations of Captivity: A History of African-American Slaves* (Cambridge: The Belknap Press of Harvard University Press, 2003), 174; King, *Stolen Childhood*, 111; Jennifer Morgan, *Laboring Women: Reproduction and Gender in New World Slavery* (Philadelphia: University of Pennsylvania Press, 2004), 9; Calvin Schermerhorn, *Unrequited Toil: A History of United States Slavery* (Cambridge: Cambridge University Press, 2018), 94.

23. Josie Jordan, *Federal Writers' Project: Slave Narrative Project, Vol. 13, Oklahoma Project, Adams-Young*, August 16, 1937, https://www.loc.gov/resource/mesn.130/?sp=165.

24. Jordan, *Federal Writers' Project*.

25. Jordan, *Federal Writers' Project*.

26. Harris, *Uncle Remus: His Songs and Sayings*, 100.

27. In an enslaved community, people typically depended on each other for survival, and though it is a part of human nature, greed typically was not tolerated. Nevertheless, there is no general rule for understanding the role of greed within an enslaved community, as sometimes it was every person for themselves. For more on this topic, please see the following: John Blassingame, *The Slave Community: Plantation Life in the Antebellum South* (New York: Oxford University Press, 1972); Brenda Stevenson, *Life in Black and White: Family and Community in the Slave South* (New York: Oxford University Press, 1996).

28. Harris, *Uncle Remus: His Songs and Sayings*, 11–16.

29. Neal Upson, interviewed by Miss Grace McCune, *Federal Writers' Project: Slave Narrative Project, Vol. 4, Georgia, Part 4, Telfair-Young*, August 5, 1938, https://www.loc.gov/resource/mesn.044/?sp=51.

30. Upson, *Federal Writers' Project*.

31. Harris, *Uncle Remus: His Songs and Sayings*, 103–7.

32. Harris, *Uncle Remus: His Songs and Sayings*, 103–7.

33. The topic of cotton weighing and consequential punishments has been covered by several historians. Please see the following source for more information and additional sources: Caitlin Rosenthal, *Accounting for Slavery: Masters and Management* (Cambridge: Harvard University Press, 2018).

34. George Womble, *Federal Writers' Project: Slave Narrative Project, Vol. 4, Georgia, Part 4, Telfair-Young*, May 8, 1937, https://www.loc.gov/resource/mesn.044/?sp=183.

35. King, *Stolen Childhood*, 72.

36. Henry Bibb, *The Narrative of the Life and Adventures of Henry Bibb, an American Slave* (New York: Henry Bibb, 1849), 17.

37. J. W. Terrill, *Federal Writers' Project: Slave Narrative Project, Vol. 16, Texas, Part 4, Sanco-Young*, https://www.loc.gov/resource/mesn.164/?sp=86.

38. Terrill, *Federal Writers' Project*.

39. Joel Chandler Harris, *Told By Uncle Remus: New Stories of the Old Plantation* (New York: McClure, Phillips, & Co., 1905), 56.

40. Harris, *Told By Uncle Remus*, 72.

41. Harris, *Told By Uncle Remus*, 53–54.

42. Mark Twain, *The Adventures of Huckleberry Finn* (1885; repr., New York: Dover Thrift Editions, 1994), 221.

43. While most of these sources came from my personal collection and contributions from the libraries of my friends and colleagues, I also received help from the following online databases. For ex-slave narratives please see https://docsouth.unc.edu/neh/texts.html; for more FWP interviews, please see "Born into Slavery: Slave Narratives from the Federal Writers' Project, 1936–1938," *Library of Congress*, https://www.loc.gov/collections/slave-narratives-from-the-federal-writers-project-1936-to-1938/about-this-collection/.

Works Cited

Ball, Charles. *Slavery in the United States: A Narrative of the Life and Adventures of Charles Ball, a Black Man, Who Lived Forty Years in Maryland, South Carolina, and Georgia, as a Slave Under Various Masters, and Was One Year in the Navy with Commodore Barney, During the Late War.* 1837; Reprint, Chapel Hill: University of North Carolina Press, 1999.

Baptist, Edward. *The Half Has Never Been Told: Slavery and the Making of American Capitalism.* New York: Basic Books, 2014.

Berlin, Ira. *Generations of Captivity: A History of African-American Slaves.* Cambridge: The Belknap Press of Harvard University Press, 2003.

Bibb, Henry. *The Narrative of the Life and Adventures of Henry Bibb, an American Slave.* New York: Henry Bibb, 1849.

Blassingame, John. *The Slave Community: Plantation Life in the Antebellum South.* New York: Oxford University Press, 1972.

"Born into Slavery: Slave Narratives from the Federal Writers' Project, 1936–1938." *Library of Congress.* https://www.loc.gov/collections/slave-narratives-from-the-federal-writers-project-1936-to-1938/about-this-collection/#:~:text=About%20this%20Collection-,Born%20in%20Slavery%3A%20Slave%20Narratives%20from%20the%20Federal%20Writers'%20Project,white%20photo.

Botkin, B. A., ed. *Lay My Burdens Down: A Folk History of Slavery.* Chicago: University of Chicago Press, 1945.

Douglass, Frederick. *Narrative of the Life of Frederick Douglass, an American Slave.* 1845; Reprint, Chapel Hill: University of North Carolina Press, 1999.

Faulkner, William. *The Days When the Animals Talked: Black American Folktales and How They Came to Be.* Chicago: Follet Publishers Company, 1977.

Gates, Henry Louis. *The Signifying Monkey: A Theory of African-American Literary Criticism.* Oxford: Oxford University Press, 2014.

Griffin, Rebecca. "Courtship Contests and the Meaning of Conflicts in the Folklore of Slaves." *Journal of Southern History* 7, no. 4 (November 2005): 769–802.

Halbwachs, Maurice. *On Collective Memory.* Chicago: University of Chicago Press, 1992.

Harris, Joel Chandler. *The Classic Tales of Brer Rabbit.* Philadelphia: Running Press, 2007.

Harris, Joel Chandler. *Nights with Uncle Remus: Myths and Legends of the Old Plantation.* Boston: James R. Osgood and Company, 1883.

Harris, Joel Chandler. *Told By Uncle Remus: New Stories of the Old Plantation.* New York: McCure, Phillips, & Co., 1905.

Harris, Joel Chandler. *Uncle Remus: His Songs and His Sayings.* New York: Appelton and Company, 1880.

Hartman, Saidiya. "Venus in Two Acts." *Small Axe* 12, no. 2 (June 2008): 1–14.

Jacobs, Harriet. *Incidents in the Life of a Slave Girl, Written by Herself.* 1860; Reprint, Chapel Hill: University of North Carolina Press, 2003.
Joyner, Charles. *Down by the Riverside: Slave Life in Coastal Georgia.* Athens: University of Georgia Press, 2011.
Joyner, Charles. *Remember Me: Slave Life in Coastal Georgia.* Athens: University of Georgia Press, 2011.
King, Wilma. *Stolen Childhood: Slave Youth in Nineteenth-Century America.* Bloomington: Indiana University Press, 1995.
Levine, Lawrence. *Black Culture and Black Consciousness: Afro-American Folk Thought from Slavery to Freedom.* New York: Oxford University Press, 1977.
Marshall, Emily Zobel. "'Nothing but Pleasant Memories of the Discipline of Slavery': The Trickster and the Dynamics of Racial Representation." *Marvels & Tales: Journal of Fairy-Tale Studies* 32, no. 1 (2018): 59–75.
Morgan, Jennifer. *Laboring Women: Reproduction and Gender in New World Slavery.* Philadelphia: University of Pennsylvania Press, 2004.
Roberts, John W. *From Trickster to Badman: The Black Folk Hero in Slavery and Freedom.* Philadelphia: University of Pennsylvania Press, 1989.
Rosenthal, Caitlin. *Accounting for Slavery: Masters and Management.* Cambridge: Harvard University Press, 2018.
Schermerhorn, Calvin. *Unrequited Toil: A History of United States Slavery.* Cambridge: Cambridge University Press, 2018.
Scheub, Harold. *Trickster and Hero: Two Characters in the Oral and Written Traditions of the World.* Madison: University of Wisconsin Press, 2012.
Stevenson, Brenda. *Life in Black and White: Family and Community in the Slave South.* New York: Oxford University Press, 1996.
Vinthagen, Stallen, and Anna Johansson. "'Everyday Resistance': Exploration of a Concept and Its Theories." *Resistance Studies Magazine*, no. 1 (2013): 1–46.

Contributors

Jayson Althofer is an independent scholar based in Toowoomba, Australia. He works as a curator and research librarian at Toowoomba Regional Art Gallery. His curatorial projects include *Breaking News: Captain Cook in 2020*. His most recent publication is "Friedrich Engels and Gothic Marxism: A Fairy-Tale Introduction," in *Critical Imprints VIII: The Supernatural in Literature* (2020). He also co-writes with Brian Musgrove; their collaborations include "Capital of Dreadful Light: Marx, Engels and Diabolic Enlightenment," in *Gothic Dreams and Nightmares*, ed. Carol Margaret Davison (Manchester University Press, forthcoming).

Chigbo Arthur Anyaduba is an assistant professor in the Department of English, University of Winnipeg, Canada, where he teaches African/Black diaspora literatures. His scholarly interests are broadly multidisciplinary and lie at the intersection of African literary and cultural studies, genocide studies, diasporic, and postcolonial studies. His current research is concerned with tracing the various modes of representing and theorizing mass violence and atrocities occurring in Africa as well as some of the tropes through which violent encounters have been understood in Africa and beyond. Anyaduba is the author of *The Postcolonial African Genocide Novel: Quests for Meaningfulness* (Liverpool University Press, 2021).

Caroline (Carly) Bagelman is a lecturer at Liverpool Hope University in Education Studies, where her research currently focuses on the ways in which refugee experience and resettlement is addressed in mainstream schools, Schools of Sanctuary, and initial accommodation provision. Her work also critically examines the role of education in both colonization and decolonization, with a focus on the Canadian context where she was raised.

She is interested in the use of children's literature to develop and nurture the critical consciousness of young people on these subjects. She received a master of arts degree in cultural, social and political Thought at the University of Victoria and a PhD in education at the University of Glasgow.

Maria Chatzianastasi is an adjunct lecturer at the University of Nicosia, Cyprus, where she teaches in the Lifelong Joint Programme with Aristotle University of Thessaloniki: Contemporary Children's and Teenager's Book: Reading Approaches and Creative Writing and in the MA Programme of Study Special and Inclusive Education. Maria is also an adjunct lecturer at the Pedagogical Institute of Cyprus, where she teaches on the critical and creative use of picture books. She received bachelor of arts (with a minor in psychology) and masters of arts degrees in education (primary education), both with High Honours, at the University of Cyprus. Maria also holds a postgraduate certificate in research training in the humanities and social sciences and a PhD in children's literature and linguistics from Newcastle University. Since 2009 she has been working as a primary school teacher. She has worked in both public and private education in Cyprus. Between 2018 and 2021 she participated as a post-doc researcher in DIALLS: Dialogue and Argumentation for Cultural Literacy Learning in Schools (Horizon 2020, https://dialls2020.eu/). Maria has previously worked as a Scientific Collaborator at the European University Cyprus, where she has taught children's literature to undergraduate students of primary education (2013–16).

Rosemary Horowitz joined the faculty of Appalachian State University in 1995. Prior to her teaching career, she worked as a writer, editor, and trainer for several organizations. In addition to teaching at Appalachian's Boone campus, she participated in several ASU initiatives in other locations, most notably in Puebla, Mexico, and at the Appalachian Loft in New York City. She co-directed ASU's Office of Judaic, Holocaust, and Peace Studies. Her publications include the edited collections *Memorial Books of Eastern European Jewry: Essays on the History and Meanings of Yizker Volumes* (McFarland Press, 2011) and *Elie Wiesel and the Art of Storytelling* (McFarland Press, 2006). She passed away in August 2021.

Megan Jeffreys is a PhD candidate in the history department at Cornell University, where she researches various aspects of American slavery. Her current research focuses on the numerous groups involved, either directly or indirectly, in the escape of enslaved individuals, illuminating their perspectives of the event, the individual(s), and slavery as a whole. This research works to understand the ripple effects surrounding the decision to escape, focusing on individual, familial, community, and national reactions. Her publications include "Freedom on the Move by Sea: Evidence of Maritime Escape Strategies in American Runaway Slave Advertisements," in *Sailing to Freedom: Maritime Dimensions of the Underground Railroad* (University of Massachusetts Press, 2021).

Barbara Krasner is a doctoral candidate in Holocaust & Genocide Studies at Gratz College. She teaches in the Holocaust & Genocide Studies program at The College of New Jersey and in the English and History departments at other New Jersey institutions of higher education. She serves as Director, Mercer Holocaust, Genocide & Human Rights Education Center, and is the author of more than forty books for young readers, including the middle-grade novel in verse *37 Days at Sea: Aboard the MS St. Louis, 1939* (Kar-Ben, 2021).

A graduate of Colorado College and the University of Chicago, **Lora L. Looney** is an associate professor of Spanish at the University of Portland in Portland, Oregon. She teaches Modern Spanish Peninsular Literature and takes groups on immersion programs to Spain. When teaching in her field, she engages undergraduates using her digital humanities website, which presents original theoretical frameworks exploring why the youth protagonist is a recurring Spanish cinematic and literary figure to depict Spain's Civil War and postwar dictatorship. She frequently reads Matute's *Los niños tontos* with students in her classroom.

Simona Mitroiu, PhD, is a senior researcher at Alexandru Ioan Cuza University, Romania. She is the editor of *Life Writing and Politics of Memory in Eastern Europe* (Palgrave MacMillan, 2015) and *Women's Narratives and Postmemory of Displacement in Central and Eastern Europe* (Palgrave MacMillan, 2018). She is also the author of two books and several papers in international journals, including *Canadian Slavonic Papers, Slavonica, Nationalities Papers: The Journal of Nationalism and Ethnicity* and *European Legacy: Towards New Paradigms*. Her research focuses on memory and life writing, communism and post-communism, vulnerability and exclusion in media studies.

Mary-Catherine Mueller earned her doctoral degree from the University of Texas at Dallas. She currently teaches Holocaust literature and writing and reasoning courses for the Department of English at Southern Methodist University in Dallas, Texas. Mueller's most recent book, *The Holocaust Short Story* (Routledge, 2020), is the only book devoted entirely to representations of the Holocaust in the short story genre. Some of her other recent work appears in *The Struggle for Understanding: Elie Wiesel's Literary Works* (State University of New York Press, 2019) and the *Journal of Contemporary Antisemitism* (forthcoming). In addition to her publications and teaching, Mueller has presented her work in the field of Holocaust studies to scholars, educators, and human rights advocates around the world. Her research and writings examine representations of the Holocaust in art, culture, and memory; Jewish studies; anti-Semitism; and representations of the Holocaust in literature.

Brian Musgrove has a PhD from the University of Cambridge, where he taught before moving to Australia and becoming head of the Department of Humanities and Social Sciences at the University of Southern Queensland. He has published articles on drug literature, aspects of drug cultures, and their relation to capital. He also co-writes with Jayson Althofer; their collaborations include "'A Ghost in Daylight': Drugs and the Horror of Modernity," in *Palgrave Communications 4* (2018) and "Capital of Dreadful Light: Marx, Engels and Diabolic Enlightenment," in *Gothic Dreams and Nightmares*, ed. Carol Margaret Davison (Manchester University Press, forthcoming). He is currently an independent scholar.

Victoria Nesfield is a lecturer in religion at York St. John University, UK. She obtained her PhD on the works of Primo Levi and Elie Wiesel from the University of Leeds, where she worked as a postdoctoral researcher on Germany's Confrontation with the Holocaust in a Global Context. Her research interests on the Holocaust and responses to the Holocaust include testimony, literature and art, memory, and education. She has published articles and book chapters on these areas in publications including *Research in Education*, the *International Journal of Public Theology*, and *Journal of European Studies*.

Kaitlyn Newman is a lecturer in the Philosophy, Religion, and Liberal Studies Department at Georgia College & State University. She earned her doctoral degree in philosophy from Pennsylvania State University. Her past research focuses on the ethical dimensions of genocide memorialization and remembrance, as well as the ethical potentialities of representations of genocide in literature and art.

María Porras Sánchez is an assistant professor in the Department of English Studies, Universidad Complutense de Madrid. She has formerly taught at Aberystwyth University and Universitat Oberta de Catalunya. Her main research areas are graphic narratives, cultural translation, and postcolonial and transnational literatures in English, with an interest in precarity, migration, and otherness. She combines her teaching and research with her work as a literary translator. She has co-edited, with E. Sánchez-Pardo and R. Burillo, *Women Poets and Myth in the 20th and 21st Centuries: On Sappho's Websi*te (Cambridge Scholars, 2018), and she is currently working with G. Vilches on the volume *Precarious Youth in Contemporary Graphic Narratives: Young Lives in Crisis* (under contract, Routledge, 2022).

Philip Smith is professor of English and Associate Chair of Liberal Arts at Savannah College of Art and Design. He is author of *Reading Art Spiegelman* (Routledge 2015), *Shakespeare in Singapore* (Routledge 2020), and co-author of *Printing Terror: American Horror Comics as Cold War Commentary and Critique* (Manchester University Press, 2021). He served as co-director of the Shakespeare Behind Bars program at The Correctional Facility at Fox Hill, Nassau. He is editor in chief of *Literature Compass*.

Chengcheng You earned her doctoral degree at University of Macau. Her work has been published in, among others, *Children's Literature in Education, Mosaic: An Interdisciplinary Critical Journal, The Lion and the Unicorn, International Research in Children's Literature,* and *English Studies*. She is co-author of *Poetics and Ethics of Anthropomorphism: Children, Animals, and Poetry* (Routledge). She is assistant professor at Department of English, Faculty of Arts and Humanities, University of Macau.

Index

Angels Wear White, 264–268
atrocity, definitions of, 1, 10, 45, 70, 72–73, 162, 180, 226, 257–258, 277
Australia, 273–296

Bosmajian, Hamida, 5, 6, 11, 47fn20, 69, 70, 76, 82, 83, 86, 89, 92fn30, 108–109, 162
Breaking Stalin's Nose, 162–163, 164–169, 173–175
bystander, 102, 106–107, 266

Caruth, Cathy, 75
catharsis, 7, 8, 51, 60, 125, 174, 215
censorship, 11, 56, 113, 153–154, 161, 179, 191–192, 194
childhood, 2, 5, 7, 10, 12–17, 39, 69–70, 72, 74–75, 77–90, 124, 129, 136, 164, 169–173, 175, 182, 207, 231, 254, 276, 298
children's art. *See* juvenilia
China, 113–114, 118fn32, 123, 240, 253–272
colonialism, 53, 62, 63–64fn9, 91fn22, 243, 225–251, 273–296
communism, 17, 129, 161–178, 206, 211, 317
communist. *See* communism

Darfur, 21–50
Deogratias, 51–68
Dicker-Brandeis, Friedl, 147–148

Einstein and Einstein, 260–264
enslavement, 53, 297–314

fairy tales, 2, 9, 125, 181, 186, 229, 298
fascism, 132, 184, 188, 196fn19, 211
fascist. *See* fascism
Frank, Anne, 10–12, 21fn57, 110, 112, 145

gray zone, the, 256. *See also* Levi, Primo
girlhood, 74, 108, 114, 121–142, 146, 170, 193, 253–272
Greece, 69–95

Holocaust, 3–7, 10–17, 19–21fns, 25–27, 29, 31, 33–41, 43–45, 46fn2, 47fn20, 48fn24, 51–52, 56, 61, 63fn45, 66fn42, 70, 75–76, 78, 83, 99–115, 116fn13, 121–126, 136, 144–148, 153–154, 203–204, 207, 227–229, 257
hope, 7, 11, 59, 73, 74, 104, 114, 126, 131, 136, 145, 148, 149, 174, 297, 306

indigenocide, 273–274, 276

juvenilia, 21–50, 143–157

Kidd, Kenneth, 2, 3, 5, 10, 13, 20fn29, 20fn33, 54, 72–73, 76–77, 83, 86–87, 89, 90, 99–100, 124, 174, 206, 207, 227, 285, 309fn7
Kacer, Kathy, 123, 126–135
Kimmel, Eric, 107–109, 111, 118fn32, 125
Kokkola, Lydia, 2, 3, 4, 5, 7, 100, 101, 112, 125, 191, 211, 215, 220fn78

Levi, Primo, 3, 117fn22, 150–152, 256
Los niños tontos (The Foolish Children) 179–200

Magic Pudding, The, 273–296
Marzi: A Memoir, 162–163, 169–175
Maus, 12–13, 63fn4, 203–204, 210, 215
Memories That Hurt, 84–89

Nazi, Neo-Nazi. *See* Nazism
Nazism, 3, 6, 8, 12, 44–45, 48fn25, 56, 76, 100, 104–114, 122–123, 126, 128, 131, 136, 144–146, 150–151, 153, 164, 211, 220fn78

Orlev, Uri, 123, 126–135

parrhesia, 227–251
photography, 7, 46fn4, 211
picturebooks, 2, 225–251, 273–296
Poland, 12, 100, 112–113, 129–130, 169–172

rape, 2, 9, 12, 18, 53–54, 74, 82, 225, 254, 257, 264–267, 277
residential schools, 225–252
resilience, 131, 242, 300, 307–308
Russia, 114, 123, 138fn23, 161–165, 167, 175fn4, 176fn12
Russian. *See* Russia
Rwanda, 14, 46fn6, 51–77

slavery. *See* enslavement
Songs of the South, 297, 299
Soviet Union, 111, 113–114, 136, 154, 161–175
Spanish Civil War, 179–198, 201–220
Spiegelman, Art. *See Maus*

Terezín Concentration Camp, 114–147
trauma writing, 2, 70, 75–78, 86, 89
Truth and Reconciliation Commission (TRC), 225–227, 243

What Does Enslavement Mean?, 74–75, 84–87
Wolves and Red Riding Hood, The, 74, 79–82
Wiesel, Elie, 3, 8, 57, 154fn5

www.ingramcontent.com/pod-product-compliance
Lightning Source LLC
Chambersburg PA
CBHW031705230426
43668CB00006B/115